SOUTH OF HEAVEN

THOMAS FRENCH

POCKET BOOKS
New York London Toronto Sydney Tokyo Singapore

PRAISE FOR
SOUTH OF HEAVEN

"Amazing. . . . French's chronicle reads like a novel. . . . Without judging, French records the speech of these kids, documents their romantic shutouts, their kamikaze driving, their cramming for tests and their foolishness. . . . Over the course of the year, the students at Largo apparently forgot about the bulky, ancient reporter hanging around writing down everything they said and did. They let down their guard in a way they rarely do with adults."

—Rosemary Armao, *The Virginian–Pilot and the Ledger–Star*

"This chronicle of high school life is both absorbing and disturbing. . . . an education for those who aren't familiar with the pressure of high school today."

—Sandra Fish, *The Orlando Sentinel*

"French does a superb job of revealing the hearts and minds of individual students, parents, and school administrators. . . . Indeed, if these tales of teen angst, parental frustrations, and valiant teachers were in a novel, French would get an 'A' for character development. . . . [a] well-written and moving account."

—Ron Davis, *St. Petersburg Times*

"French presents each character with objectivity and compassion. . . . an exceptional piece of journalism. . . . *SOUTH OF HEAVEN* is a good piece of nonfiction. It is an honest rendition of the teenage world that is no longer as carefree as many adults think. *SOUTH OF HEAVEN* is a ride into an entirely different culture, and a ride that is well worth the price of the ticket."

—Tanya Barrientos, *The Philadelphia Inquirer*

ALSO BY THOMAS FRENCH

UNANSWERED CRIES

S O U T H

O F

H E A V E N

WELCOME TO HIGH
SCHOOL AT THE END
OF THE TWENTIETH
CENTURY

POCKET BOOKS, a division of Simon & Schuster Inc.
1230 Avenue of the Americas, New York, NY 10020

Copyright © 1993 by Thomas French

Published by arrangement with Doubleday

French, Thomas, 1958–
    South of heaven: welcome to high school at the end of the
twentieth century / Thomas French.
        p.   cm.
    Originally published: New York: Doubleday, 1993
    ISBN: 0–671–89801–9 (pbk.)
    1. High school students—Florida—Case studies. 2. High
school students—Florida—Social life and customs. I. Title.
[LA229.F753 1996]
373.18'09759—dc20   95–41502
                                                  CIP

First Pocket Books trade paperback printing March 1996

10 9 8 7 6 5 4 3 2 1

POCKET and colophon are registered trademarks of
Simon & Schuster Inc.

Cover design and electronic retouching by Matt Galemmo
Photo of sky © Jake Wyman/Photonica
Photo of stars © Edward Holub/Photonica

Printed in the U.S.A.

Photographs by Maurice Rivenbark—*St. Petersburg Times,*
reprinted with permission

FOR LINDA,
HEART AND SOUL

CONTENTS

PREFACE
XI

PART I
SHOW-AND-TELL
1

PART II
DISAPPEARING ACTS
91

PART III
THE HISTORY LESSON
173

PART IV
MOTHER'S MILK
231

PART V
SOLITAIRE
303

EPILOGUE
357

AFTERWORD
364

PREFACE

In the mid-1970s, when I was in high school, it was easily the strangest and most confusing place I had ever been.

There were many things I loved about my school. Cruising the halls with my friends, bantering with my teachers—Mr. Brooks, who taught senior English and who had a special love for Dante's *Inferno,* had a sign over his classroom door that said, "Abandon Hope, All Ye Who Enter"— quietly passing folded notes from desk to desk, catching the scent of my girlfriend's perfume as she walked up behind me at my locker on Friday afternoons. Still, I was continually amazed at how ridiculous the rest of the experience could be.

To listen to the morning announcements, you'd have thought the most pressing crisis in the world was our student body's lack of school spirit. Basketball players were worshipped like minor gods; honor students were viewed as major-league geeks. In a ritual known as flushing, seniors routinely grabbed freshman boys, dragged them into the bathrooms, and dunked their heads into the toilets. The administrators, meanwhile, were addicted to the word "immature." The principal and his assistants constantly told us to act like adults, but treated us like children. They told us what we could wear, when we could move, how fast we could walk to lunch, and what topics we were forbidden to write about in our school newspaper.

When I went out for the tennis team, I remember, the coach told me to cut my hair. It was down to my shoulders and looked terrible, but I loved it anyway. I asked the coach—who, for the record, had two of the thickest, most ghastly muttonchop sideburns in history—what the length of my hair had to do with my backhand.

"Just do it," he said.

Afterward, I was so embarrassed that I wore a blue ski cap every day for weeks. If I was taught anything, it was that high school was not about learning but about keeping quiet. And when I finally graduated in 1976, I swore to myself that I would never voluntarily go back to that place.

I was wrong.

More than a decade later, while covering education as a reporter for the *St. Petersburg Times,* I decided—without any outside coercion—to spend a year inside one of the local high schools in Pinellas County, Florida. After all the time that had passed, I wanted to understand what it was like to be an American teenager at the end of the twentieth century. How have things changed? How have they stayed the same? What does it mean to be growing up at a time when AIDS is spreading and the ozone layer is disappearing and institutions such as banks and savings and loans are teetering on the edge? To be coming of age in a society that shows every sign of coming apart?

With the encouragement of my editors at the *Times,* I set out to answer these questions. After obtaining permission from local school officials, I spent the 1989-90 school year wandering Largo High, a respected school in the northern part of the county. I had never been to Largo High before, but I chose it because I knew it was the home of all sorts of students, white and black, from affluent neighborhoods and poor neighborhoods and everything in between. That fall, when Largo's principal and faculty agreed to open their doors, I began my reporting, roaming from one end of the campus to the other. I sat in classes, hung out in the cafeteria, attended parent conferences, jostled my way through the crush of bodies in the halls, had popcorn thrown at me in the stands at football games, even rode along with some kids on a toga scavenger hunt.

Though I did wear a toga on the night of the hunt—I had no choice, since the kids refused to let me in the door without this sign of good faith —everyone at Largo knew I was a reporter. I didn't pose as a teacher or a parent, and even if I'd wanted to, I could never have passed as one of the students. ("Yo, Biff? Who's that gray-haired kid scribbling all those notes next to you in trig?") In any case, there was no need to hide my identity. Students, parents, teachers, and administrators were all remarkably open. They weren't exactly eager to expose their lives to such public scrutiny, but they wanted people to see what has happened to high school and to the lives of high school students. Maybe, they said, it will make someone wake up and pay attention.

I have to admit that much of what I saw was disturbing. I was impressed with the school itself—Largo is known around the county for its committed, experienced teachers—but it was hard not to be shaken by the realities that the students carried with them onto campus every morning. Of the hundreds of kids I met, a surprising number were dealing with problems so gut-wrenching that it was hard to understand how they made it out of bed in the morning, much less came to school. Many were living in homes where no one touches or talks to one another, where happiness is something that appears only in late-night reruns. These students were under siege, fighting to hang on amid the destruction of their families, their neighborhoods, everything around them, and as I sat in class, listening to them tell the secret stories of their lives, it seemed sometimes that the entire world outside must be crumbling.

Yet when I left campus at the end of a school day, I was never completely discouraged. What gave me hope was the kids themselves. For all their struggles, there was still an abundance of wonder and joy in their lives. In the year I spent at Largo, I watched them fall in love, forge fierce alliances, escape death, get accepted to college, laugh their heads off, and dance as though there were no tomorrow. With their wits, their wild sense of irreverence, and the sheer invincibility of their personalities, they all survived and sometimes even triumphed.

When the year was over and I returned to my desk at the *St. Petersburg Times,* I was overwhelmed by what I had witnessed. But I had to try to capture some of it on paper. First I spent a year writing a series of articles for the newspaper, and then I began expanding the material into this book. The lives of these students are so incredible that what I have wound up with may sometimes read like a novel; yet this is entirely a work of nonfiction. All of the people, events, and details described in the book are real; there are no composite characters, invented quotes, or imagined conversations. I have used the real names of everyone except for one person, Andrea Taylor's friend, the girl I call Sabrina. All of the central figures in the book—Andrea and the other students who are described in the greatest detail—were written about with their permission and the permission of their parents.

Although I personally witnessed many of the scenes and recorded firsthand many of the quotes that appear on these pages, there were other moments where it was impossible for me to be present. I was not around when these students were small children; I was also nowhere in sight, obviously, when couples went on dates. When necessary, then, I have reconstructed scenes based on the recollections of the people involved. When I was done writing, I showed these reconstructions to the original sources to confirm that my descriptions were accurate.

Even now, several years after I began this project, I still don't think that what I've written begins to live up to the richness of the tapestry that unfolded before me at Largo High. I've done my best, though, and after all this time, I have come to believe that this is a story about a place that none of us ever escapes, no matter how long ago we left it. A place that stands as a reflection of everything that is good and bad in the country that surrounds it. A place where that same country's future will almost certainly be won or lost.

That's what I'd like to think *South of Heaven* is. A portrait of the place where the battle for our future rages every day.

SOUTH OF HEAVEN

PART ONE

SHOW-
AND-TELL

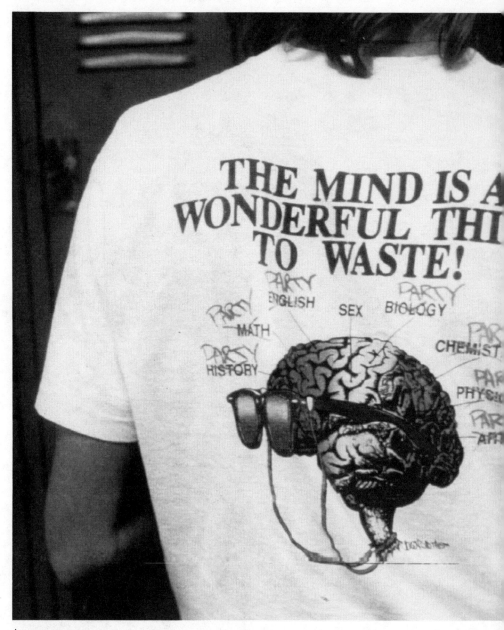

IN THE HALLS.

ONE

ME SO

HORNY

THE HORDES ARRIVE WITH THE SUN.

First bell, the warning bell for first period at Largo High, rings at precisely 7:19 A.M. Not 7:18, not 7:20, but 7:19, now and forever, or at least until the powers that be change their all-powerful minds. Which means that anyone who doesn't want to be late—and who can risk that, what with the continued terror of the hall sweeps—better drag his sorry carcass out of bed and onto campus by then.

When the first of them gets there, most of Florida isn't even out of bed yet. Sometimes it's still dark, and on certain mornings the school is shrouded in mist, swallowed almost from view by a thin gray cloud that hangs motionless over the sprawling red-brick buildings and the people trudging down the walkways toward their lockers. The scene might be pretty in a spooky, Fall of the House of Usher sort of way, if there were time to stand around and gawk and recall that whole gloomy Poe unit back in freshman English. But there isn't time.

The yellow buses pull in, faintly glowing in the early-morning light like some radioactive wagon train. They unload their passengers with rapid-fire precision, then pull out just as quickly, on their way to other routes. Those students who are old enough and fortunate enough to drive themselves follow close behind, whipping into the north parking lots, the boys revving their engines and honking their horns at the next car in line, the girls checking their makeup one last time in side mirrors and leaning halfway out the windows to call to friends in the distance. Half of the cars, it seems, are decorated with stickers for Oakley sunglasses—"Thermonuclear protection"—and many vibrate with the bass that throbs at the threshold of pain from their tape decks and from the speakers stashed in the trunk. These are the boom cars, some of which pack monster stereos with up to one thousand watts per channel, and what they're booming with now is 2 Live Crew.

> *Me so horny*
> *Me so horny*
> *Me love you long time*

Inevitably there is another line of cars inching its way up to Largo's main entrance. This is a quieter, more sedate line—Barry Manilow emanates from some of the car stereos in this line—because it is filled almost entirely with mothers and fathers dropping off their kids. Morning after morning, they kiss their children, wish them luck, then watch them disappear into a swirl of exhaust fumes.

Parents recognize that this is one of the crossroads, where lives are made and broken, where some build the foundation for a career in medicine or accounting and others stumble into an existence sustained by menial labor. Still, almost none of the parents know what high school is like nowadays. They think they know, but they are wrong. They don't have the faintest understanding of what this place has become. Without being here every day, how could anyone?

If the parents could step out of their cars and spend just a few hours on this campus, they would begin to see it. High school, they would quickly learn, is exactly as it has always been and yet totally different. In many ways, it remains the same institution, as absurd and savage and wonderful and terrible as ever. Kids still forget the combinations to their lockers, stuff freshmen into trash cans, write gushy notes in which every "i" is dotted with a tiny heart. They still shuffle to those bizarre pagan rituals known as pep rallies, where they still try, sort of, to remember the almost surrealistic words to the school song:

Oh, we love the halls of Largo
that surround us here today,
and we will not forget
tho' we be far far away.
To the hallow'd halls of Largo
every voice will bid farewell,
and shimmer off in twilight
like the old vesper bell.

If hardly any of them know what a vesper bell is, they have at least remembered to give the alma mater the obligatory rewriting. When many kids sing it, the opening goes like this:

Oh, we hate the halls of Largo
that imprison us every day . . .

They remain faithful to a host of other traditions. They still insist that no one understands them. They still moon teachers, elect student council reps, invent obscene pet names for the administrators. And for the most part, they still learn. Some of them learn amazingly well, especially at a school such as Largo, where the faculty is loaded with teachers who are fighting to make a difference.

Even the most dedicated teachers, however, would admit that high school has also become a strange and frightening place. A place where boys decked out in gold jewelry give phone numbers for their beepers instead of their homes, where skinheads stride into class daring anyone to look them in the eye, where girls who still haven't lost all their baby fat search for a secluded phone so they can make an appointment at the abortion clinic. More than anything else, it has become a place where an alarming number of students actively resist taking part in any assignment that requires them to pay attention for longer than the length of the latest video from Madonna or the Hammer.

Among the throngs milling through these halls, on their way to first period, there is a certain blond-haired girl who skips class so often that she has turned herself into a kind of ghost. Her name is on the attendance rolls, but her teachers hardly know what she looks like. She has no problem coming to school itself. It's the actual classes she avoids. Day after day, she haunts the campus, wandering from one end to the other, silently watching as all the people around her move on with their lives.

She walks down the long empty hallways, crossing under the skylights, floating past shelves filled with trophies, past rows of bright blue lockers, past signs warning that the lockers may be searched without warning at any time. She steps outside and moves along the cement walkways—battered walkways stained with ancient blobs of gum and marked with faded yellow lines—that link one building to the next. She roams beneath the shade of the live oaks that line the basketball courts. She heads back to the front of the school and cruises through the administration building, nodding to friends slumped in orange plastic chairs while they wait for bad news, moving quickly past the permanently hushed corridor immediately outside the principal's office. She walks back outside, heads across the beaten grass on the patio, slips into the bleachers inside the gym, wonders where she should go next.

Sometimes, during the six-minute break between periods, she runs into students who are scurrying toward the same classes she's supposed to be taking. When she sees them, she smiles and calls out a message for her teachers.

"I'm on my way," she says, drifting in the opposite direction. "Tell them I'm on my way."

Over in the front office, waiting to hear another lecture from an assistant principal, sits a small pale boy who will not go to class unless his parents pay him.

"We made this contract up," he says. "If I go to school, every day I get four dollars."

Down the hall of A Wing walks another boy, a boy who recently celebrated the start of the semester by joining some friends at a Back-to-School party. A party held on the beach, in the middle of a school day.

"It's, like, a relief day," he says.

In a classroom across the way, seated in the back, is a senior honor student who readily admits that in his entire life he has read only one book all the way through. Namely, Robert Fulghum's *All I Really Need to Know I Learned in Kindergarten.*

"I like his books," he says, "because the chapters are three pages long."

But these are just the kinds of things a visitor could see and hear in a single day. Spend a week or a month here—spend a year—and soon one witnesses the unmistakable signs of a larger disintegration. There are kids at this school who pass the dead time on their bus by putting cigarettes out on their arms. Kids so filled with self-loathing that they carve on themselves with knives. Kids who live under assumed names so their abusive fathers cannot find them and beat them. Kids who have been kicked out of their houses because their mothers have found new boyfriends who don't want a teenager hanging around. Kids who have run away and are sleeping wherever they can. In their cars, in picnic shelters, in all-night laundries. Anyplace but the place that used to be home.

M I K E   B R O O M E   I S   A B O U T   T O   G O   S U P E R N O V A .   I T ' L L   H A P P E N any second now. Just wait.

By now, Mike is famous for his explosions. He is fourteen, only a few weeks into his ninth-grade year, but well on his way already to failing all his classes and to relegating himself to a lifetime of diminishing possibilities. He has light blue eyes that burn, a scraggly collection of chin hairs that may someday qualify as a beard, and the fervently indifferent air of someone fighting to convince himself that the world has nothing interesting left to show him. He wears an earring shaped like a skeleton smoking a joint. His right arm bears a homemade tattoo that shows an upside-down *A* encased inside a circle, a well-known symbol for anarchy. His jeans are marked repeatedly, in dark black ink, with the letters FTW, which stand for "Fuck the World."

Mike's not stupid. If he wanted, he could do most of his schoolwork in his sleep. Occasionally he does just that. He'll sit at his desk with his head down and eyes closed, and a teacher will call on him, and he'll look up, give the correct answer to whatever's been asked, then return to his dozing. Usually, though, he's too angry to be bothered with such nonsense. He's almost always angry. At school, at home, everywhere. Sometimes it seems as though he lives inside a single never-ending rage.

At the moment, he is slouching his way through another day of earth science. Around him, other students sit listening to the teacher and leafing through their textbooks, the thin white pages rustling softly through the room. He makes no pretense of following the lesson, however. He has not even bothered to take a book off the shelf. The teacher's trying to get him to join the rest of the class, but he's ignoring her.

The teacher likes Mike. She wants him to make it, does not want to see him join all the others who have already vanished from the attendance rolls. It's true, he often frightens her. Sometimes his rage is so close to the surface that he's almost shaking with it. But beneath the anger, there is something special about him. Something promising that goes beyond the fact that he so obviously has brains. His other teachers sense it, too. They can see it when his guard is down, flickering momentarily behind his eyes. Maybe he's just lost. Maybe he's been in a tailspin for so long he doesn't know how to pull out.

So the teacher keeps trying. If Mike won't get a book, then she'll get one for him. She sets it before him and opens it. She finds the right page.

Still he refuses to work.

She looks at him. If that's the way he feels, she tells him, perhaps he shouldn't come to class tomorrow.

"Mike," she says, "this is a waste of your time."

He stares back at her. He could try to tell her what's wrong. He could try, if he wanted, to explain that she has no idea what his life is like.

Instead he stands up.

"Fuck you," he says.

The teacher is not fazed. This is not the first time these words have been hurled in her direction.

"I don't think so," she says. "What is the problem?"

"Fuck this whole school. Fuck the whole system. Fuck everybody."

Normally the other kids in the class would laugh. But this time they know that Mike has gone too far.

"What are you doing?" they ask him. "You don't want to get kicked out."

"Yes, I do. I want to quit this fucking school."

"You can't quit. You need to graduate."

"Fuck it. I can get a job."

Before he leaves, he tells the teacher to write him a disciplinary referral. He demands it. He takes the paper. He walks out the door.

TWO

WHERE THE WILD THINGS ARE

"GOOD MORNING. OUR THOUGHT for the day is: You have to learn the ropes in order to pull the strings."

The words waft through the halls early one bright Thursday. If this message has a sinister undercurrent—exactly what strings does the voice want to pull, and why?—nobody seems to notice. It's just the morning announcements. Most people are only half-awake anyway.

"Please stand for the pledge."

Groggily everyone gets up and goes through the motions.

". . . with liberty and justice for all."

So begins another day at Largo High. It's fall. Or rather, it is supposed to be fall. Homecoming and Halloween are approaching, but the temperatures insist on climbing into the low nineties almost every afternoon. Kids are sweating in the halls, fanning themselves with folders; teachers stand at the front of their classes, struggling to be heard over the low roar of room air-conditioning units.

Summer always seems to drag on forever at Largo, a medium-sized school of 1,900 students that sits just north of St. Petersburg on the center of Florida's west coast, only a mile or so from the dark green waters of the Gulf of Mexico. Home of the Packers, home of the Blue and Gold, Largo is only one of dozens of high schools scattered around the densely populated metropolitan area that straddles Tampa Bay. The region encompasses Tampa, Clearwater, St. Pete, plus more than twenty other municipalities, including the city of Largo itself, all of which run together to form a conglomeration of palm trees and pavement that bakes for six months of every year under the subtropical sun.

At least the nights are finally getting more bearable. Early in the first semester of the 1989-90 school year, the sweltering afternoons are giving way at last to cool evenings under the glaring lights at the football games. Largo is settling down for business. The pulsing energy of the semester's early days has died away; the feverish pitch of the weeks before holiday break has not yet begun. The campus, a cluster of mostly one-story buildings stretched for half a block along the rush of traffic on Missouri Avenue, is relatively quiet.

Two girls cut across the visitors parking lot, on their way to class, trading tales of intrigue.

"Did you get into any trouble this weekend?"

"Of course."

Over in A Wing, a boy storms past the lockers, fuming to a girl walking beside him.

"I'm gonna take a forty-four," he says. "I'm gonna stick it to his head. I'm gonna pull the trigger."

At the back of a world history class, a girl ignores a lecture on the Punic Wars so she can expound on life.

"The world flies by when you turn nineteen," she says to a friend seated beside her. "I'm telling you, it flies by."

At the front of the room, the teacher stands before the glowing surface of an overhead projector, his face shining in the square of light as he jots notes for the class to take down. He's trying to tell them about Hannibal and the elephants crossing the Alps in a surprise attack on Rome. But the kids keep interrupting.

"Can I please go get a drink of water?" says one girl.

The teacher pauses, sighs, musters a smile.

"Say 'please' one more time."

"Please."

"Say it real pitiful."

"Pleeease."

"Do it quick."

In a practice room behind the auditorium, a balding guitar teacher beams as he and students in a makeshift band pound through a ragged but spirited rendition of "Wipe Out," the 1963 surfing classic that was recently rereleased in a rap version. Today, though, they're doing it the old way, and the class actually seems to be getting into it. Kids are nodding their heads, tapping their feet, dropping the requisite teen scowls for guarded smiles. One boy in boots and a tattered black T-shirt—a boy notorious at Largo because a Smurf was once supposedly found in his locker, hanging from a tiny noose—stands off to the side, bent at the waist, furiously banging his long blond hair up and down as though he were in the front row of a Megadeth concert.

A few moments later, in a breathtaking shift of pace, the students put away the electric guitars, take their seats, pick up acoustic instruments, and glide through an ensemble performance of a waltz. Time slows to a gentle, almost stately, pace.

"Watch your posture," says the teacher, studying them with quiet pride. "Sit up straight."

Off in another corner of the school, during a discussion on current events, a group of kids talks about the end of the world, which they insist is imminent.

"We could die any minute," says one boy.

"There's nothing to prevent us from dying," says another.

"We could die any minute," echoes a third, picking up the rhythm, "and all these teachers worry about is homework . . ."

Largo kids are the same as students most anywhere else. They may have better tans. They may be surrounded by alligators and Disney World and sun-scorched tourists. And some of the more hard-core surfers actually keep a nightly vigil on the TV weather reports, praying for a massive low-pressure front to sweep into the area and kick up the waves in the gulf. But for the most part, there's nothing particularly unique about these kids' daily existence. If it weren't for the unremitting heat and the unbelievable size of the cockroaches, they could be living in almost any state in the Union.

They wake up every morning, or at least a good number of them do, in the same prefabricated apartment complexes and cookie-cutter subdivisions found all over the country. When they get dressed, they walk out the door and head for a school that's just down the road from the full complement of universal fast-food joints; there's a Wendy's right next to campus, and a Mister Donut directly across the street; McDonald's, Burger King, Pizza Hut, and Kentucky Fried Chicken are all only a few blocks away. They pull up to the same drive-through windows as every other kid, ordering in the same fast-food shorthand. They hang out in the parking lots of the same 7-Eleven on the corner, monopolizing the same bank of phones and avoiding eye contact with the same weary clerks.

On weekends, they do what kids everywhere have been programmed to do and go shopping at the global mall, buying their clothes at the Limited and the Gap, snacking at the Original Cookie Company and Orange Julius. They listen to radio stations where the deejays affect the same raucous but fun-loving personalities, telling the same breed of off-color gags and playing the same songs as their counterparts at other youth-oriented stations across the land. They watch MTV and Bart Simpson like everybody else; they rent the same movies and buy the same tapes and wait until their parents are asleep to watch the same late-night sex flicks on Cinemax and Showtime.

Though they do have a few bits of slang that are peculiar to their school, Largo students generally speak in the same flattened-out, vaguely midwestern dialect that so many teenagers speak after years of watching homogenized sitcoms. Even though they live hundreds of miles below the Mason-Dixon line, southern accents are almost unheard-of here, not just because of the TV shows but because so many of the kids are transplants who moved to Tampa Bay from up north. The area is such a melting pot that even the ones who were born in Florida and whose parents have lived here for decades speak as though they were from Michigan or Ohio.

It doesn't really matter what state they're from originally, though, because these kids have been raised in the same broken homes as everyone else and dragged through the same custody battles and seen their lives turned upside down by the same economy and been forced to grow up with the same set of diminishing prospects. They are all children of the post-Watergate wasteland, where presidents are expected to lie and fathers are expected to leave and the television is always switched on.

The palm trees are just decoration, designed to enhance the illusion that they are living someplace different.

EYES ROLL. A CHORUS OF GROANS RISES THROUGH THE ranks.

"Awwwwwwww, man."

"Are you kidding?" says one of them. "Get out of here."

Standing at the front of the room, the health teacher shakes her head. She is not kidding, she says. For an assignment, she wants all of them to interview their parents to find out what dating was like for them when they were young.

The teacher is leading this class through an extended unit on teen dating and sexuality. Even though they are only sophomores, she knows many of them are already having sex; they talk about it openly here in class. Especially the boys. Today she wants to continue with their discussion on sexual stereotypes and attitudes. She wants to know, she says, how long they have to be involved in a relationship before they expect their partner to sleep with them.

"Will most guys wait six months for sex?" she asks.

Several boys snicker.

"Most guys will wait a week," says one of them. "*Nice* guys."

Back out in the hall, it's another morning stuck on fast forward. A crush of bodies, fighting to make it to the next class. Slamming lockers, passing flirtations. Whoops and insults and high-pitched cries. The usual descent into chaos.

Over in C Wing, a girl wearing a University of Florida shirt and a look of homicidal fury blazes down the corridor, shaking her head.

"He's *mine*," she vows to a friend trying to keep up beside her. "She's *not* gonna have him. So you can take that to the bank."

A haze of body heat and hair spray hangs over the lockers. Sentries stand at the door of nearly every bathroom, keeping a lookout for adults, ready to sound the warning to the smokers assaulting their lungs inside the stalls. Roaming brigades of cheerleaders, decked out in their uniforms, plow through the crowd. In the center of it all stands one couple, jamming traffic in midstream as they reacquaint themselves with the contours of each other's tongue.

Another bell rings, and suddenly the halls are empty. Empty, that is, except for the principal, Judith B. Westfall, who at this instant is cruising through A Wing, her walkie-talkie in hand. She sees a piece of paper on the floor and picks it up. She sees two stray girls and stops them with a deadly smile.

"Can I see your hall passes?"

The girls produce the passes.

"Do you have your honor cards?"

The principal—the kids call her Ms. Westfall to her face, Judi behind her back—has noticed that these two strays are both wearing shorts, which means they'd better have their honor cards. This year, for the first time, Largo is attempting an unusual experiment. At every other public high school in Pinellas County, shorts are forbidden. Exactly why they are forbidden is a mystery, considering that this is Florida and schools are hot and other counties in the state let students wear them all the time. Plus, the dress code does allow girls to wear miniskirts, which show more skin than almost any pair of shorts.

The whole thing is dumb; on this, almost everyone agrees. It's one of those quintessentially mindless rules that have always defined high school. Over the years students, parents, teachers, and administrators have wasted hundreds of hours debating the issue, fighting over whether the policy should be changed. Back in 1983, in one of the more inspired protests in high school history, a group of boys at another local school demonstrated against the double standard of the rule by wearing miniskirts to class. The Miniskirt Rebellion, it was called, and it created such a stir that the boys and their infamous legs ended up on the national network news. It was all for naught, however. School officials quashed the rebellion, suspending its leader. Worse, the school board only toughened the dress code. Today, all these years later, the no-shorts rule remains in effect for all Pinellas County high school students.

Unless, that is, you go to Largo and carry an honor card. Before the new year began, a bunch of kids at the school teamed with Ms. Westfall to persuade the school board to try out a new wrinkle in the rule. Together, she and the kids got the board to agree to a one-year test program that allows Largo students with good grades, good behavior, and solid attendance to wear shorts. If they qualify, all they have to do is apply for an honor card.

There's just one thing. If the experiment's going to fly, those who wear shorts must carry their honor cards at all times. Or else.

Now one of the girls squirming before Ms. Westfall admits that her card is not on her person. Not at this precise microsecond.

"Um, it's in my purse," says the girl, trying not to sound too frantic. "Want me to go get it?"

Ms. Westfall gives the girl a withering look—a look she has mastered through years of practice—then sends her and her friend on their way. Ms. Westfall watches them go, allowing herself a smile. The truth is, she's smiling a lot these days. She's excited about the shorts program, and the fact that Largo kids were the ones to pull it off. She's also excited about the start of the semester and relieved that she hasn't had any major crises to contend with. The students are working hard, the teachers seem relatively happy, and the football team is undefeated—always good for morale —after winning the first four games of the season. So far, in fact, everything has gone surprisingly well. Certainly better than last year, which was the year Ms. Westfall and everyone else would just as soon forget.

The whole thing was a nightmare. Largo kept attracting attention for all the wrong reasons. One teacher was accused of making sexually explicit statements to some of his female colleagues. Another teacher was suspended then transferred to another school after he was accused of trying to buy a stolen handgun from a student. The teacher denied that he was really trying to buy the gun, a 9mm Beretta. Later, when he was brought up on disciplinary charges, he said that he had merely been conducting his own personal investigation into the student's suspicious activities. But when he started talking about paying $140 for the Beretta, one of the conversations was overheard by an undercover narcotics officer from the sheriff's department, posing as a student to ferret out drugs on campus.

It was a banner year, all right. By the time the undercover cop was finished, five Largo students were under arrest on charges of sale or possession of marijuana or cocaine. Almost no one other than Ms. Westfall had known who this officer was or what he was doing on campus. He was so convincing as a student that he ran afoul of some of the teachers, who were worried because he seemed to have little interest in homework and was missing so many days of class.

"Don't you want to graduate?" one of them asked him.

Then there was the mass protest. It happened near the end of the year, when the administration and faculty began a strict enforcement of the tardy policy, nabbing all the strays who were wandering in the halls without a pass and then taking them down to the cafeteria to write them all up with referrals. The kids weren't particularly thrilled with the new order. But what really sent them over the top was the language that some of the teachers and administrators used to describe the new order. The mass roundups were known as "hall sweeps," and the cafeteria was called "the holding tank." When those phrases spread through the school, the students decided to fight back by skipping class and staging a demonstration.

It was disorder on a grand scale. Hundreds of kids were standing at the front of the school, yelling and chanting and ignoring all of the usual rules that keep them in their seats. A cameraman from one of the local stations showed up, and the level of hysteria went up even more. Finally

Ms. Westfall sent the TV crew packing and waded with a bullhorn into the middle of the demonstrators. A few minutes later, order was restored and the kids went back to class. But even now, when she looks back on that mob scene and the rest of that horrific year, Ms. Westfall visibly shudders.

Never again, she tells herself. She does not ever wish to suffer through anything as stressful as that again. She doesn't think either she or the school could take it. So now she has a little prayer she says to herself during quiet moments. It's the same prayer all principals say. Just let it stay calm this year, she tells herself. Just let everything stay nice and peaceful and perfectly still, just for this one time, this one year . . .

THE GHOST FRESHMAN WHO WANDERS THE HALLS HAS materialized in a classroom. Her name is Jaimee, and she is sitting at a table inside the pod, a small building just off the end of A Wing where there are no windows and where the walls are merely temporary room dividers. Jaimee is filling out a sheet of questions her teacher has passed out. The sheet is designed to help the students set goals and formulate strategies toward reaching those goals. It begins: "My goal is to . . ."

She reads this and writes: *learn to surf.*

Question two: "What skills will you need in order to accomplish your goal?"

She writes: *good balance.*

Finally: "What should you be able to do that will demonstrate that you have achieved this goal?"

She writes: *surf.*

Sitting nearby, a skinny boy named Kurt with a Mohawk on his head and tiny swastikas marked on his high-top tennis shoes fills out his sheet.

His goal: *grow my hair out.*

What he'll need to do to accomplish his goal: *shampoo it every day.*

What he'll be able to do if he achieves his goal: *put it in a ponytail.*

A boy named David studies his sheet. David is older than most of the freshmen and sophomores who surround him in this class. Last year he dropped out of school, but now he has returned with a vengeance, determined to make it this time. He is the voice of maturity, an evangelist for education who now preaches to the other kids about the importance of earning a diploma.

David's goal: *to pass all classes with at least a B.*

What he'll need to do: *just work hard.*

What he'll do if he achieves it: *graduate!*

Here in the pod, there's another experiment going on. Here, in a part of the school other students sometimes call the Twilight Zone, approximately two hundred of Largo's most difficult students—the lost, the unmotivated, the hostile, some of the most hopeless of the hopeless cases—are taking part in a special program that might be their last chance at making something of their lives. The program is called GOALS. The acronym stands for Graduation Options: Alternatives to Leaving School, which is a long-winded way of saying that this is a place where teachers try to keep kids from walking out the door and never coming back. One of many such programs spreading around the country, GOALS is a last-ditch attempt to reach students who have spent years trying to prove that they are unreachable. It is the front line in the battle against dropouts.

Each year, tens of thousands of students disappear from Florida's public high schools. Depending on whose figures you believe—the federal and state governments keep arguing about the exact numbers—roughly 25 to 40 percent of the state's high school students ultimately quit. This is where GOALS comes in. The idea behind the program is simple. Take a bunch of kids who should be making it but aren't. Kids whose standardized test scores show they've got the brains, but whose behavior and grades and family histories make it clear that they're on the way to dropping out. Put them in smaller classrooms—no more than eighteen kids per instructor, which is half of the ratio you'll find in many regular classrooms—and give them specially trained teachers who'll be tough enough and creative enough to figure out a way to pierce the students' armor of indifference and anger.

Still, there are no guarantees. Especially with these kids.

"Do you want to work at McDonald's for the rest of your life?" someone yells out one day in the pod's one and only hallway.

Instantaneously, several voices shout the same answer.

"Yes!"

IN A ROOM AT THE OPPOSITE END OF THE SCHOOL, A SENIOR girl sits in her Latin class, feeling her stomach growl. She needs to score some sugar. A megadose of chocolate. Now.

"Do you have any M&Ms, first of all?"

She says this to the person seated beside her, the one who's selling candy for the band or the yearbook or some other no doubt worthy cause.

"And do you have change for a five, second of all?"

The answer to both questions being yes, she hands over her money and takes her change. She looks toward the front of the room, where the teacher is leading the rest of the class in an exercise from page 305 of their books.

Hostibus pulsis, tamen disciplinam nostram non remittemus.

Oh boy.

"Ablative absolute," says someone brave, diving in first. "The enemy, having been . . ."

This person pauses.

". . . driven out," says a boy nearby.

"Defeated," says the teacher.

"The enemy, having been defeated . . ."

Another pause.

"Nevertheless," says someone else.

". . . nevertheless, we will not . . ."

The senior girl is camped in her usual spot at the back of the room. She isn't really paying attention to the exercise; she isn't supposed to. She's the only fourth-year Latin student in the room, which means she usually works independently while the others slog their way through lessons she mastered long ago. At the moment, as she snacks on her M&Ms—in brazen defiance of school policy—she is translating an oration Cicero delivered to the Roman Senate in 63 B.C. against some stooge named Catiline.

"How're you doing?" asks the teacher, stopping by her desk for a moment.

"Oh, fine," she says, looking up from the text with a sigh. "Cicero's boring."

The teacher smiles. "He *is* boring."

"He's very long-winded. All he says is, 'Get out of town, Catiline! And take all your followers with you!'"

By now this girl is intimately familiar with Cicero. She has learned, she says—softly, so as not to disturb the rest of the class—everything the man ever did. She recalls what year he delivered his first speech. What country he first visited as a young man. Where he was at the moment of his first sneeze.

She laughs. Only kidding. She doesn't really know the precise location of his first sneeze. But a few seconds after making the joke, she explodes, almost on cue, with a little sympathy sneeze of her own.

"Excuse me."

Her name is Christine Younskevicius. But almost everyone calls her YY, since that's so much easier than trying to negotiate the swamp of diphthongs that makes up her Lithuanian last name. The nickname was bestowed upon her eons ago by another teacher and has stuck ever since. A perpetually dangling double question, it fits her perfectly. Somehow it captures the manic quality of her entire life.

"Tempus fugit," YY tells her friends. Time flies. And nobody knows it better. For her, time flies supersonic. It has to, just to keep up with the after-midnight sessions with the books and the honor classes early the next morning and of course the overriding imperative, which is that she must continually confirm and reconfirm that she is one of the best and brightest to ever roam these hallowed halls.

She is seventeen now, on her way to college and a future brimming with possibilities. She has dark brown eyes, a permanently tangled mess of brown hair, and an alarming shortage of eyelashes, which she tends to pull on whenever her nerves get frayed, which is almost every day. This year she is vice-president of the National Honor Society; president of the Latin Club; a member of Mu Alpha Theta, better known among the clueless masses as the math honor society; co-editor in chief of the student newspaper; and a starter on the academic quiz team, which happens to be the reigning county champ. Her specialties, the subjects where she's expected to rack up the points during the quiz matches, include calculus, physics, literature, the arts, plus assorted dusty facts from ancient Rome.

As if that's not enough to make a girl sketch out and go psycho—and YY will be the first to admit it happens from time to time—she is also an older sister and part-time caretaker of three infinitely younger brothers; a free agent in the savage arena of dating (no one has asked her out for centuries); and a high-ranking member of the most exclusive and powerful clique on campus, which can be a full-time job unto itself. Her grade-point average, meanwhile, hovers somewhere in the upper reaches of the stratosphere, where it must stay if she wants to keep the scholarship her parents are counting on for next year.

She's not a saint or anything. Known among some of her friends as the Wild and Wonderful YY, she's a regular on the circuit of A-list parties, a veteran of countless blowouts where the young and the restless and even the academically inclined have been known to incur major damage to their systems. But she is also the quintessential achiever, a top student—number six in her class to be exact—who knows when it's time to get wild and when it's time to get on task. Even more remarkable, she is one of the few teenagers remaining on the planet who love to read; sometimes, when she's not busy writing for the school paper or struggling with a physics assignment, she'll reread her favorite sections of Edith Hamilton's *Mythology* for fun.

YY loves mythology. She has loved it for so long, she can recite the details of almost any Greek or Roman myth. She can tell you which of the gods sent the two big ole snakes to kill Baby Hercules, and which god disguised himself as a swan so he could put the moves on this earth girl named Leda, and how one of the love children conceived by said Leda and said swan was none other than Helen of Troy, a.k.a. the Face That Launched a Thousand Ships. Ask about the fair Helen, and YY will snort and start in about what a worthless creature she was, allowing Paris to steal her away while her husband was out of town, then helplessly fluttering her eyelids while all these warriors fought and died over her in the Trojan War.

"A real wench," YY says. "She was hatched from an egg, which is *really* strange."

Mythology was how YY got into Latin in the first place. That's how lots of kids get into it. Either that, or through the history, which can be pretty wild as well. Cicero may be boring, but there's still the big bad lions snacking on Christians in the Colosseum; Caligula, the mad emperor, supposedly sleeping with his sister and then ripping the fetus from her womb; Cleopatra and Caesar getting horizontal among the pyramids; plus a veritable cavalcade of conspiracies and assassinations and incestuous relationships and prophetic dreams and wives poisoning their husbands and husbands beheading their wives and one wine-soaked orgy after another. Say what you will about the Romans, but they certainly knew how to hold a teenager's attention.

Their Latin teacher, Mrs. Troiano, uses the juicy stuff for all it's worth. She and the students talk at length about the factors that led to the decline of the Roman empire—the corruption among public officials, the decline of morals, and so forth—and then draw parallels to what's been happening in recent years inside the United States. Mrs. Troiano does all sorts of things to make the class come alive. Back when these kids were just starting Latin, she had each of them pick a particular historical or mythological figure and assume it as their own identity to be used during class. One kid chose Narcissus and then insisted the Homecoming Queen was in love with him. Another kid, a strange boy who always wore a black raincoat, picked Caligula and did his best to live down to it. Another boy went for Oedipus, apparently not realizing the long-term implications for him and his parents. To this day, one of the girls still refers to herself as Circe the sorceress.

"I turn men into swine," she says happily one afternoon, throwing up her hands at the nearest male, as though she's casting a spell on him. "Poof!"

"They don't *need* to be turned into swine," says YY. "They already are."

As for YY, she had a bit of a challenge figuring out who she wanted to be. She hates all those passive women in the myths—myths obviously written by men, she notes. She can't stand all those simpering fair-skinned maidens who are continually getting turned into heifers and being watched over by some giant with a hundred eyes and so forth, all because they did the wild thing with the wrong deity. YY's not the simpering type. She's strong, she's independent, she's not afraid to tussle with anyone who crosses her. Which is why she picked Juno, queen of the gods, queen of heaven, protectress of women, the top chick on Olympus.

So now here Juno sits, deigning to appear in the form of this slightly tousled girl. She munches on the forbidden M&Ms, toys with her hair, directs the beams of her eyes to the Cicero text, and tries to focus once more on the ramblings of possibly the most long-winded mortal ever to draw a breath. Without saying a word, she resigns herself to the fact that even those who wish to live among the clouds must dedicate themselves almost daily to the dreariest of tasks.

THE FILES IN THE FRONT OFFICE WOULD HAVE YOU BElieve that Christine Younskevicius and Mike Broome go to the same school. And technically speaking, this is correct. They both walk the same long halls. They sit in classrooms only a hundred yards away from each other, trapped behind weathered desks scrawled with the same declarations of love and lust. The truth is, though, the two of them don't go to the same school at all. They don't know each other; they have never even heard of each other. They are invisible to each other. They exist on different planets.

Mike sits on the steps outside the auditorium, smoking a Marlboro. A few feet behind him, posted over the auditorium doors, is a sign, weathered and chipped, but still readable:

Please—No Smoking, Drinks or Food

There are half a dozen reasons why smoking is the last thing Mike should be doing. For one thing, he has asthma—and a deep, rattling cough to prove it—and the cigarettes only make it worse. For another, he has already been caught smoking once this year, and if he gets caught again, he wins an automatic five-day suspension. Finally, he is a GOALS student, and GOALS students are supposed to be resurrecting their academic careers, not trashing them.

Why, then, is Mike out here in broad daylight, cigarette in hand? It's not just a nicotine craving. If it were, he could easily have picked someplace less conspicuous. Instead he has lit up here on the steps, probably the most visible spot on the entire campus. So why would he do something he logically cannot afford to do? Maybe Mike will be able to explain it someday. But ask him now and he'll just shrug and look away with a cryptic smile.

"I don't know. School's boring."

Almost everything is boring to Mike. He's never heard of Leda or the swan or their daughter, Helen, the wench who hatched from an egg and started a war. The notion of plodding through a book on mythology or history is completely foreign to him; he doesn't see the point. He isn't even sure he sees the point of finishing high school. Some days, he insists he's ready to quit right now. One morning, after he has been slapped with another in a long line of suspensions—a suspension he almost invited but that now enrages him—he storms into the GOALS office in the pod.

"I'm not coming back," he tells Ruth Riel, the dropout prevention specialist who heads the school's GOALS program.

She reminds him that legally he can't quit until his sixteenth birthday, which is more than a year away.

"They'll come to your door," she says.

"I won't open the door."

On other days, on the days when things go well, Mike insists he wants to stay in school. He says he wants to get through the next four years, graduate, and then join the Air Force, just like his oldest brother, Greg. There is a framed picture of Greg, in his uniform, on a table in the living room at Mike's house. At night, when Mike stretches out on the floor, staring at the TV—his mother sitting to the left in her chair, his stepfather to the right in his chair—Greg's picture looks at them all, reminding them of what a Broome boy can accomplish. During the day, when Mike is in class, he makes paper airplanes. He sits quietly at his desk, folding one blank sheet of paper after another, driving his teachers crazy.

More and more, it's looking as though this may be as close as Mike ever gets to working with a plane. He knows the Air Force won't take anyone without a high school diploma, and if he gets caught smoking again—if he gets into any more trouble, period—a diploma is going to be that much further out of reach. But that's too far away to worry about. Besides, his mother smokes. His stepfather smokes. So does Wade, Mike's other brother, who's a couple of years older and who also goes to Largo. It was Wade who gave Mike his first cigarette when he was twelve.

So now here's Mike perched outside the auditorium with some friends, puffing away. He and the others—a congregation of metalheads, skateboard cowboys, Nintendo junkies, and other dispossessed souls— meet out here on these steps every day, decked out in their standard uniforms of torn jeans and Metallica shirts. The Step Kids, the adminis- trators call them. The head-banging kid in the guitar class, the Smurf Killer, hangs out here; so does the kid whose parents pay him to come to school. They share cigarettes, keep an eye open for adults, practice kick- flips on their skateboards, trade imitations of their least favorite adminis- trators. They talk about girlfriends, about Nintendo triumphs, about the latest ridiculous thing uttered by their parents, about which of the women teachers they think are hot.

Sometimes they don't say much at all. Sometimes Mike and the others sit without saying a word, wearing their silence like it's part of the uni- form. They stare into the distance, watching other kids cruise along the sidewalks, listening to the school's flagpole clinking in the wind, hearing the warning bells and the final bells and ignoring them all.

THREE

THE TWILIGHT ZONE

DOWN IN THE FLUORESCENT REALM of the pod, in Mrs. O'Donnell's science class, it is time once again for show-and-tell.

A pale girl named Shannon passes around a picture of her dead dog.

"Her name was Whiskey," she explains. "We got her at three weeks old. And my mom's ex-boyfriend got mad at her."

It is a terrible story. Whiskey, a mix between a pit bull and a Labrador retriever, had a habit of running outside whenever the door was left open. One day, it seems, the mother's former boyfriend grew so angry at the dog that he purposely opened the door and sent her traipsing out into the cruel world, where she was promptly captured by animal control and hauled away to the pound. Before it would release her, the pound allegedly sent a letter to the family, demanding $450, which was more than the ex-boyfriend had any intention of paying and more than the mother could scrounge up on her own.

"Ten days," says Shannon. "They gave us ten days. And we got the letter on the tenth day."

She is fighting back the tears.

"They killed her," she says.

One of the boys can't believe it. "Man, if they killed my dog, I'd go in there with a gun and start shooting."

Someone else nods in agreement. "I'd take a shotgun to 'em."

Mrs. O'Donnell, listening nearby, shakes her head. "No, that's not the answer," she says. "We've discussed that before."

They are sitting in one of the pod's ten windowless classrooms. The walls are a vague shade of pale yellow; the floor is off-white. The entire room is cast in a dim and claustrophobic light that radiates from the fixtures in the ceiling. From the next room, carried through the thin walls, comes a flurry of muffled voices.

Shannon appears to be finished. The picture of Whiskey has made the rounds, and now she's holding it again, staring at it quietly. Mrs. O'Donnell turns to the rest of the class.

"Who's next?"

A girl who almost never speaks a word in class—a girl with stringy hair and bad acne and not much money for new clothes, a girl the other kids like to make fun of—shows a tattered bird's nest she has lovingly saved and protected. A boy tells about the first time he killed a deer. A girl shows a drawing she has done, modeled after the cover of an Iron Maiden album.

A couple of the others see it and snicker.

"Hey," says the artist. "I was *not* stoned when I drew that."

Another girl shows off a ring on her middle finger. The ring is formed into the letters "O-Z-Z-Y," as in Ozzy Osbourne, the heavy-metal star.

"Isn't he the guy who ate the bat?" says Mrs. O'Donnell.

"He didn't *eat* the bat," says someone else, rushing to Ozzy's defense. "He spit the head out."

A boy raises his hand and tells about a song he likes in which a young man beats his mother in the head with his skateboard.

"It's got a thrash kind of beat to it," he says. "It pumps you up."

"Do you ever listen to any other kind of music? Classical, country?" says Mrs. O'Donnell, teasing. "What about disco and John Travolta?"

The whole class groans. They stare at her as though she were a cavewoman dropped into the twentieth century.

"Jesus," says one boy, dropping his head to the table in front of him.

"That was back in the *seventies,*" says someone else.

Several boys jump up and run to the center of the room to do their best John Travolta imitation. They stand there, legs planted to the side, pumping their arms up and down and pointing their fingers toward the sky and singing in tandem.

"Ah, Ah, Ah, stayin' alive, stayin' alive . . ."

Mary O'Donnell, a tall, slender woman with brown hair and an easy smile, claps her hands and laughs. This is the whole point of show-and-tell. It's exactly what she wants. Normally she would be teaching these kids biology or earth science. But once in a while, she lets them put away their books and bring in something that's important to them. Maybe it's an heirloom their grandmother gave them. Or a T-shirt they've decorated with the name of a metal band. If they don't want to bring anything, they can share a story about their lives. Or they can cut out a newspaper clipping and discuss some world issue that's on their minds. Mrs. O'Donnell has found that show-and-tell is a remarkably efficient way of cracking the tough exterior of her GOALS students, of getting them to show how they think and what they care about. If she can understand them, then maybe she can make contact with them. If she can do that, then maybe they'll stay in school.

She turns to Kurt, the skinny boy with the Mohawk on his head and the swastikas on his shoes. Kurt tells her he has nothing to share and nothing to say. Not to be deterred, she fishes for anything to get him talking.

"What possessed you to get that haircut?" she asks him.

He looks at her as though she's insane. "Nothing 'possessed' me . . . I just did it."

"Well, how long have you had it?"

"About a month."

"What do your parents think of it?"

"They don't."

"Don't you spike it sometimes?"

A nod.

"What kind of mousse do you use?"

"I don't know."

They move on. A girl shows her teddy bear, which is so ragged it is missing an arm and a leg. Someone else gets up to show off her copy of *Sassy* magazine. She opens it to let the others check out some hot photos of Patrick Swayze. When Mrs. O'Donnell says she's not familiar with *Sassy*, all the girls in the room stare at her in disbelief.

"You've never heard of Sassy?"

She ignores them and flips through it. "What do they tell you about in here?" she says.

"Makeup tips . . . Five types of guys to avoid at all costs."

The biggest presentation of the day comes from Mickey. His real name is Steve, but he won't let anyone call him that. For as long as the kids in the pod can remember, he has always wanted to be known by the name of his hero, Mickey Mouse. This is not a joke. Mickey has a sense of humor about it, but underneath, he is dead serious.

He shows the others his Mickey Mouse harmonica. And his Mickey Mouse cap. And his Mickey Mouse doll, and his Mickey Mouse toothbrush container, and his Mickey Mouse earring. He would have brought his Mickey Mouse underwear, he says, but he doesn't think they'd really want to see it.

"Anything and everything, I've got it."

He shows them a clipping of a newspaper photo that shows a cow with spots naturally shaped like Mickey Mouse's head. According to Mickey, the people who owned the cow have already sold it to Disney.

"They got, like, a million bucks for that cow," he says.

The other kids are stunned by the sheer number and diversity of the souvenirs. Especially the Mickey Mouse fishing bobber.

"No way," says another kid, staring at the bobber. "Where would you get that?"

Mickey smiles.

"I don't reveal my sources," he says.

Mrs. O'Donnell asks him how the fascination began. It started a while back, Mickey says, when he had quit school for a time and was at home by himself. He was depressed. He was lonely. He felt like a failure. Then he found Mickey Mouse.

"I couldn't make friends or nothing," he says, "and it's, like, *this* was my friend, who would never tell me I was a loser . . . He never argues back."

A girl nearby raises her hand. "He can never talk to you, either," she says. "Have you thought of that?"

"I don't care," says Mickey. "He never tells me that I'm wrong."

When he says this, the rest of the class grows uncomfortably quiet. Some of the kids are studying Mickey with amazement. Others are fighting not to laugh. Finally someone breaks the silence.

"Is your house, like, Pee-Wee's Playhouse?" says one of the girls.

Mickey stands there with an uncertain smile, looking out at the faces of his classmates. He could take their reactions two ways. Maybe he's made a hit and they're just laughing at the oddness of his obsession. Or maybe they think he really is a loser, confirming his worst suspicions.

Before it goes any further, Mrs. O'Donnell steps in. Politely she thanks Mickey for his presentation and moves on. A few seats down, among a group of kids who refuse to take show-and-tell seriously, always blowing it off, a boy holds up a can of diet Coke he's been drinking.

"This is my can," he says with a smirk. "You can recycle it and get money for it."

"This is my pen," says the boy beside him, playing along. "It flies."

With that, he pulls the pen back and flips it into the air. It sails across the room in a graceful arc, tumbling lengthwise end over end . . .

LAST SPRING, WHEN MRS. O'DONNELL STARTED TEACHING in GOALS, she might have been surprised to hear someone like Mickey tell his story. She came to Largo from an affluent school outside Chicago. Here, teaching in classes filled with kids living on the edge, she has seen and heard things she never could have imagined before.

"I couldn't see having a father," a boy says one day. "It would just blow my mind."

This is a common sentiment in the pod. Many kids have barely met or never seen their fathers. As it happens, the father of this particular boy left the family shortly before the boy was born. Now the boy lives with his mother, who still harbors a general resentment toward men. Sometimes she gets angry at her son; sometimes, he says, she tells him she wishes she'd done what someone had told her to do when she was pregnant with him. She wishes, she tells him, that she'd had him aborted.

"I don't think she really means it," the boy says, looking away.

In one show-and-tell session, a girl tells a story about the day a strange man came to visit.

"Someone was at the door," the girl says, "and it was, like, my dad, and I didn't even know who it was . . . He only stayed for, like, a half an hour because he was getting ready to go to the airport."

"Do you look like him?" someone asks.

"I don't know."

Mrs. O'Donnell asks the eleven kids who've shown up for today's class how many still live with both of their original parents. Three of them raise their hands. Two, however, obviously have not understood the question, because they now explain that they're living with their mothers and stepfathers. The third says his parents are still together but are filing for divorce.

"They keep arguing about who's going to pay for the lawyer," he says.

One of the girls raises her hand to talk about how she lives with her mom and her mom's boyfriend.

"Do you get along with him?" says Mrs. O'Donnell.

The girl shrugs. "I don't talk to him. He's just there."

Many students talk openly in class about how their parents are alcoholics. Some of the kids themselves confess that they are struggling with their own drinking problems or other drug addictions. Some started their habits with the aid of their mother and father. In the middle of one show-and-tell, a girl talks about a birthday party she went to where the birthday girl and her mother celebrated by snorting a line of cocaine together.

One morning a boy walks up to Mrs. O'Donnell, obviously upset. She knows something is wrong—he's been seething quietly for days.

"Is there a problem?" she asks him.

"There is a problem."

"What is it? Do you want to talk about it?"

"I don't want to talk about it, but there is a problem."

"Is it something at home?"

"It's just everything."

Some of them write it down. On the outsides of their folders, they write things that give Mrs. O'Donnell a glimpse into their rage, their despair, their sense of powerlessness. Sometimes it's swastikas, drawn over and over. Sometimes it's the titles of their favorite death metal songs. Sometimes Mrs. O'Donnell isn't sure what she's reading.

A few examples:

Mommy's little monster
So far so good so what
Keep America white
Under the influence
Suicidal tendencies
My life's a mediocre piece of shit
Slap of reality
Into the pit
South of heaven

Not everyone in GOALS is consumed with such frustration. Many of the kids are remarkably upbeat about their lives, considering some of the things they contend with at home. In the hall outside Mrs. O'Donnell's classroom, a glass case will soon be going up, filled with the photos of more than a dozen GOALS students who are expected to graduate this coming June. Their photos show them standing proudly in bright blue caps and gowns, squinting into the sun, smiling uncertainly, as though they can hardly believe it themselves.

Still, the teachers know that no matter how hard they try, many of their students will indeed drop out. Even with the smaller classes in GOALS, there's no way to reach every kid who comes through the door. Some of the students who find their way into the pod are struggling with problems so overwhelming—problems that clearly began long ago, often before they even made it to kindergarten—that it's hard to imagine anything saving them.

There is a girl in Mrs. O'Donnell's sixth-period class—a pretty girl, with long blond hair and an angelic face—who has apparently convinced herself that she is a witch. Sometimes she casts spells on her teachers; when they stumble over their words or make a mistake in front of the class, she claims her magic is responsible.

"I made her say that," she tells the other kids.

This might be funny if it weren't for the other things this girl has been doing. She talks to herself about the devil, she tells other kids she can read their minds. Recently she completed a drawing, one that graces the outside of her folder in another class, of a naked man with a large erect penis.

There is another student—Mrs. O'Donnell doesn't have him, but she's heard the other GOALS teachers talking about him—who without warning will suddenly scream in the middle of class and who sometimes tries to unnerve his teachers by touching himself in front of them. He's a scrawny little kid, just a baby really, but the teachers have heard that he recently ran away from home and was living in a picnic shelter. Now back with his family, he has begun making ominous statements about not caring if he dies.

Mrs. McGraw, who has him in her seventh-period English class, has found a way to calm him down. This kid, it turns out, loves to read. As long as he's reading at his desk, he will not scream or run around the room. So McGraw gives him books—he seems to respond especially to macabre stories by writers such as Roald Dahl and Shirley Jackson—and lets him sit there, losing himself inside the pages. Mrs. McGraw is not sure how long it will work. The reading's just a stopgap, really. A way of holding back the flood for just a little while longer.

In Mrs. O'Donnell's third period, there's a boy who recently drew a picture of Satan as part of his class notes. Not long ago, he exploded in her classroom, cursing at her with an outpouring of obscenity. She sent him to an assistant principal's office, where he sat slumped in a chair, repeatedly knocking his head against the wall behind him.

"How many days for swearing at a teacher?" he asked the assistant principal.

"Three."

The boy thought for a moment. "How many days for killing a teacher?" he said.

Down the hall, in another classroom, there's a pale, sickly looking girl. She's a heavy girl, with a serious weight problem that stands as a metaphor for her inability to control anything in her life. She's waiting for an intestinal bypass operation that's supposed to make her thin and solve all her problems. She has been told that the surgery is both expensive and risky. She insists she does not care.

"If I die soon," she says, "then at least I'll be happy."

And then, of course, there is Mike Broome. Always, there is Mike Broome.

MIKE BROOME, TAKING A PUFF FROM A FRIEND'S CIGARETTE, SITS AMONG THE STEP KIDS.

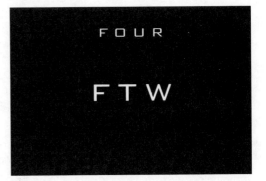

FOUR

FTW

HE CONSTANTLY INVENTS NEW ways to self-destruct.

A few weeks into the school year, he has already become a legend around the pod. He gets into fights with other students, smokes in the rest rooms and on the steps, raises havoc in detention hall, terrorizes substitute teachers. Day after day, he engages in an ongoing experiment in his classes, testing the limits of his teachers' patience and goodwill. He insults them, defies them, leaves class without their permission, refuses to lift a pencil for them. He practically dares them to send him to the office.

"Mike, don't do that."

It's seventh period, the last period in the day. He is seated at his desk in Mrs. McGraw's English class, making another paper airplane.

"Don't do that."

When he ignores her, she takes out a disciplinary referral form and puts it in plain sight on her desk. He sees her and stops. A few minutes later, he gets out another piece of paper and slowly begins folding it into another plane. He waits until Mrs. McGraw looks at him, then crumples the paper into a ball. She looks away, and he does it again.

Like some of the other teachers, Barbara McGraw has a special attachment to Mike. As much of a pain as he can be, she, too, is convinced that there's a nice boy hiding somewhere inside him. She knows there is, because she's seen it. One day someone brought a baby down to the pod, and the teachers watched with astonishment as Mike gently held the child and played with her. Suddenly all the hostility vanished. He was just this sweet kid, lost in the wonderment of holding someone even more vulnerable than he.

Now, as he taunts Mrs. McGraw with his growing fleet of aircraft, she tries to ignore him, hoping he'll stop. If she writes him up, she knows he'll probably be suspended again and will miss days he cannot afford to miss. So she does not fill out the referral. She tries to let it be.

At 2:28 P.M., two minutes before the bell rings and he's free to go, Mike walks up to her desk. He is strangely angry. Clearly he does not understand why she has refused to play her role in the drama he has been staging.

He picks up the referral.

"You can shove this up your ass," he says.

Mrs. McGraw sighs, gets out her pen, and gives him what he wants.

WHAT MRS. MCGRAW WANTS TO KNOW—WHAT ALL OF Mike's teachers in the pod want to know—is how he got so angry in the first place.

Wade, Mike's older brother, who is also in GOALS, does not offer any clues. Wade has his moments. Not long ago, furious because he wasn't allowed to sit with his friends and talk, he leveled a vague threat at Mrs. O'Donnell, telling her he was going to get her. Usually, though, Wade is not like that. He's softer and friendlier than his little brother. He's the class clown, the type who's usually busy cracking up the kids around him, telling jokes under his breath, grinning maniacally at his teachers.

Mike is not much for maniacal grins. Mike is not much for grinning, period. He can work himself up into a rage and hold on to it for weeks. He is a master of sustained animosity. Of course, the teachers know that finding the source of this animosity is the key. If they could get him to open up and reveal the secret well that feeds his rage, they might have a chance to get through to him. But any effort they make to understand him, he resists. Any attempt to coax him out of his isolation, he rebuffs.

"If you could have whatever you wanted," someone asks him one afternoon, "what would it be?"

"I don't know."

"What do you do when you're upset or mad?"

"Sit in my room, listening to the stereo."

"What do you do when you're happy?"

"Sit in my room, listening to the stereo."

"What do you care about?"

"Nothing."

"What's important to you?"

He shakes his head, laughs. "Nothing."

Mike is not a total loner. He has a few friends, kids he meets on the auditorium steps or in the neighborhood, kids who shoot hoops with him and go roller skating with him on Friday nights at Rainbow Roller Land. But they bristle with their own alienation—he's not the only one attracted to the letters "FTW"—and are just as disconnected as he is. Mike doesn't hang out at the mall, like almost every other teenager does, because he's broke and says he doesn't see the point. And even though he lives within walking distance of the campus, he doesn't go to football games either, or the lip syncs, or any of the dozens of other after-school gatherings, most of which are free or close to it. Every day, when the final bell rings, he is gone.

Usually he stays close to home, which for him is a three-bedroom rental house with peeling white paint and faded shingles and a little front step where he sits in the afternoons, smoking his Marlboros and watching the traffic roll by on Belleair Road. He likes to play Nintendo sometimes —there are two Nintendo rigs in the house, one in Wade's room and one in his mom's room—but the real fan of the game is his stepfather, Jerry, who has been known to play for hours at a stretch when he comes home from his construction job. Usually Mike prefers to lie alone in his room, strumming on his guitar, listening to his mother in the kitchen as she pours herself another glass of milk for her ulcer.

His mother's name is Jewelene Wilson. It used to be Jewelene Broome, but then she married Jerry. Even so, anybody could take one look at her and see that Mike's her son. She has the same complexion and the same eyes; when she gets mad, they burn with the same fire as Mike's. Mostly, though, Jewelene just looks worn-out. She has a good sense of humor; she's the one who gave Wade that grin. But over the years, she's been forced to struggle through more than her share of hard times. She grew up in Chipley, a little town in the Florida Panhandle. Her father walked out when she was a baby, leaving her mother to raise six kids on her own. To help make ends meet, Jewelene picked cotton and hoed peanuts in the summer; the rest of the year, she stuck it out in school, finally graduating from Chipley High on May 31, 1966. A few days later, on June 4, she and her first husband were married.

Things went all right for a while. They moved to Tallahassee, her husband got a job as a butcher, and she kept busy raising Greg and Wade and Mike. Then one day Jewelene was cleaning the house, moving the beds around—she was a fanatic about mopping every inch of the floor—when she hurt her back and had to go to the doctor. X rays revealed a tumor in the bone of her left hip, and her hip socket had to be removed. She was still in the hospital, recovering from the operation, when the next blow hit. Her husband called, she says—their kids were off at his mom's while she was hospitalized—and told her he didn't want her around anymore.

Her husband, not surprisingly, says it wasn't quite that simple. He says that he and Jewelene had been having problems long before the cancer and that her relatives were hostile to him. Either way, the Broomes were divorced, and Jewelene and the boys moved to Pinellas County, where her family now lived. It was a rough stretch for all of them. Mike was just turning two, and suddenly his world had turned upside down. Before, he'd been his daddy's boy, always wanting to be with him, clamoring to ride beside him whenever he was running out on some errand. Then his father disappeared, and Mike began to wonder if his mother was going to leave as well. The prospect terrified all of the boys. One day, when she had to go to a hospital in Gainesville for a checkup, the three of them clung to her so hard that she could barely get out the door. They were sobbing. They were clutching onto her arms and legs. In an absolute panic, they just kept asking her the same question over and over.

"Are you coming back?"

Somehow they made it through those days. Jewelene had to stay in bed for a time, but the boys took good care of her. They ran errands, took turns rubbing her leg, showered her with guileless affection. Soon she was on her feet, and in the years that followed, she met Jerry and remarried and found a job in a factory, sewing children's clothes. She couldn't work at the factory for long, though, because her hip began hurting badly. She was forced to come home and collect disability. Today, more than a decade later, she still walks with a slight limp, still feels the pain in her leg, still gets worked up every time she talks about her ex-husband.

"I'd like to string him up from the highest tree over a canyon," she says.

Jewelene Wilson sits in her chair in the living room, smoking and watching the soaps and worrying about what's going to happen if her two youngest sons don't make it through school. She doesn't have to worry about Greg; he already has his diploma. But the odds are piling up against Mike and Wade. Especially Mike. He never was the greatest student, but he was always smart enough to get by, even when he barely worked at it. Then he hit middle school, and everything fell apart. He started failing classes and had to repeat sixth grade; he kept getting in trouble. Now he's in ninth grade, and it's only becoming worse. Every time Jewelene turns around, someone from GOALS is calling, saying Mike's been suspended again. She's starting to grit her teeth whenever the phone rings.

"Do you want to dig ditches all your life?" she asks him. "Do you want to be a bum and live on skid row?"

"I don't care."

Mike didn't used to be like this. His mother is sure of it, because she has so many reminders. There are old photos of him hanging in the living room, not far from the one of Greg in his uniform; and back in Jewelene's room, under the bed, there are albums filled with snapshots from the early days. It's amazing to look at them. In the old pictures, when Mike was a little boy, there is no trace of the anger. There's just this happy kid, mugging with a toy guitar, holding a white kitten, standing in his pajamas on some distant Christmas morning. It is clearly the same person. But he looks completely different. His face is bright and open; he has a tiny galaxy of freckles stretching across his nose; his short brown hair juts up in a cowlick. And he's smiling. He is actually smiling.

But that was long ago, before the bitterness set in and changed him forever. Today Mike's face is tight and closed, a mask that shows little but a perpetual scowl. It is the face of someone who has been fighting for years to show nothing, to contain a flood of violent emotion that lingers constantly just below the surface. Sometimes, when he doesn't realize anyone's watching him, he allows himself a smile. When that happens, he looks so young it's hard to remember he's a high school student. Other times, he looks like a weary middle-aged man, tired and frayed and beaten down well beyond his years. How could he look so old? How could someone who's only fourteen possibly look that old?

At school, his teachers study him, trying to find some clue. Mike just keeps fighting them off. Whatever's bothering him, he does not breathe a word of it. Instead he offers them his curses and his rage and every ounce of resistance he can gather. Repeatedly he threatens to drop out. When he wants to taunt them in a different way, he shows them how easy it would be to breeze through their silly courses. He comes back from one of his suspensions—he's been gone from school for days—and gets a perfect score on one of Ms. DiLello's math tests. Other kids who've been in class all along are flagging it, and he gets forty points out of forty, plus all six extra credit points.

Annette DiLello can't get over it. One day she is looking through her grade book when she sees an odd brown stain on one of the pages. She stares at it, trying to figure out where it has come from. Then it hits her: This is Mike Broome's blood. He was in a fight with another kid the other day at the front of her class, and his nose was bloodied.

It is a sign. Maybe not from heaven, but definitely a sign. Mike has been bleeding in her classroom. He has been bleeding all over the pod ever since he came here. He has been forcing them to witness his self-destruction, demanding that each and every one of them watch as he tears apart his future.

Well, Ms. DiLello is tired of it. All his teachers are tired of it. And one way or the other, they are determined to put an end to it. It's not too late. It's still early in the year. If they can find a way inside the emotional fortress he has built around him, they can reach him.

Mike himself has proved it is possible.

It happens late one afternoon. Once more he is in trouble. He has been up at the office, getting another suspension, and now he is an open wound, walking through the halls. Ms. DiLello and Mrs. O'Donnell pull him into an empty classroom.

"We want to talk to you for a minute."

Mike is beside himself. He stands by a desk up front and pours out his frustrations. Everyone is against him, he says. None of the teachers understand him. None of the kids do, either.

Ms. DiLello and Mrs. O'Donnell listen, and then they tell him that they do understand, that they are on his side, that they are ready to do whatever they can for him. Looking into his eyes, Ms. DiLello puts her arm around him.

"You know, Mike, everybody likes you. We want you to stay here in school. We care about you."

It is then, at this moment, that Mike does what they will remember and talk about for so long afterward. It is then, when Ms. DiLello has made this simplest of connections, when she has broken the barrier between them with the touch of her hand and a few kind words that tell him what should have been obvious all along, that Mike shows them a glimmer of hope.

Tears well in his eyes. He stands between them, not angry anymore, just another scared fourteen-year-old kid, crying in a quiet room.

As the semester rolls forward, other lives are turning in unexpected directions.

David the evangelist, the dropout who returned to school so full of sermons about the importance of sticking it out, empties his locker one day and goes to the front office to turn in a new set of withdrawal papers. He's leaving again. Only a few weeks after announcing how determined he was to graduate, his name is added to the list of others who are beginning to vanish from the classrooms.

But there is more. Something unbelievable has occurred.

Up in the most rarefied regions of Largo's academic hierarchy, YY has run seriously afoul of her principal, Judith B. Westfall. A fundamental law of the universe has been violated. Top students, especially ones who translate Cicero and run the newspaper and ride buzzers for the quiz team, do not typically find themselves in trouble with the authorities. But that is exactly where YY finds herself. Both she and a second student— sweet little Amy Boyle, president of the National Honor Society, the other editor who runs the newspaper, and one of YY's closest pals—are now in deeper than deep.

The problem comes from two editorials that appear in the year's first issue of the school newspaper, the *Packer Press*. Down in the front office, they have struck a major nerve. In one of the editorials, Amy has attacked that perennial problem of high school, the lack of spirit. According to Amy, spirit is dismally low at Largo, much lower than in the old days before the current regime took over.

As if this is not enough, YY has taken aim in her editorial at Ms. Westfall's pride and joy, the shorts experiment. The program, YY has argued, is a good idea gone bad. It dumps too much paperwork on teachers, it embarrasses kids whose grades aren't good enough to qualify, it forces other students to jump through all sorts of hoops just so they can wear what they should already be free to wear. The program should be dropped, YY says, and kids should be treated like adults and allowed to slip into shorts whenever they want.

Now, as copies of the newspaper's first issue circulate around the school, Ms. Westfall is outraged. She is indignant. She is sketched beyond belief.

And YY and Amy are strongly encouraged to join her in the front office. At once.

FIVE

NEGATIVITY

ON ANOTHER DAY, UNDER LESS
disastrous circumstances, the office of
Largo High's principal would be a surprisingly pleasant place to visit. It's a nice
room, warm and friendly, filled with antique furniture and antique dolls and em-
broidered sayings and a general aura of
benevolence. Not to mention the midget
pigs. They're everywhere. Little pig figu-
rines, little pig knickknacks, all of them
placed around the office in honor of the
school's mascot, a wild and hairy razor-
back hog.

Normally, seeing all these tiny
porkers, YY and Amy might have per-
mitted themselves a giggle. But at this
particular moment, shortly after noon on
Friday, October 6, giggling is not advis-
able, because Ms. Westfall is venting
upon these two girls the full measure of
her fury. They have been irresponsible,
she tells them. They have crossed the
line. They have taken cheap shots.

"As far as I'm concerned," she says,
holding up the offending *Packer Press,*
"this newspaper should go in the
trash."

With that, she throws it. Not into the

trash, but back onto the table, so that if need be she can pick it up and get angry all over again.

"How can you be so negative?" she says. "I don't know how you could have been picked editor of the newspaper if you're so negative."

Amy starts to cry. YY tries to defend herself, saying she has a right to voice her opinion.

"Well, if you have your right to voice your opinion to the students," says Ms. Westfall, "then I have my right to voice my opinion to you."

She tells YY that she suspects the influence of an outside agitator. She says she believes YY's editorial does not represent YY's opinion at all, but the opinion of a consultant—a woman reporter at the *St. Petersburg Times* —who sometimes works with the staff. It is Ms. Westfall's belief that this consultant encouraged YY to target the shorts policy.

"It wasn't like that," says YY.

"I think it *was* like that. I know what's going on at this school. I talk to the kids."

YY, always on the alert for subtle hints at some larger subtext, hears this statement and cannot help wondering exactly what it means. She and the consultant did discuss the shorts editorial, and they did talk about different approaches to take on the issue. But it was YY who decided which way to go. Even so, how does Ms. Westfall know anything at all about the consultant's role on this story? Does she have some kind of informer on the staff? Is it possible this woman has her own little *Packer Press* spy?

Ms. Westfall just keeps going. She keeps saying she can't believe such negativity.

"This is the worst thing," she says, "that's happened to me all year."

When YY hears this, she wants to say, Well, Judi, if this is the worst that's happened, then you're having a pretty good year. But YY does not say that. This is my principal, she reminds herself. She can suspend me. She can take me off the newspaper staff. She can do whatever she wants.

So YY shuts up and silently endures the rest of the lecture. Ten minutes or so later, when she and Amy stagger back to the newspaper room, they're both sobbing. Amy, who has practically never been in trouble before, who hardly knows any reality but the reality of being a model student, approved by all, is devastated. But YY is made of tougher fiber. After all, she is Juno, the queen of heaven. And underneath her tears, she is shaking with her own terrible fury.

This means war.

• • •

THE VOICE OF WISDOM DOES NOT KNOW WHEN TO SHUT UP.

"Good morning," it says, floating once more through the halls like some cheerfully disembodied spirit. "Our thought for the day is: If we had more guided men, we wouldn't need more guided missiles."

It's not even 8:30 A.M., far too early for the voice to sound so perky. But the voice is always perky.

Every morning, when most of the school is still cursing the invention of alarm clocks, some bright-eyed kid down in the front office scampers onto the P.A. system and reads the morning announcements, always starting with the thought for the day. Actually there are several bright-eyed kids down there, all of them impossibly vibrant and good-natured, all of them taking turns at the microphone. They pick the thoughts themselves. Just before showtime, they open a little metal box filled with typed sayings, the official thought-for-the-day vault, and choose whichever one strikes their fancy.

What nobody around the school seems to notice is that the sayings the students choose tend to be puzzling non sequiturs, vaguely ominous warnings, rigidly archaic credos, scattered bits of slightly skewed advice. Whether the kids do this on purpose—whether they are truly attempting to enlighten or merely engaging in a sly form of subversion, saluting the start of each day with a tiny salvo of absurdity—is one of the abiding mysteries of life at Largo High. Either way, it's almost impossible to picture them reading some of their selections with a straight face.

"Ideals are to run races with," they say one day, defying all logic. "The moment we stop chasing them, they sit down and become opinions."

Another: "If you wish success in life, make perseverance your bosom friend, experience your wise counselor, caution your elder brother and hope your guardian genius."

This is rich. But not nearly as rich as the day when the kids share these immortal words: "Leisure is a beautiful garment, but it will not do for constant wear."

On a walkway outside the office, a phys ed teacher confronts a skinhead boy, trying to find out if he and some of his friends are responsible for the swastika that's just been found scratched onto one of the gymnasium doors.

"And you don't have any idea who might have done it?" she says, glaring at him.

The skinhead has this helpless look on his face.

"We didn't do it," he says. "I swear."

Down in the pod, in one of the GOALS classrooms, a slender boy with sandy hair—a skateboarder who religiously reads *Thrasher,* a magazine aimed at skateboard fanatics—talks in class about the ultimate thrasher dream.

"You can never dream about what you want to dream about . . . I've tried so hard. It's impossible."

"What do you try to dream about?" says the teacher.

The boy pauses. "There's no school," he says carefully, "and the whole world is pavement."

It is a beautiful vision. So beautiful that a big goofy grin is now spreading across the boy's face.

OUT IN THE HALLS, JAIMEE THE GHOST HAS WANDERED INTO October. The first report cards of the year are about to be handed out, and yet Jaimee remains oblivious. Though it hardly seemed possible, she has begun to lapse even further out of control. Already she has become so insubstantial, so ethereal, that she seems scarcely more than a shadow. Quietly she glides down the halls, waving at her friends inside their classes, lingering near the pay phones, hiding in the bathrooms to elude assistant principals. She laughs when nothing funny has been said. She talks to people without looking at them, her eyes gazing off at some vague point in the distance.

Her mother is at the end of her endurance. She does not know how to reach Jaimee. She used to know, back before Jaimee started acting this way. But not anymore. Her mother has tried everything. She has reasoned with her daughter, given her a dozen second chances, played the understanding and forgiving parent, played the Nazi storm trooper. Last spring, after she caught Jaimee stealing her car, she took her to the police station and insisted that she be arrested and taken to court, so she would understand that her actions have real consequences. But that didn't change a thing. Jaimee's no better these days. She keeps lying. She keeps slipping out her bedroom window at night, going who knows where. She's constantly running away. From the house, from school, from reality.

Only now it's all accelerating. Jaimee's burning through friends at an unbelievable pace. She tears through them so fast, it's almost impossible to keep up with all the names that come and go on the answering machine.

It has to stop. Her mother doesn't know how. But somehow she has to find a way to make it stop, or she's going to lose Jaimee forever. She already knows how it will happen. In her mind, she hears the phone ringing. It's the middle of the night, and she fumbles for the receiver, and there's someone official and stiff on the other end of the line. Someone she does not know. Someone who tells her . . .

YY, FACING ANOTHER DAY IN THE STRESSED-OUT SWEEPSTAKES.

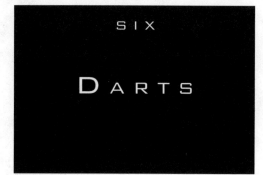

SIX

DARTS

EARLY ONE FRANTIC MONDAY morning, YY sits at the back of the newspaper room, tearing through a calculus assignment that somehow eluded her the night before. She is slaving away all by her lonesome, not a guardian genius or a bosom friend in sight, when suddenly the voice of her principal comes floating over the P.A. system.

"Largo," says Judith Westfall, "we'd like to congratulate you on the very smooth opening of school and the first six weeks of school."

Ms. Westfall is giving a pep talk. She wants students to know that today is the first day of the rest of their semesters. Or something like that.

"We have many reasons," she says, "to feel very proud of being at Largo High School."

YY fights back a groan. It's not enough that this is a Monday and already she's running behind, playing catch-up in calc, which is not her favorite subject, despite her parents' deeply held belief that she's some sort of holy vessel of mathematics. It's not enough that she also happens to be in the middle of one of her menstrual periods, which can be so intense that she has been known to issue orders of surrender to her own body.

"Down boy," she tells her uterus.

But YY's uterus never listens. Right now it's making her feel so sick that, as she so delicately puts it, she is on the verge of heaving a lung. As it is, even without her period, she is rapidly becoming a permanent contestant in the stressed-out sweepstakes, constantly chugging down the aspirin and the No Doz, fighting back the panic and the exhaustion and, yes, the urge to scream. Because nobody—none of these so-called adults, that is— has the faintest notion of what it means to be a fun-loving yet achievement-oriented young soul trying to find your way in this hyper-extended, hyper-accelerated Age of Mega-Turbulence.

When it all gets too much for her, when she starts to lose it, YY's friends will shoot her a look.

"What's your damage?" they say, using one of the ritual quotes from *Heathers,* their all-time favorite movie. "Did you have a brain tumor for breakfast?"

This is their quaint way of telling her to fire the retro rockets and calm down. But calming down is not always within the realm of possibilities. Not for YY. Sometimes—and this is only natural, given her nickname—she feels like a human yo-yo. Except yo-yos are only forced to move in two primary directions; namely, up and down. YY is being yanked around so many ways she can't even keep count. There's the looming specter of her advanced placement tests—calculus again—and the ever-present demand to keep up her grades so she holds on to that scholarship for next year, plus the high hopes of her parents—Helen and Bob, she calls them, or sometimes Helen the Hun and Bob—and the high hopes of her teachers, not to mention the uncompromising standards she sets for herself.

Her parents and her teachers seem to be under the impression that she's got it all under control. They actually make comments about it. It's amazing, they say. She juggles everything so well. She doesn't know how to break it to them that they're wrong. She's sorry, she doesn't mean to disappoint anybody, but she's just not as strong as they think she is. Sometimes she feels herself slipping toward the edge. She cries and cries. Late at night, alone in her room, she stares at the walls and stares into space and wonders if she might really fall apart.

YY never had a chance. She's been on the academic fast track since she was a zygote, swimming around inside Helen the Hun. She was raised in one of those comfortably messy homes where the closets in the children's rooms were always overflowing with books—*Charlie and the Chocolate Factory, The Phantom Tollbooth,* the collected works of Dr. Seuss, Beverly Cleary, and Judy Blume—and where the refrigerator door was hidden behind a blanket of glowing report cards, honor roll certificates, and test papers marked with those little stars that teachers have been doling out since the dawn of time.

Her parents are both exceptionally smart people. It's not exactly correct to say that they're rocket scientists, but it's close. Her mom's a software engineer for Honeywell's military avionics division. She works on things like the navigational systems of fighter jets and the Star Wars defense plan.

"My mom," says YY, "is math personified."

Her dad's an electrical engineer, also at Honeywell, who designs circuits for satellites and works on the space shuttle and does other highly classified projects for NASA and the military. At least, that's how YY understands it. She's not really sure what the man does, except that whatever it is, it's top secret. She's always kidding him, saying she knows he's a spy.

"Dad, what are you working on?" she'll ask him.

He'll smile. "You know I can't tell you that."

Together, Helen and Bob combined their gene pool to produce five highly intelligent children—YY's the second oldest—all of whom they instilled with a bedrock belief in education. The indoctrination is captured, step by step, in YY's childhood photo albums. There's a picture of her at age one, already grinning the wild and wonderful YY grin and already clutching a book, prophetically titled *Fun Days.* There's another shot of her on her second birthday, posing happily with one of her presents, a Fisher-Price schoolhouse. And yet another shot taken at age seven, flashing a shy little smile as she receives her first library card, which might be considered a minor moment in some houses, but which Helen was determined to record for posterity. Then there's the big black-and-white glossy of YY on the set of *Romper Room,* where she appeared for a couple of heady weeks in '77, playing and learning on TV with other kids. Even then she was the ideal pupil, earning a Romper Room School diploma in which the show's host, Miss June, attested that young Christine "was, at all times, a 'Good Do Bee.'"

Of course, life was a little easier in those days. Now that YY's on the verge of adulthood, being a Good Do Bee is about a trillion times more complicated. Because there's so much more to juggle than just her classes and her grades and her scholarship. She's got her after-school job on the buffet line at the Belleair Country Club, which requires her to stand over smelts and mussels—there ought to be a law against such odors—and to swallow her pride and ignore the snooty tones of some of the members, a few of whom are so old and feeble they'll point at the rice—rice, mind you —and ask her what that is. And like a good buffet girl, she tells them, because she needs the money, because it pays for lunch and shopping and of course gas for the Y-mobile, her red '83 Honda Accord with more than fifty thousand miles on the odometer and a few scattered french fries on the floor, which she absolutely has to drive because no self-respecting senior would be caught dead on one of those hulking geek transports called a bus.

There's more. With YY, there's always more. She's got all these big parties calling her name on the weekends. And her continuing attempts to establish a meaningful dialogue with these subhumans she laughingly calls men. And, oh yes, this one tiny question about her life, like what should she do with it? A career in pro football seems unlikely. Any career that requires even a minimum of physical exertion seems unlikely. YY is renowned for her stunning lack of athletic ability.

"I don't do sports," she says proudly, as though she's making a political statement.

She's not sure, but she thinks she might like to become a writer. She already does articles for the *Packer Press,* writes lovely essays for her teachers, keeps a journal at home, contributes poems to the literary magazine. Next year, when she goes to college, she wants to major in English. There's just one problem. Her parents seem dead set against it. Their official position, of course, is that they want their daughter to study whatever's in her heart. But YY is picking up a different message. She's feeling intense pressure from them to forget writing, which they've told her is totally impractical. They say there's no future in it, no stability, and worst of all, no money. They seem to want her to concentrate on math and go into some math-related field—engineering or computers, maybe—where she'll make the bucks and live prosperously ever after.

So now YY finds herself wrestling with a career crisis. Does she do what she wants, possibly invoking a major power struggle with her folks? Or does she cave in and devote her life to logarithms?

Helen and Bob don't seem to realize how strongly she feels about this. Lately they've been distracted, struggling with some problems of their own. Last year, after two decades of raising a family and building a life together, the two of them split up. YY knows it shouldn't be that big a deal. Doesn't everybody's mom and dad get divorced these days? But when it happened with her parents, YY was hit hard. She's still trying to sort through the wreckage. She can't get away from it. Her dad has moved out, but he's back at the house almost every night, seeing the kids, making sure he remains a presence in their lives, and talking to YY's mom. Only Helen and Bob don't really talk much anymore. Their lips move; words are propelled through the air between them. But it's just a clever imitation of talking. They sit at the kitchen counter and turn the TV to the Financial News Network and watch the stock quotes float by on the ticker and discuss what's happening with the market. It's so much easier that way. So much safer.

Bob doesn't seem to know what to say to YY, period. He has no trouble talking with her three younger brothers. But he seems totally at a loss when it comes to opening up to her. YY knows he tries. But it still hurts that with all his brains and all his security clearances the man can't find a way somehow to sneak through the trenches and get closer to her. Back in August, when she had her birthday, he told her he loved her and gave her a balloon with a hundred-dollar bill tied to the other end of the string.

"Thanks, Dad," she told him, not sure of what else to say. "I love you, too . . ."

But that's ancient history. Because today, as if she didn't already have a thousand and one reasons to get sketched, YY finds herself here at the back of this empty newspaper room, forced to listen to another one of Judi Westfall's pep talks.

YY is still smoldering from their confrontation the other day. It was an astounding moment. There they were, YY and Amy Boyle, the vice-president and president of the National Honor Society, their senior résumés loaded with enough awards and honors to choke any college admissions officer—two of Largo's most dedicated students, in other words—and Ms. Westfall had the gall to accuse them of being an embarrassment to the school. She'd made it sound like they were terrorists or something. Like they'd been caught hurling a bomb down A Wing.

And now, as if to taunt them further, as if she didn't already have the last word, here comes Ms. Westfall again, commandeering the P.A. system, riding the sound waves right into their faces, making them and the rest of the school sit through a soliloquy on the joys and wonders of being a Largo Packer. One of the first things she mentions—the woman can't resist—is the shorts program, which despite YY's objections seems to be a spectacular success. Attendance is up, grades are up, and most of the kids seem to be following the rules most of the time.

"One thing I'd like to remind you," says Ms. Westfall. "Applications for the second six weeks' honor card will be available on the patio today during lunch. Applications are due by—"

YY has heard enough.

"Shut up, Judi," she tells the speaker on the wall.

The thing is, YY essentially agrees with Ms. Westfall. YY may gripe about her school. She may make scathing jokes about it. But this is the way of YY. She gripes and makes scathing jokes about everything, especially the stuff she feels deeply about. She freely admits it's a defense mechanism. Turns out YY has this little problem confronting her emotions.

Still, even the most clueless freshman in the entire pathetic history of clueless freshmen could see that, for all her cutting remarks, YY is completely devoted to Largo High. She adores her teachers, takes a quiet but unmistakable pride in her classes, joins a ridiculous number of clubs and organizations, attends the football games religiously, immerses herself completely in the Packer experience. Not being the cheerleader type, however, she doesn't feel the need to brag about the place. She doesn't have to. With her academic record, she is already a walking advertisement for the kind of excellence Largo can churn out. Beneath the wisecracks, she is a true believer.

Which is why she can't stand to have Ms. Westfall—or anyone else, for that matter—shove the rah-rah rhetoric down her throat.

Judi's doing it right now. Still on the air, still surfing on the sound waves, she's talking about the many "positive aspects" of Largo.

YY hears this and begins to mimic her principal's voice. *"Positive aspects. There are so many positive things going on around Largo."*

It feels good to mock Ms. Westfall, even behind her back. It may be childish. It's probably more than a little unfair. But it's not like YY can openly confront the woman. Not without risking getting suspended. That was the lesson of the day down in the front office, wasn't it?

So on this Monday morning, YY and a few of her friends begin exacting their revenge. They commit themselves to a guerrilla campaign in which the only object is to ridicule the enemy in as many petty ways as possible. They call Ms. Westfall names. When she speaks over the P.A.

system or at assemblies, they repeat what she says in the voice of Elmer Fudd.

Most seditious of all, however, is the dart board. One day after school, YY and Amy go out and buy a dart set. They bring it back to school, back to the newspaper office, and begin covering the board with cutout photos of various people who have aroused their scorn. Old boyfriends, Dan Quayle, a couple of curvaceous girls they call the Boom-Boom Twins, and, yes, Ms. Westfall. They choose one of her official portraits—she's in a dress with a floral pattern, smiling her most positive smile—and put it over the bull's-eye.

They hang the dart board in the newspaper darkroom, where it won't be obvious. They stand back, darts in hand, then begin hurling. Maybe they're not really throwing the darts at Ms. Westfall. Maybe, on some subconscious level, she's just a convenient target for all their pent-up frustrations. Because the truth is, the severity of the girls' reaction—especially YY's—is out of whack with what happened with Ms. Westfall. Where is all the anger really coming from? Who or what are they really mad at?

Doesn't matter. The experience is still tremendously cathartic. When they nail one of their old boyfriends in the crotch, or when they score a direct hit on Ms. Westfall, they are overcome with an intense sense of gratification. They shout. They squeal. They almost jump for joy.

Of course, they don't score direct hits too often. Their aim isn't that good. YY has a hard time even hitting the board.

That's okay, though. The year is young, and these girls are hard workers. They believe in self-improvement. Practice may not make them perfect, but they know it will bring them closer to Judi.

ANDREA TAYLOR AND THE GLOW.

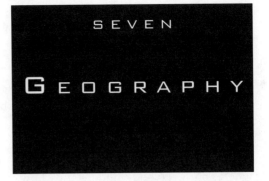

SEVEN

GEOGRAPHY

Back in the pod, inside a fourth-period American government class, Mike Broome is missing again.

"Where is he?" asks one of the kids.

"Suspended," says Mike's older brother, Wade.

The problems with Mike have not magically disappeared. Just because he opened up that one afternoon, tearfully confessing his feelings of alienation to Mrs. O'Donnell and Ms. DiLello, does not mean he is ready to make a turnaround. Mike still pushes people away, still engages in one self-destructive act after another.

Here in the GOALS program, Ms. Westfall's pep talks play a little differently. In the pod, there are times when the teachers are astounded at the progress the kids are making. But there are other times when it truly can be reassuring to hear about all the positive things happening at Largo. Sometimes, it's reassuring to hear about anything positive happening anywhere.

On the bad days, on the days when she's ready to scream, Mrs. O'Donnell will call her own home from school and leave herself a cheerful message on the answering machine. That way, when she steps wearily across the doorstep, she'll hear something upbeat. Someone telling her that she's a good teacher and she's not just beating her head against the wall. Someone promising her that everything's going to be all right . . .

THE RULES ARE CLEAR. THEY'RE NOT WRITTEN DOWN ANY-where, but everybody understands how it's supposed to work.

Geographically, it breaks down like this: The steps in front of the auditorium belong to the acolytes of the apocalypse, with their Metallica shirts and skateboards and smoker's coughs. The long metal rail down at the end of A Wing, just in front of the pod, is where black kids sit. Sitting smack in between the two, with the rail off to one side and the steps off to the other, is the patio. You can't miss it. It's the big courtyard at the entrance to the school, the one with the trees and the benches and the inspiring view of the Mister Donut across the street. The one that's crawling with patio people.

There's lots of room out on the patio, and lots of room among the patio people for all sorts of interlocking hierarchies. There's the jocks and the jock admirers, the class officers and student council reps, the mousse-and-lace-leggings brigade, the amiably air-headed, and of course those academic overachievers who come equipped with social skills. If anyone thinks it's a coincidence that these particular students have claimed this particular piece of turf, they're not paying attention.

Literally situated at the front and center of the school, with the other territories scattered around its fringes, the patio is the physical hub around which so many things revolve. It is the heart of the school's social structure, the premier stomping ground for the most popular and powerful kids in the entire school. For all their different subsets, most of them fit the same general profile. They tend to be the ones with the designer clothes and the designer hair and virtually no understanding of what it's like to be alone on a Saturday night. And usually they are white.

Andrea Taylor doesn't care about that. She doesn't worry about the general profile; she doesn't let it bother her if she doesn't have as much money or the same color skin as some other kids. Andrea—'Dre to her nearest and dearest—used to stay on the rail. But now she goes onto the patio whenever she wants. She eats her lunch out there, she stands under the shade of those cute little patio trees, she mingles and makes jokes and acts as though it were the most natural thing in the world. Some of her friends from the rail used to give her a hard time about it.

"You're turning into a white girl, 'Dre."

Eventually, though, her friends got tired of saying that. They learned to respect the fact that Andrea is the type who writes her own rules. Some of them have even joined her on the patio.

Andrea's a senior now, seventeen, a solid student, tall and slender, with startling brown eyes and a smile that could stop rush-hour traffic out on Missouri Avenue. She's one of those people who actually glow. Guys are constantly making fools of themselves over her. Last year, one boy was so crazy about her he gave her his beeper number, just so she could reach him whenever she wanted. She'd call him up at work in the evenings—he delivered pizzas—and tell him she was hungry and would he please, on his next run, stop off somewhere and get her a Big Mac and some fries. He'd do it, too. He'd do anything for Andrea. He was always hanging around her locker, staring at her like a lovesick cow.

John Boyd, an old buddy of Andrea's, used to rag her about it. He'd call her up, laughing about the sorry state of this kid.

"What have you done to this boy?" he'd say. "You got him strung out on you."

John's no stranger to lovesick admirers himself. He's a sweet guy, with a soft voice and an uncanny ability to make anybody smile at any time. He also has a body that's featured prominently on a good many Top Ten lists —he's a running back on the football team, with the muscles to prove it— all of which explains why girls are always throwing themselves at him in the halls. At the moment, he's in the middle of an on-again, off-again romance with Andrea's best friend, a girl named Sabrina, who goes to nearby Dunedin High.

Anyway, John understood about the boy with the beeper. He thought it was funny how this kid pined for Andrea. Not everyone felt that way, though. Some of Andrea's other friends didn't like the idea of her and this guy being together, because the boy happened to be one of the patio people.

"I hear you go out with white guys," someone said to Andrea one day.

Andrea looked at this person. "I date black guys, too."

Everyone's got these funny ideas. She hears them from both sides. When a black girl goes out with someone who's white, black guys at the school get all worked up. To them, there's only one reason why a white boy would want to go with a black girl. The crazy thing is, white guys jump to the same conclusion when a white girl goes out with someone who's black.

Andrea herself is not immune to funny ideas. The kid with the beeper was the first white guy she ever went out with, and when she was finally ready to grant him a kiss, she found herself wondering, as their lips moved toward initial contact, if it was going to be different from kissing other boys. Would he taste different? Was he going to shock her with some strange technique she'd never encountered before? No. He kissed just like everybody else. It was nice. Later on, she went out with another white guy, and when he kissed her, it was better than nice.

"I'd let him kiss me for days," she says.

Andrea recognizes how much this interracial stuff upsets some people. She knows how strongly they feel about her breaking all these unwritten rules. She knows how some people feel about anyone who's black, period. Sometimes, in the halls, she'll pass the skinheads and see them glaring at her. She doesn't let it get to her, though. She just looks them in the eye and smiles and keeps moving.

She's got what you call a positive attitude, which accounts for the glow. She had it when she was a little girl—her early pictures almost shimmer with it—and she just never let it go. Next year, when she goes to Florida State University, she wants to study business. She'd like to be an executive.

"I guess I want to be the boss," she says, grinning. "Like Abby Ewing on *Knots Landing*."

Andrea knows she can do it, too. She knows, because her mother has been telling her so since she was a little girl. Andrea gets plenty of emotional support from both her parents. Her mother and father aren't married and don't live together, but her dad, a phys ed teacher at another school, keeps in touch with Andrea. The two of them went through some hard times working things out between them; Andrea still recalls the sting of attending school functions as a little girl and not having her father at her side. By now, though, they've reached a point where Andrea accepts the situation and makes the best of it. And no matter what, she knows she can always count on her mother. Andrea's mom is a straight-talking, no-nonsense woman who works on an assembly line at Honeywell. Her mom wishes she could get a promotion, but they've told her that without a high school diploma it's impossible. Her mom never got a chance to finish school. She had to quit when she was a teenager, because her family needed her to work in the fields. She used to tell Andrea what it was like

in those days, what it meant to have no shoes and to wake up in the cold
—this was in Georgia, where she grew up—and to feel a gnawing in her
stomach and know there was no food in the house. When Andrea was
little, her mom used to sit her down in the kitchen and talk about those
days. She'd tell Andrea how she wanted her to learn and work hard and
stay in school, so she'd have more chances in life. Andrea heard the speech
so many times, she memorized it.

"Education is important," her mother would say. "You *need* your
education. You will *not* make it in this world without an education."

Her mother knows how hard it can be. She knows about people like
the skinheads. She tells Andrea to be strong and deal with it. She tells her
not to let other people define her.

Andrea realizes it's good advice. But it hasn't always been easy to
follow. When she was a freshman she did what was expected and stuck
close to the rail.

The truth is, black students and white students get along better at
Largo High than they do at some other places. Largo is lucky. It's one of
the few high schools in the county where the surrounding area is racially
mixed enough to avoid court-ordered busing, which means that many of
the kids have been going to the same neighborhood schools together since
they were in kindergarten. They know each other in a way that kids at
other high schools do not. Still, the African-American students don't always feel at home. There aren't many of them at Largo—only about 10
percent of the student body is black—and it's rare for them to run for
student council or apply for the newspaper or even go to the school
dances. Many of them don't feel welcome. But the rail is different. It's the
one part of the campus that's universally acknowledged as theirs. It feels
safer to sit there. It feels friendlier.

But for Andrea, the time came when she wanted something more,
when she wasn't content to stay within the boundaries somebody else had
drawn up for her. It was too limiting. Too much of a trap, both in the way
she saw herself and in the way others saw her. When Andrea sat on the
rail, balancing her weight against the metal, she'd watch the white kids
walk by and not even register her presence. As long as she stayed there, it
was like she wasn't a real person to them. Like she was just another unit
in a larger stereotype. So out into the patio she went, ready to try another
balancing act.

Some of her friends tried to stop her. They warned her she was going
to get hurt.

"Don't even think about it," they said. "Don't think you're going to go out there and be Miss La-di-da. Because they're going to bring you down."

It seemed like somebody was always predicting the worst. One year, when she ran for cheerleader, they told her she wouldn't make it because there was already one black girl on the squad and that was all that would ever be allowed.

Andrea didn't listen. She didn't see how she'd ever get anywhere if she gave in to that kind of thinking. And she was right. This year she's president of Largo's Black Culture Club, but she's also a cheerleader and a student council rep and a member of a student advisory committee that works with the county's school superintendent. She goes to dances with other black kids at a community center, but she also goes to the school dances and to the football games. She still sits on the rail sometimes. She sits wherever she pleases.

Now, though, she's trying something new that has her girlfriends shaking their heads again. She's in the running for Homecoming Queen.

Andrea has no idea who nominated her. But when she found out that she'd survived the first round of voting and was one of three finalists, she couldn't help but get excited. She knows it's just a symbolic honor, but it would still be wonderful to stand out on the field under the lights, just for one night, with the crown on her head and the people in the stands cheering her name.

Of course, she's fighting history here. In the seventy-five years of Largo High's existence, an African-American girl has never been named Homecoming Queen. Andrea does not know this. All she knows is that she's never heard of it happening before. Black candidates have been nominated before. They've even made it onto court. But never has she seen one of them win.

Already her friends are cushioning her for the blow, preparing her for the big letdown when she hears someone else's name ring out over the football field.

"Don't worry about it if you don't get it, 'Dre," they tell her. "You'll still be our queen."

The other two finalists are Louise Moffat and Shana Denton. Both are nice girls, well-liked, definite queen material. Andrea's friends, who've been factoring every angle into their calculations, do not discount Louise's chances. Still, the way they figure it, Shana Denton's probably the girl to beat. She's gorgeous, with long wavy hair and green eyes and creamy skin just like in the soap commercials. She looks like a Homecoming Queen is supposed to look, at least for those who have it in their heads that the Queen is supposed to be white. Even putting aside any possible racial considerations—if they ever can be put aside—what may really lock up the title for Shana is that she's the longtime steady of Jamie Bryant, a football player who's one of the finalists for Homecoming King.

In the senior class, Shana and Jamie are the couple of all couples. They're always together, holding hands and snuggling; people keep wondering when they'll get married. Shana's definitely got her share of fans, but Jamie's probably the most popular guy in the whole school, which means he'll almost certainly be named King. And if he wins, Andrea's friends figure, Shana will probably get voted in with him on sheer romanticism, because that would make the King and Queen a boyfriend and girlfriend.

It's not necessarily logical. But these contests never are. People are so sentimental. They're such suckers for fairy-tale endings.

JOHN BOYD, ANDREA'S OLD FRIEND, IS PULLING FOR HER to win the Homecoming crown. John knows the odds are against her, but he also knows that 'Dre is not the sort of person to let odds stop her.

Truth is, John's the same way. At the moment, he and the rest of the Largo football team are bucking the odds every time they step out onto the field. In recent years, the Packers haven't been known as one of this area's football powerhouses. Last season, they went 4–6; the season before that, they were 1–9. But this fall, something has happened. To the surprise of virtually everyone, they're still undefeated. They've reached the half-way point of the season—they've won five games now—and almost nobody has managed to touch them. The only close game they've had was against the Lakewood High Spartans, who were ranked high in their state division.

Success has not gone to the head of Pat Mahoney, Largo's coach. In fact, it hasn't even made it past his stomach. He still throws up before every game, like he always has. He keeps wondering how long this streak can last. He knows this team has plenty of talent and drive. What they've got, actually, is a surplus of aggressive energy. Annihilating their opponents once a week isn't enough to satisfy this crew's bloodlust. They can hardly step onto the practice field before they're beating up on one another.

"If we get through a day without a fight," Mahoney tells people, "it's a minor miracle."

The coach, a bearded, barrel-chested man who once played linebacker for Boston University—a man whose nose has been broken five times and who has suffered five concussions—doesn't mind a little brawling now and then. It gets the team pumped and ready for the real action. It gets them going. Once they've started, though, some of the boys don't know when to stop. During games, the extracurricular violence can get plain out of hand. A couple of the defensive backs routinely rough up the other teams, planting their cleats on the fingers of the opposing players when they're down, poking them in the eyes when they least expect it, hitting them late and hitting them hard, doing their best to knock them out cold. Mahoney keeps telling them to calm down and clean up their act, but they don't always listen. Around Pinellas County, the Packers have acquired a reputation as major-league cheap-shot artists, which means the referees are always gunning for them, which means trouble. Every other touchdown they score seems to get called back on a penalty.

Of course, they hardly know how to score any touchdowns unless it's the third or fourth quarter. For all their aggressiveness, the team tends to sleepwalk through the first half of every game. Time and again, Mahoney storms into the locker room at halftime, screaming and frothing at the mouth. He can't figure it out. Why do they have to wait until the clock is running out before they come alive? So far they've managed to pull it out every time. But how long can that last? What happens when they play somebody who doesn't let them get away with it?

Mahoney can hardly stand it. The team is so unpredictable. They've got this quarterback Jason Kylis. He's a nice kid, a strapping junior with an amazing arm; when he's on, he can drill the ball to whatever square inch of the field he wants. The problem is, Jason is not always on. Sometimes he's so off, it's like he's taken a vacation in another solar system. He keeps losing his concentration. Mahoney calls all the plays, relaying them into the game, but seconds after he hears his instructions, Jason forgets them.

"What the hell are you doing?" says the coach, yanking him over to the sidelines.

"Oh, yes, sir," Jason tells him. "I'm sorry. It won't happen again."

But it does. He stands there in the huddle, trying to remember the play, until one of his teammates reminds him what they're supposed to do. It's not that the boy doesn't try. When he's calm and focused, he does great. But if he gets flustered, that's it. After observing Jason at length, Mahoney swears he's learned a way to predict the kid's performance. Jason has a towel he uses to wipe his hands on the field, and sometimes, before the games, he has a habit of losing it. When that happens—when the coach sees his quarterback wandering the locker room, shaking his head as he searches for his towel—he knows it's going to be a rough night under the stadium lights.

Somehow, though, despite it all, the Packers have managed to come out of every game on top. Part of their success has been due to John Boyd, a gifted tailback who knows how to read the flow and cut into an open seam. He's been averaging close to ten yards a carry; in the opening game of the season, against Gibbs High, he rocketed down the field for a sixty-yard TD. John's most spectacular moment, however, came during the Lakewood game. That was the night when people started to take Largo seriously; before then, almost nobody would have thought they stood a chance against a team like the Spartans.

It was a wild evening. A late summer thunderstorm was raging over the area, hurling down so much rain and lightning that the refs stopped play for a while. The Packers, slipping into their usual first-half slumber, fell behind 10–0. Coach Mahoney was so livid, he was butting heads with the players at half-time, trying to knock some energy into them. Finally, at the start of the fourth quarter, Largo managed to score a touchdown on a long pass, which put the game at 10–6. John Boyd, who always held the ball for the kicker on extra points, looked to the sidelines to get the signal from the coach. Were they supposed to go for the kick? Or was John supposed to pick up the ball and run for the two-point conversion?

"Kick it! Kick it!" yelled Mahoney, raising both hands into the air, which was the signal.

At that moment, there was a good deal of confusion on the field. For some reason, the sprinklers in the grass had switched on just before the touchdown, and in the mayhem that followed, John could neither hear nor see the coach. So he took matters into his own hands—literally—and went for the conversion, racing for the corner of the end zone, barely eluding his would-be tacklers. Suddenly the score was 10–8. A few minutes later, when the Packers added a field goal, they went ahead by one point, which was just enough to squeak by the Spartans.

Today, several weeks later, Largo's still riding high from that victory. Now they're the ones with the state ranking. But the team knows better than to get cocky. Because a couple weeks from now, in the game just before Homecoming, they're crossing the Sunshine Skyway bridge and heading down to Sarasota County to play the perennial king of their district, Sarasota Riverview. One of the best teams in the entire country, the Rams usually squash the Packers like a palmetto bug. If John and the rest of the Largo team want to hold onto that untarnished record, they'll have to get by Riverview first.

Coach Mahoney's stomach can hardly wait.

EIGHT

THE

STRESSED-OUT

SWEEPSTAKES

ON A COOL MOONLESS EVENING, throngs of wide-eyed parents come to the school to see the place where their children's lives are being shaped.

In the old days, they would have called this Back-to-School Night. Now it's just Open House, which sounds more professional, more upscale.

The parents arrive at dusk, just as the sun sinks into the gulf. They park their cars, file into the auditorium, settle into their seats. Quietly they observe the tableau that has been so carefully prepared for them. They stare up at the stage, gazing at the unfurled flags and the blossoming flowers and the well-scrubbed faces of the student leaders seated behind the lectern. They listen appreciatively to the school's jazz band, which is playing something stirring. Some of them even cast their eyes to the right and take in the massive replica of the school seal that's painted on the auditorium's east wall.

Shaped like a shield, the seal bears three images—a cluster of oranges, a winged foot, and what appears to be an Indian maiden, waiting to serve a plate of chow to some men parked offshore in a big ship—all under the word "LARGO." To a first-time observer, it's unclear why these images have been chosen. But there can be no doubt as to the intent behind the official school motto, displayed below the seal. The motto says, *The Key to Success Is Work.*

This is good. This is exactly the kind of thing parents look for at Open House. They have come here, as parents do every year at every school in the land, to be reassured. They want to meet the teachers and tour the campus and bear witness with their own eyes that the walls of education are still standing. They want to be told that all is well with their sons and daughters, that the traditions of the past have not been forgotten, and that here, on these grounds, a solid foundation is being laid for the future of their country. They want to hear—they need to hear—that everything is going to be okay.

Of course, not everyone has come tonight. If just one parent of every student had shown up, there would be close to two thousand people in this auditorium. As it happens, there are only about five hundred, which is still a better turnout than some schools get. The funny thing—and it's the same way every year—is that the parents who are here tend to be the ones who have the least to worry about. The ones whose kids are already doing fairly well in school, many of them on the honor roll, taking the advanced placement courses, getting inducted into the NHS. And the other parents? The ones whose kids are struggling and could use a little hands-on attention from Mom or Pop? As usual, most of them are nowhere in sight. Maybe they had to work, or their car's in the shop, or they just couldn't pull themselves away from *Wheel of Fortune.* Whatever.

"Good evening," says Judith Westfall, leaning into the microphone up onstage. "I'd like to welcome you to the 1989-90 school year and our Open House activity."

With that, the rituals of hope and stability commence. The parents are introduced to the senior class president, an impressive young woman who places her hand over her heart and leads them in the pledge of allegiance. They meet the student council president, another poised young woman, who shines with enthusiasm as she briefs them on the plans for Homecoming, which is rapidly approaching. They nod with thanks toward the president of Largo's parent-teacher-student association, who waves and smiles with a modest confidence. And they pay close attention when Ms. Westfall steps back to the lectern and begins listing the school's achievements. For several years, she points out, Largo has been named a Florida National Merit School. Just last spring, it won an Outstanding School Award from the Florida Department of Education.

"You can see," she says, "why we're filled with pride this year to be Largo High School Packers."

Ms. Westfall does not realize the effect such words would have on YY and her friends. She does not know about the dart board, or the nasty jokes, or the fact that those girls can hardly hear her name without scoffing. If she did, she would probably be surprised. Almost certainly she would be hurt. Still, she is not about to apologize for how passionately she feels about this school.

Certainly there are some neo-fascist principals out there, square-jawed types who never made it out of the fifties and rule their schools like petty despots. But Judi Westfall is not one of them. High school students and principals have always found it convenient to stereotype each other. So it is only natural, perhaps even historically inevitable, for YY and the others to make assumptions about Ms. Westfall, to categorize her, dismiss her, turn her into a dragon. It's true, she was angry at YY and Amy. She still thinks that their editorials were unfair, but she wasn't trying to attack the girls personally. If she had to do it over again, she might have tried to be a little less fervent with them. But she's hardly the villain they'd like to make her.

Up at the lectern, Ms. Westfall is talking about the shorts experiment and how Largo kids won over the school board. Those students, she says, have learned a valuable lesson about working for change within a political system. To her, that's what the experiment is really about.

"It was time that Pinellas County schools listened to students," she says, emotion rising in her voice. "Students have good ideas."

Applause fills the hall. The parents look intensely happy that their children are part of the shorts experiment. It's so progressive. So democratic.

This is not the high point of the ceremony, however. The high point comes when the parents join Ms. Westfall and a choir of students in a hushed rendition of the alma mater. Some of the parents, many of whom attended Largo themselves, get a dreamy look in their eyes. A few of them appear to be on the verge of tears, especially when they slide softly into the second verse.

> *One day a hush will fall*
> *the footsteps of us all will echo*

down the hall and disappear.
But as we sadly start, our journeys far apart,
a part of every heart will linger
here in the sacred halls of Largo,
where we've lived and learned
to know that through the years
we'll see you in the sweet afterglow.

The moment is surprisingly touching. When the alma mater plays at football games, kids invariably mock its archaic lyrics. But tonight their mothers and fathers invest the song with a kind of wistful grace. They sing it with so much sincerity that it becomes something transcendent. It's a wish, really. An act of faith.

A FEW DAYS AFTER OPEN HOUSE, MRS. O'DONNELL SAYS something that stops her students cold.

It's in her fourth-period class, and she's just had her kids watch *Desperate Lives,* a movie about teens and drugs, and now they're all sitting around talking about how much pressure there is for them to experiment with pot and cocaine. When Mrs. O'Donnell points out that this is nothing new, that drugs have been around for a long time, they tell her she doesn't understand.

"Peer pressure now is not the same as what it was when you were growing up," says one of them.

"There was peer pressure," says Mrs. O'Donnell. "There's always been peer pressure."

"Not like now."

"Can't you just say no?" she asks.

For a second, the kids say nothing. They exchange knowing glances among themselves, slowly shaking their heads. Calmly, carefully, they try to lay it out for her.

"You can say no," says one of the boys, the boy whose mother talks about how she should have had him aborted. "I've said no plenty of times."

When you go to parties, he says, sometimes there's a line for the coke. You can decline the offer only so many times before people start to look at you funny.

"You get called a pansy," says one of the girls.

They start to move on, trading stories. But Mrs. O'Donnell wants to go back to the question of peer pressure. She recalls what that's like, she says. After all, she was in high school once and went through the same thing. It wasn't that hard to say no. Why should it be hard for them? She recalls what it's like to be a teenager, she says. She remembers how it felt at their age.

They shake their heads again and give her grim little smiles. They tell her she is wrong, that there's no way she could travel back through time to the reality of those days. Nobody can do that.

"You can't put yourself back like that," says a tall boy named Chris. Normally he doesn't say much of anything in class. But now he's leaning forward, staring at her, dead serious in his determination to make her understand. *"You cannot put yourself back."*

Besides, even if she could do it—if she could somehow revisit every moment with absolute clarity—she still wouldn't understand. Because being a teenager, Chris tells her, is nothing like when she and their parents were kids.

"They didn't go through what we go through," he says. "They didn't have the same problems at home and stuff."

With that, the class launches into a long spiel. They talk about AIDS and crack and all the divorces they've lived through and how so many kids are killing themselves because they live in homes where no one can stand the sight of them. Why shouldn't they get high?

"If your family hates you," says one boy, "it's easier to smoke a joint."

Mrs. O'Donnell shuts her mouth and listens. She hears this speech all the time. So do the other teachers. Inside and outside the pod, they all hear it repeatedly, from almost all the kids. The lost causes say it. The middle-of-the-roaders say it. Even the best and the brightest keep talking about how rough it's gotten. They keep going on about the stress overload, about how everything's spinning out of control.

It would be easy to dismiss this as melodramatic exaggeration—the collective whining of just another generation of self-absorbed kids who think they're the only ones who've ever felt confused or alone—were it not for the fact that the teen suicide rate has soared over the last few decades. Less than a year ago, a captain of the Largo High football team who'd just dropped out fatally shot himself in the head. In the first three weeks of last year, three teens in neighboring Hillsborough County killed themselves, one in her school's parking lot. The year before that, a student at another local high school put a gun to his head and fatally shot himself at the end of his English class. It's not just high school students, either. In Miami, a ten-year-old boy worried about getting punished for poor grades —he'd just gotten his third bad report card in a row—shot himself not long ago with his parents' .357 Magnum.

"You don't know what it's like," the kids tell anyone who'll listen. "You have no idea."

And they're probably right. The world is simply not the same as it was when their parents were sixteen. Never mind all the emptiness so many of them are dealing with. Never mind all the subtle and not-so-subtle pressures—pressures more intense and sophisticated than ever—for them to join the party and start drinking, smoking and having sex. Never mind the push for them to get an after-school job so they can drive a car, dress fashionably, buy one stereo for their room, buy another for their car and conform to all the other consumer-crazed behavior that's drummed into them daily. Never mind that these jobs often keep them busy from early afternoon until midnight, even though they've still got homework to do and are supposed to be in class at dawn the next morning.

For the moment, put all of that aside. Put aside, too, the acne attacks and the sting of rejection and all the other usual tortures of adolescence. Even if kids didn't have to deal with any of these things, they'd still have to go to school, which has been transformed like the rest of society into an unbelievable grind. Every day it's the same. Seven straight hours, not counting the time they're expected to devote to homework, with no breaks except half an hour for lunch and a few minutes to dash to their lockers. Forget study hall. There's no such thing anymore, at least not at Largo, which has so many state-mandated graduation requirements that every hour of every day becomes critical. There is literally no time to waste.

Getting out of high school is only the beginning. Anyone with an ounce of professional ambition knows it's almost essential these days to earn some kind of college degree. But gaining entry into a major university, even a state school like the University of Florida, isn't always so easy anymore. In fact, it can be extremely difficult for almost any high school senior who hasn't earned above-average grades or at least done well on the SAT, which has become one of the most powerful instruments in this nation for determining who makes it into the finer halls of higher learning and who gets left behind in the dust.

The Scholastic Aptitude Test—or the Scholastic Assessment Tests, as the two-part exam has recently been renamed—looms over the lives of teenagers. Many kids make a career of obsessing over it; some actually start preparing for it years ahead of time, before they've even entered high school. Of course, they worry about a whole slew of other tests and exams as well. And all for what? Even if they make it through the obstacle course, what's the prize waiting for them at the end? Kids are not stupid. As stressful as the world has become for them, they know it's even worse for adults. They know, because they see their parents, if Mom and Dad are still around, come home every night and collapse on the couch. They hear them moaning like wounded animals about taxes and bills and the tyrannies of their bosses and the mountainous piles of work waiting for them every morning on their desks, provided, that is, that they're lucky enough to have a desk and a boss and a job and not be out on the street, wondering how they're going to make the next mortgage payment.

It might be okay if kids had the luxury of believing the future held something better for them. But that's not exactly the forecast these days, is it? Teenagers may not read much, but in between flipping channels, they've caught a few of the latest updates on the national deficit and the homicide rate and the health care crisis and the destruction of the rain forest and the seemingly imminent collapse of just about everything on the planet. They know what kind of mess they're inheriting. And they know who's going to end up paying for it and living with it. When they see the old clips of Ronald Reagan and all the other politicians, chuckling and waving at the cameras, kids understand who's being laughed at. Ultimately the joke will be on them.

Which might help explain why so many walk away. Nothing personal, but they just don't want to waste any more time playing this little game. What's the point? If tomorrow is already trashed, why not hit the beach today? Because the alternatives aren't too spectacular. They can be mature young adults who stay in school and stay in line and do exactly what they're told, praying all the while that everything will work out fine and that they'll emerge from the whole experience with a diploma and a good job and the linings of their stomachs still intact. If they're not too hung up on being perfect, they can cheat. An awful lot of them, from kids in the National Honor Society on down, admit they cheat. And if that doesn't do it, they can get stoned or drink themselves into stupors on the weekends and hope that they destroy enough brain cells to stop them from worrying about the SAT or college or anything else.

Or they can watch *Heathers*. If they're smart then they can always turn on the VCR and let *Heathers* roll one more time.

NINE

THE

FEARSOME

FOURSOME

THEY GLIDE INTO THE CAFETERIA on another pizza-and-corn-dogs Thursday, just as first lunch is kicking into high gear. They are cloaked in the color-coded uniforms; they are exuding the requisite aura of imperial contempt. No one can touch them.

They walk up to a table. Up to one of the clueless innocents.

"So," they say to him together, reciting the ritual introduction, "this is what we call a lunchtime poll."

They draw their breaths, pause the ritual pause, then continue.

"You win five million dollars in the Publishers Clearing House Sweepstakes, and the same day that Big Ed guy gives you the check, aliens land on the earth and say they're going to blow it up in two days. What do you do?"

The innocent stares at them like a dumb animal. Poor thing. He has no idea why they have uttered these words. He has no idea why they are dressed this way, one of them in yellow, one in blue, one in purple, one all in black. But something stops him from committing the heresy of asking. Something deep inside him tells him to fulfill his role, which is to provide them with a response.

He thinks for a second. Well, let's see. If Big Ed gave him all that money, he says, what he'd do is keep two million for himself and use the rest to bribe the aliens into backing off.

A sensible answer. Not one of the answers laid down in the sacred text, but it will suffice.

They move on, pose the question to others, listen carefully to their answers. One person, reverting to basic instinct, says she would grab the cash and head for the mall. Another says he would use it to buy a weapon to annihilate the aliens.

YY, who has been assigned the pivotal role of official secretary, follows the decreed procedure and records every response on a clipboard. She is wearing a yellow top offset by a black jacket and yellow tights offset by a black skirt. She is supposed to be Heather Number Three, the yellow Heather. Even with the costume, this is a stretch. In the movie, Heather Number Three is tall and blond. Not a bit like YY.

So what? YY and Amy Boyle and their two closest girlfriends in the entire world—Meridith Tucker and Karin Upmeyer—are engaged in symbolic theater. They are reenacting a crucial scene from the movie that stands, at least in their minds, as the most underrated, most wickedly funny high school satire of their day. This is no time to get excessively literal. It is not the time to act as though they have had brain tumors for breakfast.

It's October 26, one day before Homecoming. The football team's untarnished record is no more. Last Friday, in a loss that left some players openly weeping, the Largo Packers traveled to Sarasota Riverview and were beaten 20–14. The team members, who still hope to make it into the play-offs, are now doing their best to put the disappointment behind them and get fired up for tomorrow night's game. The rest of the students, or at least the majority of the patio people, are already fired up, deep into a week's worth of pre-Homecoming activities. That's why YY and her friends are in their color-coded uniforms, conducting the lunchtime poll.

As part of the festivities, today has been designated as Character Day, when kids are encouraged to dress up and act like their favorite fictional or historical characters. Monday was College T-shirt Day, Tuesday was Hippie Day, and Wednesday was Nerd Day, which led at least one young critic—a friend of YY's, no one should be surprised to hear—to suggest that everybody should simply wear their hippie costumes again. To YY and her pals, the sixties are seen as a quaint and laughably naive era. To them, the sixties are so irrelevant that when they recently drew a giant peace sign on a teacher's blackboard, they accidentally put it upside down.

This is the nineties, or at least the eve of the nineties. What's relevant now—what YY and company have chosen to immortalize here in the cafeteria late on this Thursday morning—is *Heathers*.

The movie is so much a part of their lives, it's hard to believe that it was only a couple months ago when they stumbled across it in the video store. It had played briefly in the theaters earlier in the year, but like most other people, including many teenagers, they'd never heard of it, which made it all the more of a revelation when they watched it together the first time. The four of them felt as though they had been struck by a thunderbolt.

Once described as a cross between *Blue Velvet* and *The Breakfast Club, Heathers* is a dark and twisted comedy that stars Winona Ryder as Veronica Sawyer, a girl who discovers one day that in her quest for popularity she has joined the most vicious clique in the annals of high school history. There are only three other girls in this clique, all beautiful, all spoiled, and all named Heather; to distinguish themselves they each pick a different dominant color for their designer wardrobes. Together, they rule their midwestern high school through terror, humiliation, and lip-glossed brutality. They amuse themselves with the lunchtime poll, asking other students to play the fool and thereby acknowledge the foursome's supremacy. They have no tolerance for imperfection, either in themselves or in others; one of the Heathers is bulimic and has made a ritual out of purging in the bathroom after lunch. They torture a lonely fat girl with sadistic practical jokes. And they crush anyone who crosses them. Early in the movie, when Veronica fights back and tries to assert some independence, she finds herself at war with Heather Number One, who threatens to turn her into a social outcast and exclude her forever from "all the reindeer games."

Then Veronica meets a new kid—teen idol Christian Slater, playing a rebel named J.D., which stands for Jason Dean—who decides the time has come to begin killing off the Heathers and their allies, the thick-necked date rapists on the football team. J.D. draws Veronica into the plot as an unwitting accomplice, then leaves her no choice but to help him cover their tracks by making the murders look like suicides. It works like a dream; as the death toll rises, everyone automatically accepts that the Heathers would kill themselves. It has become the fashionable thing to do.

"Dear Diary," Veronica writes in the movie's signature line. "My teen angst bullshit has a body count."

Heathers would horrify many adults, especially those who don't know, or don't want to know, what high school has become. It may be a satire, with a fair share of exaggeration, but at the core it's unflinchingly real. With searing detail, it shows kids talking like they really talk, acting like kids really act, doing all of the things parents pretend their children would never do. Veronica and her friends roam from one kegger to the next; they joke about erotic fantasies and masturbating in the shower; they let boys tear their clothes off in cars, in backyards, in a cow pasture, wherever. Most damning of all, they're smart enough to see through all the hypocrisy around them. They have no illusions. They no longer believe in fairy tales, even the ones the adults still tell themselves.

"The afterlife is *soooo* boring," the ghost of Heather Number One complains to Veronica. "If I have to sing 'Kumbaya' one more time . . ."

As reprehensible as the Heathers may be, they're only the natural product of their Darwinian surroundings. They're just the ones who've clawed their way to the top, and for all the hate they inspire, other students are still eager to win their approval. Just about every kid in the movie is maneuvering for one kind of status or another; everyone's working an angle. At a pep rally, the young lechers in the stands peer through binoculars at the cheerleaders doing cartwheels in their short skirts. At one of the funerals, a boy is shown kneeling at the open casket, supposedly praying but in reality asking God to help him get admitted to college.

"Preferably an Ivy League school," he adds.

When they watched *Heathers* that first night, YY and her pals were instantly hooked. They laughed hysterically, totally enraptured, grateful to learn that someone finally understood just how insane high school—not to mention the rest of the world—has become. It was so real, so deliciously subversive. They began renting it over and over. One night they watched it three times in a row. They memorized the lines, analyzed the plot, even went so far as to begin a running debate—these are honor students, re-member—as to whether the character of J.D. is supposed to be a Christ figure.

"I'm totally serious," Amy insists one day in the newspaper room.

She and YY have taken this Christ figure theory one step further. They have also decided that Veronica symbolizes the woman of the same name who wiped Christ's brow as he carried his cross. Their evidence? Amy and YY lean heavily on the fact that at one point in the movie

Veronica burns a cigarette lighter into her palm, creating her own stigmata. As for J.D., they note that just before he dies—and as a true nonconformist, he inevitably must die—he stands with his arms held out and his legs crossed in the classic crucifixion pose.

"He did *not* cross his legs," says Karin, her eyes bulging with exasperation, her voice shaking with outrage.

"Five bucks," says YY, ready to bet on it. *"Jason Dean is a Christ figure."*

Karin's not buying it. After all, J.D. is a murderer. "Jesus," she says, "never laid a finger on a fly."

"He might to prove a point," says Amy.

Listening nearby, Meridith—the cautious one, the one who hangs back before committing herself—shakes her head and laughs.

WHEN CHARACTER DAY ROLLS AROUND, NONE OF THEM CAN resist the opportunity to slip into the Heathers' skin for a few hours. It's so easy. They're already so close. There are four girls in the movie, and there are four of them in real life. They call themselves the Fearsome Foursome. And though they're not the type to brag, there's no question that the girls are all heavy hitters in Largo High's ruling elite, highly placed in just about every major student power base. For starters, YY and Amy have their fiefdoms with the newspaper and the National Honor Society, which means they exert some influence over the flow of written information and the happiness of the school's top students. YY has even been known, in joking moments, to wield her honor society position like a blunt instrument.

"You guys get out of my mug," she tells a couple of uppity juniors making fun of her one night at a football game, "or I'll mess up your work in NHS. You're talking to the vice-president."

Amy, meanwhile, is a delegate on the student council, along with Meridith and Karin. Meridith, who already shows the makings of a great politician, is the council's president; in fact, she was one of the poised young women who spoke to the auditorium full of parents at Open House. For the record, Meridith also happens to be one of the bright-eyed kids in the front office who get to select the thoughts for the day, which endows her with a bizarre kind of authority unto itself.

As for Karin, in addition to her duties on the council, she's vice-president of the senior class. She also holds the unofficial title of funniest person in the school. Actually all four of them are funny. They may be smart kids, but they do not spend their Saturday nights pining away in the chemistry lab. They're quick, they're charming, they can maim with their one-liners. They are the Heathers of Largo High.

With one big difference.

YY and the gang like to think they're pretty hard-edged. But never in a million semesters could they even feign the depths of cruelty flaunted by the characters in the movie. These are nice girls. They're so nice, someone should probably report them to the proper authorities. They go to church; they lead school food drives for the poor; they truly work at making their parents and teachers proud. Still, they are human, and they are teenagers. If they were given a truth serum once a month and forced to divulge every detail of their weekends, their mothers and fathers would probably be permanent guests in a cardiac unit.

Even Amy sometimes wanders from the straight and narrow. Amy's the oldest of the four and the one who takes herself the most seriously. She is also the littlest, the bossiest—being in charge gives her a thrill, she admits it—and definitely the one most committed to the noble but preposterous notion of always being completely honest with one's mom and dad. The others like to rag her about it.

"It's your senior year," they tell her. "You have to lie to your parents every once in a while."

In keeping with her reputation, Amy really is remarkably sweet and innocent. So much so, it's possible that her folks truly may have convinced themselves that she does not drink. Amy and YY and the others are more responsible about alcohol than most kids. When they're on the road, they try to have a designated driver who stays sober. But they're all several years past their first beer, with their favorite brands and favorite drinking games. This year the big game, the one kids seem to keep playing at parties, is Suck and Blow. It's sort of an older version of Spin the Bottle. They all sit in a circle, boy-girl-boy-girl, and then one of them—say a girl —takes a playing card from a deck, doesn't matter which one, and puts it flat across her lips, holding it there by sucking air inward. The object is for her to pass the card without using any hands, pressing up against her neighbor's lips and then blowing until he has it; that person then has to hold onto it and try to pass it along. The key is not to laugh, because that scrunches up your face and interrupts your air intake and makes you drop the card; when that happens, you have to either take a sip of beer or drink a shot. Since it's almost impossible not to laugh, this is a good way to get drunk fast.

Sometimes, of course, they get too drunk too fast and end up playing

Tag-Team Puking. That's what they call it when two of them get sick at the same time and wind up in the same bathroom, one vomiting into the sink and one into the toilet, which is what happens one night to YY and Karin after they work their way toward the bottom of a bottle of tequila.

Getting their hands on beer or liquor is remarkably easy. On behalf of all of them, YY has made liberal use of a fake ID provided by her older sister; the card alleges that YY was born in 1969, which is close enough that it actually fools some people. Of course, they don't always have to rely on YY's ID. When they want to drink, there's almost never any shortage of opportunities. If they're up for it, they can head for one of the get-togethers on Party Island, a circle of sand in the middle of the Intracoastal Waterway where scores of high school kids gather on weekend days. They pay a couple bucks admission for the beer and the boat ride that gets them there, then hang out for hours, drinking and playing volleyball, working on their tans and hoping they don't get busted. YY and the others don't hit the island parties too much anymore, though; usually the sand is too crowded with insufferable sophomores and juniors.

On Friday and Saturday nights, however, they will make appearances at the neighborhood blowouts, which for some odd reason tend to be held at the houses of kids whose parents are out of town. These little get-togethers sometimes attract more than a hundred kids, which means they sometimes attract their share of trouble. At a party YY gave last summer, her guests drank enough beer to fill five Hefty bags with empty bottles and cans. Halfway into the evening, one drunken fool took the liberty of eating some live shrimps he'd scooped out of the aquarium in the family room.

"You got any cocktail sauce, man?" he asked.

YY stopped him before he ate the blowfish, which was good, since it would have been poisonous. As it happened, she didn't know the guy. She didn't know half the people there. Someone stood at the front door, charging admission. Someone else walked up to her and issued an apology.

"I feel really bad that we're trashing your house," he said. "Here's eighty-five cents."

NATURALLY, AMY AND KARIN AND MERIDITH WERE ALL AT YY's party that night. The four of them almost always hang out with one another, and not just on weekends. In fact, it would be misleading to suggest that all of their time together, or even most of it, is spent at wild affairs where they try to stay afloat amid all the beer. Usually they're busy with more mundane pursuits, going to school, studying, heading for work. But even then they are almost always together. They sit together in class —Amy and YY are enduring the same calculus and physics courses—they work on the newspaper together, they eat lunch together, they lounge around the same table and gripe about the same teachers.

They would definitely be patio people, except they tend to spend every spare moment at school inside AB-12, the room number for the newspaper office. They are all AB-12 rats. They eat there, sleep there, and constantly torture one another there. YY has received an untold number of noogies there, has had her shoes ripped from her feet there and hidden many times in the ceiling's removable panels, has even been locked inside the darkness of one of the cabinets. AB-12 is their inner sanctum, a place where they can yell, cry, store the dart board and their secret supply of No Doz, write inane quotes on the blackboard, and gather to weave the epic stories of their lives.

YY periodically collapses onto one of the tables in back and begins talking to whoever will listen. She talks about the barren tundra of her love life, Helen the Hun, her little brothers, the saga of the traumatized blowfish. She tells about the morning last year when she went outside her house and discovered that some unknown agents had covered the windshield of the Y-mobile with an encrusted layer of smooshed-up cookies. Nutter Butters, to be exact.

"So I'm out there with a spatula," she says, "trying to get them off."

YY and the gang have all sorts of after-school adventures. They drag their boyfriends—some of whom they've traded between them—onto dates together. They organize group shopping expeditions to the malls. They gather on Sunday nights to watch *Star Trek: The Next Generation* and to continue their running debate over which is superior, the new show or the old.

The four of them are a team, even when they argue. They are so in sync, they even get their periods at the same time, which isn't that surprising given how much time they spend together under the moon. Still, it's kind of spooky. When the cramps start to hit, they talk about it in code in front of other people. They refer to their little friend, the elf who kicks at their insides.

"The elf is back," one of them will say, and the others will nod, since he's kicking them, too.

All of them work together at the Belleair Country Club. Like YY, they're all buffet girls. It's a fairly easy job, except for the dreaded mussels and smelts and the snooty tones of the members, and the fact that they're forced to dress up in stupid costumes. At Easter, it's bunnies; on St. Patrick's Day, it's leprechauns. Normally they just wear uniforms with cummerbunds. Karin and YY and Meridith all wear black cummerbunds, but Amy gets to wear a silver one because she's the head buffet girl, which leads to all kinds of taunting from the others.

"Gosh, Amy," they tell her. "It must be lonely at the top."

But it's not that lonely, really, because they're all at the top and they all have one another. They're seniors, they're on their way to better things, they radiate an aura of untamed invincibility.

The girls understand each other instinctively. Except for Meridith, who's the firstborn in her family, they are all second children, each with an older sister, which means they know what it's like to live in someone's shadow. And though well-to-do surroundings are no guarantee of academic success—some of the GOALS kids at Largo have been known to drive a Mercedes to school—they all come from middle-class to upper-middle-class homes. More important, they come from homes like YY's, where the walls are covered with books and where reading and learning are as much a part of daily life as watching TV or playing Nintendo. All of their parents went to college, and it was always assumed their children would do the same. There was room to argue about what university they would attend and how many degrees they would pursue. But from the day the girls were born, they were definitely going. Dropping out was never an option.

To YY and the others, dropping out is one of the more incomprehensible mistakes anyone could make. These girls have always done what was expected of them, which was to stay and play the game. They may make fun. They may complain bitterly about the system and hurl the occasional dart at Ms. Westfall's grinning mug. But they do not walk away. They've stuck it out for almost thirteen years of school now, counting kindergarten. They've jumped through all the hoops, followed a fair percentage of the rules, done almost every single thing expected of them. To an astonishing degree, they have been ideal students.

Not surprisingly, they get pretty sick of it.

Which is why, on this Thursday, one day before Homecoming, they are having such a blast dressing up as the Heathers. To these girls, the notion of surrendering to their evil alter egos—of letting their monstrous mirror images run loose around the school, just for a day—is irresistible.

So through the cafeteria and into the halls they glide, wearing the clothes and wearing the attitude. They don't have to say FTW. They have their own slogans, from the movie. Some of their favorite lines are nastier than anything Mike Broome has probably ever dreamed of saying.

"If you want to fuck with the eagles," they proclaim, quoting from one of the picture's key speeches, "you have to learn to fly."

Almost no one knows what they're talking about, since not that many kids have seen the movie. But the girls don't care. They just keep going. They love it.

"Why do you have to be such a mega-bitch?" they say. Automatically they give the required response. "Because I can be."

They walk past the lockers, overwhelmed with an intoxicating sense of power. At this moment, they truly have been transformed. They feel as though they really do own the school. Well, sort of. Before quoting a few of the racier lines, they look around to make sure no adults are within earshot.

"Fuck me gently with a chain saw," they say, lowering their voices just a tad and laughing hysterically. "Do I look like Mother Teresa?"

But it's not really the adults they have to worry about. Because what the girls don't yet realize—what they won't figure out until later on, when they look back and try to understand what went wrong—is that a backlash is already starting among their fellow students.

Not all of the clueless innocents, it turns out, are amused by this little act. Not all of them, in fact, are convinced that it's an act. Some kids, when they find out what's going on, would argue that YY and the others are merely revealing the true essence of their natures. The girls, they would argue, are worshipping themselves and asking everyone else to join in. Who do the four of them think they are? Don't they know how they're coming off? Don't they know how they're making people feel?

They'll find out soon enough.

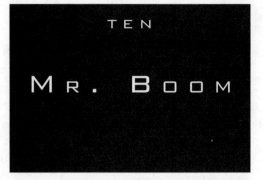

TEN

MR. BOOM

THAT SAME THURSDAY, AS YY and the others conduct their lunchtime poll, talking quietly of chain saws and Mother Teresa, the final ballots are being cast for Homecoming King and Queen. The winners will be announced during halftime at tomorrow night's football game.

Andrea Taylor tries not to think about it. She tries not to imagine what it would be like to feel that crown placed on her head. Shana Denton is looking more and more like a sure thing. Her track record is so intimidating. She's the only one in the whole senior class who's been voted to represent her class at Homecoming court all four years. Andrea was elected to court with her last year, but not in their freshman or sophomore years. There's no way around it. Shana is on a roll.

Still, Andrea is determined to enjoy Homecoming, no matter what happens. She'll go to the game tomorrow night, and then on Saturday she'll go to the Homecoming dance and let loose. The theme for this year's dance is "Sea of Love," but Andrea isn't expecting any big romantic night, because she's going with

John Boyd. She tracked him down in the weight room the other day and arranged it. It made sense. Andrea doesn't have a boyfriend right now—the beeper boy was sent packing long ago—so she figured it would be nice to go with her old pal. John's always fun to be with, plus there won't be any of the usual anxiety over whether some guy's going to lunge at her on the doorstep. That just won't happen, since John's already spoken for by Sabrina, her girlfriend who goes to Dunedin.

Of course, when Sabrina hears about the arrangement, she gets a little sketched. But Andrea tells her to calm down.

"Just friends," she says. "We're just going as friends."

JAIMEE THE GHOST DOES NOT REALLY CARE WHO WINS Homecoming Queen.

"I don't even know who's running," she says.

Her full name is Jaimee Sheehy. For the first time in two weeks, she has made an appearance in her English class down in the pod. She's the thin one, with the long blond hair and the green eyes and the clean good looks you normally see on the cover of *Seventeen*. She's sitting at a table in the back, playing a game of Sorry with a couple of boys and ignoring the morning announcements, which are full of Homecoming updates.

Almost none of the kids in the pod are going to the big game. Almost none of them are going to the dance, either. For them, the idea of attending such functions—of actively seeking to establish such a connection with the rest of the school—is unthinkable. The GOALS teachers would like to change that. They're urging their students to go to the game; at least one teacher is giving extra credit points to anyone who shows up. But it's unlikely that many of them will take her up on it. When you're a seventeen-year-old kid living in a mobile home with your boyfriend, as one girl in GOALS is doing this year, Homecoming is insignificant.

Jaimee won't be there, either. She's not even here now, in this class. Even as she sits at the table, playing Sorry and waiting for her turn at the dice, she is someplace far away. Someplace that does not appear on any map, except perhaps the one inside her head.

Just the other day, her mother discovered that Jaimee is stealing from her again. By accident, Laura Sheehy learned that her only child—the one who'd begged to be trusted again after the car theft—has taken some checks from her and used a couple hundred dollars to bankroll a little shopping spree for her and a few friends. Jaimee doesn't know she's been caught. Her mother hasn't told her yet. What's the point? Jaimee will only deny it, like she always does.

But that's it. The checks are the last straw. At last, Laura Sheehy knows what she's going to do. It'll take a little time to get everything together. She has to make arrangements with the hospital. She has to call her insurance people. But one way or another, she is determined to make Jaimee face reality.

A HANDFUL OF ZOMBIES SITS SLUMPED AT A TABLE IN THE back room of the library, their eyes glazed over, their chins resting in their palms. They are watching a videotape for an English class, trying not to fall asleep. Suddenly a buzzing fills the air, vibrating through the school with ear-splitting intensity.

Fire alarm.

None of the kids at the table get up. No one even ducks a head out the door to see what's happening. One of the boys sighs, adopts a stiff voice of officialdom and says, *"Students and teachers, please disregard the—"*

He's cut off by an echo over the P.A. system.

"Students and teachers, please disregard the alarm," announces someone in the front office. "Please disregard the alarm . . ."

A girl sits at the side of a nearby classroom, playing with her hair as she talks in a matter-of-fact voice about her drug arrest last year. The only reason she got caught, she says, was because this kid she knows told the cops about the stash in her truck. She still hasn't forgiven him.

"He narced on me," she says. "This one guy was going to kill him for me if I paid him." She smiles. "I thought that was a little bit too serious."

Over by the auditorium, the regular gang of burnouts has convened its daily meeting on the steps. Mike Broome sits among them, a cigarette in his hand.

It was risky before for Mike to smoke out in the open. It's positively stupid to do it again now, when he's racked up so many suspension days. But there he is, puffing away with his friends, when suddenly two teachers walk up and catch the bunch of them by surprise.

"Do you know who any of these guys are?" says one of the teachers.

The other one points at Mike.

"That's Mr. Boom right there."

Mike hears this and bristles. "That's not my name," he says.

"It is today," says the teacher. "Isn't it, Mr. Boom?"

The anger that simmers just below Mike's surface is about to boil over. Teachers get his name wrong all the time, leaving off the "r" or forgetting the "e," and he hates it. They should know who he is. They should know how to spell his name. And now here's someone deliberately saying it wrong, making fun of him. Why should anyone have to take this? Who does this jerk think he is?

"That's not my fucking name," Mike says, flipping a reliable middle finger at the man. "Fuck you."

A few minutes later, he is down in the office, where they know his name all too well and have no choice but to suspend him for eight days. Five for the smoking, three days for the foul language and disrespect.

Boom.

ELEVEN

SEA

OF LOVE

FRIDAY NIGHT. HALFTIME. AND the lights are blazing. They're burning with such a bright white light that they've turned the grass on the field into this supercharged shade of cartoon green.

Andrea already knows. They haven't even announced it yet, and already she knows. The first time around the track, it became so obvious. She and the other two girls are in convertibles with the tops down. They're sitting up on the backseats, smiling and waving. Shana's in one car, then Louise in another, then Andrea bringing up the rear. They're circling the track in a little caravan—the drivers are keeping the speed nice and easy—and as Shana's car goes around the fourth turn and passes the stands, Andrea hears a round of applause. Louise goes by, and there's another big round.

Then comes Andrea. She's just made the turn and is heading down the straightaway when the roar begins. The car is slowly bringing her toward the crowd, and as she approaches, the roar keeps growing. People are cheering and screaming. They're going wild.

When the three girls get out of the cars and onto the field for the announcement, Andrea is trembling. She watches as the senior class president walks up to the microphone to name the winners. First the class president announces the King, who turns out to be Jamie Bryant, just like everybody predicted. Then comes the announcement of the Queen, which anyone with at least one good ear has already guessed.

When Andrea hears her name, she does what Homecoming queens are expected to do. She gives a little jump—not too high, since she's wearing high heels—and begins to cry. The crowd roars again. People are yelling and waving their arms and firing off their flash photos. Andrea's mother and older sister and Sabrina are out there, and Andrea can actually make out her mother's voice, rising above the others.

"That's my baby!"

Everything happens so fast. Someone puts the crown on Andrea's head. She can't get it to stay. It keeps flipping off, and she keeps picking it up and putting it back on. Last year's Queen hugs her and hands her two bouquets of red roses. Ms. Westfall hugs her and tells her how proud she's made them. The senior class president hugs her. Everyone on the field, it seems, is hugging her.

Except for one person.

Andrea doesn't notice at first. She's too busy waving to the crowd and posing for the photos and riding around the track one more time for her victory lap. But when she finally gets a few seconds to catch her breath, it occurs to her that Shana is the only one keeping her distance. Other people are all swooping over, gathering Andrea in their arms and squeezing her and telling her how beautiful she looks. Even Louise, gracious as always, is congratulating her. Not Shana. As far as Andrea can recall, Shana hasn't said a word to her since the announcement.

Later, when asked about this moment, Shana would insist that she did in fact approach Andrea and congratulate her. Still, it's obvious out on the field that night that Shana is taking her defeat hard. When Andrea looks over and sees her, Shana is standing off to the side, fighting back the tears, too crushed to say anything. She's just looking off in another direction, away from Andrea and the glittering crown that was supposed to be hers.

THE REST OF THE NIGHT GOES SMOOTHLY. THE FOOTBALL team, still smarting from the loss to Riverview, takes comfort in a victory over Countryside High, this year's sacrificial Homecoming victim. The honor of the Packers is restored. All is well.

But the next evening, at the dance, things get a bit uncomfortable. As King and Queen, Andrea and Jamie Bryant are supposed to dance a slow song together. They're supposed to do "Sea of Love," since that's the theme of the night. But when the song begins to roll and they start moving in the middle of the floor, Andrea can't help but notice Shana.

The girl is still acting detached and distant. In fact, a week will pass before she can bring herself to say much of anything to Andrea, and even then there'll be a vague lingering tension. At this moment, while Andrea and Jamie dance their song, Shana is looking especially despondent. Andrea can see her over Jamie's shoulder. She's dancing listlessly with another guy, paying absolutely no attention to him, gazing off into space.

Andrea can't take it. Before the song is over, she gives in.

"Do you want to go ahead and dance with Shana now?" she asks Jamie.

He's a gentleman. He's nice about it. But the answer is yes.

So Jamie and Shana are reunited, and Andrea is cut loose. But that's okay, because John Boyd's waiting for her in the wings. The guy always looks hot. But tonight he is positively volcanic. He's wearing this black tux, and when Andrea gets near him, she discovers that he's slapped on this cologne she loves called That Man.

Turns out she has plenty of chances to smell it. They're on the floor together for every slow song. John's pulling her real close. It catches her off guard. They're swaying together, and he's holding her hand—holding it tight—and she's leaning on his shoulder, zoning in on the cologne.

Suddenly Andrea realizes she has another problem to worry about. A new and considerably more thorny problem. One that makes this Homecoming Queen business look like nothing.

There on the dance floor, as they slowly spin to the music, it hits her. She has to figure out what to do about Sabrina. She has to find a way now to save their friendship. Because Sabrina is not likely to take it well—not well at all—when she learns that Andrea, her oldest and dearest confidante, the one she was supposed to trust, has stepped off into the deepest waters of the sea of love and is now sinking unpredictably and undeniably head over heels for none other than John.

HALLOWEEN'S A FEW DAYS LATER. MRS. O'DONNELL IS walking on campus during seventh period—it's one of her planning hours —when she sees something she will remember for a long time.

It's Jaimee Sheehy and one of her friends from the pod. They're outside the gym, dancing with these big plastic skeletons.

"Am I going to see you girls in class?" Mrs. O'Donnell asks them.

They laugh.

"Oh, we'll be there. Maybe tomorrow."

Jaimee does not know yet that the missing checks have been discovered. She does not know what her mother intends to do. Still oblivious, she dances away. She and the other girl look very happy. They dip and tilt. They giggle. They move with the skeletons to a song no one else can hear.

PART TWO

DISAPPEARING

ACTS

JAIMEE SHEEHY, CAUGHT IN THE SHADOWS.

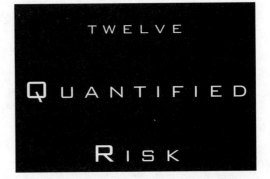

TWELVE

QUANTIFIED

RISK

''GOOD MORNING. OUR THOUGHT
for the day is: It's no use getting into a
good college if you fail tuition.''

The voice of wisdom shares this
friendly tidbit on a Wednesday in November. Once again, the thought behind
the thought for the day is open to inter-
pretation. Is the voice actively taunting
students whose families can't afford to
send them to college? Or is it just making a poorly chosen play on words? Who
knows.

It's easy to feel on edge these days.
Only a couple of weeks ago, students
were relaxing in the calm and benevolence of October, letting their homework
slide, telling themselves there was still
plenty of time to straighten up and salvage their GPAs. But now the inevitable
acceleration has begun. As the days swirl
by with increasing speed, kids are suddenly waking up to the fact that Thanksgiving is almost here, which means
Christmas is almost here, which means
exam week is descending upon them like
an angel of doom. Reality is finally kicking in. Sort of.

"I don't think he's that cute," one girl

says to another inside a B Wing classroom. "He's got a good body, but his face is not that cute."

A few feet away, another girl—a girl who has recently been thrown out of her house—leans over a piece of paper, silently writing.

I have come to a time in my life where I feel abandoned, alone, and where my time is running out. The clock keeps ticking away as more and more evil things keep happening and I have been put out in the cold. . . .

Over in A Wing, the head of the social studies department is giving her advanced placement American history class its usual grilling.

"What amendment," asks Rosa Waldrep, "provides for direct election of senators?"

It is a sneaky question. So sneaky that many lawyers could not answer it without looking it up.

A boy seated near the front raises his hand.

"Ummm, Nineteen?"

Ms. Waldrep shakes her head. "The Nineteenth Amendment gave women the vote." She pauses a beat and gives him a cutting little smile. "I'm glad you know that one, John."

She makes sure they know the correct answer (it was the Seventeenth Amendment) and then moves on. She's always moving on, always asking more questions, always pushing them harder. Some years ago, Ms. Waldrep suffered a stroke that paralyzed half of her face; even today, the paralysis makes it difficult for her to speak. But after two decades in the classroom, she's not about to stop. Known as one of Largo's most demanding instructors, she is also one of the most affectionate. Sometimes, when she's probing her students' minds with her endless queries, she stands beside them, gently stroking their hair. "Dear children," she calls them, without a trace of irony.

"Who can name for us—look me straight in the eye—and name the first seven presidents?"

She calls on a girl sitting off to the side. The girl casts her eyes upward, as though the answers might be scribbled on the ceiling.

"Look at me."

The girl does as she's told, then—miraculously—reels off Washington, Adams, Jefferson, Madison, Monroe, Adams, Jackson.

Sitting at the lectern, Ms Waldrep rewards her with a nod of approval.

She knows how tough the kids think she is. But today, as on so many days, she wonders if she's too easy. There's so much they need to learn. So much to etch into their brains . . .

Across the way, a dark-haired boy with an enigmatic smile sits in a booth inside the cafeteria, surrounded by female admirers as he rearranges what's left of his lunch into some kind of sculpture. He is an artist who specializes in works constructed out of food and food containers. Once it was *The Leaning Tower of Milkshakes.* Another time, *Portrait of a French Fry.* Today he places a straw inside a milk carton and attaches a rectangular section of crumpled foil to the straw.

"It's abstract. Very abstract," he says. "It's a representation of the American flag in a hurricane."

DOWN IN THE POD, SOMETHING HAS COMPELLED JAIMEE Sheehy to make her way into Mr. Taylor's seventh-period world history class. She takes her seat and begins taking notes. Mr. Taylor is at the overhead projector, going over some review material on Tribune Tiberius Gracchus, a reformer in ancient Rome.

Jaimee squints up at the screen.

"I can't read your writing," she says.

Renny Taylor is not surprised. "Because you're not here enough to know what my writing looks like," he tells her. "Jaimee, this is the first time you've been in here to take notes in—"

He doesn't remember how long it has been. He looks at his roll book and informs her that she has not shown up for this class since October 20. That was a couple of weeks ago, which means that in that time period alone—forget all the earlier absences—Jaimee has missed more than the nine days allowed each semester.

Other kids hear this and stare.

"You've already failed," one girl tells her.

"What are you doing here?" says another.

Jaimee says nothing. She fixes her eyes ahead, up at the projector as Mr. Taylor returns to his lecture. A few minutes later, when he's done and the bell is about to ring, he looks back at her. "You're going to come back tomorrow?" he says.

She smiles. "If you're lucky."

• • •

AFTER ALL THIS TIME, JAIMEE SHEEHY REMAINS A MYSTERY. To her teachers, to her friends, possibly even to herself. Despite all the evidence to the contrary, she claims she wants to graduate from high school.

"I have to," she says, sighing as though someone is forcing her to state the obvious. "I don't want to work at McDonald's or something."

She insists she faithfully goes to class. She knows that everyone knows this is not true, but she insists it anyway. When people ask, she tells them she's headed for college. She has ambitions, she says.

"I want to be like . . . What do I want to be? Um, maybe be a horseback rider, like a Grand Prix rider."

She already owns a horse, she says. His name is Shoney. She loves to ride him.

"My favorite is jumping," she says.

She did once own a horse named Shoney, and she did love to ride and jump with him. But that was centuries ago, before she became Jaimee the ghost. Back when she was still just Jaimee the fairly normal kid.

At home, in her room, she has a paperweight from an insurance company. The paperweight has an equation written on it. *Quantified risk = 0 risk.* On her bulletin board, not far from the paperweight, she has a drawing of a skeleton skateboarding through Armageddon. In the background it shows a huge mushroom cloud, decorated with a smiley face; in the foreground is the skeleton, grinning on the board, riding over a landscape of graves and toxic waste. Hanging nearby are Jaimee's old ribbons, the ones she won when she was still jumping at shows with Shoney. There's one shot of Jaimee in the black hat and the black jacket and the rest of her riding gear, standing next to the horse, smiling shyly for the camera.

Her mother doesn't know what went wrong. Maybe the change was coming all along. Maybe the ghost was always inside Jaimee, waiting for the right moment to come to the surface. But Laura Sheehy didn't see it.

In the beginning Ms. Sheehy sympathized with her daughter. Laura was no angel herself in high school. When she was growing up in Long Island, she was a master at cutting classes. She was a fairly good student; usually her report cards were packed with Bs, sometimes even As. But she used to go on mini-vacations and take off from class for a few days. She would skip with Jaimee's father, who went to the same school. The two of them were close back then, dating until graduation, then eventually marrying and having Jaimee. Within a few years, though, it was over. Once the divorce papers went through, Laura packed up Jaimee and moved down to Florida. Laura was sick of New York winters, sick of getting robbed every time she turned around, ready for someplace new. Her parents were already living in Pinellas County, so she and Jaimee came down and moved into a nearby duplex.

When the time came for school, Jaimee did all right, although she wasn't the greatest student in the world. She never much liked to read, and her attention span was always short. It wasn't that obvious at the time, but there were already hints of what awaited over the horizon. Jaimee's elementary school teachers kept sending home reports of how easily distracted she was, how she was reading below grade level, how she constantly had to be reminded to stay on task. One day in fourth grade, Jaimee and another girl terrified their teachers when they sneaked out of class and vanished for a while, playing in some woods behind the school.

Still, as frightening as the disappearance was, it was only an isolated incident. And if Jaimee wasn't particularly dazzling in the classroom, she was rapidly developing into a hardworking, dedicated athlete. She played in the youth leagues outside of school. She went out for both baseball and soccer; the only girl on her soccer team, she was picked for the all-star squad. And when a kids' hockey league started up at a local skating rink, she grabbed a stick and joined that, too, chasing pucks on the ice with the boys. Her dream, she told her mom, was to be a goalie.

Riding Shoney was what she loved best, though. Jaimee got the horse when she was ten. As a single mom, Ms. Sheehy had a hard time scraping together the five hundred dollars to buy him, but she thought it would be good for her daughter. Shoney, her mother thought, would give Jaimee something to love, something to take care of, something to be responsible for. When they went to the ranch where he was up for sale, the horse immediately came over and began nudging his nose against Jaimee's arm, as though he'd known her forever. When Jaimee climbed up on his back and rode him for the first time, she couldn't stop smiling. She didn't want to get off him.

It was Jaimee who taught the horse to jump. She was remarkably patient, coaxing and pushing and bribing him with treats until they were soaring together day after day. Jaimee was so determined, she even built her own jumps. She and her mother would collect old boards and barrels and hammer them all together, just so Shoney would have something to clear. Jaimee was always willing to work hard for that horse. Knowing how tight her mother's budget was, she took a job cleaning the stables where they kept him; that way, she could pay for Shoney's feed and for riding lessons.

Other girls her age kept horses at the same stables, and as time passed, Jaimee grew close to them. They'd ride together, brush their horses together, and clean the stalls together. There was a little lake at the stables, and during the day, when the horses needed cooling off, the girls would swim with them in the water. Sometimes they'd even spend the night with the animals, giggling in the dark, sneaking up and scaring each other, sleeping on blankets stretched across fresh hay.

Then Jaimee hit fourteen, and something happened. Suddenly she lost interest in all of the things she'd loved. She didn't want to go to baseball practice. She didn't want to play soccer or hockey. And she had almost no time for Shoney. She didn't want to ride him; she didn't want to see him. She didn't want anything to do with him, period.

At school, where Jaimee had never been that interested in the first place, it was even worse. As she left eighth grade and entered high school, she fell into a downward spiral. Once she found out that the school rules allowed her to miss nine days a semester without any penalties, she immediately skipped until she reached the limit and then kept it up until she was in so deep there was no chance of an appeal. She skipped so many days, she failed every course in her freshman year; furthermore, she lied repeatedly to her mother, saying she was doing fine. One day she even brought home a doctored report card that showed her receiving mostly As and Bs. That's why her mother put her in GOALS during the second semester. She hoped the special attention down in the pod would help Jaimee. But the problem only intensified.

The low point came late in the second semester. The day Laura Sheehy discovered that her black Firebird was missing from the parking lot at the Largo Medical Center where she works as a respiratory therapist. She had just called the police when a coworker, looking out the window, pointed across the way.

"There's your car," the coworker said. "It's over there."

The Firebird had returned. Only now it was in a different parking space. Laura went out and felt the hood; it was hot. The car was dirty, even though she'd just had it washed. French fries were scattered on the floor in the back. The radio had been switched to another station.

That was it. Laura took her daughter to the police station and insisted that she be charged with the theft. She stood and watched while Jaimee was fingerprinted and photographed. A month or so later, the two of

them were in juvenile court together as a judge placed Jaimee on probation. But that didn't help, either. Jaimee was supposed to complete some
community service, cleaning desks at the school, but she didn't do it. She
didn't take the probation seriously. Truth was, she didn't take much of
anything seriously. Not anymore.

Laura Sheehy wasn't giving up, though. One way or another, she was
determined to turn the situation around. She pored through a book called
Theories of Adolescence. She even tried getting professional help. In the
evenings, after work, she'd take Jaimee to a woman at a local counseling
center. The counselor put Jaimee in front of a sandbox and asked her to
draw a story in the sand. Jaimee made little horses and little jumps for the
horses, and she drew herself and her mother and made them a house. The
counselor couldn't help but notice how small Jaimee drew herself. Even
though she was on the verge of becoming a young woman, Jaimee drew
herself as a small child, someone who clearly had not yet grown up.

As revealing as the sessions were, they ultimately didn't seem to do
much good. Jaimee wasn't showing any signs of getting better. For all the
horses she drew in the sand, she still had no interest in Shoney. She kept
promising to take better care of him, but she never followed through.
That summer, her mother decided the time had come to sell the horse.
She thought Jaimee would be crushed, but when they sold him, she barely
noticed. It was nothing.

Now, only partway into this new school year—Jaimee's second stint in
the ninth grade—the downward spiral is only picking up speed. Jaimee's
still skipping. When her mom's at work, she's having parties at the house.
Just the other day, Jaimee bought a new poster. It was of Jim Morrison,
the doomed lead singer for the Doors, which made sense in an odd kind
of way, given Jaimee's running flirtation with the void. She gave the
poster to her mother, as a gift.

"I love you, Mom," she told her.

Laura Sheehy was touched, but she couldn't understand how Jaimee
had managed to buy the gift. Where did she get the money? She didn't
have a job, and her mother certainly hadn't given it to her. Ms. Sheehy
looked around and discovered other new things in Jaimee's room. Some
clothes, a cassette tape, another poster. Then Laura looked in her check-
book and noticed some checks were missing. She went to the bank and
found that a couple of hundred dollars had been withdrawn from her
account. Ms. Sheehy couldn't believe it. For months, she'd been working
overtime, saving to buy a house. Jaimee knew it, too. And yet she'd taken

the money. Not to buy anything major, either—it's not like Jaimee has been trying to make a living out of this—just some little trinkets for herself and her friends.

What Ms. Sheehy couldn't help notice was the name of the cassette tape Jaimee had bought with the stolen money. It was by the Red Hot Chili Peppers. It was called *Mother's Milk*.

Laura Sheehy thought back to how she'd nursed Jaimee as a baby. In those days, it wasn't widely done. Her doctor had tried to talk her out of it. Jaimee was jaundiced, and the doctor told Laura that it was because she had insisted on being different and nursing. Laura, who had studied the literature and consulted with her Lamaze instructor, ignored the stupid man. She held the baby in her arms and felt her drinking from her and saw her looking up into her eyes, contented and safe, and it didn't matter what the doctor said. So what if Jaimee was yellowish-brown because of the jaundice. That could be treated easily. Besides, she was so beautiful. She'd been born with a tan . . .

Laura knows that beautiful child is still there. And she has decided how to bring her out of whatever wasteland she's wandering. She's not going to bother having Jaimee arrested, since they already tried that route. No. This time, she's going to put Jaimee someplace where she'll get the help she obviously needs. She is going to place her daughter in Charter Hospital of Tampa Bay, a mental health facility that specializes in, among other things, working with troubled teens.

Jaimee won't hear of it.

"I'm not going to go," she says.

Her mother tells her she needs help. She tells her they've got to do it. The decision is final.

"You are going to Charter," she says.

THIRTEEN

SECRETS

ANDREA TAYLOR KNOWS A HOPE-
less yearning when one hits her. And
what she's yearning for now is more
hopeless than hopeless.

There's no way around it. Andrea is a
practical girl. As much as she'd like to go
out with John Boyd, she knows it would
be crazy to try. If Sabrina found out,
she'd probably never forgive her. So Andrea is keeping her feelings to herself.
She is determined not to let this get out
of hand. Of course, it doesn't help that
John has already tempted her with a
kiss.

It was after the Homecoming dance,
when John took her home. He didn't
mean to tempt her. He just gave her a
little peck while they were standing beside the car. Nothing passionate. The
kind of kiss someone gives a friend out of
politeness. Still, Andrea was taking no
chances. The next day, when she provided Sabrina with a rundown of the
night—and a rundown was required, so
as not to arouse suspicion—she conve-
niently skipped over the close encounter
in the yard.

"And then he brought me home," she
told Sabrina, "and that's about it."

The problem is, that's not it. As the fall semester barrels toward that balmy stretch of the high fifties that Florida jokingly refers to as winter, Andrea can't get her mind off John. She knows she should be happy. Ever since she was named Homecoming Queen, all the rules at school seem to be under revision. It wasn't just her winning the crown—for years now, other kids have been chipping away at the barriers, too—but Homecoming didn't hurt. African-American kids are still doing the balancing act together on the rail, but they are also venturing onto the patio in greater numbers. They sit under the patio trees with other black students, but they also sit with white kids. It's the same in the lunchroom. In the cafeterias at so many other high schools, there's a persistent social segregation, with blacks eating only with blacks and whites eating only with whites. But in Largo's cafeteria, there are bunches of tables where everybody mixes and hangs out together. It's not the end of racial problems, not by any stretch of the imagination, but at least it's a step in the right direction.

None of that, however, helps Andrea with her current dilemma. She can't help it. She thinks about John all the time. About how it felt to be wrapped in his arms that night on the dance floor. About how sweet he is.

About how he can make her laugh with just a look. Plus, let's be honest here, she can't take her eyes off the boy when he's walking down the hall. Especially when he walks in front of her, giving her a chance to discreetly check out his moves. She's human, isn't she? Is it written somewhere that Homecoming queens aren't allowed to lust a little like everyone else?

Of course, Andrea can't really talk openly about this particular object of desire. Sabrina can, though. Sabrina goes on about John all the time, and as her best friend, Andrea is naturally called upon to listen. It's terrible. Andrea sits there with her after school, trying to smile, trying to look supportive, while Sabrina talks about how wild she is about John. When she's had enough and can't take it anymore, Andrea changes the subject.

"Yeah," she says, burning inside. "Whatever."

EARLY ONE DEAD NOVEMBER AFTERNOON. SCATTERED SUN-light fighting its way through the window of a tiny cluttered office. Phones ringing endlessly somewhere in the distance.

Mike Broome sits against the back wall, slouched in a chair, studying his fingernails and dodging questions from yet another adult with a fancy title.

"Mike," says this person, sighing across a desk, "aren't we trying to work things out?"

"Yeah."

He keeps looking at his nails. He gazes at them as though his eyes have never beheld such an intriguing sight.

"Am I going to get suspended for this?" he says, still not looking up.

"No. Should you?"

"I don't know."

Behind the desk, a sign hangs on the wall:

A new broom sweeps clean.

Mike does not appear to notice these words. He's too busy these days to notice much of anything. He is on a mission. A quest for a special place in the history books of Largo High. If he continues on his present course, he may soon set a school record for the number of disciplinary referrals received by one individual in a single semester. Today has been especially eventful. Mike has scored a double play. In the space of one half hour, he has been given two referrals. One was for allegedly picking on another kid and then insulting his teacher when she tried to stop him; the other was for cursing and causing a disturbance when he was sent to the office for the first incident. His specific words during the disturbance, according to the second referral, were, "I don't know why the fuck I was sent up here."

Now Ruth Riel, the dropout prevention specialist, sits on the other side of the desk, trying to understand why Mike does these things. Through it all, they have always kept their tempers. They have been extremely reasonable. So reasonable, Mike can hardly stand it.

Miss Riel looks at him.

"Why do you use 'fuck'?"

"Because I want to."

"That is the worst word that you can use. It gets you in trouble."

No response. Miss Riel is still looking at him, but he won't return her gaze.

"Are you going to work with us, Mike?"

Mike keeps studying his nails.

"Mmmmm-hmmm."

"I told you before, we can't help you if you're not working with us . . ."

Miss Riel goes on. She says she doesn't want to suspend him. She knows what it's like to be in trouble, she says. When she was in high school, she tells him, she always had to stay after school for detention. She goes on, trying to establish some sort of bond, but Mike hardly seems to hear her. He doesn't particularly care what it was like in the old days. What he wants to know is what's going to happen to him right now.

"I don't want to get suspended," he says, finally looking up. "Because my mom said if I get suspended again, I got to go live with my dad . . . I ain't going to live with him."

The moment Mike mentions his father, he drops the boredom act. The air of feigned indifference disappears; an edge immediately slips into his voice.

Miss Riel hears the change and pauses. Quietly she studies this strange boy across the desk from her. She does not know that much about Mike's family or his childhood, since he still resists revealing anything about himself to her or his teachers. But she senses that he has lowered his defenses, if only for a moment, and shown her something real inside him. She doesn't push for more details, though. Pushing never works with

Mike. Instead she lets it go, quietly filing it away in her mind, saving it for a later date when it might come in handy.

She turns to a computer screen beside the desk, scans through Mike's disciplinary record. He hasn't done anything terrible for a few days now, she says. If he'll apologize to his teacher, if he'll tell her he didn't mean to insult her, they're willing to make an exception this time. They'll let him off with a few demerits. Will he do that for them?

Mike looks down at his lap.

"All right."

MIKE IS RUNNING OUT OF TIME. ALREADY HE HAS MISSED SO many days due to suspensions that it will be nearly impossible to pass any of his classes this semester. He could still turn it around, though. He could fix it so easily. If he'd just talk to them. If he'd drop the armor and tell them what's wrong, they could help. But he won't do it. He opened up that one time, with Mrs. O'Donnell and Ms. DiLello, but he has not done it again. Either he does not have the words, or he is not willing to use them.

"I don't care," he says, over and over. "Fuck it."

If Mike ever ventured out into the open, there's no telling what he'd share with the teachers. He might talk about how alone he feels. He could try to describe the ache of always looking in from the outside. He might even try, maybe, to explain how hard it is for him to breathe here at the school. Not just because of his asthma, either. It's the walls. And the walls around the walls. And all these ridiculous rules, which are more walls unto themselves.

But Mike tells them nothing. He hides his secrets as though they were treasures. He guards himself with silence, just like his dad does. At least that's what Mike's mom says. According to Jewelene Wilson, her ex-husband shares the same reluctance to open up and share his feelings. He's the one who gave that trait to Mike. It was one of his more enduring gifts to his youngest son.

"What's the matter?" Mrs. Wilson asks the boy.

Always, the answer is the same. "Nothing."

She keeps trying to figure it out. She sits in her easy chair in the living room—it helps to sit, since her leg still hurts all these years after the cancer—and she listens to the traffic out on Belleair Road and she tries to piece everything together. She knows it all started with the divorce, when

Mike was only two and watched his dad walk away forever. This is the secret Mike's teachers have been longing to learn. At least, it is part of the secret. Mrs. Wilson recognizes that her son's problems probably can't be explained away so easily. She knows that everything that's happened with Mike cannot be traced back to one single factor. Still she's sure that this is at the heart of it. She looks back to those early days and remembers how torn up Mike was when his dad first left. The real change, though—the bitterness, the rage, the explosions—came afterward, when he got older and started to understand that he had lost his father in more ways than one.

All these years later, Mr. Broome still lives in north Florida. He's remarried, too, and he works as the manager of a Swifty convenience store. Though he keeps in touch with his sons, there is a kind of descending order to the relationships. He is closest to Greg, who was the oldest and whom he knew the best and who came to live with him for a time before Greg enlisted in the service; he is the most distant from Mike, who was just learning to talk when they separated. Now they hardly speak at all. Sometimes Mr. Broome calls on Mike's birthday; more often, says Mrs. Wilson, he does not. (Again, her ex-husband says it's not that simple. He does try to stay in contact with Mike, he says. He insists that he regularly remembers the boy's birthday, and he notes that when Mike was in the eighth grade, he came to live with him for a month or so. But the boy soon left, he says, because he missed his mother and because he bridled at the strict rules his father set.)

Now Mike feels a deep detachment from his father. He says it doesn't bother him. But when the subject comes up, it's easy to see the lie in his face.

A few years ago, when he was more open with his mother, Mike used to talk with her about it. So did Wade. The two of them would go on and on about how their father didn't love them. They knew he cared about Greg, but they could see no signs of their father caring about them. Their mother tried to make them feel better, telling them that their dad loved the two of them in a special way. But they didn't believe her. Why didn't he call? Why didn't he write?

Finally Jewelene Wilson phoned her ex-husband and told him what the boys were saying. So Mr. Broome drove down from the Panhandle one weekend and came by the house—the boys' stepfather politely slipped out to a movie—and spent a couple hours with them. He told them he did love them. He tried to get them to talk with him. But Mike and Wade clammed up. They sat beside him on the couch and refused to say anything. They shut him out, just as they felt he'd done to them.

Now Mrs. Wilson has no idea what to do. The school keeps calling, reporting some new bit of trouble that Mike has created for himself. It seems like they call almost every day. They're always talking to her about Mike, asking her questions, pressing for details about what he's like at home. She knows they're trying to help. She knows they have Mike's best interests at heart. But sometimes she thinks she hears something underneath their voices. Some suggestion that maybe she's to blame for what's happening.

"I'm doing the best I can," she tells them.

She wishes she could go to school and secretly watch Mike in class. She wishes they had a classroom with a two-way mirror, so she could sit in the next room and observe without his knowing it. Maybe then she'd understand and know what to do. She wonders if Mike's taking drugs. She has asked him, and he denies it. She's taken him to the doctor and had him tested, but the test came out negative. She searches his room, but she can't find anything. So what's making Mike act like this? Is it just his father? Or is it her, too? She sits in that chair in the living room and wanders through her memory, hoping to figure out what she might have done wrong over the years. Did she make a mistake? Is it something that can be fixed?

She's so tired. She has been tired for almost as long as she can remember. Like her son, her face is taut with tension, lined with worry. She's only forty-two, but she looks much older.

"Sometimes," she says, "I feel like I'm one hundred and forty-two."

FOURTEEN

GIDDY-UP

"TINA."

No answer.

"Tina, speak to me."

The frizzy-haired girl behind the wheel does not dare take her eyes off the road. She is concentrating so hard, gripping the wheel of the burgundy Lancer, that she can barely say a word. The car keeps stopping and starting, cruising forward and rolling backward.

Another lurching day in driver's ed.

"Go ahead," the teacher tells her, coaching from the passenger seat. "That's pretty good."

They are a mile or so away from campus, practicing road maneuvers along a quiet neighborhood street lined with tidy houses and immaculate green lawns.

"Stay in your lane now . . . You're going toward that car."

She's having trouble backing up straight. She's also far too timid on her sudden stops. The teacher keeps cueing her, yelling every few feet for her to stop, but she can't seem to hit the brake with any force.

"Just be quick as a cat," he tells her. "You got to really jump on that baby. Okay, do a three-point turn."

She makes the mistake of pausing for a second in front of a driveway. Never do that, the teacher says. Never, ever, block a man's driveway . . .

Back at school, in a classroom on the second floor of the AA building, the health teacher who made her kids interview their parents is now passing out a worksheet on menstruation. Me-Me Panzarella, a straight-talking young woman with a heavy Bronx accent, stands in front of the room, waiting until all the worksheets are distributed. She tells the males in the room they better pay attention, too.

"Guys, you need to know this stuff so you can understand us. So you can deal with us," she says. "It's very important, especially for people who are sexually active and who do not want to get pregnant."

Some parents grow faint when they hear the things their kids learn in health nowadays. Not that it's all sex ed. Ms. Panzarella covers alcohol and drugs, diet and nutrition, mental health and first aid. At one point every semester, she hauls out the mannequins with the inflatable lungs and teaches CPR.

"My class is about life," she says.

Still, if Ms. Panzarella's going to get any angry calls from home, it's usually when her classes hit the human sexuality unit. So many parents still cling to the fantasy that their kids are little innocents who save themselves for marriage. But she doesn't have the luxury of such fantasies, especially when one national study after another confirms that many teenagers are sexually active by the end of high school. She doesn't particularly like it—just get her talking about why so many kids turn to sex out of a lack of love in their lives—but she also understands that no matter how much she or anyone else preaches, teens will still be fumbling with each other's clothes in the backseats of their cars.

"I hate to say this," she told one group of wide-eyed mothers and fathers back on Open House night, "but a lot of my students are already having sex before they ever get to my class."

Ms. Panzarella refuses to play make-believe. If she's not willing to face what their lives are like, how can she help them? How can she teach them to help themselves? So she does what she can. She tries to help them avoid getting hurt, getting pregnant, contracting the HIV virus, making choices that can haunt them for the rest of their lives or even kill them. She covers it all, with no holds barred.

She quizzes them on how to figure out the days of the month when it's stupid for them to have sex without a contraceptive and the days when it's insane. She shows them drawings of circumcised and uncircumcised penises, so they'll understand the difference. She describes for them, in graphic detail, what can happen to fetuses whose mothers smoke or drink or take other drugs. During one of her most revealing exercises, she tells them to get out a scrap of paper and anonymously write down any question they're dying to ask the opposite sex, but don't dare. Then she reads the questions aloud and lets the boys answer the girls' questions and the girls answer the ones from the boys. The guys usually ask why so many girls tease and play games; the girls ask why so many guys want to use them and then throw them away.

She turns now to one of the boys.

"What's ovulation?"

"Release of the egg."

"How long can sperm live in the uterus?"

"Three days."

Ms. Panzarella nods.

"Six to eight hours in the vagina," she says. "Up to three days in the uterus."

Over in the cafeteria, as lunch moves forward, a couple wrapped in a passionate embrace quickly disentangle themselves under the stare of an assistant principal.

"I didn't touch her," says the boy, visibly blushing.

Not far away, at another table, a gaggle of puny freshmen joke about all the older women who are dying to meet them and fall into their arms this weekend. As the others giggle, one of the boys dips the tip of one finger into the ketchup on his tray and tastes it. He does it again. And again.

IN AN OFFICE NEXT TO THE WEIGHT ROOM—A CRAMPED LITTLE closet of an office, with cement-block walls and an odor of stale sweat in the air—Coach Mahoney sits and stares at the game films for the hundredth time, trying to figure out what's happened to his football team.

They lost again last week, this time to the Northeast High Vikings. It wasn't even close; the other squad outscored them by twenty-one points. Worst of all, Mahoney had to apologize after a couple of Largo players, the two defensive backs with the notorious taste for blood, tried to nail the Vikings' quarterback with an unnecessary hit to a bad knee. At first, when the irate Northeast coach called to complain—it didn't help that the injured quarterback was his own son—Mahoney didn't want to believe any of his players could sink so low. But then he reviewed the film and saw it for himself.

Ouch. It's bad enough to be caught playing dirty. But to play dirty and still lose? Team morale is dropping like a rock. The early days of the season, when they were climbing the polls, seem so far away now. Mahoney hasn't given up, though. He still does everything he can to keep his players psyched. He screams, pounds on lockers, butts a few heads now and then. And every Friday, before the game, he still pumps them up with movies. He's been doing it forever. One year, when they were playing on Halloween night, one of the guys asked if they could watch *Evil Dead 2* beforehand. Okay, said the coach, always willing to try something new. A psycho horror flick, however, didn't cut it as a motivational tool; after watching the movie, the Packers were so out of kilter that they played like zombies, losing to a team they should have creamed. Now Mahoney plays it safe and sticks with NFL highlight tapes.

For all the frustrations, this year hasn't been without its own unique entertainment value. The players may drive Mahoney insane, but they never bore him. It's not just Jason Kylis and his disappearing towel. There's a senior named Frank Ruffner who seems to believe he's the reincarnation of Jim Morrison. One time Frank stood up in a movie theater and yelled, *"I am the Lizard King!"* Famous for his unbridled behavior, he's constantly breaking things, offending girls, getting kicked out of parties, pouring beer down his throat, consuming the contents of the nearest refrigerator. Once when he was at McDonald's with one of his teammates, he went scavenging at other tables for leftover food.

"You done with those fries?" he asked a stranger.

Frank is the team's official wild man. The other players don't know whether to laugh or run away. They can't get over it. What makes him act this way? What goes on inside his head?

"He means well, guys," the coach tells them.

The same cannot always be said of Jermaine Stephenson. Off the field, Jermaine is a charming young man. But when he puts on his uniform, he can be positively brutal. He's one of the two defensive backs who took the cheap shot against the Northeast quarterback and who have given Largo the outlaw rep. Furthermore, he is proud of it. When he plays, he says, he enjoys inflicting pain. To him, it's part of the game. He likes to knock the wind out of receivers and then stand there, taunting them as they scrape themselves off the grass.

"Yeah, motherfucker," he tells them. "I bet you won't want to come this way again."

Jermaine pushes the rules as far as he can, and then some. When he's out of the game, standing on the sidelines, he'll kick and try to trip any opponent who ventures within range. When he's on the far side of the field, near the other team's bench, he'll insult the coaches, telling them to put on some shoulder pads and get into the game so he can kick their asses, too. During one game, he wore a hand towel marked with the word "ruthless."

His coach and his teammates do what they can to keep Jermaine in line, especially when he goes too far and the refs are on the verge of slapping the Packers with another penalty. When that happens, John Boyd —an old friend who grew up with Jermaine—plays the diplomat and asks him to back off. Out on the field, John's the opposite of Jermaine. He's an old-fashioned, squeaky-clean player who crosses himself and offers thanks to God whenever he scores a touchdown. And when he tackles people— like most of the team, John plays both offense and defense—he reaches down and gives them a hand up.

Jermaine can't get over it.

"Damn, man. You're too nice," he tells him. "This is football. You have to be *mean*."

John can't help it. He's just no good at being mean. He has always been the type of kid who works hard and does his best to follow the rules, especially when it comes to football. He's wanted to be a running back since he was a little boy—his dream was to be the next Tony Dorsett— and now, after years of working in the weight room and sweating under the Florida sun, his efforts are finally paying off. The way he sees it, football is his ticket. He doesn't know if he's got the moves to play pro. But if he keeps breaking free of tacklers here at Largo, he might wind up with a scholarship to college. Either way, John's happy just to be playing. He loves to run with the ball. He loves to run, period. His friends some- times call him Giddy-Up. He got the nickname a couple years ago when he started wearing a big funny cowboy hat to school and trotting through the halls, acting like he was on horseback. Afterward, the name just stuck. His teammates see him streaking down the field, his chest heaving, his eyes wide open, and they can't help but think of him as Giddy-Up.

John's one of the leaders of the football team. It's not just the speed and the moves; it's his personality. Like Andrea, John has a glow. He's so calm and steady, so at ease with himself, that it's almost impossible not to look up to him. Maybe that's why he always offers the team prayer before the games. Other guys might seem stiff or uncomfortable conducting a group prayer, but John seems born to it. They do it just a few minutes before kickoff. John and the other players gather in one of the end zones and kneel quietly in the grass, and then he asks the Lord to watch over them and allow them to play up to their potential and to please make sure that no one gets hurt.

Coach Mahoney watches on, wondering if the whole thing's such a good idea. He doesn't have anything against praying. But he winces every time he hears John bring up the possibility of injuries. The coach doesn't want his boys worrying about pain and suffering just before they head out onto the field. Is that really the right frame of mind for cracking heads? Would General Patton, he asks himself, have talked about death and dismemberment moments before a major battle?

Of course, John's not always so serious. Most of the time he's just as crazy as the rest of the team. For instance, he and some of the others—including Jermaine and a handful of other friends who all grew up together in the same neighborhood—have a long-term commitment to barking. They call themselves the Raw Dogs, or just the Dogs for short, and it seems like they're continually munching on Kennel Rations, or sticking out their tongues and panting, or getting down on all fours and barking and howling and yapping away. Now John's got the rest of the team doing it, trying to become honorary Dogs. The funny thing is, each kid has a distinctive bark. John's is deep and slightly mournful, like something out of a bloodhound. There's another Dog named Carlos, a scrappy kid, smaller than most of the guys on the team, who yips like a Pekinese. And then there's old Frank Ruffner, who sounds like a pit bull.

One day at practice, they take the canine routine to a new level. It's a blistering afternoon, and after a lengthy workout, the boys are pouring with sweat. John is standing in line for the water spigot when suddenly he gets an idea. He looks over at a big puddle of runoff water from the spigot sitting on the track beside the field and decides there's no point in waiting in line.

"Come on, Dogs!" he yells, dropping onto his hands and knees before the puddle. "You want to be a Dog, do it!"

Others drop beside him. Together they lower their heads and begin to lap up the water, snorting and laughing all the while.

"Are you guys done?" says the coach, shaking his head in disbelief.

• • •

ANDREA TAYLOR IS GETTING TIRED OF BEING PRACTICAL. She is rapidly reaching the point where practicality is tearing her in two.

At school, Andrea walks beside John Boyd, dying to tell him how she feels. But she knows she can't. Normally, when it comes to something like this, she'd confide in Sabrina. But obviously that's out of the question, too. So who can she tell? Andrea has to confide in somebody, or she'll burst. At last she decides to share the secret with another friend of hers, this guy named Shawn from the Black Culture Club. A guy who can be trusted to keep his mouth shut. A guy who, once he's heard the facts, makes no bones about what he thinks Andrea should do.

"Go for what you want, 'Dre," Shawn tells her.

This would be good advice, if what Andrea wanted were possible. Because what she'd like is to have it both ways, to be with John without torching her friendship with Sabrina. Which, as far she can tell, would never happen. Which puts her back where she started.

She thinks and thinks. She tries her best not to think at all. Finally she can't stand it anymore. She has to do something. The time has come, she decides, to let John in on her little melodrama. Maybe he'll know what to do. He might even talk some sense into her.

Andrea drops the news one day after school. She and John are standing at the rail, down near the library, when suddenly she blurts it out.

"You're probably not expecting this," she tells him. "*I* wasn't expecting this. But I like you."

John stares at her, dumbfounded.

"You do?" he says.

She nods. "You couldn't tell?"

"No."

She says she knows it's wrong. But she can't hide it any longer.

As usual, John is a gentleman. He tells her it's okay and promises to keep quiet. Still, he seems to be in a state of mild shock.

A few days later, though, after the surprise has worn off, he gives Andrea a jolt of her own. He sends her a note, confessing that he feels the same way she does. He likes Sabrina just fine. She's a sweet girl. But the truth is, he says, that he wants to be with Andrea.

So much for talking sense. Now they're really in trouble.

FIFTEEN

INCANTATIONS

HE LEANS UNCOMFORTABLY ON the edge of his chair. He keeps gesturing with his hands. He is trying to find the right words.

"If you don't come out with an education, you can't prepare yourself," the man tells his daughter, staring into her eyes. "There's not too many choices for you. You can hustle hamburgers or work at a car wash."

His voice trails off. Something in her face, maybe a hint of a blush, tells him he has made her feel self-conscious.

"I'm just talking out loud," he says. "I'm not trying to embarrass you, honey."

The two of them are seated beside each other in a small and cluttered office in the administration building. Outside, it is a gray Thursday morning, with a hard rain that keeps falling in thick waves against the window. This is the office of Patricia Palmateer, an assistant principal who is seated across the desk from them, listening to the rain and silently watching as a father struggles to make some kind of contact with his little girl.

Mrs. Palmateer lets the man talk. She has already explained to his daughter April what will happen if she continues skipping. She has informed April that she is now officially over the nine-day limit for absences and that unless she appeals to the attendance committee she will automatically fail the entire semester. Mrs. Palmateer has even tried to inject April with a small dose of reality, suggesting—though she does not put it in these exact words—that if the child goes on this way, the day will come when she may not be able to afford all the little niceties to which she has so obviously become accustomed. For instance, those L.A. Gear sneakers she's wearing. The expensive ones with the black and hot pink laces.

As usual, Mrs. Palmateer has tried every approach. She has recited the entire litany, verse for verse. But then, April probably knew it all by heart before she and her father ever walked into the room. April has already dropped out once; this year, when she came back and enrolled in the GOALS program, she made honor roll for the first six weeks. But those days are over. Once again she is only making sporadic visits to her classes. She is becoming a tourist at the downward slide of her own life.

April is sniffling now, biting the inside of her lip. She keeps looking away from her father, who is still trying to talk, still fighting to get through to her. He wants so much for her, he says. He's not ashamed of what he has made of his life, he says—he's a technician who fixes machines for Xerox—but he wants her to have more choices than he did.

"If I knew when I was eighteen what I know now, I really would have tried to stay in school longer," he says. "Because I didn't know how tough it is out there. By the time you get out of school, out on the street, in the real world, either you make a living or nobody cares."

He gazes toward the window, where the rain is still falling against the glass. For a moment he looks as though he has gone somewhere far away. He begins to talk about when he was a young man, when he graduated from technical school and went into the Navy and was stationed on a ship at sea. Every evening, he'd go up on deck, up to the rear of the ship, and watch the dark waves veering away in their wake. That was when he began to understand.

"I'd stand there, looking at the water passing by, thinking "There's *got* to be a better way," he says, pausing. "The ship was getting somewhere, but I wasn't."

A quiet falls over the room. The incessant ringing of all the phones outside seems to die away. Mrs. Palmateer looks over at April's father with a kind of awe. If only she could hire this man and have him tell his story to all the students who sit in the chair where April is sitting now.

Because there are so many of them. There are several hovering outside Mrs. Palmateer's door right now, waiting their turn. They're always hovering out there, holding the referrals that summarize exactly what they have done to be sent to this office. In addition to other duties, Mrs. Palmateer is the assistant principal who oversees Largo's GOALS program. On this morning, almost every student she sees is from GOALS. One after another, they drop into the chair and watch her read the referrals.

Just before April, it was Melissa, who yawned and played with her hair while Mrs. Palmateer recited the litany of what happens to those who do not go to class. Then, immediately after April and her father leave, she meets with John, a boy who fidgets in his chair as she informs him that he has been withdrawn from the rolls as a student.

John nods. "My mom told me. Why?"

"What do you think?"

"I don't know."

"You've been missing for three weeks."

Just after John comes Laura, who was sighted with some other kids skipping up at the Burger King near the school. After Laura comes Stephanie, who slipped out of class to talk to a friend and who rolls her eyes when Mrs. Palmateer tells her that's not such a good idea. A few minutes later, Mrs. Palmateer finds herself in the middle of a sobering exchange with a girl named Tabatha Turner, who collapses in the chair like a rag doll.

"You have come so far," says Mrs. Palmateer. "Do you want to go back to where you were?"

Tabatha stares at the floor and considers the question for a moment. In one ear, she is wearing an earring shaped like a skull and dagger; in the other, a tiny dangling pair of handcuffs. Hanging over her shirt is a necklace that bears the words *Oh Shit.*

"No," she says finally, sighing.

"Where do you want to be?"

"I want to stay in school."

"What do you want to have in your little hand three and a half years from now?"

"A diploma."

"That's right. And how do you get that diploma?"

"Going to school."

"How often?"

"All the time."

Last year, Tabatha was a nightmare. She rarely spent a whole day in class. Sometimes she'd head with her friends for a big drainage pipe behind the school. They'd sit inside on a piece of plywood and smoke cigarettes; Mrs. Palmateer isn't sure, but she thinks some of the kids might have had sex out there in the pipe. Later on, Tabatha turned around—she was one of the bright successes down in the pod—but now she is drifting again. Turns out she was one of the kids sighted with Laura up at the Burger King. A police officer saw them, and they ran.

"Running from a police officer is very, very dangerous," Mrs. Palmateer tells her. "It can get you hurt. It can get you taken off to JDC." She means the Juvenile Detention Center. "I don't want you there. Do you want to be there?"

Tabatha shakes her head.

"You deserve good things," says Mrs. Palmateer. "And they'll happen to you. Hang in there. Pass all your classes. Get that diploma and then go on and become whatever you want to be. Because you can do anything you want."

Still slumped in the chair, Tabatha has begun to cry. She's trying not to, but it's no good. The tears run down her cheeks, glistening faintly beside the dangling shadows of the handcuffs and the skull and dagger.

THE REVELATION VISITS THE HEATHERS LATE IN THE SECOND half.

They are up in the stands, in the section filled with shivering seniors. They have been busy on this chilly night. Already they have butted heads and spoken in tongues and played Pick a Noise. They have shamed a member of the boys' swim team, sitting nearby, into pulling up the cuffs of his pants and giving them a peek at his freshly shaved legs, the sight of which prompts them to hoot and stomp their feet. They have twisted their bodies into a bizarre series of contortions that spell out the word "Largo." In homage to countless generations of teenagers before them, they have even cupped their hands over their mouths so they could pretend to be coughing as they yelled "Bullshit" at an assistant principal patrolling the main aisle below.

They have just finished doing all of these things, and many more, when suddenly Karin Upmeyer fires the retros and makes a solemn pronouncement.

"You want to think of something really scary?" she says to the others. *"This is the last home football game . . ."*

YY, sitting a few inches away, fending off the cold with the sleeves of her sweater pulled over her hands, picks up the beat and completes the sentence with her. The two of them speak the last few words in tandem, ever so slowly.

". . . of our whole entire lives."

The first semester isn't even over yet, and already YY and Karin and Amy Boyle and Meridith Tucker are waxing nostalgic, immortalizing every moment of their final year at Largo High. Before you know it, they'll be issuing commemorative mugs for their last pop quiz, their last hoagie smuggled from off campus, their last party raided by the police. Right now, though, they are so overwhelmed by Karin's terrible observation that they fall into a state of shocked silence. They say nothing for a good long time, maybe even two or three full seconds, before they launch back into the torrent of wisecracks, running gags, gossip bulletins, chimp imitations—featured prominently in Pick a Noise—along with assorted beloved quotes, not just from *Heathers,* but from an astonishing number of other movies, songs, cartoons, and late-night TV ads.

"Shhhhhhhhh," they tell each other in a stage whisper, repeating the timeless words of Elmer Fudd. "Weah hunting wabbits."

"Is that *Freedom Rock?*" they say, reliving their favorite campy moment from their favorite campy K-Tel-type commercial. "Well, turn it up, dude!"

It's Friday, November 10, one day after Tabatha broke down in Mrs. Palmateer's office. Tonight, as the Largo Packers face the Patriots of Pinellas Park High, the girls are gathered with a gang of their fellow AB-12 rats and miscellaneous senior cohorts. They don't know how lucky they are. They remain blissfully unaware, without the faintest idea how wonderful it is that they can sit here singing and laughing under the stars, huddling together against the cold. Intellectually they recognize all the advantages that allow them to be so happy. They know, for instance, that not all kids have so many friends or live in nice big homes or enjoy the shelter of families as loving as theirs. But on an emotional level, they don't fully understand how good they have it and how bad it can be for others. They cannot imagine the depth of the sorrows that run through the lives of some of their fellow students.

How could they imagine it? YY and Karin and the others are still just teenagers who have their hands full trying to make sense of their own lives. They're just kids, doing their best not to look too frightened as they stumble forward into the future. They work extremely hard, both in school and out. Why shouldn't they have fun sometimes? Plus, it's not like the girls have had their GPAs handed to them on a proverbial platter. Other kids probably like to think so. That's usually the rap against those who do well, isn't it?

But YY and company have all paid the price for their success. For years, they have been pushing themselves past the point of exhaustion; sometimes they get so overwhelmed, it seems as though they're going to collapse under the load. Meridith will just start sobbing; Amy puts on her jogging shoes and tears off into the night, running away from it all. The Wild and Wonderful YY keeps pulling at her eyelashes and laughing that nervous laugh and biting her nails. Not long ago she wrote a poem defending her right to chew on her fingers. Sort of an ode to the wages of stress.

> *The earth will still turn, on its axis still bent,*
> *And I'll still bite my nails, and I'll be content.*
> *Don't become nit-picky, a harpie, a fighter,*
> *Don't pick on a habitual nail-biter.*
> *So all of you hecklers please decease,*
> *I want to bite my nails in peace.*

It's not exactly Emily Dickinson, but it will do. Especially now that the girls are seniors and are working up a monster dread over the pressures they'll encounter next year at college. What if they can't cut it? What if they're not good enough? Karin's probably the most worried. She doesn't know what college she'll be attending—unlike the other three, she's only an average student and has yet to be accepted anywhere—or what she's going to study if and when she gets there.

"She's gonna major in Karin," says YY, trying to get her to lighten up.

Karin giggles. "I'll major in YY. Oh my God, that's really scary."

They try to act so tough. They laugh, they shoot off their one-liners, they pretend that they have never heard of doubt or insecurity. But they all have moments when they want to sit alone in their rooms and stare at the walls. Amy, the quintessential perfect kid, torments herself by wondering if she can measure up to the towering precedent of her older sister, who was perhaps an even better student than she is. Karin, the loudest and funniest and most outrageous of them all, the one with the big hair and the bigger smile and the voice that doubles as a sonic boom, has worried since she was a little girl that her mother—a graceful, beautiful woman who was once a contestant in the Miss America Pageant—thinks she's overweight and unattractive. The thing is, Karin's not fat. She has been known to put on a few extra pounds now and then; even so, she is a pretty young woman. Still, she feels as though she'll never be quite pretty enough.

As for YY and Meridith, they're both still nursing wounds from the divorces of their parents; when the subject comes up, Meridith sometimes gets this distant look, as though she has drawn an invisible curtain across her face. YY, meanwhile, has her career crisis to contend with. She knows that Bob and Helen the Hun are pushing her to take the math route only because they're trying to look out for her, because they want her to be able to take care of herself. So she avoids forcing the issue and tries not to dwell on it too much.

It's almost always there in her voice, though. It's in all the girls' voices. Beneath the invincible exteriors, beneath even the frustrations and the stress that fuel the wisecracks, the Fearsome Foursome are scared just like the rest of us. Scared of failing, scared of letting their parents down, scared of college and jobs and marriage and mortgage payments and all the blank pages of their lives waiting to be written. You can hear it tonight, at the Pinellas Park game, as they joke and patter and fire away with their assorted beloved quotes, repeating them together in one voice like so many incantations recited against the dark, against uncertainty, against loneliness. They're doing everything they can to hold on. They're trying so hard to have a deliriously good time . . .

It's working, too. When they're together like this, they truly are invulnerable. Nothing from the past or the future can even scratch them. Of course, it helps that so many of their friends are at their sides, laughing and snorting and making chimp noises right along with them. Flounder is here. So's Peace Dog. So's Jason Davenport, one of their best male-type buddies. Jason is so tight with YY and the others that when they go into their Heathers mode, he has been known to play the crucial role of J.D. Naturally it has not escaped the girls' attention that Jason happens to have the same initials as his character. How perfect. How very, as the girls in the movie like to say. At this particular moment, though, Jason is not playing J.D. He is taking advantage of yet another opportunity to make fun of the cheerleaders. He keeps talking about how lazy they are. He makes it sound as though they're slugs in short skirts.

"Wait," he says, feigning breathless anticipation. "They're going to do something."

Down on the track, in front of the stands, the girls in uniform are trying to pump up the crowd with a rousing chorus of "Let's go, Largo!"

"Original cheer," says YY.

"They can't say more than two words at a time," says Jason.

As usual, YY and company are doing the old outside-but-inside routine. Here they sit, mocking the concept of cheerleading—and a strange concept it is, when viewed from a distance—ridiculing any administrator who wanders within range, snickering when some poor receiver dives for a pass and comes up with nothing but a mouthful of turf. Still, YY and Karin and the others have all shown up tonight, as they do at almost every football game. They've paid their money, and they've stuck it out to the finish, even though their cheeks are reddening in the cold. For the record, half the cheerleaders are their pals.

When a Largo runner breaks loose from the line of scrimmage and barrels into the end zone, the girls jump up and let out wild, ear-splitting screams. When the play gets called back on a penalty—still a problem for the Packers—they flip into a sarcastic spiel about how their school always gets robbed of its TDs.

"Let me get this straight," say YY and Karin, speaking in tandem again. "Their touchdowns count, but ours don't. Okay, rules are rules. Every time we score, it doesn't count. Okay, got it."

And when the final seconds tick away and Largo has lost 24–14, YY and the gang moan about how unfair it was, then quietly join the crowd shuffling out of the stadium. They don't even smile when the school band serenades their departure with the customary postgame rendition of the *Flintstones* theme. It's the last time the girls will hear this song on this field. Their last chance in their entire high school lives to dance under the lights with Fred and Barney, and all they do is get in their cars and drive away.

JAIMEE SHEEHY IS GONE.

It happens on a Saturday. On the same day when her mother is set to take her to Charter. Laura Sheehy intends to do it that evening, after she gets off the day shift at her own hospital. Jaimee is still fighting it, still insisting that she will not go. So that day her mother calls the apartment repeatedly from work, making sure her daughter's still there. Since Jaimee knows what time her mother normally gets off work, Laura leaves a little early, calling the apartment one more time to make sure Jaimee's around.

When Laura gets home, though, Jaimee is nowhere to be found. She must have missed her by only a few minutes.

Hours go by, and still no sign of her. It's getting late. It's way past dark. Laura Sheehy starts to panic. She gets on the phone. She calls emergency rooms, calls Jaimee's friends, calls the police, gives them one of Jaimee's Little League photos so they'll know what she looks like. One of Jaimee's friends asks around for her and finds somebody who talked to Jaimee this very evening, just a little while ago. She was up near the Pizza Hut on East Bay Drive. She was with the girlfriend who danced on Halloween with her and the skeletons. The two of them had packed some clothes and were carrying a little money. Supposedly they were talking about going to the Clearwater bus station and heading for Cocoa Beach, on the other side of the state.

Laura Sheehy checks at the bus station. No one has seen the girls. All night, she tries to find them. No luck. They have vanished.

SIXTEEN

SPROUTS

IN MRS. O'DONNELL'S CLASS, they're climbing back on the deathmobile. It's time again for show-and-tell, and it seems that's all the kids want to talk about. Their dreams of death. Their premonitions of death. What they think awaits them after death. How Armageddon is just around the corner.

"I think the end of the world is coming," says one boy.

"I do, too," says someone else.

"Too many things are happening."

Someone brings up the subject of the spirit world, which leads to the predictable discussion of Ouija boards.

"I burned mine," says a boy named Eric, a tall blond-haired kid with deep-set eyes that look as though they could cut through metal. Some of his friends call him the Dragon.

Mrs. O'Donnell, who knows a hint when she hears one, presses for more details. Why exactly did Eric burn his Ouija board?

"I didn't like what it told me."

"What did it tell you?"

For a moment, he doesn't answer. He just gazes at the table.

"It told me when I was going to die."

The other GOALS kids stare at Eric with a quiet intensity that borders on admiration. Death is always in the Top 40 here in the pod. It surfaces constantly in the kids' conversations, floating through so many of their favorite songs, swirling silently in the overwhelming grimness of their wardrobes. Black is the color du jour every jour. They wear black shoes, black shirts, black jeans, black dresses, black jackets, black hats, even black motorcycle helmets. If it comes in black, they want it.

No one carried this infatuation further than the Smurf Killer. He's not in GOALS anymore—he only stayed a year before it was decided he should leave the program—but his former teachers still talk about him with a kind of morbid fascination.

"He was smart," one of them says. "Very creative."

By now the stories about this boy have taken on an almost mythic air. It wasn't just the Smurf allegedly dangling from the noose in his locker. The teachers in the pod aren't prigs; they have enough of a sense of humor to appreciate the genius in such a gesture. And if he'd left it at that, if all he'd done was string up an innocuous blue-skinned doll, they probably would have just laughed. But the child showed signs of deep psychological disturbance. As best as they could tell, he was actively worshipping the devil. The word among the teachers is that a possum skull adorned with a candle was also found in his locker. In class, he was obsessed with death and despair, constantly writing on those themes in English. At one point, he wrote mock obituaries for himself and the other members of his family, inventing horribly violent ways for all of them to exit this world.

The teachers tried to talk to his mother, describing his behavior to her, but she didn't seem overly concerned.

"His mom didn't think that was abnormal," remembers one teacher.

Today the Smurf Killer's legacy lives on. Although there's no doubt that he was an extreme case, the same horrific themes that consumed him hold considerable power for many of the kids in the pod. Many teenagers —indeed, many adults—are interested in death, but not to the pervasive degree found with so many GOALS kids. It's not just the gruesome songs and the black clothes, either. They wear necklaces and rings and earrings adorned with skulls and skeletons. They draw ghouls and monsters on their folders. They carve pentagrams and other satanic symbols on the tops and bottoms and even the legs of the wooden tables in their classes.

When they're bored, they have been known to sketch portraits of the Grim Reaper.

Maybe it has something to do with their feelings of powerlessness. Or maybe they're just young and especially eager to shock their teachers and parents. But they are especially fascinated when they hear something macabre that hits close to home, like Eric the Dragon's story about the Ouija board. Or like the Prom Queen ghost.

Today, as on so many days, the kids in Mrs. O'Donnell's classes are drawn to the subject of Largo's most famous spirit. Many schools have their own version of the Prom Queen ghost. This one is supposed to be the ghost of a Largo student who died in an accident seven years ago. She wasn't the Prom Queen. But she was on her way home with some friends late one May night when the car crashed into some trees on a dark section of Alternate Keene Road, killing her and the driver. The story goes that if anyone drives along that stretch of road with their lights turned off, they'll see this girl's ghost in the rearview mirror, floating behind the car. The legend is well known throughout the school. Lots of kids have tried it, including YY and her friends. Some swear they've seen the apparition.

Now, in Mrs. O'Donnell's show-and-tell session, a girl suddenly volunteers that a friend of hers knows a way to lay the spirit of the Prom Queen ghost to rest. There is a spell, she says.

This girl is serious. Normally she's quiet in class, but today, amid all this talk of death and spirits, she wants to tell stories about her excursions into black magic. She and a friend, she says, once used a special book called the *Necromonicon* to compel a Ouija board into communicating with them. It spelled out the word "evil," she says. The room went cold; a wind rushed through the house, even though all the windows were closed; a Bible was set on fire.

She swears it.

"If you're into black magic," she volunteers to the rest of the class, "there is a way for you to meet the devil."

"Would you *like* to meet the devil?" asks Mrs. O'Donnell.

"No."

For all its popularity, though, death is only one of many subjects that comes up during show-and-tell. The kids talk about everything. About their dreams that turn out to be prophecies of the future, their jobs that never work out, the endless arguments with their parents. One boy tells Mrs. O'Donnell's fourth-period class about the time he nearly died while driving drunk. He has the scars to prove it. He parts the hair on his head and shows them off.

By no means is show-and-tell always so serious. When the kids get rolling, they crack jokes and reveal strange but true facts about their families and regale each other with elaborate tales about their boyfriends and girlfriends, most of which end with someone getting dumped. One morning a girl stands up and gives a moving speech about the importance of Earth Day. Another kid gives a hilarious account of his mother's out-of-body experience. Then there's the clean-cut boy on the football team who gets other kids to make thumping bass sounds with their mouths as he performs a rap number—the lyrics of which, he informs the class, he wrote himself.

> *I'm a bebop maker,*
> *a girlfriend taker,*
> *a rhyme creator.*
> *When the beat come out,*
> *it sounds so sweet.*
> *When the beat kick out,*
> *it will be neat.*

To keep the sessions going, Mrs. O'Donnell asks a myriad of questions. What do they do on Saturday nights? What do they want to make of their lives when they get out of school and are trying to scrape by on their own? Mrs. O'Donnell listens intently to their answers, laughs at their jokes, plays along, plays dumb, does anything she can to keep them talking. If a kid brings in a motorcycle helmet, Mrs. O'Donnell will try it on and let the class laugh at her. If someone brings in a skateboard, she'll kick off her shoes, step onto the board, and ask how to position her feet.

"Show me," she says to a kid one day who's just finished doing kick-flips for the class. "I'd like to try it."

After rolling tentatively between the desks, she steps off the board and shakes her head. She says it's too hard. She says she can't believe how easy this kid makes it look.

Suddenly the class is urging her on, telling her to give it another shot. Suddenly they are the teachers and she is the student.

"You just can't do it because you think you can't do it," one of them tells her, echoing the words she uses so often with them. "Just get on it real confident. Jump on that thing and take off."

Back on the board she goes. Her knees are wobbling. Her arms are waving. She's laughing.

"You just want me to kill myself," she says, "so you won't have class."

• • •

ONE DAY, WADE BROOME ENTERTAINS MRS. O'DONNELL'S sixth-period class with an account of his adventures from the previous Saturday night, when he and some friends went cruising from one fast-food joint to the next, stealing ashtrays. They're starting a collection, he says. A collection of ashtrays, all taken from McDonald's and Burger King and so forth.

A girl across the room informs Wade that this is not a good idea, since he and his friends could get arrested and find themselves in JDC.

Wade laughs. "Some of my best friends are in JDC," he says.

Mike Broome, who happens to be in this class, too, listens silently to his brother. This is the way it usually works with the Broome boys. Wade keeps playing the comic, telling his jokes and stories. Mike keeps his mouth shut, almost never saying a word. One November morning, when show-and-tell is scheduled, he raises Mrs. O'Donnell's hopes by bringing his guitar from home. But once the class starts, he changes his mind and sits in his usual slouch, emanating a hostility so intense that you can almost feel it rolling across the room in waves of white heat.

Wade tries to get him to lighten up.

"Mike," he says, nodding toward Mrs. O'Donnell, "she wants you to show-and-tell your guitar."

Mike stares at the desk in front of him, frowning.

"I ain't showing-and-tellin' nothin'."

That would seem to be the end of it. But a little while later, after some of the others have made their presentations, Mike calms down, pulls the guitar out of its case, and sits there, quietly strumming for the rest of the class. All at once, he's a different kid, open and approachable. When he's like this, Mrs. O'Donnell and his other teachers think there's still a chance to reach him. But there's no telling when the other Mike, the Mike who specializes in trashing his future, will return.

On another day, after he comes back from one of his many suspensions, Mrs. O'Donnell tries to give him a test. He knows the material; he was here for the review. But he refuses to take it. Trying to make it easy, Mrs. O'Donnell offers to let him use her review notes, which will include the answers. Still he refuses.

"Do you want to take the test later?"

"No."

He sits with the test in front of him, ignoring it, glaring at her. At the end of the period, he tells her he's ready to turn it in. She picks it up and finds the test blank except for his first name.

Mrs. O'Donnell doesn't know it, but Mike has encountered a setback. Earlier in the semester, he was talking about how he wanted to go into the Air Force like his oldest brother, Greg. But the other day, while Mike was home during a suspension, he talked to Greg on the phone and found that he might not be able to make it into the service anyway, even if he straightens up and graduates from high school. It's Mike's asthma. The Air Force, Greg told him, might not accept him because of it.

Mike says he doesn't care. But as usual, it's glaringly obvious that he does.

What the teachers can't seem to get across to him—what he seems unwilling to accept—is that he cannot continue this way without paying the consequences. They hate resorting to that kind of bombast. *Pay the consequences, Mike.* They don't like falling back on all those turgid old phrases that used to make them gag when they were kids and had to suffer through lectures. But they can't help it. They don't know how else to put it.

"What can you do with yourself if you drop out?" Ms. DiLello asks him.

"I don't know."

Mike is hardly the only one in the pod hiding from reality. Not long ago, Miss Riel found herself trying to talk some sense into a girl who had decided to drop out and move in with her boyfriend.

"He's going to support me," said this girl, whose name is Diane. "He's going to take care of everything I need."

"What about five years from now, when you and this guy aren't together anymore?" said Miss Riel. "What are you going to do then?"

"I don't care. I'll marry somebody."

The scrawny boy in Mrs. McGraw's seventh-period class, the one who screams without warning, is slipping further and further away. He's running around his classrooms, burning cigarettes into his arm, telling wild stories about people holding knives to his throat.

The angelic-looking girl in Mrs. O'Donnell's sixth period, the one who believes she is a witch, had a breakdown recently and went away for a few days. Now she's back in class, staring at people.

"I forgot who I was," she says, giggling.

Eric the Dragon sits in class and stares into space. He's a friendly kid, with a quiet charm, but when he talks about his life, it's clear he feels a profound sense of isolation. One of his favorite pastimes, he says, is to climb this one tree by the beach and sit there for hours, watching people go in and out of a nearby bar, wondering if their lives are better than his.

"I build a wall to hide everything," he says softly one morning at the back of a classroom. "Eventually it will break."

Many GOALS students feel just as removed as Eric does. They don't have the faintest idea how to do the outside-but-inside routine. These kids, or at least a large number of them, exist only on the outside. Like YY and the rest of her gang, they see the pettiness of the rules—just ask them about the logic of bathroom passes, if you dare—and the farcical nature of certain school policies. They sense the same smothering qualities of the system. But they have trouble seeing beyond these limitations. They don't understand that any system they enter, any school, any business where they'll ever work, has its petty rules and smothering qualities. It's hard for them to accept that high school offers something worth their time. YY and her friends have the long-range vision. They laugh and make fun, but they stay, because they know that eventually staying will be rewarded. The kids in the pod tend to act on the moment; they get mad and walk away. To them, school is just stupid and unfair. It's not a place that deserves their patience or endurance. It deserves only their contempt or, at best, their indifference.

"They can't hang with the system," says one girl, trying to explain. "They give up. They quit."

Many of them quit because others have quit before them. They're caught in all sorts of self-destructive patterns established by their friends, their older brothers or sisters, their parents, the entire society. Not just patterns of dropping out. Patterns of anger. Patterns of addiction, abuse, rejection. YY and her pals may have to cope with their own painful problems and frustrations. But they're flexible enough to compartmentalize. Even if they're upset about something, they can put it aside for an hour or two while they study for tomorrow's exam. GOALS kids have a hard time slicing up their emotions like that. Some of them, struggling with the wrenching emptiness in their lives, are left with almost nothing extra to help them cope with smaller problems. They are so volatile, almost anything sets them off. If a teacher looks at them funny or if another student says something that hurts their feelings, they may walk away and not return to class for a week. They hunger for stability, for quiet, for routine.

• • •

THE TINIEST CHANGE CAN UNHINGE THEM. MRS. MCGRAW, for instance, has found that she has to be careful about when she rearranges the desks in her room, or else she'll rattle her classes. One weekend she goes to the beauty salon and gets her hair done. When she returns the next Monday, the kids are shaken up. They want to know exactly what she's done.

"Did you color your hair?"

"No."

"Yes, you did."

"No, I didn't."

Mrs. McGraw, a stout woman with a slight twang to her voice that hints of her upbringing in Tennessee, is no novice when it comes to dealing with kids. She has taught for fourteen years; she has also raised three domestic terrorists of her own, all boys. "There aren't any more of these at home, are there?" someone at one of her sons' schools once asked her. Now all three are grown, and one is even making noises about becoming a teacher. So she knows firsthand that even the most difficult kids often turn out fine in the end. Still, what Mrs. McGraw is seeing at Largo these days has unnerved her. Every day she has five classes, with about ninety kids total. In her grade book, where she keeps track of them all, she puts a little star by the name of every kid who's dealing with serious difficulties, either at home or at school or both. Well before the end of the first semester, the number of stars has burst into a galaxy.

"It just tears me up," she says.

Mrs. McGraw and the other GOALS teachers do their best to make their classrooms a place where the students can feel safe and secure. None of it flies without the parents, though. If Mom and Dad aren't willing to work with their kids and with the teachers, then the odds of turning any of these students around are next to hopeless. But if the parents are on board, then there's at least a chance. That's why they're all asked to sign the admission agreement. If they want their kid in GOALS, the parents—as well as the student in question and at least one teacher—must sign a piece of paper promising to go the extra mile.

Some of the parents are ready to go a hundred extra miles. Some, even though they've signed, will barely move an inch. Others are simply oblivious. Earlier this semester, the mother of one GOALS student came to Open House so she could meet her son's teachers. She was sincere, she was concerned, she had taken the time to show up. But as she left the meeting with Mrs. McGraw, the mother turned and said something incredible.

"Good luck with your sprouts!" she said.

Mrs. McGraw smiled and nodded and was already talking to someone else. She probably didn't even register exactly what the mother had said. But that last word hung in the air. Sprouts? *Sprouts?* What kind of problems did this woman think the teachers in the pod were dealing with? Did she think she'd stumbled onto the set of *Leave It to Beaver?*

If Mrs. McGraw had the time, she might have found a way to straighten her out. Maybe she could have told her about the boy who grabs his crotch and shakes himself at her. Or maybe she could have told about the two girls who were chatting it up in class the other day, talking about having sex with their boyfriends in a park. They were going on about how sex outdoors is so messy and how dirt and sand are always getting stuck in the most sensitive of places. Mrs. McGraw told them to stop it, that it wasn't polite to discuss such things. The girls just rolled their eyes and told her to get real.

"That's life," they told her.

Or maybe, if she'd had just a moment more, Mrs. McGraw could have cornered the mother and insisted that she come to the school this coming week, when GOALS will be sponsoring another parent workshop. This is one of the new things they're trying this year. One evening every week or so, a different speaker visits the pod and tries to enlighten parents on what's happening in the lives of their children. The first session was on family communication. The one next week will be on teens and drugs; Nancy Hamilton, the director of juvenile services for Operation PAR, a local drug treatment and rehabilitation program, will be the guest.

A major push is under way to round up a good crowd. Calls are being made to parents; fliers are being sent home with the kids. The teachers are very excited.

NANCY HAMILTON DOES NOT DISAPPOINT. FOR MORE THAN an hour one Tuesday evening, she stands in front of a GOALS classroom and rivets the members of the audience. She does not speak to them only of drugs; instead she paints a portrait of how drugs are a symptom of a larger ailment. She tells them that the average age of onset of drug use among the adolescents who come to Operation PAR is around ten or eleven, but that it's not unusual to see them starting as early as seven or eight, often with cigarettes.

"We've had kids," she says, "whose moms have been rolling joints for them since they were five."

She talks about parents who let their kids drink at home, naively hoping it will keep them from drinking somewhere else. She tells of kids who are introduced to the concept of getting high by their grandparents. She acknowledges that crack is a serious problem, but points out that alcohol is still the drug most commonly abused by high school students.

"I can't believe how alcohol-centered these kids' lives are," she says.

She tries, without getting melodramatic, to describe how difficult it is to be a teenager these days. She talks about how the drugs that are available are ten times stronger than they used to be; how incest is on the rise; how so many teenage girls are having babies; how most kids not only are having sex but having it with multiple partners—this is a shift, she says, from the serial monogamy they practiced not so long ago—and about how an increasing number of the young are living on the streets and leasing their bodies to some stranger, just so they can eat or have a place to sleep. "Survival sex," she calls it.

At the heart of her talk, however, is a simple plea for parents to listen to their children.

"Most kids," she says, "just want to talk to you."

There's just one problem with Ms. Hamilton's presentation. Almost no one's on hand to hear it. There are plenty of teachers here—six of them, which is about half of Largo's GOALS faculty—even though they've been at school since 7:00 A.M. But for all the calls and fliers sent home, the audience is filled with a grand total of two parents.

A WEEK AND A HALF LATER, THE NEXT WORKSHOP ROLLS around. This one's on satanism and cults; again there are six faculty members in the room and only two parents.

ONE WEEK AFTER THAT, AT A SESSION ON FAMILY DYNAMICS, the teachers find themselves sitting with one mother.

It makes no sense. There are a couple hundred kids in this program, and most of them presumably are living with at least one parent. Yet tonight they are down to a single solitary mother.

At least this woman's here, though. At least she's trying. She listens closely, taking in every word, hoping to hear some clue as to how to reach her son, a boy so intelligent that he used to be in the gifted program in elementary school. Now he's in GOALS, struggling just to make it through high school. His mother doesn't understand it. The boy, she says, doesn't want her to touch him. She tries to hug him, but he keeps pulling away . . .

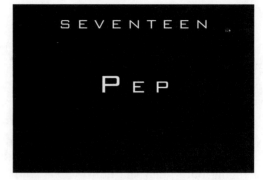

SEVENTEEN

PEP

ANDREA TAYLOR AND JOHN BOYD
are trapped in the shadows.

They are more than friends, but not
quite a couple. They talk on the phone,
they exchange notes and longing glances,
they spend time with each other constantly. But that's it. No hand-holding.
No kisses by the car. Despite the lingering heat between them, the two have
agreed they have to keep their distance.
For Sabrina's sake, they have decided
that it's impossible for them to become
boyfriend and girlfriend.

At least that's what Andrea has decided. John isn't so sure. He tells her
there must be a way. Maybe, he says, they
could work it so Sabrina wouldn't want
him anymore. Maybe they could make up
some story about how he's been cheating
on her with another girl and then have
Andrea leak it to her during one of their
heart-to-hearts.

"Call her up, 'Dre. Call her and tell
her I'm scamming with somebody else,"
says John. "Tell her that, so she'll just
leave me alone. So we can be together."

Andrea won't hear of it.

"We can't do that," she says. "It just
wouldn't be right."

Still, what they're doing isn't completely aboveboard, either. No matter how hard they try to avoid it, the situation breeds all sorts of tiny betrayals. Sometimes Sabrina will call Andrea's house after school and talk happily away, unaware that at that moment John is at the house, too, sitting a few feet from her best friend. Or she'll call John, not realizing that Andrea's visiting him.

One day Sabrina nearly stumbles on the truth. She's over at Andrea's, hanging out, when she notices that Andrea has recently put a photo of John in a place of honor on her bedroom wall. It's a fairly incriminating piece of evidence—if she'd thought about it, Andrea would have probably hidden it—and for a moment, it appears as though Sabrina might catch on. But Sabrina obviously doesn't suspect a thing, because there are other photos on the wall, too. In fact, when she sees John's face among the others, she breaks into a smile.

"That's my baby," she says.

Andrea feels her heart skip a beat.

JAIMEE SHEEHY HAS OFFICIALLY BEEN WITHDRAWN FROM THE rolls of students. She's okay, though. The Largo police found her and the other girl the day after they disappeared. Jaimee said they'd spent the night at a friend's house, but they were so dirty it appeared they may have slept out somewhere, maybe in a park. When they were caught, they were in front of St. Patrick's Catholic Church, hanging out with some friends.

Laura Sheehy picked up her daughter at the police station that day and took her straight to Charter Hospital in Tampa. Even then, Jaimee couldn't bring herself to face what was happening. She told her mother that she wanted her friend, the one she'd run away with, to go with her. But Ms. Sheehy told her no. Jaimee was going to a hospital, not a slumber party.

"This isn't supposed to be fun," her mother told her.

So now Jaimee is off at Charter, working with the counselors and the doctors and living in a unit with other out-of-control kids. She will stay for an undetermined number of weeks. However long it takes before her mother can trust her again.

Down in the pod, where Jaimee was once supposedly a student, the parent workshops have been canceled due to a lack of parents. One of the teachers, however, was just invited by a student to attend a satanic ceremony. Another student, asked to join in a class discussion, recently offered her nails as a current event. And in her room near the end of the hall, Mrs. McGraw has been trying to get tough with her freshman English students. But they keep making her laugh.

"You know you love us," they tell her.

"That's beside the point," she says, fighting back a smile.

A few doors down, in one of Mrs. O'Donnell's classes, one of the boys has handed in a form listing his goals for the year. His number one goal: *drive Mrs. Odonnel in sain.*

ON THE DAY OF THE BIGGEST FOOTBALL GAME OF THE YEAR, something happens. Two things, actually, which when taken together come close to a definitive explanation of the place high school has become.

It's Friday, November 17, the day the Largo Packers will wrap up the regular season—they didn't make the play-offs but will appear in a post-season bowl game—by playing their archrivals, the Tornadoes of Clearwater High. In honor of the game, this has been declared Farmer Day, which is an affectionate nod to the old days, some forty or fifty years ago, when Clearwater and Largo were about the only two public high schools in this corner of the county. Back then, Clearwater was known as the city school, and Largo was supposedly filled with nothing but farmers. There is apparently some truth to this. Mrs. Badders, one of Largo's math teachers, still talks about when she was a student here—a surprising number of Largo faculty members graduated from this school, which helps account for their deep loyalty to the place—and how one day she actually rode her horse down one of the halls.

Anyway, in honor of that history, many of the teachers and even a few of the students are walking around in overalls and straw hats, dangling oats from their lips and debating whether they'll whip those sissified city boys from Clearwater at tonight's game. It's a loose kind of day, a day when even the administrators are lowering the walkie-talkies for a second and enjoying themselves, and everything's going fine until fourth period, when the girl in the pod starts rambling on about the devil.

It's the blonde girl who thinks she's a witch. The one who reads minds. In the middle of Mr. Howard's math class, she bursts out with an ominous question.

"Is there anybody here who can take me to the hospital?"

Tracy Howard asks her what's the matter, but it's as if she doesn't hear him. She stands up and walks toward the door.

"If nobody is going to take me to the hospital," she says, "then I'm going myself."

With that she takes off down the hall. People run after her; people run for help. Somehow they get her to the office, where she launches into a speech about how she's God or at least a messenger from God and how she can't breathe because the devil has been sucking her blood. She says she needs to get to a hospital and get a transfusion, so she can breathe again. Finally the police arrive and take her to a hospital for psychiatric care.

What happens next, though, is what really makes the day so remarkable: The Farmer Day pep rally goes on just as planned.

There's no reason it shouldn't. No logical reason at all for the school to suddenly stop in its tracks. Still, there is something surreal about the fact that these two events can occur in one place in the space of a single day. They are so alien to each other, it seems as though they could not exist in the same universe.

The pep rally gets under way late that afternoon, just before the end of the school day. Students are summoned from their classrooms and called to the stadium, where they listen to the band and watch the cheerleaders and stare at Coach Mahoney. It sounds strange to hear him talk about a game of football only a short time after the witch was taken away ranting about the devil. Maybe he doesn't know. He probably hasn't even heard.

Mahoney stands there in front of the microphone, his back ramrod straight, his close-cropped beard bristling with purpose, facing the crowd like a general surveying the troops. He reminds them how long it has been since Largo has beaten its north county nemesis. But he wants them to know that the members of the team—"our young men," he calls them —have assured him victory is at hand.

"If you really want to see something tonight," he says with a grin, "after we beat Clearwater, they're going to shave my face on the fifty-yard line at Tornado Stadium."

He looks up at the kids in the stands, looks them in the eye, and says he expects each and every one of them to be at the big game.

"There's no excuse for you *not* to be there tonight."

THAT EVENING THE LARGO PACKERS VENTURE INTO THE EN-emy's stadium and vanquish the Tornadoes 13–6. The players follow through on their promise and shave the coach on the field. YY and the gang join a horde of other students swarming onto the field in a mass celebration.

Why shouldn't they celebrate? No matter how silly or overblown it may be in the larger scheme of things, this moment will never come again. If they're going to revel in it, they'd better do it now. So, for a few minutes, YY and company abandon the outside-inside routine and give themselves over entirely to their school. They chant, they bark like dogs, exchange high fives. YY sits atop someone's shoulders, twirling triumphantly under the lights.

EIGHTEEN

IN THE

DARK

YY SITS ALONE ON HER BED, PEN-
cil in hand. Above her, Van Gogh's *Starry
Night* hangs on the wall, endlessly spinning. Beside her, the bulletin board
is disappearing beneath a maelstrom
of academic ribbons, certificates of
achievement, and who knows how many
goofy snapshots of her and Karin and
Amy and Meridith and the rest of the
AB-12 rats.

She opens her notebook and begins
with a simple sentence.

> *I was fourteen when my parents got
> a divorce.*

She is trying to get it all down on
paper.

> *I had started my first year of high
> school, which is a scary experience for
> anyone. But also around this time, I
> started getting warnings from my par-
> ents. They never seemed to talk to each
> other anymore. They wouldn't fight, in
> fact a raised voice was never heard. Ev-
> erything was normal, but something was
> wrong. You couldn't place your finger
> on it, you just had a feeling of dread.*

YY has altered a few details. She was not fourteen when it happened; she was sixteen. She was not a freshman; she was a junior. She has made other changes, too. She writes that she has only an older sister and a younger brother, when actually she has an older sister and three younger brothers. She has also streamlined the facts, taking moments that occurred separately and combining them into one scene.

> One day, my parents sent my sister and me to get pizza for dinner. We got into the car and started heading for the pizza place, having a regular conversation, but my sister had a weird expression on her face, and she didn't talk much. I asked her what was wrong.
>
> "Well, Mom and Dad have been talking to me," she said in a quiet voice. "They've definitely decided to get a divorce. The trial's in two weeks."
>
> I started to cry. I hadn't even really thought about what was happening, but I started crying just the same. We pulled over at the place and she held me for a long time.

She tells herself that she is only trying to make the story simpler, to make it more dramatic, to make it easier for people to relate to. But there is a small part of her, deep inside, that recognizes that perhaps she is changing details to keep some distance between herself and the girl she's describing. To keep it from seeming too real. To protect herself, just a little, as she walks through the shadows.

Doesn't matter. The essence of what she writes is true.

> After a while, we went back home. I walked in the door, and then made up some excuse and left. Glancing over at my parents, I knew I couldn't stay there.
>
> I took my bike out of the garage and started riding down the road towards a small park about a mile away. I hadn't even gone bike riding in ages, it just seemed like the thing to do. Finally, I reached the park and sat down on the grass. For the next hour I stayed there, huddled in a ball, because I had convinced myself that nothing could hurt me as long as I stayed in that position.

She takes the piece to school and works on it there. When her physics teacher gets too boring, slogging his way through his lectures, she pulls it out at her desk and scribbles away, pretending she's still taking notes. She erases parts and rewrites them, gradually shaping it all into something smooth and alive. When she reads it over, it gives her a comforting kind of clarity. Before, her feelings about the divorce were all mixed up; she did not know exactly what she felt. Now she has captured those emotions on paper and given them a structure and order and shape. It still hurts to think back on those days, but at least she has found a way to start putting it all behind her.

> *People say that you pattern your future relationships after your own family, but I haven't had a serious enough relationship yet. I've promised myself that when I get married, I'll never get a divorce. However, if I've learned one thing from this situation, there are just some things that you can't control.*

It feels good when she finishes. It reminds YY of why she loves to write. Now if only she could make her parents understand.

NOT FAR AWAY, INSIDE ANOTHER HOUSE, MIKE BROOME LIES in the darkness of his bedroom, alone with his Guns n' Roses photos and his Miller High Life beer poster and the weight of his isolation.

The room is small and cluttered, with a single-size bed surrounded by walls with fake wood paneling and dirty clothes scattered across the floor around the bed and cassette tapes lying among the clothes and kits for model airplanes and model cars piled on top of the dressers. Towering around the bed, stacked on top of one another, stands a collection of mismatched stereo speakers—sixteen total—all of them hooked up together in a tangle of spliced wires that feed into a guitar amp and a busted Sanyo receiver. Beside the amp, an electric guitar sits in its black case in the corner. Above the stereo, two .22 rifles and a shotgun hang on their racks.

In the middle of it all, Mike remains flat on his back on his bed, staring up at the circling blades of the ceiling fan, feeling the claustrophobic press of the walls. He hears cars cruising past on the street outside, on their way to places he will never know. He hears his mother in the kitchen, opening the refrigerator to get a glass of milk for her stomach.

Smoking another Marlboro, he pops a tape into his cassette deck and listens to *Theatre of Pain,* one of his favorite Mötley Crüe albums.

The idea of putting his own thoughts on paper seems laughable to

Mike. He doesn't like to write; he has no interest in reading. His mother does, though. At night, when everything gets too much for her, when her leg hurts and her back hurts and her head is pounding from all the worrying, Jewelene Wilson loves to settle in her easy chair with one of her mysteries or romance novels and tune out the rest of the world. If she gets her hands on a really good book, it's almost impossible to make her look up until she finishes the last page. For an hour or so, she is taken out of herself and transported to someplace far away, a place where questions always have answers, where plot threads are always tied up, where the possibilities know no end.

But Mike wants nothing to do with it. None of Mrs. Wilson's boys ever did. Not even Greg. When they were young, she tried to read aloud to them, but they just didn't care. They were always jumping up and running away to find some toy. So she gave up. Why try to force it? Now, all these years later, Mike does not even have the refuge of books. About the only things he does have are his skateboard and his cigarettes and the driving anger of his music.

He gets so tired of everyone asking him what's wrong. He can't stand it when Miss Riel and Mrs. Palmateer and the others sit him down and tell him how worried they are about him and ask him to please try, just try, to explain what exactly it is that has made him this way. He doesn't know what to tell them. He's not sure he can explain it to himself. Why should he waste his breath trying to make sense of it for them? They wouldn't understand anyway. They say they would, but they're wrong. They're so transparent. So . . .

Mike feels the pounding rhythms of the Mötley Crüe songs washing over him from the wall of speakers. Only half of them are actually pumping anything out. He bought most of them secondhand not long ago, then brought them home and jerry-rigged them all together so he could crank up the volume. But the other day, when he turned up the power full blast, he blew out the receiver. Now the only speakers playing are the ones feeding off the guitar amp.

Doesn't matter. He takes another puff on the Marlboro and closes his eyes.

His mother wonders what will happen when he turns sixteen. She doesn't want him to quit school, but there doesn't seem to be anything she can do about that, either. Wade seems to be doing okay in class. He always has his sense of humor, always seems able to flow with the tide. Not Mike, though. The doctors have told him that cigarettes are the worst possible thing for him, especially with his asthma. But he smokes them anyway. He does it openly, even in front of her. For years he sneaked out and smoked behind her back; she knew because she could smell it on his clothes. But now he lights up in the kitchen while she's sitting right there at the table.

He's starting to scare her these days. He acts as though he doesn't care what happens to him. He keeps telling her, when he tells her anything, that he wishes he were dead . . .

"GOOD MORNING. OUR THOUGHT FOR THE DAY IS: WE ALL didn't come over on the same ship, but we're all in the same boat."

Out in the long halls, a sophomore boy has just realized that his girlfriend has broken up with him. She doesn't use words to tell him; she resorts to momentum. The two of them are strolling together past the lockers when suddenly he stops for some reason and she keeps walking. That's the way she does it. That's how she tells him that he is now relegated to the status of a nonentity. No goodbyes, no nothing. She just keeps going, never looking back.

"Her name is Heather," he says afterward, still mourning her departure. "She's a bop. She's a patio person . . . It's like, 'Your dad doesn't drive a Ferrari, so you can't hang out with me.'"

Mrs. Palmateer walks across the patio, on her way to make an unannounced visit to the girls' bathroom by the gym. She slips in so quietly and unobtrusively that the lookout at the door doesn't even notice her until it's too late. Seconds after she goes in, a stream of girls comes pouring out, coughing and clearing their throats and doing their best to fade into the landscape. Mrs. Palmateer emerges behind them, smiling.

She looks over toward the auditorium steps, where the usual suspects are gathered once again. The Smurf Killer is seated behind his girlfriend, his arms wrapped around her. Ignoring the presence of authority only a few feet away, he casually cups the girl's breast with his hand.

Mrs. Palmateer apparently doesn't see it. However, she has heard the bell go off.

"Let's go," she tells the Smurf Killer and the others. "You're late."

"WHEN YOU DO LIP SYNC," says the familiar BRONX accent at the front of the room, "you have to wear appropriate clothing. You can't show your butt or your boobs . . . You cannot do 'Me So Horny.'"

Out in the audience, sprawled among the rows with their guitars and hand-scrawled lyric sheets, the children of MTV make no comment on these limitations on their artistic freedom. Dozens of students have gathered here in the auditorium after class today to try out for the school's upcoming lip-sync contest. Eager to make the cut, they listen carefully as Me-Me Panzarella, who has been appointed to organize the show, lays down the law of lip sync in her usual no-nonsense style. No nudity. No simulated sex. And stay away from 2 Live Crew.

Come the night of the show, the students who survive these auditions will appear onstage in a swirl of fog and flashing lights to act out their favorite music videos. As the original versions of their chosen songs blast through the speakers, they'll ham it up with a vengeance, mouthing the lyrics, pretending to thrash away at their guitars and drums, doing everything in their power to adopt the persona of whomever they're imitating. For one night, they will become blazing stars—Madonna, the Hammer, the members of Public Enemy or the Cult—and strut their stuff in front of what probably will be a packed audience.

In many ways, the teens of today are essentially the same creatures that teenagers have always been. Still, there is something fundamentally different about them—something connected to television. Actually, it's more than just TV. Almost everyone under age fifty was raised with TV. With these kids, it's something more pervasive. From the day they're born, they roam in a blizzard of visual images, directed their way from film and video and computer chips. As so many social scientists have shown, it changes them in a thousand tiny and not so tiny ways. It alters their sense of time, the way their brains process information, their expectations about the world and what it owes them, the shape and color of their imaginations, their fears, their fantasies. And, of course, their relationship to music, which has long been one of the defining relationships of any generation.

Kids don't just listen to a song anymore. They watch it, they tape it, they replay it in slo-mo, they fast-forward through the verses and scenes that bore them. To them, music is something that enters not just the ears but the eyes. In fact, most of the music they watch on MTV is a visual performance in which the actors move their lips to prerecorded voices, which may or may not be their own, and pretend to play their guitars and drums to prerecorded instrumental tracks, which may have been originally performed by someone else or by a computer. The music these kids usually watch, the music that makes up the sound track of their lives, is already a lip sync, which probably explains why they emulate the concept with such fervor. Over the past five or ten years, lip-sync contests have become wildly popular events at high schools around the country. Largo High holds two of them every year. This semester's contest promises to be especially intense; already, more than twenty acts have signed up for two days of auditions, hoping to make the cut.

"There's a lot of competition this year," says Ms. Panzarella. "It's going to be difficult to pick."

YY and Karin are trying out with "Closer to Fine," a jangling folk song by the Indigo Girls. They know their chances aren't that good; the song's a bit too quiet and serious and not nearly as visually dramatic as others. But they're giving it a shot.

There's no question, however, that Andrea Taylor will make the cut. Andrea is an exceptionally talented and dedicated dancer. She's been taking ballet and other lessons for years; on weekends, she performs in Point Blank, a local dance troupe. For the lip sync, she and some friends are performing Janet Jackson's "Miss You Much," a cleverly choreographed number that's been a big hit on both the radio and MTV. A real crowd-pleaser. Andrea, who's taking on the Janet Jackson role, will undoubtedly be the highlight of the evening. Plus, in the second half of the show, after she's done with the song, Andrea will serve as co-emcee with John Boyd.

Appearing onstage together will be hard. Andrea and John have grown tired of hiding. They're not being fair to Sabrina; they're not being fair to themselves. And now they're going to have to walk out onstage together at lip sync, laughing and smiling and acting as though nothing's going on between them.

Andrea thinks it's time to stop the charade. They have to make up their minds. Either they're going to be together, or they're going to be apart.

"All or nothing," says Andrea. "I don't want to be half-stepping."

NINETEEN

THE V CLUB

By now, you'd think there would be no surprises left down in the pod. After all this time, it would seem impossible that the kids could do anything that would catch the GOALS teachers off guard.

In Mrs. McGraw's seventh-period English class, the scrawny boy who screams without warning keeps complaining that other kids are showering him with spitballs. Mrs. McGraw sees the spitballs dotting the carpet around him, a minefield of paper and saliva, but she can't seem to catch anyone actually shooting them at him. Then, one day, she nabs the culprit. It's the scrawny boy himself. She catches him chewing on paper, making a spitball. He's the one who's been making them all along. Mrs. McGraw doesn't understand. Does he think it's funny? Is he trying to win sympathy? What is going through this child's head?

In the room at the end of the pod's hallway, in Mrs. Frye's family living class, there sits a girl who wears a necklace decorated with metal tabs pulled off soda cans and beer cans. There are dozens of tabs on the necklace—107 of them, to be exact. One day a visitor asks this girl why she collects them.

The other kids snicker.

"Calm down," she tells them, laughing. She hesitates for a moment, trying to find a polite way to put it. Finally she decides there is no polite way. Every time a guy gives her one of these tabs, she says, that guy supposedly is entitled to, as she puts it, "a free fuck."

"That's really what it means," she says, still laughing.

Eric the Dragon has begun talking about guns. He has a collection of them, he says. One day, when Ms. DiLello gets annoyed with a kid who's always pestering her—this big, gawky freshman named Jim, who's harmless but irritating—Eric walks up to her and offers a suggestion. He is willing, he says, to eliminate the problem of Jim.

"I'll take care of him for you, if you want."

Ms. DiLello looks at Eric. He is not smiling. He appears absolutely serious.

"No," she tells him. "That won't be necessary."

Next door, in Mr. Klapka's American government class, a debate is under way. To help them understand how laws are made, Mr. Klapka has assembled his students into their own House of Representatives. Now they are arguing the merits of a bill one of them has proposed, a bill to ban anyone older than sixty-five from driving.

Toward the back of the room, Mike Broome sits without saying a word, studying his own list of proposed bills.

the drinking age to 15
driving age to 13
tobacco age to 14
the law that if a kid quits school they can't get a license

What he means by that last proposal is that he would like to repeal the Florida law that allows the state to suspend the driver's licenses of young dropouts. This is not an academic issue to Mike. More and more, it's looking as if he will in fact quit school when he turns sixteen. He's already doing his best to get kicked out. He's admitted it to the teachers. At least, that's what he says on some days; on others, he still swears he wants to graduate. It's like he's riding the longest roller coaster in history, and he wants to drag them all along with him.

One day Mrs. O'Donnell, who has not given up hope, pulls Mike aside and tells him it's got to stop. She reminds him how she and Ms. DiLello stood up for him early in the semester. They've tried so hard to help him. Why does he keep slapping them in the face?

"I don't care if I'm hurting your feelings," he tells her. "I don't care if I'm hurting anybody's feelings. Just screw it."

Mrs. O'Donnell and the other teachers in the pod can be forgiven if they sometimes take such things personally. They knock themselves out to make it as easy as possible for the Mike Broomes of the world to succeed. Even though GOALS teachers cover the same basic material as their counterparts in the regular classes—they teach from the same textbooks and follow curriculums guided by the same state requirements—they try to make learning as effortless as possible for the kids. They assign little or no homework. They keep reading and writing assignments to a minimum. If the kids finish their work, they reward them by letting them play computer games or by giving them a free day or letting them watch TV.

Outside the pod, there's considerable hostility toward the program. Regular students, who resent the special breaks given to GOALS students, constantly rail against the kids in the pod, calling them stupid and lazy. There's a whole series of GOALS jokes. Like with the Video Highlights. This year, for the first time, Largo High will offer not only a traditional yearbook but also a video yearbook—a videotape, filled with scenes shot around the school—and some of the GOALS kids have been given the responsibility of putting it together. Crews of GOALS kids have been roaming the school with a camera for months, talking to everyone in sight, collecting all kinds of footage. So now regular kids have these lines about how bad the whole thing's going to turn out.

"When you put the videotape in, the screen's going to be black," says one junior honor student, reeling off the lines, one after the other. "When you put the videotape in, it's going to be Beta."

Kids aren't the only ones who rip GOALS. In the faculty lounge, there are more than a few teachers who love to privately trash the program. As far as they're concerned, it's a giant step in the wrong direction. Too many students, they say, already want their diplomas handed to them without an ounce of effort. They already come to class every day expecting some kind of entertainment extravaganza, some kind of elaborate TV game show, where the questions aren't too taxing, where no one's expected to read, where the contestants are automatically handed big cash prizes just for showing up and spelling their names correctly. And now, they say, here comes GOALS, surrendering to those expectations.

Some teachers can barely speak politely about the program. They resent all the money and time and attention that go into GOALS; they resent that the teachers there are given smaller classes, when almost every other teacher is struggling to breathe—struggling to do anything—in the crush of students who fill their classrooms.

In the pod, the criticisms sting. The GOALS teachers know the program is far from perfect. Sometimes they wonder themselves if they're too easy on the kids, if they're always striking the right balance, if they're really making a difference. But at least they're trying.

"You are *not* going to fail," Mrs. McGraw tells her kids. "I won't let you."

Still, the enormity of what they're up against can be overwhelming.

In her room at the pod's east end, Leah Whitehead, a veteran teacher who does not think of herself as one who is easily shaken, has almost lost hope with her sixth-period English class. One afternoon, as she attempts to lead them through a vocabulary assignment, they badger her because she won't let them put their heads down and sleep.

"My sleeping rule is cut-and-dry," she tells them. "I'm not going to negotiate on this."

"I think we need a democracy," says one boy.

"I think we need a vote," says another.

Mrs. Whitehead is not impressed. "You haven't earned the right to have a democracy. It's a right that is earned."

They hardly hear a word she says. They're too busy telling her what's wrong with her class. It's boring, they say. It's no fun, they say. It has nothing to do with life.

"It's not our fault if we fall asleep."

"You should make it interesting."

"If they paid us three or four dollars an hour," one of them says, turning to the argument many of them use, "maybe I'd stay awake."

Mrs. Whitehead looks at the boy who has made this last statement. He is sitting with his feet propped on the table. She tells him to take them down. He tells her his feet are not really on the table, they're on the edge of the table.

"Get them down," she says.

She's not giving up. She's still trying to make them understand.

"Education is not about doing page 176," she tells them. "It's about listening and learning and finding out. Maybe you won't use it today. But maybe down the road ten years from now, twenty years from now, you will use it . . . I didn't understand William Faulkner when I was in high school. I thought he was pretty boring."

One of the boys interrupts her with an upraised hand.

"Who's William Faulkner?" he says.

For the rest of the hour, they show no mercy. They say they don't have a textbook. They say they don't have their folders. They dare her to send them to the office. They ignore her, carrying on a loud debate among themselves about whether the members of Metallica are or are not devil worshippers. In a stroke of perverse genius, they begin whistling the theme to *The Andy Griffith Show*.

Through it all, Mrs. Whitehead never breaks. But slowly a look of defeat creeps into her face.

Amid the clamor, some students are actually working on the day's assignment, a vocabulary list. The final word on today's list is: *devastate*.

Flipping through a dictionary, one of the boys writes down a definition: *to lay waste*.

IN A ROOM AT THE END OF B WING, AN ENGLISH TEACHER with short gray hair and a sly smile sits perched on a stool in front of one of her senior advanced placement classes. By tomorrow, she says, she wants the class to have read the final act of Henrik Ibsen's *A Doll's House*.

A collective moan rises from the desks.

"Is that so much?" says Lucia Anne Hay. "One lousy act?"

Down the aisles, the kids mimic her in high-pitched, singsongy voices usually reserved for imitating parents.

"Is that so much? One lousy act?"

Mrs. Hay fights back a smirk, trying her best to look stern. This is a game that she and her seniors play. She assigns a reading, they pretend to pitch a fit, she pretends to be shocked. But tomorrow, when the bell rings and they take their seats, she knows—and they know she knows—that most if not all of them will have read the one lousy act and will be prepared to dissect it with ruthless efficiency. These are advanced placement kids. This year they will read, among other things: *Hamlet, Macbeth, Othello, Antigone, Medea, Lord of the Flies, Wuthering Heights, Lord Jim*, and Albert Camus's *The Stranger*. Furthermore, some of them will like it.

YY's in this class, sitting over in the front left corner. So's sweet little Amy Boyle, sitting directly behind her. Carolyn Hanson, the quiet young woman who will be this year's valedictorian, is seated next to Amy. The entire room is a teacher's dream. Sometimes Mrs. Hay can almost see the neurons firing inside their brains. Like right now, as she talks about Ibsen. She tells them how old Henrik once said that the search for truth can make you lonely. She tells them how he said that the majority is never right until it does right. She even relates a little story about how the dear man used to keep a live scorpion—stinger and all—on his writing desk. It was a way of injecting venom into his plays.

"That's what he was doing," she says. "Getting out the venom."

When Mrs. Hay sits in front of a class like this one, bouncing ideas and questions off the kids, she looks so happy. If the whole school were filled with students like these, maybe she'd always be happy. Maybe she wouldn't worry so much about what's going to happen five or ten years down the line.

Mrs. Hay is not a doomsayer. She has taught at Largo High for two decades now, and she is proud of its record and accomplishments. But beneath the surface, something has gone wrong. It has been going wrong for years. Only now it's getting worse. Not just down in the pod, either. To one degree or another, the same disease that is ravaging Mrs. Whitehead's sixth-period class—the apathy, the withering of curiosity, the almost palpable frustration and anger—already has infected the rest of Largo High, as it has infected so many other schools.

In some parts of the campus, it may be better hidden. It may not reveal itself so dramatically. But it's still there. It comes from outside. From all those thousands of TV screens, endlessly flickering through all those childhoods. From countless homes where no one talks to each other and where happiness is something that appears only on late-night reruns. From an entire society addicted to lottery tickets and get-rich schemes and miracle drugs and magical solutions and who knows how many other forms of instant gratification. The teachers don't particularly care where you put the blame. But they know it's out there, and for a long time now, they can't say exactly how long, it has been slipping into their schools— even schools such as Largo, where the walls in the front office are covered with awards and plaques and letters of commendation—and into every classroom.

The teachers talk about it. They stand in their empty rooms during their planning periods, when the kids are gone, and they talk about how scared they are.

"There *is* a problem," says Mrs. Hay.

They've got to get kids reading again. They have to find a way, she says, to make them understand that reading and writing and stretching their minds will eventually bring rewards that cannot be measured in dollars and cents. Somehow, she says, they have to show them that effort is its own reward. That's why Mrs. Hay is among those who believe GOALS is on the wrong track. She knows how hard the teachers in the pod are trying. Still, she doesn't understand the point of steering the kids away from book work. Books are at the heart of it all. Work is at the heart of it all. If you take away those things . . .

Mrs. Hay has stepped down off the stool. She has finished talking about Ibsen, and now she is standing in front of YY and Amy and the others, distributing entry forms for something known as the PRIDE writing competition. Every year, one senior is chosen as the best writer in the school; that person then goes on to compete with the winners from other schools. Of course, she says, it would help to know how to use apostrophes. It would help, she says, casting an eye in YY's direction, to know the difference between "it's" and "its."

YY puts her head down on the desk.

"I know," she mutters, laughing. "I know."

Mrs. Hay says she wants them to give it a shot. She turns to the only boy in the class that day. With all these females around, she says, he'll probably be able to share something different in his entries. He'll be able, she says, to give the male perspective.

YY snorts. "Skip the male perspective," she says.

YY WILL TELL YOU WHAT SHE THINKS ABOUT MALES. SHE has composed her own thought for the day about them: "All men are islands, and some should be deserted."

The problem is, men keep deserting her. Weeks after the fact, YY is still wincing from the disastrous date at this year's Homecoming dance. She went with this guy from the yearbook staff. Afterward, when they were alone, he told her he wished he were with this other girl. His timing was perfect. When he made the confession, he had just begun kissing YY.

"I can't believe I'm here with you," he said. "I like somebody else."

Unfortunately, YY gets into these situations regularly. Foul creatures are always popping up in her life. It's like she's in some bad horror movie where the monster never dies.

"YY's gotten worked over so many times," says Karin Upmeyer, "it's not even funny."

One legendary night, the Heathers were at a party when some jerk came up and started blatantly hitting on YY. He was so transparent, it was a joke. So YY dug into her Latin reserves and started conjugating *exeo,* which means "to leave." She literally went through the list of verb forms—*exeo, exis, exit, eximus,* etc.—until this lower life-form got so bored and confused that he slithered away. The girls burst out laughing.

Only YY. No one else would ever brush off a guy in a dead language. The others love to rag her about it.

Last year was the worst episode yet. That was when YY fell hard for this one senior boy. They had a big romance. He used to sit in his trig class and write her notes in which he'd leave out all the vowels. Or at least try to.

> *Hw r y? Tdy I m gng t hv fn n trg . . . f y cn ndrstnd ths nt I wll b vry mprssd . . .*

Silly, yes. But deciphering this boy's notes gave YY something to do. And when he broke up with her, she was crushed. The official reason— what he told her over the phone—was that it was nothing she'd done, that it was just him, that things weren't working out. The real reason—what he told other people—was that with the divorce of her parents, which was happening around then, YY just wasn't her old wild and wonderful self anymore. She'd changed. She wasn't any fun.

But that's not even the best part. The best came the day after this guy ended it with her, when he called and asked if she wanted to go out that weekend. YY was confused. Was it over between them or wasn't it? But she was willing to give him a second chance. So she went to his house that night. When she arrived, though, he gave her the arctic treatment. He told her he had to go somewhere and then climbed into a car with some of his buddies and took off, leaving her there looking like a stooge.

The memory cuts even now. For solace YY turns to Karin, who can always be counted on to give the guy a healthy rip.

"How could his parents be so nice," says Karin, looking back on YY's days with him, "and spawn such a thing from hell?"

What made the whole thing even worse was that YY had slept with this boy. He was her first, which meant that their relationship had forced her to revoke her charter membership in the V Club. That's the term that YY and the others use for girls who are still virgins. They make jokes about it when they're sitting around together, getting drunk. They joke because they don't know how else to talk about it. So they drink, and they laugh, and they go on about who's still in the club and who's not. Of course, the membership ranks are rapidly shrinking throughout the school. Among the Fearsome Foursome, only Amy and Karin still qualify. Amy, in typical Amy fashion, has vowed not to sleep with anyone until she's married or at least until she graduates from high school. Karin, meanwhile, says she's just not ready yet for sex.

Turns out Meridith and YY weren't ready, either. Meridith took the big step late in her sophomore year, when she was fifteen. She was involved with an older boy from Largo, and he pushed repeatedly for them to sleep together, and eventually, after they'd been seeing each other for months, she said yes. They did it at his family's apartment after school, while his mother worked. They used condoms—Meridith insisted—but even so, she was still uneasy about it. After they finished, she'd find herself sitting in bed, feeling lost and confused. This is what grownups do, she'd tell herself, and I'm not a grownup.

Once Meridith started sleeping with the boyfriend, though, it wasn't easy to stop. He didn't suffer any of the same qualms she did. Whenever they saw each other, he kept pressing for sex, and reluctantly Meridith would give in. Finally it reached a point where she was trying to figure out how to put an end to their sessions without ending the relationship as well. Then something happened that made the question moot. She had a dream one night in which she saw this boy selling marijuana and cocaine to a crowd of customers from a van in the parking lot of his apartment complex. It was an extremely vivid, detailed dream—to this day Meridith can recall, for instance, that the van was tan-colored—and afterward, she was severely shaken. Although her boyfriend did experiment with drugs in real life, as far as she knew he'd never sold them. But after the dream, she realized that she could easily picture him doing it. Suddenly she recognized a disturbing quality in this boy that in the past she had either overlooked or found it convenient to ignore. When she woke up that day, she broke up with him.

That was almost two years ago. Since then, Meridith hasn't slept with anyone else. She dates lots of guys, but does not allow her relationships to go that far anymore. It'll be fine when she's older, she says. But not now. Not yet.

YY feels the same. Last year, when she had sex with her longtime boyfriend, the one who wrote the notes with no vowels, she did it because she thought she was in love. He kept pressuring her, and she kept saying no, and then finally she relented. Immediately she wished she hadn't. She didn't like the backwash of mixed-up emotions that hit her afterward. YY didn't feel comfortable with sex. She didn't feel she was mature enough for it. She didn't know what she felt, except for being sure that she didn't want to keep doing it. When she and the boyfriend broke up, her waning interest was one of the tensions hanging in the air between them.

Like Meridith, YY hasn't slept with anyone else since then and doesn't plan to until she's out of high school. She doesn't completely regret trying it, though. At least now the mystique is gone. At least she understands what sex is like and that she can live without it. Some people, especially if they're still in the V Club, think they can't. They build it up into such a big deal that it makes them act stupid. YY knows better. Sex can wait.

Besides, she's got other things to worry about these days. She's still staring down her math-vs.-writing career crisis, still trying to figure out whether she should point her life in the direction she wants or kowtow to the wishes of Helen the Hun and Bob. It's kind of funny. For years, her parents have been drumming it into her skull that she should make decisions for herself. When she was growing up, they always let her pick her daily wardrobe, no matter how outlandish she looked as she headed out the door. They were so eager to encourage her intellectual freedom that they didn't give her a middle name; instead, they let her choose her own. A few years ago, she made her selection: Cecelia.

"She's the saint of music and poetry," YY explains, "and I thought that was pretty cool."

But now, when it really counts, her parents seem to be pulling rank. She tries to talk to her mother about it. But Helen doesn't seem to want to hear it.

"You're doing math," she tells her.

Helen says this as though she were repeating an immutable law. As though it were the preordained equation of her daughter's life, scribbled indelibly on her birth certificate. *Christine + math = fulfillment.*

Her mom has always had it in her head that YY was destined for a life of numbers. She talks about how easy math is for Chrissie—that's what both parents still call her—how she never has to think about it, how it just flows naturally into her head. Her mom has one anecdote she loves to tell about when Chrissie was a little girl. She was a late talker, it turns out. Other kids made fun of her because she stumbled over her words and didn't really begin speaking until she was three and a half. (She's been making up for it ever since.) But when she started, Helen remembers, one of the first things out of Chrissie's mouth was a story problem.

"Five forks and five knives," she said, watching her mother as she set the table one day. "That's ten."

YY rolls her eyes at the very mention of this incident. It's true that math comes easily to her. But though she doesn't have the heart to say this to Helen's face, it has never really thrilled her. What makes YY happy is writing. Like with the piece she did on the divorce. She's shown it to some of her teachers. They told her it was good, so now she's decided to enter that PRIDE competition, with the divorce story as the centerpiece of her collection. She hasn't shown it to her parents, though. She doesn't want to hurt their feelings; also, she's still trying to avoid forcing the career question to a head. Maybe if she waits long enough, it will blow over. Maybe it will just go away.

In the meantime, something else has come up. Something strange. Weeks after YY and the others dressed up as the Heathers for Character Day, parading through the cafeteria as they conducted their lunchtime poll, the clueless innocents are starting to take revenge. The inevitable backlash has finally begun.

The first sign shows itself down in AB-12, the Heathers' home turf. There's an old wooden lectern at the front of the room, and on the lectern, the girls had written the words "Fearsome Foursome forever." But then one day, when they're not around, someone scratches over those words and replaces them with a new name for the girls. Now the lectern says: "Breakfast Club Bitches Forever."

YY and company don't understand it. If someone wanted to slam them, why do it with a reference to *The Breakfast Club* instead of *Heathers?* Did they get their movies confused? There was that one character in *Breakfast Club,* the Molly Ringwald character who was so superior. Is that where it comes from? Is there someone out there suffering under the delusion that the Fearsome Foursome wants to be a bunch of Molly Ringwald clones?

"Just forget it," YY tells the others. Whoever's doing this is just being stupid. It's not worth worrying about it. "They're geeks."

But forgetting turns out not to be so easy. Because after the day with the lectern, the backlash gets worse. The girls are starting to hear nasty comments, passed along secondhand. They're finding things written about them on the blackboard. At home, they're starting to get anonymous calls.

Amy and Mer and Karin and YY discuss it when the four of them are alone together. They wait until they're in a place where no one else can hear them—they don't want to give their attackers the satisfaction of seeing them squirm—and then they hash it all out. They talk about what to do; they debate whether it's wise to do anything at all. Suddenly they are the clueless innocents.

"Who the hell would have done this?" says Karin, shaking her head. "We've got to find out who it is."

ANDREA AND JOHN CAN'T PUT IT OFF ANY LONGER. ONCE and for all, they have to figure out whether they're going to try to be together or not.

They make the big decision on Friday, December 1, the same day the lip sync is scheduled. They meet early that morning. They both find a way to slip out of their second-period classes and head down to the library. They talk the whole period, going over everything forward and backward, being as logical about it as they can. Finally it becomes clear what they've got to do. They're going back to being strictly friends. No more longing glances. No more secret notes.

"We're going to stop it right now," they tell each other. "It's wrong."

TWENTY

ATMOSPHERIC

ENHANCEMENT

GODZILLA IS SNIFFLING. HE HAS a cold, which means he's not feeling especially sunny, which is not good. Even in the best of moods, Godzilla is not to be toyed with.

He stands stage left, just behind the curtain. He turns to his minions, who are poised at their stations, awaiting his command.

"OKAY!" he roars. "THIS IS IT! PLACES, EVERYBODY!"

The auditorium goes dark. Then, as the first strains of an INXS song come thumping out of the speakers, the chase lights begin to flash. The strobes begin to flash. A mind-boggling number of lights —lights of almost every color, lights that spin and rotate and fade in and out from somewhere high above—set the stage on fire.

Godzilla roars again.

"GIVE ME A LITTLE FOG!"

Nothing happens.

"EMILY! WAKE UP! EMILY! FOG!"

At the back of the stage, the minions have erected a large rear-projection screen, on which they'll be showing slides. Behind the screen, lying on the ground so her shadow won't be seen by the crowd, the aforementioned Emily finally gets the word and starts the fogger. Immediately swirls of white vapor—by chance, tonight's batch is scented to smell like piña colada—drift outward, spreading across the floor.

The audience erupts. There are at least three hundred kids out there —YY and Karin, who did not survive the auditions, are seated together toward the front with Amy and Meridith—and every one of their vocal cords seems to be working overtime to form the same high-pitched scream. They are so loud they threaten to drown out the two emcees for the first half of the show, who are now launching into an extended explanation of the rules. They're introducing the judges; they're telling lame little jokes; they're driving Godzilla crazy.

"Come on, dudes," he says, muttering under his breath behind the curtain. *"The show is dyin'."*

Godzilla's real name is Mark Granning, but he prefers the nickname. Actually he prefers several nicknames. Lordzilla, Godzilla, almost anything imposing-sounding with "-zilla" stuck at the end. And when it comes to lip syncs, it's best to call Mr. Granning whatever he wants.

At the incredibly ancient age of thirty-four, he is still a towering figure in high school circles. Turbulent, intimidating, and intensely talented, he's a topflight journalism teacher at Lakewood High in St. Petersburg. For the past several years, he has been conducting his own mini-revolution in multimedia education. He teaches kids how to work with video cameras, light boards, computers, and a massive sound system, then coaxes them into applying what they've learned in LAMP Productions, the school's own student production company. Together he and his gang of young hotshots travel around the state, using their expertise and $150,000 worth of equipment, paid for entirely out of the group's profits, to stage impossibly elaborate shows.

They bill themselves, without exaggeration, as "masterminds of extraordinary audio-visual odysseys." They do video dances at proms and at state conventions. They do computerized eleven-projector slide shows for school boards and teacher associations. And in one auditorium after another, they are begged to do lip syncs. The individual schools provide the acts, for better or worse. LAMP—it stands for Lakewood Associated Media Personnel—supplies the hardware and technical know-how to pull it all together.

Which is what brings them tonight to Largo, where the emcees are still onstage, hogging the mikes.

"Are you ready?" they shout, trying to pump up the crowd. "Are you ready?"

The crowd is ready. In fact, they have been ready for some time. Knowing what's expected of them, though, they respond with a gratuitous round of cheers.

With that, the lights dim again, and the contest officially begins with "Disposable Heroes," a Metallica song performed by a GOALS student named Charles and a couple of his friends. It's a typically relentless heavy-metal number, and the guys pound their way through it in typically humorless heavy-metal style, spitting out the lyrics, banging their heads up and down in the requisite display of rhythmic hostility.

The audience doesn't take this assault personally. They understand the anger's part of the act. Yet they do not warm to Charles and his friends. Down the rows, kids are sitting with a detached look in their eyes, waiting for the song to end. There's nothing wrong with heavy metal; like all types of music, it includes tons of mediocre songs and a handful of brilliant ones. But it's so sullen, it doesn't usually play too well at lip syncs. Mr. Granning's students, who know this from experience, are dying with laughter as they watch from behind the curtain. Mocking the predictability of metalhead acts, they, too, have begun to bang their heads up and down. They're pointing at the drummer, some hapless skinhead stuck behind a single cymbal, trying to make it look like he's playing an entire drum set. Granning's kids shower him and the rest of the band with scathing insults.

"How'd this guy get in high school? He must have paid off his middle school teacher."

"They're slobbering!"

"Make these guys disappear!"

When the song shows no sign of letting up, the crew does in fact make them disappear. Showing these heroes just how disposable they really are, they hit the fogger and engulf the group in a piña colada cloud until they virtually vanish from sight. "Atmospheric enhancement," the LAMP kids call this. It's one of their standard procedures for dealing with acts that bore them. It works, too. Caught inside the haze, Charles and company eventually get the message and leave the stage, grumbling about how they didn't get to finish.

One by one, the fourteen acts on tonight's bill show off their moves. The kids drop to the stage and twirl, flirt with the fans in the front row, enact little dramas of love and rejection, desire and betrayal, all in step with the music. The crowd, which by now has snapped out of its Metallica-inspired coma, goes nuts. People are out of their seats, waving their arms and singing and chanting. Dozens of them run down the aisles so they can dance in front of the stage and yell out words of encouragement. The hysteria reaches even greater heights during a Heavy D number, when one of the performers falls to his belly and begins making pelvic thrusts, thereby violating one of the show's ground rules, not to mention the ground.

"Oh!" says Granning, shaking his head in mock horror, as though he has never seen a kid try such a thing before. "Sex on the stage!"

"That's *scary*," says one of the girls in the crew, standing nearby. She's not offended by the explicit nature of the move. She just thinks that making it with the floor is unbelievably cheesy.

Out in the auditorium, the audience is finally revved up. But off in the wings, the backstage critics from LAMP are verbally strafing almost every act.

"Ten bucks says they're cheerleaders. *Definitely* cheerleaders."

"That's got to be the weakest song of all time."

"Oh my God. Did he have a lobotomy for breakfast?"

"Fog 'em! I'm tired of looking at 'em."

"They're doing 'Flashdance'? It's for real?"

Altogether, there are about fifteen kids in LAMP. There's Rashida the Mixmistress, who runs the sound board. And Alison and Kristin, the Switchzilla Goddesses, stationed at the light board. Virtually all of them have nicknames and titles as audacious as Granning's. Without question, they are a merciless, superior bunch. And why shouldn't they be? Ten or twenty years ago, kids who handled the audio-visual equipment were usually the most hopeless nerds in the school, the ones with the broken glasses and the plastic pocket shields who were always wheeling a dusty film projector down the hall. Today, the pecking order is reversed. LAMP starts out with kids who are already cool and then molds them, under Godzilla's fiery attentions, into young techno-wizards who produce the wildest, hardest-rocking high school shows around, shows that blow the roof off their peers' obsession with the visual image. These kids are dream merchants with acne.

Of course, now that they're on top, encamped along the upper tiers of the status pyramid, they've copped a major-league attitude. All of them have devoted themselves to fulfilling the same unspoken pledge, a pledge that requires them to constantly make fun of everything and everyone in

the universe, starting with one another. Granning, who presents the larg-
est and most inviting target, comes in for an almost breathtaking amount
of abuse. They rip his age, his taste in music—at home he prefers Vivaldi
and Chopin, if the awful truth be known—the expanding bulk of his
belly, the ongoing departure of his hairline.

By comparison, they are almost gentle with outsiders. Almost, but not
quite. As they roam from one lip sync to the next, they constantly crack on
the kids at other schools, whom they automatically assume are drooling
hillbillies compared to anyone from Lakewood High. If the acts don't
measure up to their standards, they tear them apart. They're professional
about it. They don't let it interfere with their jobs, and they generally do it
discreetly, so none of the natives will hear them and be offended. But they
still stand off in the wings, sneering at the other kids' disastrous attempts
to dance like Michael Jackson, snickering over their hopelessly outdated
song selections, cranking up the fogger and making them disappear whenever it all gets too tedious. It's a kind of payback, really. A way of returning all the scorn heaped upon their predecessors behind the dusty film
projectors. The final revenge of the A/V geeks.

"Bimbos, man," one of them says now, watching some Largo girls
preparing to vault across the stage in leotards.

"From hell," says another. "Bimbos from hell."

The most notable exceptions of the night—the acts that earn the praise
of even the LAMP crew—are the ones anchored by Andrea Taylor and
John Boyd.

"These guys are *good*," says Mr. Granning, watching John and a few
other kids slink through New Edition's "N.E. Heartbreak." Even better is
"Miss You Much," the Janet Jackson song, in which Andrea leads a squad
of other dancers through an intricate routine that starts and stops and
starts again, all with the same precision as the original video. They are
such a beautifully synchronized machine, the audience goes silent with
awe.

"The class act of the evening," Granning whispers.

Andrea is especially amazing. Dressed in black, just like Janet Jackson,
she prowls across the stage with a lethal grace. Inside, though, she's a total
wreck. Because just now, in the middle of the act, as she executes one
flawless move after another, she has gazed out into the audience and
found herself staring into the eyes of the one and only Sabrina.

• • •

SHE'S SITTING OFF TO THE LEFT, UP FRONT. MAYBE THE third or fourth row. Almost on top of the stage.

Her presence is no surprise. She told Andrea she was coming tonight; in fact, Andrea's giving her a ride home afterward. Still, there was no way to predict how unnerving it would be to see her out there so close. In a little while, after Andrea's done with her act, it'll be time for her and John to go onstage together and emcee the second half of the show. And when they do, Sabrina will be right there, checking out their every move.

Wonderful. Andrea's already torn up tonight, trying to accept, once and for all, that she and John just aren't going to happen. On the very same day they sealed the pact, she has to stand beside him in front of all these people and try to act happy. And now, just to stir things up a bit more, she has to worry about Sabrina watching the two of them standing together onstage. It's too much. Can it get any worse?

It can, and does, a few minutes later. In fact, it gets infinitely worse. It happens when Andrea and John are offstage. They're standing outside the auditorium, outside one of the stage doors, waiting until they're called in to take over the emcee duties, when suddenly John leans over and gives her a kiss. Not a polite little kiss like he gave her after the Homecoming dance, either. One of these long and lingering numbers that would almost get you arrested in some states.

Breathless, Andrea pulls away—not too quickly, mind you—and stares at him.

"Why did you do that? I thought we had an agreement."

John gives her this deadly smile. "It wasn't like you didn't want me to."

He knows he's right, and he knows she knows it. So much for the pact.

Right about then is showtime, when they have to go inside and take the stage. Andrea is really losing it now. Just when she needs all the poise and composure she can muster, she's ready to slide over the edge. It's impossible. Still feeling the kiss, careening toward sensory overload, Andrea feels herself walking out under the lights in front of all those faces. She stands next to John, forcing herself to smile and joke and do whatever emcees are supposed to do. She's trying to switch to automatic pilot. Fighting to remain calm, to just get through this and to make sure, whatever she does, that she does not make eye contact again with Sabrina, who is no doubt scoping her and John at this very instant.

The girl has known Andrea for so long, she can read her better than anybody. What if she's doing it right now? What if she can tell, from her seat a few feet away, what's just happened outside? What if she figures out everything that's been going on behind her back, just by the way Andrea and John are looking at each other?

SOMEBODY BETTER TURN ON THE AIR-CONDITIONING. Because Andrea and John aren't the only ones burning up the place. As the lip sync tears toward the end of the night, Jason Davenport—best male-type buddy to the Fearsome Foursome—is leading his band through a scorching version of the Cult's "Fire Woman." Jason is a willowy figure, stalking across the stage in a cowboy hat and a long black duster. He throws off the hat, swings the mike stand like an overgrown baton, spins like a tornado in sync with the others in the band.

The crowd is whipped into a frenzy. YY and Karin and the others are up in front now, joining the other screamers. Even the cynics in LAMP are getting into it.

"Yeah!" says Mr. Granning, nodding his head and tapping his feet in what appears to be a primitive attempt at dancing.

Suddenly a blonde girl in a bright red mini-dress that follows neither the letter nor the spirit of the school dress code comes prancing out in her bare feet, twisting suggestively. This is the Fire Woman—for the record, her real name is Heather—and her role is to exert her wiles upon Jason. He's on his knees when she slides up to him and begins literally hanging on the boy.

The act is so hot that when the contest is over and the judges tally their votes, Jason Davenport and the Fire Woman and the others in the Cult act win first place in the rock category. In dance and rap, John Boyd and his group take second place for "N.E. Heartbreak," and Andrea's group receives top honors for "Miss You Much." Andrea doesn't feel like a winner, though. Standing onstage, posing for a photographer, she watches helplessly as Sabrina, who has already given her a hug, rushes toward John and disappears with him.

Andrea feels her instincts for emotional self-preservation kicking in. Her heart's working overtime, doing that skipping business again. The moment the photographer's done, she takes off in pursuit of the happy couple. She finds them outside, not far from where John surprised her with the volcanic kiss. Only now he's holding Sabrina's hand.

Andrea turns to her girlfriend and unwitting rival and tells her it's time to go home.

"Let's go. Now."

Sabrina doesn't understand. "What's wrong?"

"Nothing. Let's just go."

John, who knows perfectly well what's wrong, wisely keeps his mouth shut. But in the car, as she's being spirited away, Sabrina keeps pressing Andrea for clues.

"What's wrong with you?"

Andrea stares straight ahead at the road. "Nothing. I'm upset."

"What are you upset about?"

"Nothing. Just don't worry about it."

Easy for Andrea to say. Because once she drops Sabrina off, she heads right back to school, finds John, and drags him to a Denny's to try to figure out what in the world they're going to do. After extensive and solemn deliberations—there's something sobering about a Denny's after midnight—they return to Planet Earth and agree once again that they have to keep away from each other.

"It's hard for me," says John.

"It's hard for me, too," says Andrea. "But we've got to just leave it alone, because we know it's not going to work."

The two of them are serious this time. They mean it. They don't want any more misunderstandings. The pact is back in force. It is not to be broken.

Bending it, however, is another matter. Because when Andrea takes John home, he ends the entire confusing evening the only way it could end, which is with another kiss. A friendly kiss this time. But still a kiss that's honest enough to acknowledge, no matter what they've vowed or how many hours they've spent vowing it, that no pact can ever be trusted with something as dangerous as a human heart.

Now that December is here, the countdown to the end of the semester is about to begin. With it, of course, will come the usual period of pre-finals dread, which will soon escalate into the usual pre-finals panic, which will then evolve, in the days immediately before the tests, into the usual tide of pre-finals fatalism.

In the pod, the scrawny boy who screams without warning has just consumed one of his interim report cards. At least that's what the other kids told Mrs. McGraw when they came into her room, howling with laughter.

"He got it, looked at it, and ate it," she says, shaking her head in wonder.

Across the hall, in another classroom, a girl named Jesi talks about her wild weekend. She told her parents she was headed for Disney World, but instead she and a friend drove to New Orleans.

"My mom tells me she's not stupid," she says. "Well, she's stupid enough to believe me."

Jesi's teacher—her name is Mrs. LaVassaur, but the kids sometimes call her LaVassaurus—does not hear Jesi say this. Mrs. LaVassaur is worried about one of her other students, a girl in her fifth-period class. This girl's a wonderful kid, struggling against incredible odds. She's the youngest of eight children, and all seven of her brothers and sisters are dropouts. Both parents, too. Still, this girl was doing well. She seemed to have found a way out of the pattern. Then her boyfriend broke up with her, and she fell apart. She let her classes slip; she started talking about suicide and was finally taken to Horizon Hospital, a nearby psychiatric institution. This past Saturday, when she was allowed one four-minute call from the hospital, she called Mrs. LaVassaur. She just wanted to talk to someone she trusted.

Another one of Janet LaVassaur's students recently withdrew from school for a couple months so she could have a baby. This girl's planning to keep the child; her family's going to help. On Saturday, the same day Mrs. LaVassaur got the call from the student at Horizon, she and other teachers from the pod went to a shower for the pregnant girl.

"We bought her a baby monitor," says Mrs. LaVassaur.

The girl's lawyer was at the shower, too. The lawyer who is now pressing the baby's father to acknowledge paternity . . .

So much happens here in the pod. The world happens here. In a day or a week, in the space of a single hour, so many things transpire that it's impossible to keep up. Kids come into the GOALS office crying because their father has beaten them the night before. They come in wanting to talk because they're about to get an abortion and they're scared. They come in, confused and angry and depressed, because they're thinking about suicide and aren't sure who to tell. They come in, not knowing where else to go.

One day a rumor makes its way around the pod. It concerns the girl with the free-fuck necklace. Someone has heard that she's carrying drugs and is supposedly willing to sell them. Mrs. Palmateer locates the girl, searches her, finds a small supply of LSD in her purse. The police are called, and the girl is taken away to the Juvenile Detention Center.

Meanwhile, in her room at the end of the hall, Leah Whitehead has been trying something new with her sixth-period class. In her ongoing struggle to get them to read at least something, Mrs. Whitehead has turned to Zen Buddhism. She has written a Zen expression for them on the blackboard.

chop wood
carry water

She tells them that they need to learn how to exist in the here and now. When a Zen disciple chops wood, she says, he doesn't worry about what he's doing later that afternoon. He pays attention to the strength in his arms. When he carries water, he thinks about the water. That's the kind of concentration she's after in their reading. As they read, she wants them to think about the words printed on the page.

This new approach stuns them into a kind of confused silence. For a few moments, they try it. They pick up their books and read.

"Was that so awful?" she asks.

Half of the class blurts out the same answer.

"Yeah!"

Two boys, seated at opposite sides of the room, return now to their regularly scheduled programming. They start by exchanging Heil Hitler salutes, over and over.

Mrs. Whitehead and the other teachers hold on the best they can. They know GOALS can work. They've seen it. Every year, they ram their heads against the wall for months, never seeming to get anywhere, and then, just when it seems they're past the point of no return, some of the students will make an incredible recovery. It's like one of those sappy inspirational movies where the children in the wheelchairs stand up and walk five minutes before the final credits. Only it really happens. Not with every kid. Not by a long shot. But it happens.

Usually it hits when the teachers least expect it. They'll be standing at the overhead projector, explaining photosynthesis or working through some equation, and suddenly they'll look out into the scattering of faces before them and realize that some of their most mind-bending cases—the ones who should have been written off long ago—are sitting quietly at their desks, pencils out, eyes directed intently toward the screen.

When the teachers repeat these tales of salvation, a glint of almost religious fervor enters their eyes.

"You should have seen this kid a year ago," they say. "He was a monster. He was like a creature from another planet. Now look at him."

The turnaround cases are easy to spot, too, because they're usually the ones who've made good grades and have been granted honor cards and are therefore wearing shorts, even when it's cold. Kids like Bonnie Kaseman, who used to be a queen of the absentees—she once missed close to forty days of class in a single semester—but who now regularly makes honor roll. Kids like Michelle Fletcher, a talented writer who's so smart you wonder how she ever could have needed turning around in the first place.

Still, even with students like these, there's no telling when they'll change their minds and shift into reverse. Lately Michelle Fletcher has been talking about how bored she is. She's been making ominous entries in her class journal.

> *I'm really sick of school. Everyone's changing to the worst. So am I. . . . How can I run about being cheery when all these rules are stopping me? . . . I want to get out of here so fast!!*

THANKSGIVING COMES, AND SOME OF THE GOALS students are asked to write essays on what they're thankful for. Jesi, the girl who took the wild weekend foray to New Orleans, says she's thankful she can control her parents.

CHRISTMAS COMES, AND ONE OF MRS. O'DONNELL'S students—the boy who displayed his DWI scars during show-and-tell—tells her afterward how he spent the holiday getting drunk on beer. For a present, he says, his father gave him a cigarette lighter. His mother gave him lighter fluid.

JANUARY COMES, AND WITH IT THE WEEK OF SEMESTER EXams. Some of the kids in the pod bear down and do well; others fake their way through it, singing the traditional "O Christmas Tree" as they decorate their standardized exam forms with randomly selected answers. The GOALS teachers are already reeling. Michelle Fletcher has just walked in and announced that she's ready to quit. She has a note from her father: *Michelle has permission to withdraw from school effective this date. Thank you.*

That's it. With those two sentences, Michelle can throw it all away. Miss Riel and the other teachers are beside themselves. They tell her they won't sign her withdrawal form. They beg her to reconsider. They point out how hard she's worked over the years. She's so close to graduating, why stop now?

Michelle won't budge. She has locked herself away.

"I've made up my mind," she says. "You can't talk me out of it."

Finally they have no choice but to let her go. Before she leaves, though, they manage to talk her into taking her semester exams. She argues that it's a waste of time. She's just going to Christmas-tree it, she says. But they persuade her that there's no point in wasting an entire semester's worth of work. Reluctantly she takes the exams.

Then she leaves.

As the first semester ends and the second begins, all sorts of familiar faces at Largo High are disappearing.

Jaimee Sheehy is still gone, off at Charter. The witch who lost it on the day of the big pep rally, the one who talked about the devil sucking her blood, is still gone, too. In fact, she is not expected to return; she's headed for another school, perhaps to cast her spells on someone else. Farewells have also been exchanged with the high-spirited Jesi. Not long after she wrote her Thanksgiving essay, she filled out her withdrawal papers—officially she said she was headed for night school—and cleaned out her locker. Before she left, Miss Riel asked her what kind of career she wanted to carve out for herself. Jesi wasn't sure. She'd heard that there's big bucks in cosmetology. Or perhaps, she said, the field of perfume design.

And the girl with the seven brothers and sisters, all of them dropouts before her? The suicidal one who called Mrs. LaVassaur from Horizon? She's gone as well. She piled up a mountain of absences and decided she was tired of school. The scrawny boy who screams without warning? Soon to be gone. He's transferring to a special school where someone might know what to do with him. The girl with the free-fuck necklace? Gone but definitely not forgotten. Diane, the girl who once told Miss Riel that her dream boyfriend was going to support her for the rest of her days? Long gone. Gone for months now at another program at another school. And April? The one whose father sat in that cramped little office on a rainy day, trying so desperately to get through to her? April and her L.A. Gear shoes with the pink and black laces vacated the premises not long ago.

Even Wade Broome—the smiling, joking, relatively easygoing Wade —has dropped out. He did it just before the end of the first semester. He was sick of the teachers. He was sick of everything. So one day, when Mrs. O'Donnell wrote him up again—a few days later, he had already forgotten what for—he slammed the door and walked away for good. He enrolled in night school, made plans to get his GED, found a job at a car wash. But soon he left that, too.

"There's just no future in drying off cars and doing windows," he says, sitting at home with his mother.

Wade's little brother, however, is still here at school. The GOALS teachers can hardly believe it, but it's true. The entire first semester was a washout for Mike, but he's still plugging away. In fact, as this new semester begins, he appears to be making a turnaround. Mike—the angry, explosive, impenetrable Mike Broome—has stepped out from behind the wall. Suddenly he's paying attention, doing his work, controlling the rage. If this radical behavior continues, he'll soon be on the honor roll.

He's not sure, he says. But he thinks he might like to be a teacher.

As Largo plunges into the second half of the year, something else has happened. John Boyd—the gentleman who leads his teammates in solemn prayer, the sweet and soft-voiced guy who's sent Andrea into perpetual meltdown—has gotten himself a gun. He keeps it at home, fully loaded. John doesn't want to use it. But if he is pushed hard enough, he is ready to do whatever's necessary.

PART THREE

THE

HISTORY

LESSON

JOHN BOYD, READY TO DO WHATEVER IT TAKES.

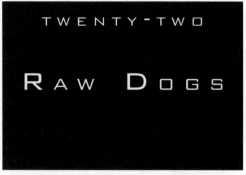

TWENTY-TWO

RAW DOGS

THEY ARE PAST THE TIRESOME formalities, past the introductions and the cautious glances at their opponents' faces and the usual droning explanation of the rules. They have just finished with the first substitution break—no coaching allowed—and are now deep within the thicket of the five-point round. YY sits beside her teammates, her hand poised near the buzzer.

"Abraham Lincoln won the 1860 presidential election by receiving a majority of the popular vote," says the adult up front. "True or false?"

YY hits the buzzer. "False," she says.

The questioner nods—five points for Largo—and moves on. He asks them about ordinates and abscissas, about Verdi and *La Traviata,* about coulombs and electrons and minor arcs and equal circles, about Attila the Hun and Genghis Khan and the oratorios of George F. Handel.

"Name the Christian missionary and theologian," he says, after they have ventured at last into the ten-point round, "whose former name was Saul of Tarsus and whose—"

YY and the buzzer cut him off.

"Paul," she says.

Another nod. "Paul is correct."

It's late on a slightly chilly January afternoon. As the school year rolls from the first semester into the second, beginning the long slide toward graduation night in June, Tampa Bay is enjoying yet another impossibly gorgeous winter day. The sun is just now setting toward the gulf; everything in the landscape—trees, buildings, even the blocks of bumper-to-bumper traffic—seems to be floating in a benevolent amber haze. Still, it is no time for idle reverie. Not now. Not for the Largo High quiz team.

YY and a handful of the school's other top students are huddled at a table in the library of Dunedin High. Around them, huddled at their own tables, hands poised near their own buzzers, are the quiz teams—now officially referred to as "academic teams"—from Dunedin, Seminole, Countryside, Clearwater, and Tarpon Springs high schools.

This convention of brains and reflexes is another match on the quiz team schedule. But it's really just a warm-up, sort of like a regular-season NBA game. Everyone knows that the real action doesn't kick in until the play-offs, or in this case, the district tournament in late February. That's when quiz teams from all fifteen Pinellas high schools will battle it out for the title of county champ.

YY and the rest of Largo's team—Carolyn Hanson, this year's valedictorian; Jennifer Belzel, the salutatorian; plus several other remarkably intelligent students, including Bret Harper, a sleepy-eyed senior otherwise known as Elvis, the King of Suede—are determined to go all the way this year. Largo won last year's tournament, and they are eager to defend their title and establish their own academic dynasty, thereby silencing any doubters who think their first championship was a fluke. Plus, if they lose, there's a good chance it will be at the hands of Seminole High, a thought that makes YY and Carolyn and Elvis and the others want to heave a lung.

"They're from hell," YY says of the Seminole squad. "They're from the depths."

Why do they despise Seminole so much? First, because the Seminole kids are good; the word among the coaches this year is that they're the team to beat. Second, because they know they're good, which makes them unbearably cocky. Third, because they are led by the notorious Timothy "I Challenge" Burrows, their not-so-secret weapon.

Burrows is this pale stick of a kid who possesses one of the most

impressive brains that Pinellas County has seen in years. He's like a walking computer. During a match he can shuffle through vast mountains of
mental files and quickly retrieve almost any obscure fact. But what really
gets to YY and her colleagues is how much of a pain Burrows can be
during a match. He repeatedly interrupts the flow of the competition,
challenging the knowledge of the judges or the accuracy of the answers,
especially when he guesses and is told he's incorrect. It's his right to
challenge; it's in the rules. But Burrows does it so often that the Largo
team would like to throttle him.

"I *totally* hate this kid," YY says during a break in the meet, glaring
across the room. Her teammates try to calm her, but she brushes them off.
"You don't understand. I am getting *so* mad."

She gets even madder when the match is over and Seminole wins with
155 points, leaving Largo to finish in the middle of the pack with only 100.
It is a bitter defeat, made all the worse by what happens a few minutes
later.

YY and the others have just walked out to the parking lot and gotten
into their cars, headed for home, when suddenly two of them find themselves smack in the middle of a quiz team's equivalent of a brawl. It's
some of the Seminole kids. They're in another car and have just pulled in
front of Jen Belzel when a couple of them turn and flip their middle
fingers through the rear window at her.

If YY were here, and not already tooling away in the Y-mobile, she'd
probably jump out and disembowel these creeps. But Jen is different. She
is so innocent, so wonderfully good-hearted, that her mind has trouble
processing what has just occurred. She can't believe it. She doesn't *want* to
believe it.

"Oh my God, Gayle," she says, turning to a teammate sitting beside
her in the car. "What did they do? They didn't really flick us off, did
they?"

In the next few minutes, Jen is repeatedly forced to confront brutal
reality. As the cars head out and drive down the street, the Seminole
kids—Tim Burrows, for the record, is not among them—pull alongside
Jen's car and flick them off again. Over and over. With an abundance of
glee.

"Why'd they do that?" says Jen, still trying to reason it out. "That
wasn't really nice."

The Seminole car pulls beside them again and again. Its occupants are
laughing and pointing; they are using their middle fingers to hound poor

Jen down the road. She flees as best she can, trying to pull away. But they're too fast. Finally, after who knows how long, they come to their turn and leave the Largo girls in peace.

That evening, Jen and Gayle get on the phone and report the incident to the others. There are cries of anger, howls of outrage. Another challenge, that's what this is. Maybe not one specifically described in the rules of academic competition, but definitely a challenge, issued with the impunity of ones who apparently believe themselves unbeatable. YY and Elvis and the rest of the team have their work cut out for them now. They're not just defending their title anymore; they're defending their honor. They must go to that tournament and kick these finger flickers in the teeth. They must humiliate them. Grind them into dust. Drop them, once and for all, onto the dung heap of quiz team history.

IF SOMEONE TOLD JOHN BOYD ABOUT THE QUIZ TEAM INCI- dent, he'd probably just laugh and shake his head. He wouldn't bother trying to tell about the challenge he's been facing lately.

It's these dealers in John's neighborhood. Somewhere along the line, they've gotten it into their heads that John and the rest of the Raw Dogs— Carlos and Jermaine and the other football players who grew up here together—are trying to move against them and clean up the area. The Raw Dogs don't particularly like seeing crack sold on the street, but they also aren't looking for trouble. Still, the dealers are protective of their business, and if they think someone's out to mess with them, they get worked up. For months now, they've been scrapping with the Dogs; they keep coming after them with bottles and sticks, 'fronting them in the street.

John wants no part of it. He doesn't think it makes any sense to go up against these people.

"This ain't really about it," he tells his friends. "This is stupid, right?"

In the neighborhood, things are different for the Raw Dogs. It's not like the fun and games they have at football practice. Because the dealers aren't backing away. In fact, they're starting to carry some heavy firepower. One night not long ago, when the Dogs were walking home from a party, one of the dealers cruised by in a car, making sure they saw the glint of the gun in his hand. One of John's buddies, Marlon, was so mad when he saw it that he stood out in the middle of the street, daring the guy to do something.

"Why don't you shoot, punk?" Marlon yelled. "If you're gonna shoot, then why don't you shoot?"

John and the others tried to get Marlon to calm down. But he wouldn't hear of it.

"No, man," he said, looking toward the gunman. "He's got to shoot me or show me what he knows."

Luckily the guy didn't do anything. But it's only a matter of time. Which is why John has started carrying a little firepower of his own. It's this .32 revolver that John bought at a pawnshop. He got the idea, he says, from a sheriff's deputy who knew what was happening and didn't want John to get hurt.

"I'm not telling you to go out and get a gun and shoot somebody," the deputy told him. "But I'll tell you this, take it however you want: Do whatever you have to do to protect yourself."

So John got himself some protection. He keeps it in a closet in his room or in another closet downstairs. He tucks it in his pants when he walks around the neighborhood. He takes it to parties and other people's houses. He's even taken it to church a couple times.

If people knew, they'd be shocked. John's not the type they'd expect to do something so dangerous. John's a solid guy. Everybody knows that. He's active in his church; during the summer, he does community work with little kids. At school, he's only an average student, not honor roll or anything, but when he stays focused, he does fine. Judith Westfall is one of his biggest fans. She knows how much other kids look up to him. When the tension starts to rise in the halls, she calls him to her office sometimes and asks him to calm people and persuade them to keep their fists to themselves.

When he's not at school, John likes to shoot hoops, mess with the Dogs, flirt on the phone, hang out at the community center. At home, he hears the same standard lectures as any kid. When he heads upstairs to bed or to do his homework, he sometimes actually considers the plea that's taped to his door: *John, please clean your room.* His mom put it there years ago, and he never had the heart to take it down. He likes to look at it and grin. John's dad died when he was four, after a blood clot burst in his head. Even if the man had lived, John doesn't know how close the two of them would have been. John's parents were not married, and after John was born, his father didn't have much to do with him. It was okay, though, because John's mom took good care of him. Today she's a house-keeper for a retirement home in Clearwater. She calls him John-John; she smiles at the mere mention of his name. John has a little brother, but he also has four older sisters, and all of them love to dote on him. He has photos of them taped up in his locker. Whenever he opens it to get a book, there they are, beaming.

Of course, he doesn't breathe a word about the .32 to his mother or anyone else. He doesn't tell Andrea, either, because he doesn't want to alarm her. She and John still aren't a couple or anything; with Sabrina in the picture, the two are still trapped in the shadows. But John knows Andrea well enough to understand how she feels about this stuff. Just a few weeks ago, not long after the lip sync, she was disappointed in him for getting into a big fight outside a McDonald's. The whole thing was stupid. John's not even sure how he got caught up in it. It was a payback against some guys from Seminole who had supposedly jumped a Largo kid. Who knows? Anyway, John and some of his buddies, who happened to be black, ended up in the parking lot of McDonald's, swinging away at the Seminole guys, who happened to be white. When Andrea heard, she was mad. Andrea hates fights, especially ones between black kids and white ones. Half the time, as far as she can tell, there's no real racial tension involved; it's just an excuse for boys to go at it. But anytime blacks and whites mix it up, it seems to her that the blacks get accused of starting it. Why play into people's hands that way? Why feed the stereotypes?

John cares deeply for Andrea, but he doesn't think she completely understands what it's like for him. She lives in a nice neighborhood on a quiet little street with quiet little houses that sit in the shade of big oak trees. Nothing fancy, but nice. And at school, she hangs with an upwardly mobile group of friends. "The good-girl clique," John calls them. For John, things are more complicated. He lives in a public housing project a few miles south of Andrea's neighborhood. It isn't a bad place; in fact, it doesn't look that different from any other subdivision, except for the bits of trash scattered across the grass and the shards of broken glass that lie along the streets, shining in the sun, and the vague sense of weariness that hangs over everything. In the afternoons, children play in the yards, and the adults sit on the porches of their stucco houses, and everyone does their best to keep cool in the Florida sun. Almost all the people who live there have normal jobs and families and bills just like anybody else. But for years, the dealers have been hanging out on the street, selling their goods. Most of them are in their late teens or twenties—John grew up with most of them—but there's always a few young ones hanging on the fringes, waiting their turn. The little wannabes, John calls them.

Time was when John qualified as a little wannabe. When he was in middle school, he was dying to join the dealers and make some quick money. He used to beg the older guys to let him help out.

"Man," he'd say, "when are you going to let me serve for you?"

Things didn't work out like that, though. The way John sees it, God didn't want him to become a dealer. John thinks about God a lot these days. He's involved with Young Life, a Christian group that reaches out to teenagers. It keeps him out of trouble, just like football does. That was the choice he made. Either he was going to be a dealer, or he was going to stick with football and try to use it to get a college scholarship. That's the choice many of the Raw Dogs have made.

The Dogs were formed last year, after they all fell in love with the Spike Lee movie *School Daze*. It's their version of *Heathers*. The picture is about this bunch of guys in a black college fraternity, Gamma Phi Gamma, who are also known as the Gamma Dogs. So John and the others decided they wanted to start their own fraternity. They called themselves the Raw Dogs. One night they initiated each other—again, just like in the movie—by shaving their heads.

That was when the trouble started with the dealers in the neighborhood. To them, the shaved heads were an ominous sign. They thought the Raw Dogs were forming a rival gang, a gang dedicated to kicking the dealers off the corner. John and the others tried to tell them differently, but it didn't work. The dealers started looking for excuses to fight. One night at a dance, one of the Dogs tried to joke with one of them.

"You're looking at an all-conference football player," he told him.

The guy didn't laugh. "You better get your all-conference ass out of the way."

From there it just got worse. The dealers would wait until one or two of the Dogs were alone and then come after them. Not long ago, they ambushed one of John's friends as he got off his school bus, coming after him with bricks and a metal bar. And now they're waving guns.

"We're going to stand our ground," the Dogs have told them.

"You ain't got no ground," the dealers say back. "We'll take you out."

No shots have been fired yet. It's going to happen soon, though; it's in the air. So John keeps the .32 close at hand. He knows it's risky. After all, he's still hoping for that football scholarship to college. And if something happens, he might never make it. He could end up in prison. He could end up wounded or worse. What's he supposed to do, though, call the police and ask for a twenty-four-hour guard? He'd rather get arrested for self-defense than get killed. Plus, it was a cop in the first place who told him how to handle this. So now he's handling it as best he can.

John always keeps the gun loaded. A couple of times he's shot into the woods behind his house, so he'll be ready for how it feels, so he won't be surprised by the kick. At night, he stands with it in front of his bedroom mirror, checking himself out, practicing his determined look. If he ever has to point it at anyone, he doesn't want there to be any doubt that he's willing to use it . . .

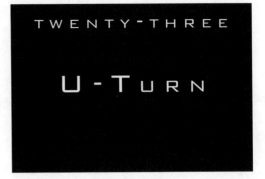

TWENTY-THREE

U-TURN

"Good morning. Our thought for the day is: Some people have a good aim in life, but they never pull the trigger."

The voice of wisdom just won't stop. Even now, after all these months, it's still bombarding the school with one bizarre line after another, always delivered with the same chirpy verve.

A bell has rung, and once more the halls are quiet. Over in A Wing, two teachers shuffle slowly past the lockers. They are on patrol, conducting a hall sweep. Teachers aren't supposed to use that term anymore, not since it proved so volatile during last year's demonstration. But they do anyway.

"Excuse me," one of them says to a spike-haired boy who wanders into their line of sight. "You got a pass?"

"No, I don't," he says, starting to back away. "I'm going to class."

They tell him to hold it. But before they can catch him, he runs in the opposite direction.

"I'm late!" he yells, glancing back at them over his shoulder. "I'm off to class!"

The teachers watch him go, sighing.

They'd rather be in their classrooms, working on their lesson plans or grading papers. It's bad enough that in addition to teaching they're expected to play babysitter and classroom cop and child psychologist and family counselor and surrogate parent. Now they're supposed to be hall monitors as well?

"This is really a waste of time," one of them says. "You know?"

A FEW DOORS DOWN, IN A ROOM AT THE END OF A WING, Mr. Feazell is leading one of his American history classes in a discussion of World War II. He has just begun talking about the Axis powers and their first conquests of Europe when he realizes that in the back of the room there is a boy gently snoring.

"Where's my Walter Mitty?" he says.

That's what Mr. Feazell calls the sleepers.

"Mitty?"

He's speaking loudly, but there's no response. He turns to those seated around the boy.

"Wake him up."

The sleeper is nudged back to consciousness, and Mr. Feazell returns to the war. He questions them about the Atlantic Charter and the Maginot Line and the Battle of Britain. He asks them to tell him what they know about Neville Chamberlain, the British prime minister who tried to negotiate with Hitler.

"Who was Chamberlain?" he says. "What did he say he wanted?"

Someone raises a hand. "Peace in our time. Policy of appeasement."

What about Hitler? says Mr. Feazell. Which country was it that joined Hitler in a nonaggression pact?

Another raised hand. "Russia."

James Feazell nods. After teaching at Largo High for twenty years, he still loves it. He has shaped so many young lives by now. Sam Ford, one of Largo's health teachers, was once among his students. So was Rudy Falana, one of the assistant principals at Clearwater High. All of them have come under the spell of Mr. Feazell, a showman who leads his classes with humor, common sense, and unabashed affection for his students.

"I'm the salt man," he tells them. "I can't make you drink, but I can make you thirsty."

One of the first black teachers at Largo High, Mr. Feazell is a remarkably nurturing figure. For years now he has spent nearly every spare moment working with African-American kids, coaching them on youth football and baseball teams, tutoring them at community centers, finding them jobs as they get older, helping them apply for scholarships and financial aid when they are ready to go to college. More than anything else, though, he listens to them. By the time they reach high school, many students—particularly black students—feel alienated from the system. It's hard for them to confide in an adult, especially since there are no black administrators at Largo. So they come to Mr. Feazell and tell him things they tell no one else. The stories they share can be appalling. Stories about drugs, pregnancy, abuse, a thousand forms of neglect. So many of them are suffering from emotional starvation. So many feel the same aching void.

"When you're dealing with a kid with those kinds of problems," Mr. Feazell says, "it's hard to start talking about colonialism in America."

One of the things he hears from black students—one of the things he sees with his own eyes, over and over—is how the system grinds them down. Usually it starts to hit them around third or fourth grade. It's probably not conscious. But beneath the surface, in the words that are spoken and the looks that are exchanged, runs a widespread expectation that African-American students will fail. Not just among the teachers and administrators, but among the students themselves. By high school, he says, these attitudes are so entrenched that many black kids are suspicious of anyone who does well in school.

"Right now," he says, "I don't think it's an acceptable thing among the black students at Largo High School that you should want to excel."

That's why Andrea Taylor is such an important role model. Mr. Feazell can't believe how strong Andrea's been, carrying the load all these years. When she was in ninth grade, eight or nine other black students in her class had just as much potential. But now, Mr. Feazell says, those others are gone; they all dropped out. Not Andrea. She's still doing great. She knocked down the walls at Homecoming—seeing her win the crown was the highlight of the year as far as Mr. Feazell is concerned—and now she's getting ready to go on to better things at college. Of course, she's had to endure other kids hinting that she's sold out and turned white.

"I know they're just kidding," Andrea says, taking her usual positive attitude. She smiles nervously. "I think. I hope."

Mr. Feazell doesn't know about the frustrated romance between Andrea and John Boyd. He also doesn't know about John's .32. But he is aware that this is a perilous time for that young man. John's another one of his favorite kids. Mr. Feazell's been looking out for him since John was seven. He coached him in youth football when John was a stubby fourth grader; now, all these years later, he's a junior, taking Mr. Feazell's seventh-period American history class.

John has so much potential. He could go so far. But in the past couple years, he's slipped. His grades have dropped; not long ago he wound up in that fight outside the McDonald's. He's walking on the edge, and if he makes a mistake, he could fall. It's easy for that to happen at this age, even for a good kid like John. One wrong step, and he could fall forever.

THE TEACHERS IN THE POD ARE STILL IN AWE OF THE MIRA-cle.

They're not sure how it happened. They don't know if it will last. But Mike Broome has made a sudden reversal. Somehow, he has become this fantastic kid who can't wait for class to begin.

"What are we going to do today?" he says eagerly as he walks into his classrooms.

Independent witnesses confirm that Mike actually smiles these days. He laughs. He jokes. He finishes his classwork, then asks for more. He is clearly the same boy, because he still wears the FTW jeans and the Metallica shirt that shows a sword coming out of a toilet, accompanied by the slogan "Metal up your ass." But now, when he's not busy, he offers to clean the blackboard. Now, when he asks for a pass to get a folder, he stuns his teachers by coming right back, folder in hand. These things are nothing, however, when compared to the historic events of Monday, January 29.

"I want to be a teacher," he tells Mrs. O'Donnell, talking with her that morning at her desk.

"Oh," she says, doing her best not to let her jaw hit the floor. "Oh." She's staring at him. She's trying to think of what to say.

"That's . . ."

She's almost too stunned to finish the sentence.

". . . great. I hear you're good with young kids."

This is true. For months, she and Mike's other teachers have clung to the memory of how sweet he was on the day when he held that baby who was visiting the pod. Now Mike tells Mrs. O'Donnell how much he loves children. During the summer, he says, he works with them at a public pool, teaching them how to swim. Swimming, he says, really starting to open up now, is one of his favorite things in the world. Especially the butterfly stroke.

He goes on and on like that, bubbling. Mrs. O'Donnell just keeps looking at him, not sure she believes what she's hearing. This is too good to be true. It's like Mike's been snatched by one of those alien seedpods and been replaced by an imposter with the same face and name. It's almost scary.

What accounts for the change?? No one can say for sure. Maybe Mike just decided it was time to get serious. That happens sometimes with GOALS kids; they'll resist their teachers' efforts for years, then suddenly something clicks in their heads—who knows what does it—and they make a U-turn and change for the better almost overnight. Perhaps Mike's been thinking about what it's been like for his older brother Wade since he dropped out at the end of last semester. Wade's already had a couple jobs. For a while he was washing dishes at a restaurant, but they fired him because he was going to night school—he still plans to get his GED—and couldn't work on Monday and Wednesday evenings. At least that's the way Wade tells it. Then he was hired as a dishwasher at a motel. But they got rid of him there, too, after he left early one day because he was violently ill.

Mike's still talking to the kids at school about it. What happened to Wade wasn't fair, he says.

"He started throwing up at work," he explains to a girl in one of his classes, "and they *fired* him."

The whole thing seems to have made an impression on Mike. If nothing else, it has shown him that the teachers aren't making it up when they talk about how tough it is out in the world. Especially if you're just a kid and don't have a diploma.

Mike's mother has lit a fire under him as well, informing him that she has run out of patience and sympathy. If he doesn't straighten up, she has promised to make good on her long-standing threat to kick him out and send him to north Florida to stay with his father, a thought that does not appeal to Mike. He may long for more attention from his father, but he doesn't want to live with him.

So now he's trying to pull it together at Largo. He's doing particularly well in Ms. DiLello's general math class. He likes the subject; he likes her. Right now, he's getting an A in her class. He plows through the assignments like a machine; Ms. DiLello could double the work, and he'd be happy. He's looking ahead now, too, thinking about the future. One day he tells her that next year he might take pre-algebra. On another morning he points to a statue on her desk—it's one of those little figures in a cap and gown, holding a diploma—and announces to the class that someday he'll be holding a diploma, too.

One of the other kids snickers.

"Why are you laughing?" says Ms. DiLello.

The kid looks at Mike. "Because he's never going to get one of those."

Ms. DiLello gives this jerk one of her intense stares.

"Yes, he is."

Outside, in the halls, Mike asks her if she really thinks he can do it. Yes, she tells him. She believes he will pick up a diploma someday.

He smiles. "Yeah. I will get one."

It's a good time all around the pod. Despite all of the kids who dropped before, a new semester is always a chance to start over. Plus, plenty of new kids have been brought in to fill the empty desks. For instance, there's this new girl named Lisa who is determined to get an education but has some hurdles to overcome.

"I'm a little embarrassed about being in here," she told Mrs. O'Donnell on the first day, as she sat among a bunch of freshmen and sophomores.

"Why?"

"Because I'm 17."

"That's okay. Nobody in here knows how old you are."

"I'm a dropout."

"No, you're not. You're back in school."

Turns out that Lisa quit a couple of years ago, in ninth grade, because one of her teachers supposedly kept coming on to her. He'd ask her to come up to his desk, she says, and then make some excuse for her to lean over so he could look down her blouse. But when she complained, she says, no one believed her. So she quit. While she was out of school, she was living on her own, supporting herself with different jobs. She painted houses, she laid carpet, she even babysat for exotic dancers. That's the term Lisa prefers.

"Not strippers," she says. "Exotic dancers."

She knew several of them who had kids and needed someone to watch them at night while they worked. She sat with the kids in this one house. Some nights she'd work from six in the evening until five in the morning. She didn't care, she says. These women were nice. Plus, as long as they paid her on time . . .

TWENTY-FOUR

NEXT TO PERFECT

THE LETTER ARRIVES AT THE house one day like a slightly garbled message from the other side. It is filled with misspellings and grammatical fumblings, which come as no surprise from one who has been such a stranger to the concept of sitting in class.

Jaimee Sheehy is writing her mother again, telling her how much she hates her doctor at Charter Hospital and how much she longs to come home. The pages of the letter are populated with dozens of hearts, drawn in the margins and all over the last page. The rest is one long stream. No paragraphs, no breaks, just words flowing together through Jaimee's declarations of love, her promises of improvement, her pleas for understanding. She can't stand it any longer at Charter, she says. She needs to be with her mom, she says. She needs her mother at her side.

Laura Sheehy wants to believe it. But she's still not sure she can trust her daughter, not after that terrible night when Jaimee and the other girl from the pod disappeared. Ever since then, Jaimee has been inside the tightly controlled cocoon of Charter. The staff there tells her when she gets up, when she goes to bed, when she can use the phone, whether she can leave the unit. They push her to think about what's happened to her life. They talk to her in one-on-one sessions, in group sessions with other kids and their parents. Occasionally they give her a pass and let her mother take her out somewhere.

It seems to be working. Jaimee seems calmer, more willing to talk honestly. She admits she was out of control. She says that she was selfish, that she chose the wrong people to hang out with, that she lied because she felt trapped. But she's better now, she says, and ready to come home. She says she'll make good grades, do chores around the house, pick better friends, work hard to make something of her life. All she needs is a chance to prove it. She can do it, she says, if only her mother will get her out.

The doctor thinks it's too soon. Jaimee's not ready yet, he says. To remove her from Charter's structured environment would be a mistake.

Ms. Sheehy doesn't know what to think. She misses Jaimee so much. She reads over the letter, wondering when she'll be able to believe her daughter's promises.

DOWN IN AB-12, IN THE CONTROLLED CHAOS THAT SERVES as the newspaper office, YY and Karin Upmeyer and the rest of the elder newspaper rats are starting to feel the effects of senioritis. They're snapping rubber bands on one another's arms, locking one another in the closet, declaring noogie wars, dropping onto the tables and wailing about deadlines, homework and how they can't wait until graduation. One day, as YY sits trying to finish another calculus assignment, Karin sneaks up behind her, snatches the paper away and hides it. As she watches YY search the room, Karin shakes her head.

"I'm sick of her doing her dumb calculus," she mutters. "Not only does she do it, she does it out loud."

Karin is joking, but beneath her smile there's an edge. Sometimes she feels so inferior when she sees YY and Amy huddled over their calc homework. Karin feels dumb compared to them and Meridith. She's quick enough—she fires off the most clever one-liners of any of the Heathers—but in class she feels like she's always muddling through. YY and Amy are already mastering college-level calculus, Meridith's taking analytical geometry, and yet here's old Karin, still suffering through Algebra II. She'll probably be in that class for the rest of her life.

"I'm there forever," she says.

Karin tries hard. She stays after school for extra help, she goes to Amy for tutoring. But she just can't get past this math thing. She received a D in the subject last semester, and she's not doing any better this time around. Her parents, better known as Ernst and Gene, are not going to be happy. Especially her mom. When Karin received the D, the woman was taken aback.

"We don't get D's," she said.

"Well, Mom," said Karin, "I got a D."

Sometimes she feels as though she must be a major disappointment to her mother and father. It seems like she just keeps messing up, letting them down, over and over. Not just when it comes to math, either. Karin still shudders when she thinks back to the time early in her junior year when her parents discovered that she had snuck her boyfriend into her bedroom.

That night, when it happened, Karin and this boy weren't engaged in any carnal act. They'd had a fight earlier that day, and though they did neck a little, they were mostly talking, patching things up between them. But still, it was after midnight and Karin was in a T-shirt, and the boyfriend had climbed in through the window. He was lying there next to her in bed, no shoes, no socks, not even a shirt, just a pair of shorts, when suddenly Rembrandt, the family dog, heard something in another part of the house and began barking. To this day Karin does not know what set Rembrandt off. But that night, she found herself quietly sending him telepathic messages, reminding this mutt that she was the one who fed him and bathed him, and asking him to please be quiet, just this once please, before her parents woke up. The messages apparently did not get through, because Rembrandt kept barking until Karin's mom and dad got out of bed and started searching the house to find out what was wrong. Soon Karin heard them walking down the hall toward her room.

The boyfriend jumped out of bed and bounded into the closet, sliding the door shut with a bang. He made so much noise, bumping against the wall and clattering the hangers, that there was no way it could have gone unheard. A second or two later, Karin's mother and father were knocking at the door to the bedroom.

"Oh my God," said Karin.

The door was locked, so she had to get up and let them in, which only made them more suspicious, since she never locks her door. Karin stood there while the two of them looked around. Her father checked the window and noticed that the screen had been removed and was lying on the floor.

"Something's not right here," he said.

He opened the closet door, and there was the boyfriend, crouched down beside Karin's laundry basket.

It was a terrible moment. Karin is crazy about her father. She will tell you that he is the coolest, funniest, most understanding man in the world. But at that instant, when she saw the disappointment clouding his face, she felt like dying.

"Dad," she told him, "we weren't having sex."

Her father did not look relieved. In fact, he looked more upset than Karin had ever seen him. But he did not lose his temper, even as he turned to the boyfriend.

"I think it's time you leave," he said quietly.

The boy got dressed and quickly made his escape, never to show his face before her parents again. Karin's mother cried. Her father just sat there with a horrified expression. Somehow, though, the family survived the incident. Karin was grounded for months—she couldn't go to Homecoming that year—and was forced to live with her guilt for even longer. She hated hurting her parents that way, hated watching as all their trust evaporated into nothing.

Things are better now. Even though the memory of that night still lingers, Karin and her folks have moved on. Not long ago, her father even got a card for the boyfriend on his birthday and had Karin give it to him, to let the poor guy know there were no hard feelings. Talk about thoughtful. How many other fathers would go out of their way to wish happy birthday to the boy caught in bed with their daughter?

That's Ernst all the way. He may be an executive for Florida Power, one of the biggest utilities in the state, but he's got to be the most easygoing power company exec who ever walked the planet. He's laid-back, he's reasonable, he has this incredible sense of humor. He's the one who gave Karin that wild booming laugh. In fact, Karin's just like him. If she'd been a boy, she says, her parents would have named her after him. She would have been the latest in a long line of Ernsts.

"I would have been named Ernst Arnold Upmeyer the Fourth," she says. "Can you believe that? I would have had *no* social life."

Karin's dad is heavily into music. At home, he's always driving his wife and daughters crazy, pumping up the volume on the stereo so he can hear his operas and his symphonies and his show tunes. Actually, the whole family's into music; Karin and her sister both play the piano, and their mother's a mezzo soprano who still performs in public and who teaches music at a nearby private school. Even their pets appreciate a good melody. They have this parrot named Captain Morgan, a big blue-fronted

Amazon, who sits on his perch in the family room and sings along with the opera records. When Karin's dad puts on Pavarotti, Captain Morgan chimes in, holding the high notes with a bizarre vibrato. People who've never heard him do it before just stand there, staring.

"Is that the bird?" they say.

Without music, there may have never been an Upmeyer family. When Ernst and Gene were first dating, back in the fifties, one of the qualities she admired in him—one of the things that set him above the crowded field of her other suitors—was his love of music. Gene was a stunningly beautiful young woman, but she was also a gifted singer; in those days, she was singing with the opera company in Charlotte. Time and again, she has told her daughters that she was originally drawn to their father because he appreciated the music and valued her for more than just her looks. A bona fide Southern belle, Gene was quite the prize. Elegant, serene, keenly attuned to all the social graces, she was raised in a conservative Baptist home in Charleston, where she eventually won the local beauty pageant. From there she went on to become Miss South Carolina and then a contestant in the Miss America Pageant, where her singing won the talent competition. She was so striking, they asked her back the next year to sing in the pageant.

All these years later, Gene is still gorgeous. You can still picture her up there on the stage, gliding down the runway and waving at the judges. Karin has always been in awe of her. When she was little, she used to stare at the old pageant photos. Her mother still has her crowns and the long white gloves she wore in those days, and sometimes Karin would take them out of the drawer and put them on and stand in front of the mirror. imagining what it must have felt like to be such a star. That's how Karin thought of her mother. To her, Gene was a celebrity.

Of course, celebrities aren't always easy to live with. Karin just wishes things weren't so complicated with her mom. She knows Gene loves her, but they seem to exist on different wavelengths. Like with their senses of humor. The woman does know how to laugh—sometimes Karin gets her going so hard her eyes tear up—but in general she's just not the type to cut loose with a roaring guffaw. At heart, Gene is still the Southern belle. She is so prim and proper, so imbued with an old-fashioned sense of decorum, that it's hard to get through to her. In the mornings, Karin will crack up over something in the comics, usually "The Far Side," and she'll show the strip to her mother, and the woman will just stand there with a puzzled look on her face.

"I don't get it," she says. "Why is that funny?"

Where they really clash, however, is over this business about Karin supposedly being fat. For years now, her mom has seemed determined to put her on a diet. It started when Karin was still a little girl. Her mother wouldn't come out and say she thought Karin was fat. She'd let her know in other ways. Karin would ask for a tunafish sandwich, and her mom would serve her plain tuna. No mayo, no relish, no bread, just a naked chunk of fish on a leaf of lettuce.

"Here," she'd say, "eat this."

Now that Karin's older, the struggle has moved a little more into the open. Her mother is never cruel; she's too nice for that. Still, she makes these comments that drive Karin up the wall. Things like, "That skirt looks a little tight, Karin."

Karin deals with it as best she can. She tries to keep it in perspective, tries not to get paranoid about her waistline. She reminds herself that she's only a little overweight. But when she gazes into the mirror, it's hard not to compare herself to her mother, who all these years after the beauty pageants remains slender and stunning. The woman is perfect.

Sometimes it seems as though Karin is surrounded by perfect people, as though she's constantly in the shadow of someone who's either prettier than her or thinner than her or smarter than her or just more disciplined than her. It's as though she's in a never-ending pageant and always being named the second or third runner-up. She continually feels like she's being compared and coming up short. Especially when it comes to school, where she hangs out with the likes of Amy and Meridith and YY. How could she possibly hold her own against them? She can't even deal with algebra. That's where it really hits her, where she is forced to consider the fact that maybe she's not that smart or that good or that special. In Ms. Fish's seventh-period.

Day after day, Karin sits in that class—she sits right in front of Bret Harper, the kid on the quiz team, the one known as Elvis—and listens to Ms. Fish talk on and on about synthetic division and inverse variation and negative reciprocals. She barely understands a word of it.

"Where are we? Wait," she says, frantically trying to keep up. "Please."

Karin might have a chance if only she weren't stuck in the middle of the pack, jammed into crowded rooms like this one. That's the problem. If she were a wonderful student like YY and the others, she'd be in those honor courses, where the classes are usually kept to a reasonable size. And if she were a failing student, she'd probably be down in the pod, where the classes are also small and where individualized attention is always the specialty of the day. But Karin doesn't fit either category. She's average, so she's forced to fight for air inside regular classes, where the rest of teen humanity is assigned. Sometimes, there are more than thirty-five kids jammed into one room, which means that the teacher hardly has time to take the roll, much less answer individual questions. In those classes, it's survival of the fittest.

Lots of times, if Karin has trouble understanding something, she doesn't even bother raising her hand. What's the point? She knows what happens to kids who are lost and try to take up too much class time with questions.

"If you don't get it," some teachers say, "we'll just have to move on."

So Karin lets it go and hopes for the best. These days, about all she thinks about is whether she'll make it into a decent college. YY and Amy and Meridith have nothing to worry about. The three of them have already been accepted to the University of Florida. But then, they had the killer SAT scores. Not Karin.

She can't believe it. She has slaved away in school for more than ten years now. She has learned to read and write, suffered through fractions and state capitals and the definition of the GNP, endured the whims of who knows how many teachers, assistant principals, crossing guards, and hall monitors. But none of that matters. What matters, as far as she can tell, is whether or not she can hit somewhere above 1,000 on her combined SAT score.

"Schools say, 'Hey, if you don't get 1,000 or 1,050, too bad,' " says Karin. "They don't even look at you."

Many college admissions officers would argue that this is not true, that the weight supposedly given to the SAT has been exaggerated over the years. The first thing they look for in an application from a high school student, they insist, is that person's overall grades. But a grade point average, as any teenager can tell you, is not the same as a standardized test score. A GPA is built up gradually, through hundreds of assignments and papers and exams tackled over a period of four years. The SAT score, which also counts for a great deal with most admissions officers, is earned in a single, unforgiving moment of truth.

The amount of pressure attached to that moment can be almost unbearable. The way students see it, it's like this: Unless your GPA is already dazzling enough to get you into your college of choice, it's absolutely crucial that you soar on the SAT. If you can't come up with enough correct answers on this one test, on this one day, some computer in New Jersey—the computer that reads the marks you make with your regulation number-two pencil—will see to it that you are sent a little form consigning you to oblivion. The computer doesn't care if you were having a bad day when you took the exam. It doesn't care if you're a good person or a creative person or even a genius who just happens to lapse into a cold sweat during tests. It doesn't care if you were raised in a house or a neighborhood that did not fit the white-bread profile that so many people believe so many of the test questions presume. It does not care, period. It's a computer.

All of education, then, is reduced to one ridiculous task. No matter what else they do, many kids believe they must beat the computer.

Karin and countless other students will tell you it's insane. But if they want to go to college, they don't have much choice. So they take the test several times, just to learn more about the enemy and how it operates. They buy books filled with vocabulary lists and sample questions and all sorts of advice on what to eat before the test and how to relax during the test and what to do if their brains go blank at the very instant they open the test. If their parents have the cash, they even enroll in special courses —some of which cost hundreds of dollars—to help them get through the ordeal.

Karin has tried all that. She has studied the vocabulary lists. She has taken one of the special tutoring courses. But still, she's not cutting it. She has taken the SAT three times now, and the best she's managed to come up with is a score of 930.

Sorry.

Now she is waiting to see if any school will overlook her score and her GPA, which isn't spectacular either, and take her anyway. She has written to several colleges, but the one she's really hoping for is Florida State University. Her grandmother went to FSU, and she knows how much it would mean to her parents if she made it in, too. She doesn't want to disappoint them again. She doesn't want to make them think they've raised some pathetic failure. She's trying not to panic, but the waiting is killing her. Weeks are going by, her senior year is drawing to a close, and still she hasn't heard from FSU's admission office. She comes home every day and stands there in the front hallway, searching through the letters and postcards that have been dropped through the mail slot. But there's no word yet.

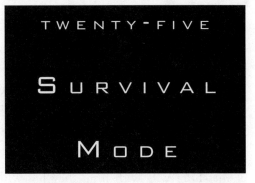

TWENTY-FIVE

SURVIVAL

MODE

"SHUT UP, YOU DUMB BRAKES."

YY, resplendent in her fluorescent green sunglasses, sits at the helm of the Y-mobile. She is trying to ignore the persistent squealing coming from under her car.

"They sound real good," says one of the girls in the backseat.

YY lets the sarcasm pass. "I think I've run out of brake fluid or something queer like that," she says.

Deep into another amber January afternoon, she and several of her academic team colleagues are headed for another quiz match. Alas, the Seminole squad will not be among today's competitors. But with the county tournament only a few weeks away, the Largo kids are gearing up to defend their title and wreak vengeance upon the finger flickers who hounded poor Jen Belzel. They are also longing, more than ever, to muzzle Timothy "I Challenge" Burrows.

As it turns out, YY and Jen are not the only ones who want to silence Burrows. A guy on the team from Clearwater High has confessed to YY that he and his compadres find Tim just as irritating as the Largo kids do. Together they are forming an anti-Burrows sect; already there are whispers of visiting his house one night and rolling it with toilet paper.

"He's *so* clueless," says one of the Largo students.

Burrows is not the first quiz kid in history to generate such hostility. A couple of years ago, there was a prodigy at nearby Countryside High who drove the other academic teams so crazy that some of them finally struck back with psychological warfare. It was the old honey trap; instead of matching wits with him, they hot-wired his hormones. According to the version now circulating through academic circles, this boy had a thing for a girl on the Pinellas Park High team. He thought she was a babe, and others knew it. So just before the final round of the country tournament, the girl was persuaded to walk up to him and stuff a piece of paper in his pocket. On this paper was a phone number, allegedly hers.

"Why don't you call me?" she told him, presumably with her most devastating smile.

The ploy worked beautifully, or so the story goes. The wizard went into instant meltdown, and another team won the title.

So far, no one appears to be setting any honey traps for Burrows. The fact is, YY and the others should be grateful to the kid for the extra degree of intensity he brings to the contest. Every competitor needs an archrival, someone to get the juices flowing. Where would Batman be without the Joker? Timothy Burrows has given YY and Carolyn and Elvis and the rest of the gang another reason to spring out of bed in the morning.

Burrows, as it happens, has no idea that he figures so prominently in the imaginations of the Largo kids; he's unaware that he's been trans-formed, in their minds, into a diabolical adversary. Much later, when he is informed of how YY and the others felt, Tim—who turns out to be a well-spoken, personable young man—seems quietly amused. The funny thing, he says, is that he never thought much about the Largo team at all. He never felt, he says, that they were good enough to worry about.

Touché.

YY and the other kids, of course, would take issue with that view-point. They don't deny that Burrows is talented. Still, in these weeks before the tournament, they believe they have the brainpower to take him on. And maybe they do. Their heaviest hitter is probably Carolyn Hanson, the sweet and utterly serious girl who was born to be a valedictorian. Carolyn is the quintessential straight arrow. She claims, not very convinc-ingly, that in her spare time she likes to "just act really wild." Her GPA is somewhere over 4.28, on a 4.0 scale. (Some honor classes, in deference to the special difficulty of their subject matter, are "weighted," which means they can be used to add extra points to grade averages.) Like most valedictorians, Carolyn downplays the academic competition for the number one spot in the school. Now that she's locked up the title, she tries to assume a laid-back attitude; she alleges that it wouldn't particularly bother her if she ever received anything less than a perfect grade. YY, however, still talks about the six-week period last year when Carolyn got a B and nearly lost it until she pulled it back up to an A in time for the semester grade, which is what affects the GPA.

"She can't get a B," says YY, "or she'll be destroyed."

A couple of years ago, when Carolyn took a standardized aptitude test given to high school sophomores nationwide—the ASVAB—she received a bit of a blow.

"They told her she wasn't college material," remembers YY.

So much for standardized tests.

The Largo team also has Jennifer Horner, a terrific junior kid who's bearing down like a cruise missile on next year's valedictorian slot, and Trina Kavula, a soft-spoken sophomore who's about to be named one of the top science and engineering students in the United States because of this little project she's been working on, *Electroosmotic Irrigation: Part One of a Three-Year Study.* In case that title conjures some image of Trina as a pimply geek, let the record show that she's a charming girl with long blond hair and a sly sense of humor who, like so many other kids, listens to the Power Pig, a local radio station.

Still, there's no question that YY hangs closer to the edge than anyone in this crew. Today, only a few minutes after hearing her wonder about the Y-mobile's brake fluid, Trina, Carolyn, and Jennifer Horner are holding their breath in the backseat as YY demonstrates the finer points of kamikaze driving. Heading out of the school parking lot, on their way to the quiz match, she cranks up the stereo and peels down the street.

"Number one rule in my car," she says, speaking loudly over the music. "Don't complain about the speed I'm traveling at."

The girls in the back appear too frightened to complain about anything. YY's right foot is glued to the accelerator; her long brown hair is swirling in the wind of her open window. She zips from lane to lane. She yells at a pedestrian who moves out of her way too slowly.

"This is what sidewalks are for, dork!"

All the while, she's flipping channels on the radio. For a moment she lands on a heavy-metal station and pauses to sing along with a song by Mötley Crüe called "Wild Side." Then she glances in her mirror and catches the poisonous look Carolyn and the others are giving her.

"So you guys aren't, like, Mötley Crüe fans, huh?"

They make it to the match safely—they take second place this time—but none of it's as memorable as the ride over. YY is the token wild child of the Largo squad. Perhaps the only member of the team who even comes close to YY's more extremist sensibilities is Elvis, the King of Suede. Poor Bret Harper. No matter what he does, he can't shake the nickname. He's had it since that fateful day, earlier this quiz season, when he stumbled during one of the matches.

Up at the lectern, the questioner had just asked for the identity of the King of Swing. A couple kids, including YY, were reaching for the buzzer, but Bret beat them to it. Something inside him, perhaps some deep-rooted survival instinct, caused him to pause for a moment and ask the others if they wanted to take it. But since this one was so easy—doesn't everybody know that the King of Swing was Benny Goodman?—they told him to go ahead. And so he blurted out the two words that would haunt him for so long.

"Elvis Presley!"

The audience erupted. Bret looked around, confused.

"Why is everybody laughing?"

YY and the other Largo kids were not among the amused. In fact, they were staring at him as if he were a war criminal. They were slicing and dicing him with the ginsu knives of their eyes. Scrambling for his honor, Bret quickly tried to account for the blunder. He said he'd misheard. He thought the questioner had said King of Suede. Not Swing, *Suede*.

This won him no sympathy.

"*Stooge*," the others hissed. "You are *so* stupid."

Even now, months later, the stigma lingers. He still fends off the insults and ridicule, all stemming from that one humiliating moment.

"It was an *honest* mistake," he says, for the umpteenth time.

But no one cares. For the rest of Bret's days, or for at least as long as anyone remembers, he will be the King of Suede. Or, when his persecutors are feeling more charitable, the King of Rock 'n' Roll. Or sometimes just the King.

Perhaps it's appropriate, then, that Bret was the one who supplied YY with a ticket to the recent Rolling Stones concert at Tampa Stadium. The two of them weren't on a date or anything, but by the end of the show, YY did find herself in a budding romance with a college guy who went with them. The relationship didn't last long, though. Apparently this boy likes his girlfriends to be a bit more subdued; YY's personality was too much for him to handle.

"You're really major," he told her.

Also, he said he didn't like the idea of hanging out with Karin and Amy and Meridith and all of YY's other high school friends. In a classic male-type power move, he pushed her to choose between him and her girlfriends. YY told him to forget it. Say what you want, but the girl is not a traitor to her pals.

Truth is, things have been going okay for YY. Turns out she won that PRIDE writing award Mrs. Hay wanted her to enter. YY thinks it was her divorce piece that helped her clinch it. Still, she hasn't shown it to her parents. She's not sure how they'd feel if they read it.

"It's my mom's birthday today," she tells some of her friends. "Guess how old she is."

"Forty?"

"Higher."

"Fifty?"

"Almost. She's forty-seven. Four. Seven. She's ancient."

YY and Helen have been getting along well. Lately, in fact, YY has stopped griping about their dispute over her future career. Now that the stressed-out sweepstakes is entering its final and most intensive stages, YY has retreated into a protective shell. She's focusing on the essentials, such as making it through these last months of exams and papers, and forcing herself not to worry about any problems that don't need to be dealt with right now. She's rationing her emotional energy, flipping into survival mode. She doesn't have time to worry about anything else; she barely has time to think about anything else. The career crisis will just have to stay on hold.

JOHN BOYD SITS IN CLASS, TRYING NOT TO THINK ABOUT THE gun in his locker. But he can't help thinking about it. Today is the day. He can feel it.

Last night, in the neighborhood, there was another bad moment with the dealers. John was on his front porch, and a bunch of them were gathered outside on the street, like they all wanted a piece of him. One of them had a gun, and he stood there holding it in the soft glow of the streetlight, just staring at John. That was the signal. That was how they let him know they were coming for him. He thinks they'll be waiting when he gets off the school bus. They've jumped him at the bus stop before, and there's no reason to think they won't try it there again. Only who knows how far they'll take it this time?

Which is why John has brought the .32 to school this morning. When he steps off that bus, he has to have it with him. Still, he knows he's taking a terrible chance. If Ms. Westfall or someone else finds out, he can forget college and his football scholarship and the rest of that; should he be caught, he'll be arrested and taken to court, plus he'll be automatically expelled. No excuses will save him, either. Guns have always been forbidden at school, but never more so than now. It's because of the shooting at Pinellas Park High, one of the neighboring schools. A couple years ago, two boys brought handguns onto the Pinellas Park campus; when school officials confronted them, one of the boys opened fire, and he ended up killing one assistant principal and seriously wounding another.

The effects of the shooting were felt across the county, rippling through every school. It was particularly traumatic at Largo High. Before he was transferred to Pinellas Park, Richard Allen, the administrator who was killed, worked here on this campus for years; many people on the faculty knew him well. And Nancy Blackwelder, the assistant principal who was wounded, happens to be married to Sonny Blackwelder, one of Largo's phys ed teachers. The dangers of guns, in other words, are all too real to the Largo faculty.

The trouble is, that's exactly John's problem. He, too, knows how frightening guns can be; considering what's been happening in his neighborhood, he probably knows it better than most of the teachers. That's why he does not want to be unarmed when he gets off the bus. The way he sees it, he didn't have any choice but to bring the .32. He can't think about what Andrea or his other friends would say. He can't worry about approval. He has to be ready.

He has done his best to play it safe, though. He has wrapped the gun in a pillowcase, then placed it inside an empty cologne box—a box for the same cologne that had so bewitched Andrea at the Homecoming dance— and stored it inside his locker, where it stays all day.

Except for when it falls out in front of Ms. Westfall.

It's in the middle of a class period. The halls are empty, and John's at the locker, getting a book, when he accidentally knocks the box to the ground. It opens, but the pillowcase does not unfold. The gun is still covered, but just barely. John's reaching for it when he realizes that at that very moment fate has chosen to send his principal strolling by.

Picking up the pillowcase, he tries to smile at her.

"Hi," he says, his heart pounding. "How you doin'?"

Ms. Westfall smiles back. She likes John. She trusts him. He's one of her favorite students. And since she has not seen the outline of the metal under the cloth, she keeps walking.

TWENTY-SIX

BOOK

LEARNING

THE BUS PULLS OUT OF THE school parking lot and heads south on Missouri Avenue. John rides near the back, waiting for his stop.

So far he has been lucky. Despite the close call with Ms. Westfall, he managed to make it through the day without anyone finding out about the gun. Not even the other Raw Dogs knew he'd brought it. In fact, two of them are with him now on the bus, unaware that he is armed. The .32 is still inside the cologne box, tucked into a book bag. A few minutes later, though, when it's almost time to get off, he quietly takes it out of the box and the bag and tucks it into the waist of his pants.

John sits there, discreetly covering the gun with his books. He stares out the window, watching the rows of houses whip past. He's so sick of thinking about this. Whatever's going to happen, he wants to get it over with. Just let it end, once and for all.

THEY'RE READY FOR HIM WHEN the bus pulls up.

John steps off with one of the other

Dogs, a boy who lives right there at the corner. The two of them look over and see the dealers standing in the street. There's a bunch of them, maybe eight or nine altogether.

The other Dog asks John if he wants to come into the house, where he'll be safe. But John doesn't want to go inside. He's done hiding.

"Giddy-up," asks his friend, "what you going to do?"

"I'm going home, man. I'm all right."

John turns and begins walking. He is not afraid. He feels energized. This is it. This is the moment.

They come up behind him, some of them carrying sticks and bottles. In the corner of his eye, John can also see the little wannabes and other neighborhood kids running up to witness whatever's about to go down.

One of the dealers decides to get things rolling. He steps forward with a clenched fist, dancing around on the balls of his feet—dancing, it occurs to John, like he thinks he's Muhammad Ali or somebody.

"What you all waiting for?" he says to the others. "Let's get him."

John pulls out the .32, turns, and points it at him. "You don't want to do that," he says.

The dancing boy stares at the gun and freezes. Behind him, the others freeze, too. Time itself freezes.

John just stands there, pointing and waiting and wondering what will happen next. Suddenly he hears several sharp pops, like firecrackers going off. At his left side, where he's carrying a textbook for Mr. Feazell's history class, he feels the impact of something hitting the book. On his right arm, he instantly feels a second impact, this one softer than the first.

More pops.

He doesn't actually see the gun that's firing at him. But from the sound of it, he guesses it's probably a .22 or .25. He turns toward where he thinks the shots are coming from and pulls the trigger of his .32.

Click.

Oh my God, John tells himself. In that split second, a dozen things race through his mind. Maybe his mother found the gun in the closet and took out the bullets. Maybe it's just not working right. But whatever's happened, he is standing in the middle of a gunfight without any way of shooting back. And in case that wasn't obvious before, a girl who's been watching now broadcasts this fact to the world.

"It's empty!" she says.

John turns and runs, tearing off through the yards between the houses, sure that he's about to get shot in the back. Knowing how fast he is, some of the dealers pile into a blue Impala and go after him. When they catch up with him, John ducks behind a parked car and waits until they drive by.

By the time he reaches his house, his fear has turned to anger. He can't believe this stupid gun. Still breathing hard, he looks inside the chambers and sees them loaded with bullets. He steps out his back door, points the .32 toward the woods behind the house, and pulls the trigger again.

Boom.

He goes back inside, opens the gun, checks the bullet that should have fired during the confrontation with the dealers. He sees a mark in it, where the hammer hit.

Now he's furious. Why didn't it shoot like the other bullet? Why didn't it fire when he really needed it?

He calls his mother at work and tells her what's just happened. He's all pumped up. He wants to take it right back to those punks.

"I'm going back out," he tells his mother.

"No," she says. "Don't leave the house. Just stay there."

She tells him she's on her way and hangs up. Meanwhile, some of the other Dogs have shown up. They've heard about the shooting. They want to make sure John's okay.

"Did you get hit?" they ask him.

"I don't think so."

Suddenly John remembers the two impacts. He rolls up his sleeves, and on his right arm he finds a light bruise. The second impact. But he can't find any other wounds, not even on his left side, where he was hit first. Then he remembers that he was carrying the textbook. He picks it up and sees the lead marks, still there. In the space of a microsecond, a bullet has ripped its way through hundreds of years of American history. It penetrated the hard cover and tore through the tops of all the pages, finally bursting out the other side. By then it had slowed enough that when it deflected into John's arm, it barely touched him, not even breaking the skin. Somehow, he emerged with nothing more than an overgrown mosquito bite.

John can't believe it. He was holding the textbook by his chest. If it hadn't been there to absorb the force of the slug . . . It's one of the oldest clichés in the world. It's like a headline dreamed up by some hack on a newspaper copy desk. *Book Stops Bullet, Saves Boy's Life.* But there's no other way to look at it, and the fact that it's a cliché does not make this moment any less wondrous to John. He has been rescued by history.

Spared by a book. Protected by Mr. Feazell, who always manages to look out for him, even from a distance.

IN HIGH SCHOOL, NEWS TRAVELS FAST.

"You okay, brother?" Mr. Feazell says to him the next day. "I heard about your incident."

The two of them talk about it. About John pulling the trigger and nothing happening. About the bullet hitting the textbook. Mr. Feazell listens carefully. He doesn't lecture. He tells John he understands, and to prove it, he shares some stories of the foolish chances he took when he was young. But before he lets John go, he stares him in the eye and gives him something to think about.

"God is trying to tell you something," he says, knowing the depth of John's faith. "He has a plan for you."

John takes these words and carries them inside him. He can't believe how smart Mr. Feazell is. The man knows so much. In the meantime, John has another small problem. It's his history book; the police, who are investigating the shooting, have taken it into evidence.

That's okay, though. Let the police have it, Mr. Feazell says. They'll get him another book.

THE FEARSOME FOURSOME. FROM LEFT TO RIGHT: MERIDITH TUCKER, YY, KARIN UPMEYER, AMY BOYLE.

ONE OF THE SEMINOLE QUIZ KIDS
sits impassively, listening to the man who
is leaning over him and growling directly
into his face.

"Get mean," says this person, presumably his father. *"Get an attitude."*

The day of reckoning has arrived. It
is Wednesday, February 21, and here at
Pinellas Park High, the county academic
tournament is about to begin. Timothy
Burrows and the rest of the Seminole
High team are seated together in the Pinellas Park auditorium, waiting to seize
the title. Around them, other teams are
psyching up as well. Down the rows, kids
are quietly hurling practice questions at
one another; one student is flipping
through a copy of *Test Your Cultural Lit-
eracy.*

Some kids obviously have more on
the ball than others. A few minutes ago,
the members of another team—though
they were wearing their identifying jer-
seys, the name of their school shall be
withheld here to spare them the shame—
actually encountered difficulty figuring
out how to enter the building. They
stood at the outside double doors, repeatedly pulling on one that was locked until

someone else walked up and suggested that they try the other half of the door, which was open all the time.

At least they've set foot on the premises. It is now 3:48 P.M., only twelve minutes before the tournament is to begin, and still no sign yet of YY and Elvis and the rest of the Largo team. A few minutes later, they finally arrive, stepping breathlessly down the aisle, reporting for duty to their coach, who was beginning to wonder if they'd show. What kept them? The details are muddled, but there was some kind of mix-up in the travel arrangements, and YY was forced to push the Y-mobile to the limits of its endurance. Anyway, they've arrived safely now and are ready for action.

YY feels confident. She likes the fact that the tournament is at Pinellas Park. That's where Largo won it all last year; it's also where the team won a double-header match earlier this year.

"This is, like, our place," says YY.

The way she and the rest of the team figure it, the top three seeds in the tournament are Largo, Seminole, and Clearwater. As if to confirm this speculation, each of these three schools is now sent to a different room to compete in separate preliminary heats with other teams. The top two finishers in each heat will then meet in the finals. If they want to go head-to-head against Seminole, in other words, the Largo kids will have to get through the first round.

YY and Elvis and the others are in Group B, which is dispatched to a large classroom in G Wing. Quickly they take their seats alongside the four other teams in this group—St. Petersburg High, East Lake, Pinellas Park, and Lakewood—and dive into the five-point round.

The first question is perfect for YY.

"Which classical work," asks the woman at the front of the room, "did Spenser and Milton imitate by dividing their epics into twelve books?"

YY hits the buzzer.

"The Aeneid," she says.

"Name the form in which the following three poems are written: Tennyson's 'Ulysses,' Browning's 'Porphyria's Lover' and 'My Last Duchess.' "

It is a vicious little question. But once again, the buzzer sounds at the Largo table, where YY and Carolyn Hanson are grinning at each other. This is too much. It's uncanny. Just this morning, in Mrs. Hay's English class, they were discussing "My Last Duchess."

"Dramatic monologue," Carolyn says.

It's too soon to get cocky, though. Because over the next ten minutes, Largo stumbles repeatedly. They keep guessing incorrectly. And when they do have the correct answer, they hesitate a split second too long, allowing another team to buzz in first.

"I'm getting mad," says YY, working herself up during the first substitution break.

She pauses. "I'm *definitely* getting mad."

Another pause. *"Now I'm mad."*

It only gets worse. As they fall further behind, heading rapidly for last place, Carolyn buries her face in her hands.

"This is death," says one of her teammates watching in the audience.

As they enter the final fifteen-point round, YY leads a last-ditch comeback that would make Mrs. Hay proud. YY nails one on John Steinbeck and Flannery O'Connor. She nails another on the figure of speech known as synecdoche. And another involving the terms "double-cross" and "double-negative."

"Yesssss," she whispers, making a fist.

The queen of heaven is back. She's adding points to their total like a prodigy possessed. Still, it's not enough. When the round is over, they have clawed their way up to third place. But they're one spot shy of making the finals.

Bye-bye.

"Can we start over?" says YY, trying to hide her disappointment.

The top two schools in their heat, St. Pete and Pinellas Park, move on to face Seminole and Clearwater, both of which have performed according to expectations and triumphed through the first round. And later that afternoon when the whole thing's over, Tim Burrows and the finger flickers of Seminole are the new county champs.

So much for revenge.

YY and the others take it as gracefully as they can—remarkably gracefully under the circumstances—and then head home for yet another glorious night of homework. No time to mope, licking their wounds. They have a calculus test tomorrow.

THE DART SLICES THROUGH THE AIR.

Thunk.

Inside the AB-12 darkroom, the Fearsome Foursome lets out a cheer. On the dart board hanging from the far wall, sweet little Amy has scored a direct hit on the photo of a boy she dated last year. The Prom Date from Hell, she calls him.

Another dart goes flying.

Thunk.

More cheers as Karin nails a picture of Mrs. Palmateer, who stopped Karin in the hall a few months ago and gave her detention because she was wearing a skirt that was supposedly too short for the school dress code. To this day, Karin denies the charge. Vehemently.

"It was a nun skirt," she says. "A skirt a nun could wear."

Thunk. Meridith, still serving her term as student council president, lands one on the council sponsor, a teacher who has been driving Mer to the brink of insanity all year. *Thunk.* She lands another on her irritating little brother. *Thunk.* YY, whose aim has in fact improved with practice, nails Ms. Westfall, who is still positioned over the bull's-eye, smiling her most positive smile. One of the boys on the yearbook staff has meanwhile put up a photo of his mother—a woman widely known as Bonnie Ballistic, on account of her famous temper—and now he lets her have it, too.

All the while, other AB-12 rats are outside, knocking at the door, begging to be allowed inside so they can nail their own favorite targets.

"As long as you don't tell anybody," YY and the other Heathers say, letting them in.

By now, the hurling of the sacred darts has become one of the most revered of all AB-12 rituals. Though Ms. Westfall's photo still occupies the place of honor, she is joined now by an increasingly crowded field of targets. The kids stick photos of their teachers up there, photos of class rivals, sometimes even photos of each other. In a strange way, it has become a kind of honor to make it onto the board. The whole thing's not just about sticking it to Judi anymore. It has become more of an all-purpose escape valve, designed to let off any number of frustrations. A way of maintaining one's sanity in the middle of the stressed-out sweepstakes.

As the school year careens toward its end and the conclusion of their high school careers, YY and the others are hanging on as best they can. They are all in survival mode, and so far it's working. They don't even seem to be letting the backlash get to them anymore.

In the beginning, when they first learned that people were making snide remarks about them, calling them stuck-up wenches, referring to them repeatedly as the Breakfast Club Bitches, the girls were stung. The idea that people saw them that way was hard to accept. They certainly didn't think of themselves in those terms.

Perhaps they should have been more quick to recognize the signs of what was coming. Early in the year, it should have been obvious that some kids were not particularly enamored of the Heathers routine; when the girls adopted the imperial attitude and fired away with their beloved quotes, there were those around them who sighed and rolled their eyes and grew strangely quiet. From there, the reactions soon evolved into something nastier—the slurs written on the lectern and other places, the whispers that went back and forth behind their backs. Almost no one, even the kids who worked with them in AB-12, ever had the guts to say anything to their faces.

"It's because people don't know us," Karin says. "They think we're snobs."

That's the frustrating part. If the rest of these snipers would just come out and take their shots in the open, the girls could defend themselves. They could explain that the Heathers act was supposed to be a joke. But nobody will really talk to them about it.

It's okay, though. After months of dealing with this stuff, Meridith and Karin and the others are finally starting to get used to it. They're learning to laugh it off and walk away. They even seem to have accepted that they'll never know for sure exactly who's behind it. They're pretty sure it's a bunch of underclassmen, but there's no way to prove it. It doesn't matter anymore. The girls keep telling themselves that it's not worth the energy, that they need to just let it go.

So now the Fearsome Foursome is trying to forge ahead. They're all fired up these days about the upcoming Sixth Annual Toga Scavenger Hunt. Over the years, such contests have become major outings at high schools around Pinellas County; at Largo, it has grown into one of the biggest social events of the year. It's always wild. Last year the contestants were asked to find, among other things, a live gecko; they were also asked to locate a prom date for some poor girl named Nicole. One team did find a gecko, purchasing it at a pet store. Another team abducted a kid working at a Taco Bell and had him give roses to Nicole at the end of the night. This year, there has been a rumor floating around for days that the list for the hunt will require contestants to pick up a road kill and bring the animal's carcass to the finish line. It is also rumored that people will be encouraged to steal something from the lawn of Judith Westfall.

YY and the others can't wait.

•   •   •

ONE AFTERNOON NOT LONG BEFORE THE HUNT, KARIN GOES home and finds a letter waiting for her from FSU. She's so excited, she tears it open right there in the hallway. The letter is polite, but as she reads it, she hears the sound of another door slamming shut on her future. It's another disappointment, another confirmation of her own mediocrity. How's she going to tell her mother and father?

She decides not to tell them anything. Fighting back her tears, she neatly folds the letter, places it back in the envelope, and takes it out to her car. She puts it in the glove compartment, wondering when she'll find the courage to break it to her parents.

"Did you get accepted?" her dad asks one day.

"I don't know yet," says Karin. "I haven't heard."

BACK IN THE WINDOWLESS WORLD
of the pod, the new teacher is slowly being devoured alive. She's teaching ninth-
grade English. She's the one they called
in to take over the classes assigned to
Mrs. McGraw, who took over the classes
that used to be assigned to Mrs. Whitehead, the teacher whose students tortured
her with the whistling of the "Andy
Griffith" theme. At the semester break,
Mrs. Whitehead decided she'd had
enough; she asked to be transferred into a
position outside the pod, in regular
classes.

The budget didn't allow the school to
hire another full-time teacher to fill Mrs.
Whitehead's slot, so they did the best
they could and hired a long-term sub.
Her name is Laura Trimm. Actually she
prefers it without capital letters. Like e. e.
cummings. Most of ms. trimm's students
have undoubtedly never heard of e. e.
cummings. But they know enough to
have already dubbed her the Hippie. The
title is not quite accurate, since ms. trimm
is only twenty-two and was still toddling
around in diapers at the time of Wood-
stock. Still, she is about as close to a hippie as anyone gets these days. She report-

INSIDE THE POD.

edly does not eat meat. She does not wear makeup or shave her legs—the kids are astounded, despite their alleged commitment to nonconformity— and she wears soft black shoes decorated with tiny peace signs. Around her neck, she keeps a yellow tiger's-eye crystal. She loves crystals. Not just for their beauty, she says. For their energy.

"I work with them and meditate," ms. trimm explains. "I study Eastern philosophy on my own. Taoism and Buddhism."

She is an easy target for a teenager. The fact is, though, that she's an intelligent and well-meaning young woman. Just last year, she graduated from the University of South Florida with an English degree; before that she was a student at Largo. The Class of '85, to be exact. Mr. Klapka was one of her teachers; so was Mrs. Hay. In fact, ms. trimm has all sorts of ties with this school. Her mother is Mrs. Badders, one of the veteran math teachers; also, ms. trimm has a younger sister, Pauli Badders, who's a senior this year and scheduled to graduate in June.

Although ms. trimm had been subbing in other classes for months, she'd never taught in GOALS. During the job interview, which took place on a Friday, three days before she started, Mrs. Palmateer tried to prepare the novice for the challenges that awaited her. She tested ms.

trimm with hypothetical situations, asking her what she would do if, for instance, she were confronted by two kids on the verge of a fistfight. This was a good hypothetical, because on ms. trimm's fourth day on the job, a pair of boys came into her room preparing to rip off each other's limbs.

"I'm going to kill you," one of them told the other.

They were on top of each other, ready to go at it, when ms. trimm asked them to separate.

"Please," she said. "Don't do this." She had to ask them repeatedly, but finally they stepped apart.

With every ounce of patience inside her, ms. trimm has tried to treat her classes with the respect she always craved when she was a student. Wonderfully, stubbornly idealistic, she subscribes to the commendable belief that kids will act like adults if they are treated like adults.

"I try," she says, speaking in a soft and nonjudgmental voice, "to be a very caring and positive person."

In a perfect school—in a school, say, created by Hollywood—these good intentions would win over her classes and usher in a golden era of growth and understanding. But this is not Hollywood. This is the pod. The kids in ms. trimm's classes are not grateful for her gift of respect. What they're grateful for is this once-in-a-lifetime opportunity to go wild. Her daily struggle is best summarized by a T-shirt one of her students wears. The shirt shows the Tasmanian Devil, happily chewing on a huge peace sign.

It probably doesn't help that ms. trimm is not much older than the students, or that she has no classroom of her own and must therefore float between different rooms from one period to the next, or that without any capitals in her name she robs herself of a certain degree of authority automatically available even to freshmen. It certainly does not help that in the early days she invites the students to call her by her first name, a tactic that one of her supervisors soon persuades her to abandon. Even then, she is placed at a disadvantage because the only other name available to her—her last name—happens to be a nasty slang term for the female pubic area.

The kids, of course, have all sorts of fun tossing that word around. They mock her, call her names, hurl pennies at her back, play Roller Derby with their desks, lock her out of class, send her crying down the hall. Time and again, they club her with her own good intentions.

"Nothing personal," one of them says, "but why are you such a bitch?"

And every day, when she walks into fifth period, Mike Broome is waiting for her. Mike has always hated English with a special passion, no matter who's forcing him to learn it, and though he may be new and improved for other teachers, he can still instantly revert to his old infuriating self.

"Let me see that thing," he says, grabbing for her crystal as she walks past him.

She backs away. In only a few days, she has learned enough to know when to back away.

"Are you going to do your work?"

He grins. "I don't know. That's a tough question."

Something on the floor catches his eye.

"Hey. Somebody dropped a cigarette." He picks it up and tucks it behind his ear. "It's mine now," he says.

She tries to take it from him. But a second later the bell rings, and he is gone.

As painful as all this must be for ms. trimm, it's Mike who probably gets hurt the worst. At this moment in his life, when he is finally showing signs of pulling out of the tailspin, the last thing he needs is a teacher whose inexperience is too great a temptation to ignore.

One day, trying to trigger the best in them, she gives a special assignment titled "Create Your Environment with Positive Thinking." She passes around a list of twenty statements designed to build self-esteem; statements such as "I am an open channel of creative energy," "I am the master of my life," and "Perfect wisdom is within my heart." Then she tells them to pick one statement for themselves and make a poster illustrating their choice. To help with their artwork, she passes around some crayons.

Mike looks at his copy of the sheet and picks the first choice on the list:

I am what I think I am.

But when he writes it down on his "poster"—the only illustration he makes to accompany the text is a few scrawled crayon marks—he makes a small change in the sentence:

I am what you think I am.

Something about this woman sets Mike off. As the days slip by, he stares at her with growing contempt. The old fires are ignited inside him. Once more, his blue eyes are burning.

• • •

JOHN BOYD IS BACK ON TRACK NOW. LITERALLY. AS THE second semester rushes forward, John is speeding along with it, running the mile relay for Largo's track team, his eyes focused on the long trail before him.

Since the gunfight, things have quieted down in his neighborhood. A crisis point has passed. The dealers are no longer trying to fight the Raw Dogs; they're too busy fighting among themselves. One day a police officer who was working the shooting came to school to talk to John. The officer had heard that John had also been seen holding a weapon.

"I don't suppose you're going to tell me where the gun is now?"

"I threw it in the lake behind my house."

That was the end of that line of questioning. As it happens, John truly does not have the .32 anymore. He left it one night in a friend's car, and for some reason the police stopped the car and found the gun and took it away. Just to be safe, John went to a pawnshop and bought another—a .32 automatic this time—but the way things are going it doesn't look like he'll have to use it.

Meanwhile, an arrest has been made. A fourteen-year-old boy was charged in the shooting and taken to the Juvenile Detention Center. Since then, this boy has been going through some tough times; during his weeks at JDC, his father died. Now, with all these changes, he supposedly has turned himself around. He wants to go back to school. Through emissaries, his mother has encouraged John to let it go, not to pursue the charges. John sends word back that he will do as she asks. If her son is willing to stop this thing between them, so is he.

John does have a score to settle, though. One day not long after the shooting, he looks over at the neighborhood basketball court and who should he see but the other kid, the one who bounced like a boxer and was so eager to lead his associates on the charge against John. Only this time, Ali's associates are nowhere in sight.

He's shooting baskets when John walks over and promptly hammers his fist into the boy's mouth.

"Let's dance," John says.

As the punches start to fly, some of the little wannabes who are also shooting hoops see what's happening and stop to watch. Out of the corner of his eye, John can see his mother in the distance, standing on their porch, silently watching.

He turns his full attention back to the boy.

"Y'all are bad with your friends," he tells him as they circle each other. "But now it's just you and me, straight up."

The two of them spin and turn and push each other off the basketball court and onto the grass. John sees the other kid eyeing a big stick on the ground, so he maneuvers over, picks up the stick, and hurls it away.

"Straight up," John tells him. "Straight up."

A few minutes later, when they're still going at it, someone breaks it up. John is exhausted, but he sees the blood on the other boy's lip and the shame in his eyes, and for that he feels a measure of satisfaction. It is enough.

Now the only thing left is to understand. Late at night, John sits in his room and thinks it all through. He remembers what Mr. Feazell told him. He replays those moments when the bullets were hurtling past him and wonders what might have happened if his gun had actually fired. Would he have killed someone? Would he have been the one arrested? But it didn't fire. There was a bullet in the chamber, the hammer hit it, and yet it did not shoot. Why?

That's not the question that gets John the most, though. What really puzzles him is why he was carrying that history book. John does not know what made him bring it home from school that day. He didn't have any homework in Mr. Feazell's class; he was caught up in the reading. So what compelled him to be holding the book at the instant when the bullet came tearing toward his heart? There's no logical reason for it. No logical reason at all . . .

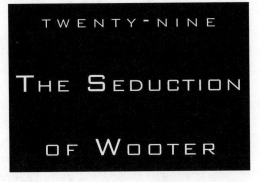

TWENTY-NINE

THE SEDUCTION

OF WOOTER

Hold on now. Take a deep breath as Karin hits the brakes on the Beast, a.k.a. the Van from Hell, and makes a last-second left turn across wet pavement. In their passenger seats, the other girls try not to yelp.

"Ooooohhhhhhhh!" cries Amy. "We were almost one with that ditch."

It's been like this all night. The tires on the Beast, which is Karin's nickname for her parents' hulking Econoline van, have been perpetually squealing. Karin and Amy and YY and Meridith have been forced to race around like madwomen, dodging puddles and trying not to drag the hems of their togas in the mud. The rain has been falling since dusk; it just won't stop. Still, this evening in early March is turning out to be one of the more wild and wonderful moments of their lives. It is a night for the archives. A night they should store away in their memories so they can look back on it, years from now, and treasure it as one of the last times the four of them were still together.

The night they kidnapped the freshman.

It's one of the extra credit options in

the toga scavenger hunt. There are thirty-five other teams competing tonight, all from Largo, all wearing the required togas—bed sheets, actually, some of them painted with glow-in-the-dark colors—as they roam the area in pursuit of the one-hundred-dollar first prize. If a team wants extra points, the options include obtaining a speeding ticket, delivering an old woman at the finish line (the rules stipulate that she must be at least sixty), and providing the judges with physical proof that a sexual encounter has transpired during the evening. Preferably, the rules state, an encounter involving one of the team members.

Or, for one hundred points, the girls can kidnap a freshman, bind and gag him, then deliver him at the finish line like some gift-wrapped slave. The question now, for YY and company, is which freshman do they nab?

Various candidates are considered, not just for their availability but for the entertainment value in seeing each of them bound and gagged. Finally they decide to go for Wooter Buxton. His real name is Scot, but when he was a baby, he preferred to squirm across the floor rather than crawl, so his family started calling him Worm and Scooter, both of which were combined into Wooter, which is what he has gone by ever since. YY and the other Heathers know Wooter well. They think they can lure him into the Beast with no trouble. The only problem is, they have to get him before his older brother—Doug Buxton, a senior who happens to be on another team in tonight's hunt—snatches him away. Which is why YY gets to a phone as soon as possible.

"Hey, Wooty," she says sweetly, already buttering up the poor child with a pet name for his pet name. "It's YY. Have you seen your brother tonight?"

On the other end of the line, the sacrificial freshman says no.

"Wooter, stay at your house." YY lowers her voice into a seductive purr. "Can we come get you? We *need* you."

"Just tell him why," whispers Amy, who's fidgeting nearby, eager as always to do the upright thing.

"No," says Karin. *"Don't* tell him why."

YY, no fool, decides it's better to leave Wooter in the dark. No point in risking full disclosure. What if the kid tries to weasel out of it?

"We're on our way," she tells Wooter. She hangs up, then turns with a grin. "Let's go get him."

Back out into the night they go, piling once more into the Beast. They pull out of the driveway and tear down the road, hooting and yelling.

"He doesn't have a *clue,"* says Karin, gunning it in the direction of

Wooter's house. "He thinks a bunch of senior women are coming to pick him up."

"He said he was going to take a shower," says YY.

"A wet freshman!" says Karin.

This is beautiful. It's too much. Not only are they going to obtain their freshman, they are going to steal him away from the competing clutches of his very own older brother.

"Doug is going to roll," says YY. "I totally want to get a picture of Doug finding out. I'd just totally lose control of all bodily functions if I saw him."

"We're rocking!" cries Karin. "We're rolling!"

The toga scavenger hunt began at seven-thirty in the parking lot of a shopping center just north of the school. As the rain fell around them, close to two hundred Largo High students—seniors mostly, bunches of patio people, almost no one from the pod—milled across the lot in their togas, gossiping, flirting, waiting until the organizers handed out the super-secret list of the items to be scavenged. In case it's not obvious, it should be pointed out that part of the thrill of these hunts is that they are not officially sanctioned by the high school. In fact, they are semi-forbidden events, frowned on by the administration and organized entirely by the kids; this year, one of the Fearsome Foursome's best friends, a fellow AB-12 rat named Troy Vaughn, is in charge. Other high schools in this area organize their own toga scavenger contests, sometimes at their own peril. A few weeks ago, some Dunedin High kids were arrested during their hunt because one of the items they'd obtained was a manhole cover. At Largo, the organizers of tonight's hunt have been careful not to include any items that would require contestants to break the law. Unless, of course, you count the fifty extra credit points to be awarded for the speeding ticket.

So here are YY and Amy and Mer and Karin, plus two other girlfriends, Tracy and Louise, all of them careening around the area inside the Beast. Though she is not actually trying to get a speeding ticket—in fact, she's keeping her eyes peeled for cops—Karin is heavily into kamikaze driving. Curbs are being crossed. A light pole is narrowly missed. Repeatedly, they are almost one with a ditch. At this very instant, Karin is yelling at a man in a bicycle cap who's crossing in front of them.

"I'm going to ram that guy!" she says. "Come on, get in my way! I don't like that hat!"

"Road kill!" says YY.

They are listening to the Power Pig on the radio, rapping together to their favorite songs. They are sipping on sodas and munching on Ruffles and Cool Ranch Doritos, Cool Ranch being their all-time favorite snack option. Amy is sitting up front beside Karin, serving as the official navigator, reading aloud from the list so they'll know what they need other than a bound and gagged freshman. Not counting the extra credit options, there are thirty-two possible items to be gathered during the hunt. A road kill, it turns out, is not among them. Nor are they being asked to steal anything from their principal's lawn. There is Item Number Eleven, however. When Amy reads it to the others, she can hardly contain her excitement.

"One cooked pepperoni in a stamped envelope," she says, "addressed to Judith B. Westfall."

Amy then reads the address given on the list—the correct address, it should be pointed out—for Ms. Westfall's home.

"They give her address?" says Tracy. "No way."

Wait a sec. Thirty-five teams are being asked to mail this woman a cooked pepperoni?

"Judi is going to have the surprise of her life," Karin says with a grin.

"Oh my God," says Meridith, looking slightly worried.

"She'll get over it," says YY.

"What are they going to do," says Karin, piping back in, "expel us all for mailing her a pepperoni?"

Good point. As usual, these kids—not just the Fearsome Foursome, but the organizers of tonight's hunt—have correctly gauged how far they can go without getting in serious trouble. As thrilling as it may have been to contemplate stealing something from Ms. Westfall's lawn, that particular prank might well have landed half the senior class in jail. The pepperoni gag, however, is perfect.

Obtaining the cooked pepperoni is no problem. By chance, YY and her family had a pizza earlier this very evening. So Karin and the others dash over and pluck a pepperoni from one of the leftover pieces.

"How'd they get Judi's address," YY says afterward, still trying to figure it out.

"Honey," says Karin, "all you gotta do is look up 'Westfall.' There's only one Judi Westfall."

"In the whole wide world," says Louise.

Many of the other items on the list are just as simple to obtain as the pepperoni. The girls have been instructed, for instance, to track down the name of the waitress of the month at the Denny's near the school. To collect a sample of seawater. To list their favorite brands of beer shown on the huge Great Bay Distributors sign on Ulmerton Road.

"That's easy," says Amy.

"Michelob," says YY.

They are asked to purchase a package of Marlboro Light cigarettes, since that's Troy Vaughn's favorite brand. To find a Barbie and sheathe it inside a condom. To identify the top six officers of the Starship *Enterprise,* which is right up these girls' alley, since they still watch *Star Trek: The Next Generation* religiously. To locate a 1969 penny.

"Gee," YY says with a grin. "I wonder why they picked '69."

Amy, reading down the list, makes a face when she reaches Item Number Sixteen.

"Gross," she says. "Oh, they're gross. I can't even say this."

She is persuaded to say it. Turns out the list requires a member of each team to pluck a pubic hair and tape it to a piece of paper. If it's a blond hair, they get forty-five points. Any other hair is worth thirty points. No red ones are allowed.

Hearing this, the girls are all disgusted. The item was obviously spawned in the piggish imagination of some male.

"I'm not doing that," says Karin.

"I'm not, either," says Meridith.

"We *have* to," says YY.

In the end it's not that big a deal. Meridith discreetly waits for a moment alone, then does what's necessary.

"Got it," she says, back in the Beast.

The others are still making faces, like she should be embarrassed or something.

"Oh," says Mer, defending herself with impeccable logic, "like you never cleaned your mom's bathroom?"

By the time they call Wooter and tell him they're on their way to collect him, the girls have already acquired many items. But they're still working on the Barbie inside the condom. They have the condom. Just a few minutes ago, two of the girls ran inside a 7-Eleven and bought a pack of Trojans.

"Should we get lubricated or regular?" one said to the other as they stared at the prophylactic section.

"I don't care."

Laying their hands on a Barbie—a relic from days of innocence—

turns out to be a far more difficult proposition. Most of the girls don't
have theirs anymore. Meridith still had one until last year, when she and
Louise used it in a little revenge scheme. They'd found out that Louise's
boyfriend was allegedly cheating on her with some pale-skinned redhead,
so they took Mer's Barbie and turned it into a voodoo doll. They dyed its
hair red, painted its lips, sprinkled it with baby powder—all so it would
look like the wench in question—then hung it from a noose on the outside of the boyfriend's mailbox.

"The girl was really mad," says Meridith. "She never talked to us after
that."

Which is why that particular Barbie is not available this evening. No
one should be surprised, however, to learn that Amy still has her Barbie
around somewhere, packed away. So on their way to pick up Wooter, they
drop off Amy at her house so she can dig around and find it.

Barreling toward the Buxton home, the girls wonder aloud whether
older brother Doug will have somehow beaten them to the freshman.
They're also worried about the reaction from Wooter's mother; this happens to be Bonnie Ballistic, the one with the temper. Mrs. Buxton might
not take it well when she hears what these girls have in mind for her baby
boy. Thankfully, when they arrive, Bonnie is off shopping somewhere.
But Wooter's father is there to greet YY at the door.

"Excuse me," she says, "can I speak to Wooter?"

Mr. Buxton smiles and asks her in. Little Wooty is just getting out of
the shower.

"He's almost ready," says the dad.

At this moment, YY takes a bold step. As long as they're here, she
might as well ask.

"Do you guys have any rope?" she says, smiling.

Mr. Buxton looks confused. "Rope?"

YY apologizes, pulls him aside, tells him why they need it. Mr. Buxton
laughs. Who says there are no fun-loving parents on the planet? Of course
he'll give her some rope to tie up his boy. How much does she need? Will
twenty feet be enough?

Wooter, who has been getting dressed in the other room, is still clueless when he walks out. Before he has a chance to ask any questions, they
hustle him outside. YY, bringing up the rear, carries the rope.

"We'll bring him back in one piece!" she yells to Mr. Buxton.

Only then, when Wooter is inside the van, with the doors closed, do
they tell him why he is sitting on the floor beside all this rope.

"All right," he says, not batting an eye. "So where do you have to bind and gag me?"

"At the finish line."

Wooter grins. He doesn't mind. It is a Friday night, and he is surrounded by older women, all fawning over him so they can tie him up and do who knows what with his freshman body. Are you kidding? He's in heaven.

"Wood, you're a buddy! You're a pal!" Karin tells him. "For this, you're blood! You're family for life!"

The Beast carries them back toward Amy's house, its tires squealing again around the curves. Karin leans on the horn, and Amy comes running out, Barbie in hand.

"Do we *have* to put the Barbie in the condom?" says YY.

"Yeah," says Tracy. "It's a total waste of a good Barbie."

Wooter, who has been asked to lie on the floor so no other team can see him and try to snatch him away, watches as they perform the procedure. He looks even more ecstatic than before. Barbies! Condoms! Senior girls in togas! It's like he has been admitted into some secret female world full of more lustful promise than any boy's fantasy.

They're singing to him. His bevy of captors is actually serenading him with a song of appreciation.

> *We love you Woo-oo-ter*
> *Oh yes we do.*
> *We don't love anyone*
> *As much as you.*

He stares up at them with an unmistakable look of love and gratitude. He is deeply impressed—he admits it—that a freshman is worth one hundred extra credit points. After suffering so much abuse throughout ninth grade, it's wonderful to be wanted. When he hears that extra points are also given for elderly women, he volunteers his own grandmother. Maybe they'd like to kidnap her, too? But no. They've decided to skip the grandmother option. It's 8:38 P.M. They're running out of time.

"Have you ever even come close to winning?" Wooter asks them. He means the hunt.

"NOOOOO," they say together. "Not even close."

It doesn't matter. Sure, they'd like to win. But on a night like this, when everything clicks, they don't have to care about anything. They cruise down streets slick with rain, stopping at traffic lights that sway above them in the wind. They navigate by the pale shimmering lights of convenience stores, keeping an eye open for familiar 7-Elevens and Pik Kwiks so they know where they're going.

Just like Wooter, the girls are ecstatic. Their faces are glowing with an indescribable radiance. They're screaming out the window at other teams they see on the road. Singing more songs. Snorting and belching without shame, honking at cute guys and tossing the communal bag of Cool Ranch Doritos from one end of the van to the other, digging toward the bottom for the last chip fragments, for once not worrying about their diets or their mothers or their SAT scores or college or the vast uncertainties of their future. Tonight they are truly fearless. They are immortal. As long as they are together inside the Beast with their grinning freshman and their twenty feet of rope and the bonds of their friendship, nothing can hurt them. If only they could be this united and invincible forever.

Onward they ride, hurtling through the darkness, crossing items off the list. They have found a way to obtain a speeding ticket. Not a real one, of course. Remember who these girls are. If they're going to break the rules, they'll do it carefully. It happens at Rainbow Roller Land, where they stop to satisfy Item Number Twenty, which requires each team to pose for a photo with the roller rink's disc jockey. They have just taken the picture when they see a Pinellas County sheriff's deputy parked in the lot, sitting inside his cruiser.

Meridith walks up to him. She is a pretty girl, wrapped inside a toga. She doesn't have to do anything terrible; she barely has to smile. She tells the deputy about the hunt and how they'll earn extra credit if they get a ticket. Can he help them?

The deputy takes out his pad and starts scribbling.

A few seconds later, Meridith is back in the van, holding the fake document.

"Oh my God," she says. "That cop was so nice."

"He was killer," says YY, who watched the whole thing.

By now it's 9:36 P.M. They want to be at the clubhouse by ten, which means they'll have to hurry. The time has come, in other words, to bind and gag their little freshman. They begin to chant his name.

"Woo-ter! Woo-ter! Woo-ter!"

Wooter whistles while YY ties him up. Cooperative to the end, he holds his wrists up together to make it easier for her.

"Twenty feet of rope your father gave me," YY tells him. "Twenty feet of rope."

"Your father loves you," says Tracy.

A few minutes later, when they pull up outside the clubhouse, they discover that their little freshman is too heavy to carry. So he hops across the finish line.

But wait. Who's that walking toward them along the sidewalk? Why, it's Doug, Wooter's big brother. And he's got someone with him. An older woman with gray hair. A woman whose presence has won Doug so many extra credit points that his team will place first in the hunt, despite the kidnapping of Wooter underneath their very noses.

Doug grins.

"We got Grandma!"

PART FOUR

MOTHER'S

MILK

THIRTY

THE

RETURN

THE PLAN IS SO SIMPLE. IT'S SO easy. Now if only Andrea Taylor could bring herself to do it.

For some time now, Andrea has been keeping a secret about her friend Sabrina. A secret that, if disclosed to the right person, would allow John to gracefully break it off with Sabrina and finally get together with Andrea. The secret is that the three of them are not just caught in a romantic triangle. It's really more of a romantic rectangle.

Sabrina is a popular girl. While she's been seeing John, she has also been seeing someone else who goes to Dunedin High with her. No reason she shouldn't date around. She and John aren't pledged to each other for life or anything; it's not like they've exchanged rings or taken vows of exclusivity. Why shouldn't she see someone else if she wants? Still, John is totally in the dark about the other guy, and if someone were to enlighten him, that would give him a natural opening to bow out and start dating Andrea without leaving Sabrina any legitimate grounds for argument.

Just one problem. Andrea, being the nice girl she is, doesn't think she can live with the plan's undeniably Machiavellian overtones. After all, the only reason she knows about this other relationship is because of her heart-to-hearts with Sabrina, her best friend, who's unknowingly torturing her by dating John, who's unknowingly playing second fiddle to this other guy from Dunedin.

It's all so complicated. She almost needs a diagram to keep it straight . . .

Then it happens. One day, before Andrea is ever forced to make a decision, she gets a phone call that takes her off the hook. It's John. Through the grapevine, he's heard Sabrina's with someone else; in fact, he says, he thinks it's this guy he knows who runs on Dunedin's track team.

"Is she still going out with him?" John asks.

Andrea pauses for a second, consulting her conscience. John already knows the truth. What's the harm in confirming it? Besides, if she tells him no, she'd just be lying.

So she does it.

"Yeah," she says. "She is."

That's it. That's all it takes. John, never the type to dawdle, gets a number for the other guy from Dunedin and immediately calls him to compare notes. Turns out this guy didn't know he was part of a rectangle, either, and he's not too happy about it. So that day, both of them call Sabrina to end it with her. In fact, they call her at the same time. Sabrina's got two lines at her house, and as she switches from one to the other, she finds herself getting dumped by two people almost simultaneously. It's horrible for her. A double-barreled disaster.

Of course, the first person she calls afterward for sympathy is Andrea. Andrea can't talk, though. She's already on the line with John.

"I'll call you back," she tells Sabrina.

The phone lines must be sizzling. Andrea hears all the details from John, then calls Sabrina and gets them again from her.

"Do you believe this?" Sabrina says. "They both broke up with me."

Andrea listens, trying to soothe her feelings as best she can. She feels bad for Sabrina; nobody deserves that kind of rejection. Besides, she never meant for her friend to lose both guys. All she wanted was John.

And now she has him.

No need to be brash about it. They'll have to be discreet and wait a bit before they actually start dating. They'll need to give it a little time. But there's no stopping them now. Andrea and John won't be hiding in the shadows much longer.

• • •

''GOOD MORNING. OUR THOUGHT FOR THE DAY IS: HE THAT lives on hope has but a slender diet."

Late March, nearly halfway through the second semester. Soon spring break will be here, then prom, then suddenly it will be June and another year will have gone.

"Okay, take everything off your desks except a pen or pencil."

On the second floor of the AA building, a health teacher stares out at his class. Time for a test.

"All talking will cease at this time. Please keep your eyes on your own paper."

A soft rustling fills the room as copies of the test are passed down the rows. All of the students begin writing. All of them, that is, except one. At the back of the room sits a girl with freckles and long blond hair and an unmistakable sense of solitude about her. Jaimee Sheehy watches her classmates with a look of wistful detachment. She's not taking the test because she was not here to learn all the material. It was only a few weeks ago when she returned to school.

Now that she has materialized once more inside the walls of Largo High, Jaimee seems slightly tired. She gazes off to the side, doodles on her folder, unwraps a chocolate bar and eats it with a quiet sense of purpose, as though she's trying to make herself more substantial. As though she is determined this time not to fade away into the atmosphere.

In class, waiting for the others to take their test, she says nothing. Outside, she says only a little. When people ask her what it's like to be back, she tells them it's strange. Inside Charter Hospital, she had all that structure, that constant supervision. Now, back on the outside, she finds the freedom slightly overwhelming.

"It was weird coming home," she says softly, avoiding eye contact as she always does.

Still, she was eager to return. Jaimee stayed at Charter from November until mid-February. For months, she cried to her mother over the phone and wrote her pleading letters, begging to be allowed to leave, vowing to change and improve and finally make good.

"I promise I'll go to school," Jaimee would tell her. "I really learned a lot here."

She hadn't meant to lie, she'd say. She'd only done it because she was afraid of getting in trouble. But now she knew better. She knew she had to follow the rules and pay attention and go to class.

Laura Sheehy was never sure what to believe. She could hear something different in her daughter's voice, something that suggested maybe this time Jaimee really had changed. But the people at Charter kept telling her that it was too soon, that Jaimee wasn't prepared to leave yet, that Ms. Sheehy was too close to evaluate the situation with any objectivity. Finally they said Jaimee was almost ready to come home. But first they transferred her to Tampa Bay Academy, a residential treatment center for troubled kids, where she'd live and study as she made the last few transitional steps toward returning to the outside world.

From the start, Ms. Sheehy didn't like the academy. She thought the other kids were scary. One day someone reportedly tried to commit suicide; another time, a boy tried to get Jaimee to duck out and smoke a cigarette with him. Convinced that it was a mistake to expose Jaimee to such things, Ms. Sheehy decided to take her out early against the staff's advice.

"You're making the biggest mistake," they told her. "You think you're going to rescue her. She's not ready."

Ms. Sheehy didn't care. She knew she wasn't giving the academy a chance, but still she didn't think it was healthy for Jaimee to stay. Besides, she thought she could see definite progress in her daughter. Jaimee seemed calm, polite, restrained. So Ms. Sheehy brought her home and prepared to send her back to the high school.

She didn't make Jaimee go back immediately, though. She'd stockpiled some days off from her job so she could spend a little time with her daughter. The two of them went to the beach, went out to eat, talked and talked. Jaimee said that when she returned to Largo, she wanted to be in regular classes, not GOALS. The kids in the pod were wild and lazy, she said. They were a bad influence. Her mother, who already harbored similar suspicions about GOALS, agreed. But before she sent Jaimee back, Ms. Sheehy made sure she understood how crucial it was that she concentrate on her studies. She'd been taking classes at Charter and at the academy; if she worked hard, she could still earn credits for the spring semester.

"Jaimee, this is really important," Ms. Sheehy told her. "You'll be able to salvage half a year out of this. All I ask of you is to go to school and get passing grades. I'm not asking for As."

So now Jaimee is here at Largo High once again, starting her way down the long road back. She has so far to go. So much lost time to make up. But at least she's made a start. Over and over, she tells her mother that she's not skipping anymore, that she's truly attending class.

"I'm going," she says. "I'm really going now, Mom."

Slowly Ms. Sheehy is allowing herself to believe it. She doesn't want to be overly optimistic; she doesn't want to raise her hopes only to have them dashed all over again. But Jaimee is obviously slipping back into the flow and learning things. At night she comes home and shows her mother her math assignments; she gives detailed accounts of what happened that day in English. Not that she's chaining herself to her books or anything. That would be too much to expect. Jaimee is learning to bear down at school, but she is also enjoying her new freedom.

She's going to see Aerosmith when the band hits town in a couple weeks. She's already talking about going to see the Ramones. Just the other night, she says, she and a friend were at Tampa Theater, seeing a group called the Sleeze Beez. Jaimee was excited afterward. A camera crew was at the theater, filming a video, she says. She's not sure, but she might even be in the video. She might actually make it onto MTV.

''ALL RIGHT, LET'S SEE NOW.''

Mr. Feazell leans intently over his desk, gazing at a row of figures in his grade book as he quietly reads each of them aloud. A boy sits beside him, entering each number into a calculator, hoping the news won't be too bad.

Every year around this time, Mr. Feazell conducts his grade conferences, calling his students forward one at a time to let them know where they stand. He has the students add up the grades themselves on the calculator; that way, there's no misunderstanding, and they can see the reality of the situation for themselves.

The boy beside him finishes entering his numbers on the keyboard. He stares at the total, his face betraying neither disappointment nor elation.

"Okay?" Mr. Feazell says. "You got it, boss man?"

The boy nods and takes his seat, then Mr. Feazell calls another student up front for another conference. This is his seventh-period history class. John Boyd, whose textbook is still in evidence at the sheriff's department, sits a couple desks away from the front, working from a replacement book. Just behind him, bent over her own assignments, sits a junior girl with porcelain skin and long flowing brown hair and an air of uncommon radiance. Her name is Heather Pilcher—yes, another real-life Heather—and like John, she's one of those kids who seem to know everybody. She's an honor student and an alto soprano in the school's Madrigal Singers, she routinely lands parts in the school plays, and she belongs to Logos, the school's Bible studies group. Early every morning, just before class begins, the group meets on the patio to read scriptures and to pray together. The others don't know it, but lately Heather has been praying for something special. She's been asking God to grace her with the gift of her menstrual period.

At this point it's too early to know if Heather's really pregnant. Her period's not due yet, and so far she hasn't suffered any morning sickness or other nausea. Her boyfriend's a nervous wreck anyway, growing more agitated as the days go by; a week or so ago, at his insistence, she took one of those home pregnancy tests. She knew it would come out negative—it was too soon to take a reliable reading—but she took it anyway, just to calm him down. She keeps telling him there's no reason to worry.

"It's *okay*," she promises. "I'm going to start. Everything's going to be fine."

It's not okay, though. Heather's sure of it. She can't explain how she knows, but she does. She can just feel it.

Now she has to figure out what to do. Not about the baby; that's already decided. A born-again Christian, Heather would never consider abortion. She knows lots of other girls do it, but she could never live with herself if she made that choice. She's having her baby, and she's keeping it, and no one better try to change her mind. The question is, how does she break the news to everybody else?

Heather is about the last girl most adults would expect to wind up pregnant, what with her Bible studies and all. If kids such as her—not to mention kids such as YY and Meridith—have already begun having sex, who hasn't? As far as Heather can tell, just about everyone in school is fooling around. Nobody has to take a poll or anything. It's simply understood. The news of her pregnancy, then, is not likely to shock many students. It's the grown-ups who might have a hard time facing reality.

She lives a mile or so east of the school, in YY's neighborhood. She and YY grew up together. They used to jump rope, climb trees, play Truth or Dare. The two of them still see each other around the school, but they've gone their separate ways. Heather was raised more conservatively than YY. She comes from a family of Southern Baptists. Her grandfather's a preacher, and her mother's a secretary at the First Baptist Church of Largo, which the family has attended for years and where Heather has been singing since she was a little girl. Sex was never discussed much around their house; it was just something she knew was expressly forbidden until one was married.

Early in her ninth grade year, Heather went against that rule and slept with a boy for the first time. Looking back, she can't believe she was so naive. But at the time, it had seemed like the right move. This boy was a senior, and Heather felt grateful that someone was actually interested in an insignificant freshman like her. So when he asked, she said yes. They skipped school one day and did it at his cousin's house. When they finished, Heather felt a terrible letdown, similar to what YY and Meridith had experienced. A sense of emptiness. That's all there is to it? she wondered. That's what all the fuss was about? It got worse soon afterward when the boy dumped her, telling her she was too young and wasn't mature enough for him.

This particular senior also turned out to be a braggart, spreading the word about his adventures with the little freshman, which left Heather with a reputation for a while. Any magical aura she'd attached to sex soon vanished. She didn't sleep with anyone else, but she was left with a fatalistic attitude toward boys and relationships in general. Eventually, though, things got better. They improved especially this past summer, just before the start of her junior year, when Heather went to a church youth camp in Georgia and was saved. She had always relied on her faith, but now it gave her renewed comfort and strength. One night she and the other students at the camp sat around talking about how the new school year was soon to begin and how it was going to be harder to resist temptation once they were back mingling with so many members of the opposite sex. Somebody suggested that anyone who felt up to it should take a pledge of celibacy. Some of the kids stayed sitting, but others, including Heather, stood up and took the vow. In front of the others, she promised God to keep her body holy and to abstain from sex until she was married. If she broke this promise, she said, she was willing to accept the consequences.

When classes started up again at Largo High, Heather felt good about her vow and the revitalized intensity of her faith. She felt she was moving closer to God, and that made her happy. She still felt that way in November, when she finally agreed to go out with Chris Wainscott, a senior boy she knew in Madrigal Singers. For the longest time, she'd refused to date Chris, reminding him that she already had a boyfriend, a guy who lived in Georgia and whom she'd met at the youth camp.

"I can't," she'd tell him. "I'm dating this other guy."

Chris didn't care. He asked Heather out repeatedly, wearing her down until she gave in. It was almost no time before their relationship took off. Chris had a great deal in common with Heather; like her, he had been raised in a fundamentalist Christian family and was interested in pursuing a career in gospel singing. Plus, Chris had the home-court advantage. The guy in Georgia, hundreds of miles away, never had a chance.

For the longest time, Heather and Chris resisted the urge to have sex. The two of them dated for months, but they did not sleep together until one Monday in February. They didn't plan it; it was just one of those moments when hormones take over and something unexpected happens. They did it at her house immediately after school; Heather's parents both worked outside the home, and so they had the place to themselves. They went to her room, which was strange for Heather, since it was the same room where she had once played as a little girl. Now, as she and Chris made love, she found herself staring at the wall, gazing at a Raggedy Ann and Andy picture her mother had painted there long ago.

There was another problem. Since this encounter was spontaneous, neither of them had brought a contraceptive. It all happened so quickly, Heather didn't even have a chance to glance at the calendar and calculate whether this was a wise time of month to be having sex. Instead, they improvised, with Heather searching through her father's closet until she found one of his old condoms.

This was the first time she'd had sex with anyone since her freshman year—it was Chris's first time with anyone, period—and as they finished, Heather felt a familiar wave of disappointment. It was nice enough, especially now that she was with someone who cared about her, but the same letdown was there. The actual event still could not match the anticipation. Though he didn't say so, she could tell Chris felt the same way.

A few seconds later, when Chris pulled out, a look of panic came over his face.

"Oh my God," he said, looking at the condom. "No. It *broke*."

LATER, HEATHER WOULD REMEMBER THE VOW SHE'D MADE AT the church youth camp. She would think back to those words, and she would torment herself with them. The day she slept with Chris, she would say, was the day she started to fall away from her walk with God. But on that awful February afternoon when it happened, she had no time for such introspection. She and Chris were both crying. Chris had to go pick up his sister from middle school and couldn't stay, but for a few minutes he cried and paced back and forth. He kept saying he couldn't believe that the condom had torn. It couldn't be, he said. It could not have happened.

"It just doesn't seem real," he said.

Heather tried to make him feel better. She told him it was all right, that nothing was going to happen. But she knew that wasn't true. Already she was overcome with a certainty that she was going to be pregnant. She was so sure that after Chris left, she kept jumping up and down, trying to dislodge the semen. All that afternoon and into the evening, she refused to lie down. That night, she prayed to God, promising that if she wasn't pregnant, she would never have sex again until her wedding day.

THAT WAS ONLY A FEW WEEKS AGO. HEATHER HAS BEEN praying ever since. She still feels sure she's pregnant, but inside she clings to the smallest hope. She tells herself that her intuition might be wrong. Maybe it will all work out in the end.

Soon they'll know. She'll wait a little longer, and she'll take another home pregnancy test, and then they'll know for sure.

THIRTY-ONE

FOND FAREWELLS, PART TWO

DAYS OF TICK-TOCKING BOREDOM. Days of waiting for another day to end. This is the dead zone, the last interminable weeks before spring break, when time suddenly stalls and the students grow so restless they can hardly stay in their seats. It's especially bad inside the pod, where the kids are always on edge anyway. Names have begun to disappear off the rolls again. Familiar faces are vanishing from the classrooms. Already the teachers are fighting to remember them all.

Eric the Dragon is gone. He dropped out in February. In the weeks before he left, Eric seemed to have withdrawn into a world of his own creation. He kept hinting about the presence of elaborate cocaine rings that were spreading around him; he claimed to be forming some sort of vigilante group that patrolled the streets on motorcycles. It was hard to tell how much of this was real and how much elaborate fantasy. Clearly Eric's homelife was a mess. He had been living with his mother and stepfather, had trouble getting along with them, had run away, camped out in his car for a while; at one point, he broke into an empty house and slept there. When anyone could get him to talk, he would go on about how he was close to "going redline" and how he woke every morning wondering if he should kill himself. Once, he said, he had punched a tire until his hand bled.

One day Eric directed his anger toward Ms. Westfall. She saw him walking on campus in the middle of class and stopped him.

"Where are you supposed to be?" she asked.

"Go fuck yourself," he told her.

Not long after that, Eric officially withdrew from school. He did it on Valentine's Day. Before he left, his teachers asked him about his plans for the future. He was thinking, he said, of becoming a gourmet chef.

The boy who loved Mickey Mouse is gone too, and all his mouse mementos gone with him. So is the thrasher boy who dreamed of a world covered with pavement. Not long ago, the teachers also said goodbye to a senior girl who had only one credit left to fulfill before she would have graduated. One lousy credit to go, and she walked out the door. Another senior girl, a girl who insisted earlier in the year that she would never quit, who vowed that she would cross that stage in June and pick up her diploma, walked out, too.

In the pod's cramped little office, the GOALS attendance clerk—Lois Welch, a sweet-tempered woman who treats the students as if they were her own children—keeps a list of all the kids who've withdrawn. She adds new names to the list almost every day.

"Shane Clark . . . Sabrina Wells . . . Jason Downs." She shakes her head as she reads aloud the names of the latest departures.

"Jason, too?" says a teacher standing nearby, checking her mailbox. "He was doing *so* well."

The kids in the pod are bored and listless, whining and complaining even more than usual. One day, when Mrs. O'Donnell starts to write a disciplinary referral for a girl who's talking trash, the girl tries to black-mail her. She says that if Mrs. O'Donnell writes her up, she'll concoct some story about Mrs. O'Donnell having an affair with another teacher and then report it to the administration. Mrs. O'Donnell tells her to go ahead and then writes her up anyway.

Such bravado is better than nothing. At least that kid was using her imagination; at least she'd taken the trouble to come to class, which is more than many are doing. With all the kids who've quit for good and all the others who are merely skipping out and getting a head start on their vacations, the pod seems almost deserted. One morning Mrs. O'Donnell finds herself standing in the middle of her fourth-period earth science class, staring at rows of empty seats. According to her roll book, there are supposed to be thirteen kids in this class. But only five are here today. And at this moment, a couple of those same five are doing their best to escape, pleading for a hall pass so they can head for the bathroom and slip away to other unspecified destinations.

"I'm going into labor," says one girl.

"Yeah," says another. "We're going into labor."

Mrs. O'Donnell ignores them, but they're not ready to give up.

"What if we *were* going into labor?"

"Yeah."

It's the same in the other GOALS classrooms. Ms. DiLello's classes are so devoid of warm bodies that one day she decides to reward the kids who have shown up by giving them a ridiculously simple quiz. She asks them to tell her the name of their favorite comic strip. To name the current month. To add two plus two. To identify the color of the pants she's wearing that day. To look at the clock and identify the correct time. Then she tells them to correct their own papers, to mark at the top that they've scored a perfect ten points—two points for each of the five questions—and turn the papers back in. To her surprise, one kid awards himself only eight points. Turns out he wrote down that the current month was June.

"I guessed," he tells her.

Ms. DiLello can't believe it.

"You can't even give away points to these kids," she says afterward. "You just can't do it."

She is particularly frustrated these days with Mike Broome. Only a couple of months after he made his spectacular turnaround, Mike has slipped back into his old ways. In the early part of the semester, he was doing wonderfully in Ms. DiLello's class; even now, if he bothers to show up, he usually gets every question right on her quizzes and assignments. The problem is, he almost never bothers.

"Where have you been?" she says one day when she spots him in the hall. "You always did so well in math."

He shrugs.

Ms. DiLello doesn't know what else she can do for Mike. She and the other teachers have tried so hard to reach him, and now he seems to have retreated further away than ever.

"He's blowing it again," she says, standing in the door of her class, shaking her head. "He had an A in here. He had a *straight A . . .* Now he's going to fail. It's really ridiculous. I can't believe he's wasting his life like this."

As impressive as it may have been, Mike's turnaround was never complete. From early on, even when he was making a new name for himself in other classes, he was still raising havoc in ms. trimm's fifth period, taking advantage of the freedom created by her good intentions. Then, in mid-February, he began self-destructing in most of his other subjects as well. He wasn't erupting as much as he used to; his anger seemed to have given way, at least for a time, to resignation. It was as though he'd decided he simply did not have the energy to hold everything together for an entire semester, as though he'd looked off into the distance toward the end of the school year and told himself he'd never make it that far. So he stopped. He wouldn't complete assignments; he refused to join in class discussions. One day in earth science, when Mrs. O'Donnell was passing out a worksheet, he told her not to bother giving him one.

"I won't do it," he said.

"Mike, what is wrong?" she asked. "Why aren't you doing anything?"

"I don't feel like it, man."

In recent weeks it's gotten even worse. Mike has reached the point where he almost never comes to class at all. In the old days, he at least made an effort to show up, even if it was just to glare at the teachers. Now he rarely gives them even that small satisfaction. He has taken refuge in the sanctuary of the auditorium steps. He's stationed on the steps almost permanently now. Unless one of the administrators chases him away, he'll sit there for hours.

Occasionally Mrs. O'Donnell takes her fourth-period class, Mike's class, on a mini-field trip to the steps to try to coax him back inside. Since he won't come to them, they go to him. Mrs. O'Donnell leads the class out across the patio and over to Mike's scowling presence on the steps. They tell him they miss him. They ask him to please come back. But it never works. Usually he either runs away or curses them.

Still, they refuse to give up. The other kids miss Mike. At least that's what they say. Maybe they're just willing to jump at any chance to get out of the classroom and roam the campus with their teacher. Either way, they keep forming search parties, trying to track Mike down and lure him back into the fold.

"I just seen Mike Broome up on the stairs," a boy tells Mrs. O'Donnell one morning at the start of class. "He said, 'See ya, dude.' "

"Let's go up there and say hi to Mike!" says someone else.

"Let's ask him to come to class."

"You know what he's going to say. 'Fuck you.' "

They look toward Mrs. O'Donnell for the go-ahead. She nods, but tells them to calm down. They're not to laugh at Mike or make fun of him, she says. They're just going to tell him, she says, how much they want him back.

"I don't even *know* the kid," says one boy who's fairly new to the class. "Who is he?"

Off they go, out of the pod and into the blinding sunlight of a bright spring morning. Together they walk past the rail, past the gym, across the patio, and over to the auditorium steps.

Mike may have been there a few minutes before, but he's nowhere in sight now. They must have just missed him.

Sometimes, just to keep the teachers guessing, Mike mysteriously appears in class. One Friday morning finds him sitting inside the classroom of ms. trimm, who is still fighting a losing battle to maintain even a semblance of control over her students. At this instant, in the middle of her fifth-period class, Mike is ignoring her and that day's assignment. Instead he is bouncing a tennis ball on his desk. He stops just long enough to call out to her across the room.

"Can I get a drink of water, ms. trimm?"

"No."

"Why?"

" 'Cause you already were down there. You wasted your chance."

He scowls. "Dumb bitch."

Perhaps she does not hear this. Perhaps she merely chooses to ignore it. Either way, she says nothing. But a few seconds later, she is forced to take action when Mike tosses the ball at the ceiling.

"Put it away," she says. She is smiling, but it is a rigid, nervous smile.

She looks tired these days. Beaten down. The past two months have been a long and bitter lesson for laura trimm. She has watched twenty-three of her students—almost a third of them—withdraw from school. She knows she has made mistakes. She admits she was not prepared for what these kids are like. As cruel as they can be to her, she thinks they're even more cruel to each other. She listens to them talk, and what she hears makes her sad. She's astonished at their apathy, at how little they seem to care about their future. Watching them, feeling the sting of their scorn, she can't believe that before these kids entered GOALS they signed contracts pledging to work hard in their studies.

"I was under the impression," she says, "that the students voluntarily came into the program with a desire to graduate."

She is appalled at how much the other teachers here are asked to give of themselves—at how hard they work, struggling to hold back the flood—and how little they are paid in return, both in respect and in money. She's not talking about herself. She's talking about the veterans such as Mr. Klapka and Mrs. Hay and Mr. Feazell and her mother, Mrs. Badders, the longtime math teacher. The ones who stick it out, year after year.

"Defense contractors can make more money building bombs than you can for educating students," she says. "I think that's ludicrous."

People can smile at her idealism if they want; ms. trimm does not care. She knows she's right on this. She also knows that the time has come for her to leave Largo High. Next week will be her final week. She has had enough of teaching for, oh, maybe a thousand years. She needs to figure out what to do with her life, she says. She plans to spend the next couple of months joining some activists on a cross-country march for peace and justice. Until then, she has a few more days of riding out the storm.

She does the best she can. On this day, Mike Broome and her other students are supposed to be working on an assignment. Instead, most of them are sleeping, playing Hangman, scooting around the room in their desks and toppling the desks onto the floor. One boy stands at the board, drawing a stick figure of Michael Jordan, soaring toward a hoop. From the back of the room, other kids cheer him on.

Mike Broome hurls his tennis ball at one of them.

"Shut up," he says.

He turns to ms. trimm, who is staring at him, clearly trying to hold her patience.

"Why are you giving me that psycho look?" he says.

She does not reply. What could she possibly say to this boy that would make a difference? What could anyone possibly say to him?

MS. TRIMM'S LAST DAY IS THURSDAY, APRIL 5. PREDICT-ably the level of chaos in her classes seems to rise almost by the minute. By the end of the afternoon, the kids are turning out the lights, wandering freely into the hall and back, ordering pizza, hiding in the supply closet, playing Black Sabbath on a tape deck, throwing chalk at each other, throwing erasers, staging mock fights, trading imitations of Ronald Reagan, turning on the overhead projector and using it to make shadow animals with their hands.

"We're going to trash this room!"

"This is the deadest party I've ever been to."

"Can we play Strip Pictionary?"

"Excuse me, ms. trimm. We're never going to see you again, right?"

"Isn't it a fun last day, ms. trimm?"

"Hey, ms. trimm? Who you going to miss least of all?"

Quietly she watches on. She told them they could have a party; after all, this is the last day before spring break, and some other teachers are relaxing the rules as well. She's doing her best not to let it get too far out of hand. She stops the boys when they try to fight, tells them to avoid screaming if possible, refuses to allow them to play Strip Pictionary. When they order pizza, she insists they order at least one vegetarian pie for her and other noncarnivores.

Finally the last bell of the day rings, and they all file out the door. Some shake her hand, some give her hugs, others just wave over their shoulder as they race down the hall.

"Have fun on the peace march!"

She stands at the door, smiling and waving. When the last of them is gone, she turns around and faces the wreckage of her classroom. With a sigh, she begins a one-woman cleanup operation, straightening the desks, picking up the trash.

"I'm not planning on having any kids," she says.

Still, the experience has not been a total disaster. Something nice has happened. Something that tells ms. trimm maybe all her good intentions weren't wasted after all. This week, after she told them she was leaving, she gave her students one last writing assignment. She asked them to do a paragraph describing her. As usual, some of them blew off the assignment. But others got out a piece of paper and scribbled away with uncharacteristic fervor.

One girl wrote:

Ms. Trimm is not a hippie or a freak. Ms. Trimm is an art form . . . I guess its okay if I say I look up to her and the ways she sees life.

A boy wrote:

You are the neatest teacher I ever had. You are the only teacher I ever had that plays catch with us and 4 square with us and plays wall ball with us and lets us draw pictures and hang them on the wall and all kinds of other neato things.

Another boy:

You're my favorite teacher . . . Don't leave or I will kill you.

They gave her carnations, a balloon, guava juice. And a card, too. A card that showed a bunch of animals in a zoo, looking sad.

We got this card because it is just like us. (Goals) Have a great time.

They signed it, of course, with their names. And with tiny peace symbols.

MIKE BROOME IS NOT ON HAND TO SAY GOODBYE TO MS. trimm. Earlier this week, while the other kids were describing her in their paragraphs and preparing for the spectacle of her last day, Mike was serving a sentence in the detention hall, otherwise known as the intervention center. Who knows where he was this afternoon.

With each passing day, Mike sinks deeper and deeper. His teachers are more worried about him than ever. On the rare occasion when they catch a glimpse of him in the halls, they can't help noticing how unhealthy he looks. He has grown increasingly thin; his hair has become scraggly and dirty; he usually appears to have arrived at school without a shower. It's not just that he doesn't care about his classes anymore. He doesn't seem to care about anything.

"He's *really* skinny," says Mr. Gerber, Mike's shop teacher. "I think he's undernourished."

Like the other teachers, Mr. Gerber has talked to Mike, trying to get him to open up and say what's wrong. But Mike is shutting them all out again. He hasn't told any of them, for instance, about what has been happening lately with his dad.

It has to do with Mike's birthday. He turned fifteen on March 29, late last week, and though he'd probably never admit it to anyone at school, he's been upset ever since. He's hurting, because he didn't get a card or a phone call from his father in north Florida. This doesn't excuse Mike's behavior; it doesn't even completely explain it, since he's been slowly reverting to his self-destructive ways for several weeks now. But it might account for the fresh infusion of bile he's brought to school in recent days.

Even after his birthday, Mike was still hoping to hear from his father. With the impending arrival of spring break, he was especially eager to talk to him; he wanted to see if his dad might come get him so they could spend the week together. But with no word from the man, Mike didn't even have a chance to ask. Finally, when he could wait no longer, Mike put aside his pride and picked up the phone himself. His dad told him not to worry. He had remembered Mike's birthday, he said; in fact, he said he'd already mailed him some money for a present. As for the two of them spending the week together, Mr. Broome said he was busy—he'd been working seven days a week at his convenience store job—but that he'd try to find a way to make it happen. He told Mike to call him back on the Friday when spring break starts.

Friday comes. Mike calls, and his dad tells him he's still trying to work it out.

Next morning—Saturday morning now—the phone rings.

"Tell Mike I'm not going to be able to come and get him," Mr. Broome says to his ex-wife when she picks it up. "He's old enough to understand."

Later, when asked about this sequence of events, Mr. Broome would explain that he truly did want to spend the week with his son, but that he couldn't get a day off work to drive down and get him. He offered to send bus fare, he says, but his ex-wife told him Mike was too young to ride a bus alone. Mr. Broome also says that he did send the birthday money, but that the envelope was returned because he mistakenly put down a wrong address. But he mailed it again, he says.

Either way, the money never arrives.

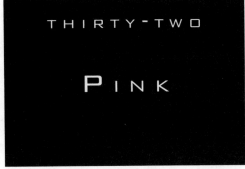

THIRTY-TWO

PINK

PLEASE, NO. PLEASE.

Heather Pilcher stands in her bathroom early one Wednesday evening, staring at the tiny circle that's about to change her life. She has just taken another home pregnancy test, mixing a sample of her urine with some chemicals provided in the kit, then pouring the mixture into a plastic container roughly the size and shape of a thimble, then adding a few more drops of another chemical solution into the mix. Sitting in the center of the test container is the small paper circle that will show the results of the test. Now, as Heather watches, the circle is doing about the worst thing possible, which is to turn pink. In fact, it's turning bright pink. Desperate to make it change back, desperate to do something—anything—Heather picks it up and blows on it with tiny puffs of air.

She knows it won't do any good. She has known all along, ever since that afternoon when the condom broke with Chris. This is simply the proof she lacked before. What is she going to do? How is she going to tell her parents? What will she say to everyone at school, to the others in the Bible studies group? What kinds of prayers will they offer for her and her baby?

No.

Still in shock, she goes to her bedroom and calls Chris, who knew she was taking the test and is waiting to hear the word.

"Well . . . ," she tells him.

"What?"

"It was positive."

Chris starts to cry. "We can't do this," he says. "We *can't.*"

"It's too late," she says, crying now, too. "We already did."

She can't talk for long. She can hear her mother down the hall, calling her to dinner. She hangs up the phone, tries to collect herself, then joins her parents at the table. They know she's been talking to Chris, and now she's having trouble hiding the fact that something is wrong. Her eyes are puffy and red.

Her father looks at her.

"Well, if he's the kind of boy that makes you cry all the time," he says, "then I don't think this is going to work out."

Heather doesn't say a word. Even if she wanted to reply, she wouldn't know where to start. She stares at her plate and begins to eat.

ANOTHER DEADLY MORNING IN FOURTH-PERIOD PHYSICS. Once again the teacher is stationed at the front of the room, droning on and on. YY and Amy, seated together in the third row, are only half-listening. Bored out of their minds, they have decided to play another round of the Line Game.

Amy scribbles something on a piece of paper, then shows it to YY.

"What you give is what you get."

YY studies the paper, then writes down her answer: *Derrick.*

Amy nods. Correct.

YY takes the paper, scribbles something of her own, then shoves it back toward Amy.

"It's not you, it's me."

Amy stares at the line, writes another answer: *Justin.*

YY nods.

Back and forth they go, exchanging quotes that have been addressed to them by various slime molds of the opposite sex. The object of the game is to guess which slime mold had the audacity to utter which line. Some of their favorites include:

"I really want to be friends."

"Believe me, things will work out, and for the better."

"I missed you, and I'm not driving all this way because you're a last resort."

"Try and be sober next time I see you."

Most of these lines were originally inflicted upon Amy. Though she's still a proud member of the V Club, Amy is notorious for the number of guys she dates. Like Meridith, who has avoided getting too close to the opposite sex ever since that bad experience during her sophomore year, Amy plows through boyfriends, drawing them in and then slipping away at the last second. The two of them are different in this respect from Karin and YY, who take a more serious approach to romance—probably too serious, since they tend to get attached to one guy and then eventually take the big fall. Amy and Meridith are more playful about the whole thing. Keenly aware that they are only in high school and that there will be plenty of time later to get serious about men, they revel in all the age-old games. They love to chase and be chased; they feint and parry and play hard to get; they have no reservations about discarding anyone who gets possessive or tries to latch on too tight. The two of them are always scamming on someone new. Especially Amy. When it comes to getting boys, nobody can keep up with Amy.

"She's like a satellite dish for hot guys," says Karin.

One day, just to humiliate her, YY and Mer and Karin and Jason Davenport and some of the other AB-12 rats compile the names of all the boys Amy has gone out with since her freshman year and write them down on the blackboard in the newspaper room. Accounts of the final total would later vary. Some said the number was only in the low thirties. Karin insists that there were fifty-two names in all; she also says that Amy later complained, not because she was upset over the list, but because they'd forgotten to include one guy.

"I did *not*," says Amy.

"She did," says Karin. "I *swear* it."

Tormenting Amy remains one of the Fearsome Foursome's favorite pastimes. Karin is particularly ruthless. She plays with Amy's hair, twisting and pulling it. She burps in Amy's ear, serenades her with annoying songs, pokes her in the ribs, honks the horn of her car, gets out the old yearbooks and points out what a geek Amy was in her freshman year, mocks her when she's angry, bugs her when she's trying to talk on the phone. Karin also taunts her with incessant clucking.

". . . bawk-bawk-Bawk-Bawk-BAWK-BAAWWWK!"

"Karin!" says Amy, finally getting mad.

That's the whole point of these exercises. Amy is so perfect, so insistently and infuriatingly flawless, that it's reassuring to push her over the edge and watch her lose it. So the other girls do it all the time. They make fun of how fashionable her clothes are, how effortlessly slender she is, how pathetically helpless she looks when she's feeling sick.

"YY, did you see her lip tremble?" says Karin, riding Amy when she comes to school one morning complaining of an alleged fever.

"I'm sick," says Amy, begging for mercy. "I am. *Listen* to me."

The girls are willing to take their laughs wherever they can these days. They blow off steam whenever possible, hurling the sacred darts, teasing each other without mercy, arguing over the existence of the Christ figure in *Heathers,* dropping onto the tabletops at the back of AB-12 and ranting away at the ceiling.

"I want to sleep," says YY, rubbing her eyes. "In my own bed. By myself."

They continue to rip Ms. Westfall, gagging and rolling their eyes every time she comes over the P.A. system and delivers her pep talks. But the edge to their attacks is gone; the fiery anger of the old days has died away. They may still skewer Judi, but they do it now out of habit, with a sense of duty, as though it's just part of their jobs. The girls are so busy with their classes, they don't have much energy to spare for hating their principal. Even YY has mellowed. Despite what she wrote in her editorial at the beginning of the year, Miss I-Want-Nothing-to-Do-with-the-Shorts-Program has broken down and applied for an honor card so she can wear shorts like all her friends, most of whom, for the record, never understood why she objected in the first place. It was easy taking a stand back in October, when cold weather was on the way. But now it's April and the heat and humidity are creeping back up.

"Leave me alone," says YY, laughing wearily when someone calls her on it.

Karin remains hopelessly lost in her Algebra II class. She still sits in front of Bret Harper, who's doing just as miserably. By now, Karin and Elvis are both coming to terms with the fact that they'll undoubtedly flag the entire course. It won't stop them from graduating; the two of them already have all the credits they'll need. Still, it's no fun feeling so lost.

Elvis seems to have achieved a kind of inner peace on this subject. Sometimes he doesn't even bother listening to the teacher's lectures or filling out her worksheets. He's so far gone, he just sits calmly at his desk, leafing through issues of *Baseball Digest*—while the others work on their algebra assignments, he tries his luck at the magazine's trivia quizzes—and playing with his Nintendo Gameboy. He's no help at all to Karin, who is nowhere near inner peace. She still stares in bewilderment at the teacher, sighs, tries without success to understand the finer points of parabolas and polynomials.

"Say that again," she asks Ms. Fish. "Huh?"

Good news, though. The other day, Karin discovered that she'll be going to college after all. She received a letter of acceptance from an actual institution of higher learning—Florida Southern College, which is fine with her.

Considering the pressure they're under these days, this is not a bad time for the Heathers. Despite the waves of fatigue that keep washing over them, they all seem to be holding up remarkably well. All of them, that is, except YY. She has so much work to do between now and the end of the semester. The countless deadlines, the endless preparation for her upcoming advanced placement exams, the homework sessions that stretch toward dawn. She's not sure she can make it. She has suffered this kind of crushing anxiety before—sometimes it seems as though she has spent every moment of high school feeling this way—but this time is different.

Some mornings, she comes to school so completely shattered, suffocating in such a state of near hysteria, that she shuts herself off from the others. She doesn't want to speak to anyone, doesn't want to look at anyone, does not care to hear a single word from even her closest friends.

"Go away," she tells them, flipping through the pages of her books, pulling frantically at what's left of her eyelashes. *"Go away."*

She does not reach her breaking point, however, until the Latin convention. That's the weekend in late April when she finally loses it, when the fragile order that she and the others have maintained begins its inevitable collapse.

The moment when everything starts to go wrong.

ANOTHER OFFERING AT THE SLAVE AUCTION.

THIRTY-THREE

DECLINE AND FALL

THE HOTEL IS CRAWLING WITH Cyclopes. They stalk across the grounds in their loincloths, one-eyed giants dripping with blood as they move past the ice machines and the soda machines and the sparkling pools lined with sun-baked bodies. Generally they steer clear of the front lobby, avoiding the watchful attention of the bellmen and the rigid smiles of the desk clerks, heading straight for the hotel's convention center. They lumber through the courtesy lounge, growling, swinging their clubs, dragging behind them the corpses of their hapless victims.

Occasionally they stop and pose for photographs.

Across the lounge, over by the complimentary juice table, barefoot maidens in flowing gowns stroll hand in hand with warriors wearing breastplates and swords. They coo, flirt, gaze longingly at each other, do whatever they can to pass for Dido and Aeneas.

"Dido and Aeneas?" says a spectator, obviously confused. "Who were they?"

"Well, you know the Trojan War?" says one of the Latin teachers judging this year's costume contests. "Aeneas was one of the survivors who left Troy. His destiny was to get to Italy so his descendants would go on to found Rome. But first he got blown off course and ended up in Carthage, where Dido was the queen, and he dallied with her for a year or so."

"Dallied?" says another judge, listening on. "I like that."

"So Aeneas and Dido were, like, a hot couple?"

Both judges smile. "Very hot," they say, answering in tandem.

Outside the hotel, across the front parking lot, in a meadow that has been designated for the day as the Olympic Field, they're about to start another chariot race. This is one of several qualifying heats, with six chariots entered in this heat, and now their teams inch them forward into position at the starting line. The charioteers stand ready in the back, slightly crouched, staring into the distance.

"I'm going to start you with a whistle," calls out an official. "Remember, we want the top three."

The whistle sounds, and suddenly the chariots hurtle forward, their carriages bumping up and down across the grass, their drivers swaying and tilting as they fight to keep their balance. Standing at the finish line, some fifty yards or so away, the judges call out the winners, who are already hooting and yelling. Within minutes other teams roll forward into position, ready for the start of another heat.

All of the chariots in today's competition are handmade, constructed of plywood, particle board, and sheet metal—one particularly impressive vehicle boasts elegant faux gold trim—and are pulled not by horses, but by crews of sweating, grunting students, including one boy who sports what appears to be a studded leather tunic, just like a young Ben-Hur. These races can be a rough business. Despite the required safety inspections, some of the chariots still crack apart, and in the past there have been a few minor injuries. In the headlong rush of the heats, team members have been known to fall and get run over by their own chariots.

"All right, then," says the official. "This is the final heat."

Another whistle, and once again the chariots dash down the field, leaving tiny dust swirls in their trail. The pounding footsteps of the runners, straining at their harnesses, ripple together into a rolling thunder that sounds remarkably like a herd of galloping horses.

''MEDEA'S A WENCH.''

"Medea's cool. So she killed her kids. So what?"

YY and a friend stand in their togas beside the Olympic Field, debating the merits of the famed enchantress who married Jason and used her magic to help him and the Argonauts lay their greedy paws on the Golden Fleece. YY is speaking up for Medea. Putting aside for a moment the nasty business of how she offed her own children—she did it to get back at Jason, after he dumped her for another woman—YY argues that Medea was actually an early feminist. At least she had the backbone to stick up for herself, she says. She certainly didn't take any crap off her ex-husband, Jason.

"She took a stand," says YY. "She got him."

It's Friday, April 27, the second day of the annual state Latin Forum. YY and seven other members of the Largo High Latin Club, including Elvis—the man seems to be everywhere—have joined more than fifteen hundred other Latin students from schools across Florida. They have all gathered here at the Hyatt Orlando, a sprawling hotel that sits beside the rush of traffic on Interstate 4, not far from Disney World. Under the watchful eye of their teachers, these kids are taking part in a whirlwind of activities, all dedicated to proving that Latin, and the history and mythology surrounding it, are very much alive.

The forum kicked off last night over in Florida Hall, a huge cattle barn of a room with walls draped in black curtains, where the kids and their teachers stood up in the opening ceremony and raised their voices together in the pledge of allegiance. In Latin, of course.

Fidem meam obligo vexillo Civitatum Americae Foederatarum et Rei Publicae, pro qua stat, uni nationi, Deo ducente, non dividendae, cum libertate justitiaque omnibus.

Since then, the forum delegates have done their best to turn the Hyatt into a modern-day version of Rome, with nearly everything but the orgies and the executions. They're dressing up for costume contests, competing in quiz bowls, running themselves ragged in the chariot races and other Roman games, showing off their knowledge in a series of rigorous written exams, including the Cicero exam for which YY has been studying all year. Last night they had a talent show; tonight they're going to head back to Florida Hall and let down their hair at a video dance and lip-sync contest, put on by none other than Mark Granning and LAMP Productions, the same audio-visual wizards who staged Largo's lip sync last

December. On the final day, LAMP will also kick the awards ceremony into high gear with a spectacular computerized slide show.

The students love the Latin Forum, not just because of all the events, but because they get to spend three days cavorting around a hotel with hundreds of scantily clad members of the opposite sex. The togas are just the beginning. Many of the kids, male and female alike, spend hours at poolside, scoping each other out in their bathing suits and bikinis. That's the best thing about this Hyatt; the rooms are scattered around the grounds into four clusters, and each cluster has its own pool and hot tub. For years now, kids at this convention and others—the state's high school journalism association also meets here every spring—have been stuffing themselves inside those hot tubs. Just last night, kids from one school managed to squeeze twenty-five bodies into one tub.

The adults try to keep everybody's libidos in check, constantly patrolling the halls outside the rooms. Even so, the convention is charged with an undercurrent of teenage sexual tension. The kids trade juicy stories about adultery and incest and other sex games enjoyed by the emperors, invent double entendres that play off their knowledge of both Latin and English, decorate their T-shirts with mottos and sayings that sound vaguely indecent.

"Habeat orgeam," proclaims one shirt at this year's convention. Rough translation: "Let's party." *"Just fac it,"* says another. It doesn't really mean anything, but it sounds good. *"Fac,"* the irregular singular imperative for the verb "to make," is always popular at the forum. A couple years ago, the Largo students created a minor stir when they hung a bed sheet off a balcony hotel room adorned with the words *"Fac me."*

"Lies, lies," says one of them now, laughing as the incident is recalled. "All lies."

For pure bawdiness, however, nothing can touch the forum's annual sex slave auction. No one has the audacity to call it that—according to the convention program, the event is officially known as Rent-a-Roman—but that's exactly what it is, or at least aspires to be. The auction is a fundraiser in which the Florida Junior Classical League makes money by selling off various kids to the highest bidder. Naturally most of the slaves are girls—girls in togas, usually wearing very little underneath—and naturally their selling price is determined by their desirability and by their willingness to please whoever buys them.

"We're going to start the bidding at ten dollars," says the student auctioneer, directing the crowd's attention to one of the first slaves, a girl named Angie. "Come on, ten dollars. This is a fox here."

Angie is indeed attractive, with a deep tan and a figure that might have tempted Caesar himself. She stands before the crowd, offering herself with a smile. She turns slowly around, giving them a full profile and a good view of long bare legs. But so far, no one is ready to bid more than half the asking price.

"Take off the toga," says the auctioneer.

With a little coaxing from him and the audience, Angie is persuaded to perform a striptease. She pulls down a shoulder of her toga, flashing her cleavage. She reaches for her rope belt, pulls it untied, and flings it dramatically into the air, then wiggles her hips until her toga drops to her feet. Suddenly she is wearing nothing but her bikini.

"Now *this,*" says the smiling auctioneer, "has got to raise the bidding."

In the crowd, boys hoot and whistle. "Take it off! Take it off!"

Soon Angie is sold. Others are sold as well, with the repeated suggestion that they will be required to do whatever their masters demand. No one is expected to take this literally; the students all understand that the auction is just an elaborate tease, since their adult chaperones would severely punish anyone who was caught having sex. Still, if the slaves are willing to play along with the game and show their stuff in front of the crowd, then that's more than enough to get money flowing out of the kids' pockets.

"We're going to start the bidding at three dollars," says the auctioneer, pointing to a slender blonde girl named Sara.

She is pretty enough, but not as pretty as Angie and her bikini. At least, that's what the auctioneer believes, or he would not have set the starting bid so low. Even worse, Sara is not willing to remove her toga or otherwise perform. She stands there quietly, obviously chagrined as she waits for someone to bid.

"You got to make them want you!" yells one of the boys.

"She don't put out!" says another.

Finally someone takes pity and shells out the three bucks to get her off the block. Another girl takes her place and is immediately subjected to similar remarks from the crowd.

"What can she do?"

"She can do a lot," says the auctioneer.

"Can she talk dirty?"

"Of course she can talk dirty."

The afternoon stretches on. Each slave waits quietly in line for his or her turn. One of the boys—Ben-Hur, the guy in the studded tunic—strips to the waist and flexes his muscles, prompting the audience to scream and whistle. A group of girls pool their money and buy him for $37.55, reportedly the most ever paid for a slave at one of these auctions.

"Tonight he's ours," says one of his new owners, grinning as they lead him away.

YY and Elvis and the rest of their contingent stand to the side, looking on.

"No one wants to be auctioned off this year?" says Mrs. Troiano, their teacher. "I don't blame you."

In past years, YY and other Largo girls have offered themselves as slaves at the auction. But they found it distasteful and are not willing to do it again. "I guess I should be flattered that a couple of us went for twenty dollars a couple of years ago," says YY, shaking her head with disgust.

The official hypocrisy here is a little tough for her to swallow. As a teenager, she's used to getting double messages from the adults, but this one is too much. Since last night's opening ceremony, the teachers who run the forum have been continually reading the riot act to her and the other students, reminding them that boys are forbidden to enter girls' rooms and vice versa. Yet in the name of raising precious funds, these same moral guardians have allowed the staging of an event that runs on the illusion of sex for sale, on fantasies of erotic submission and domination. Apparently it's okay for the kids to act the part of strippers and whores, just so long as nobody sets foot inside the wrong hotel room.

YY and the others aren't in the mood for this kind of nonsense. Exhausted from all their schoolwork, they were hoping this weekend would be a mini-vacation, a chance to sit in the sun and take it easy for a few days. But so far, the forum is turning into a disaster. One of the Largo girls, Janice Rooney, broke her thumb last night in the doorjamb of their room, and they had to take her to a hospital to have the hand put into a splint. To make matters worse, the forum's organizers have canceled Pompa, the annual processional that traditionally opens the chariot races and the other games on Olympic Field. It's usually one of the forum's highlights, a mass spectacle in which all the delegates put on their togas and other costumes and march together under the banners of their schools with their chariots out in front. But this year the organizers decided that Pompa was just too much trouble, and the Largo kids are sorely disappointed. To them, it's just another sign of vanishing spirit at the forum.

"Half the people aren't even wearing togas this year," says Janice, looking sadly around Olympic Field.

Not far away, on the side of the meadow, the slave auction is going strong. The auctioneer is still calling up new slaves; the crowd is still hooting and calling out for them to take off their clothes. When two slaves are auctioned at once, it's advertised as a "two-for-one" special. When three girls are sold together, they are referred to as a "harem."

"That would be pretty degrading, wouldn't it?" says one of the Largo kids.

Finally the last slave is called up. A slender black girl, she steps forward silently, staring at the ground. Maybe she's just embarrassed; maybe she has suddenly been struck by the historical antecedents of this moment. But once the bidding starts, she covers her face with her hands.

''OKAY! PLACES!''

Mark Granning, still reigning as Godzilla, lord of sound and light, stands in the darkness at the back of Florida Hall, his arms folded across his chest, his voice ascending to the ceiling as once more he calls his minions to their stations.

"JOSHUA, ARE YOU READY?"

Granning has taken his command position backstage, behind a giant rear-projection screen and directly in front of the control consoles. Wires snake across the floor at his feet; banks of VCRs and power amps and slide projectors and video projectors—not to mention the video editing system, including the special-effects generator—surround him. Walls of speakers rise above his head, threatening to bury him.

"EVERYBODY READY?"

He looks one more time at his watch, which shows eight-thirty.

"ROCK AND ROLL!" he yells. *"DO IT!"*

Strobes begin to flash, the music begins to play—the first number is "Good Thing," by Fine Young Cannibals—and at the other end of the hall, the locked doors are finally opened. A sea of young bodies pours inside, rushing for the open floor in front of the video screen.

Within moments the dance is in full swing. As the songs hurtle forward, one melting into the next, the screen flickers with their accompanying videos, the ones that normally show on MTV. Granning's kids, meanwhile, are shooting live footage of the crowd with several cameras—two of them stationary, plus one mobile unit wading through the mass of flesh on the floor—and putting it up on the screen next to the videos. The result is a pulsing sensory overload. When Granning cues up "Love Shack," by the B-52's, for instance, the kids dance to the music, watch the video, and stare at the screen so they can watch themselves dancing and watching, all at the same time. It's like an electronic hall of mirrors.

Off to the side, viewing the frenzied festivities with a look of school-marmish disdain, sits the official censor of the dance. She has already alerted the LAMP crew to her presence; her job, she informed them, is to make sure nothing unseemly occurs. Last year, during one of the lip-sync skits, a student mooned the audience, and the powers that be are determined not to allow a repeat performance.

Granning looks over at the censor, smiling. He doesn't want any kids dropping their pants, either. But if a couple of them try it, he's not sure how this woman plans to get there in time to stop them.

"What's she going to do," he says, "run through the crowd?"

"These people are so paranoid," says one of his assistants. "They're such snobs."

Prudishness is nothing new among the Latin teachers. One year, at an earlier forum, there was a priest who stood vigil at the side of the dance floor. The padre was hard to miss, since he was in his black shirt and collar. He was the adviser to a bunch of kids from a parochial high school. Granning walked up and asked him if there was anything wrong.

"No," he said. "I'm just here to make sure my students don't touch each other during the dance."

Granning still laughs when he thinks back to the priest. Godzilla and the LAMP crew have been handling the audio-video gigs at this convention for years now, and though they're grateful for the work, their usual cooler-than-thou attitude makes it impossible to resist making fun at every chance. It's one of the forum's fringe benefits. All weekend, they've been going on about how pitiful this whole thing is, calling the teachers a bunch of argumentative tyrants and the kids a bunch of clueless geeks. Who else, they ask, would waste years of their lives studying a dead language? Who else would drive all this way to take voluntary exams?

"There are some nerds in this place," Granning says with a grin. "Fifteen *hundred* nerds in one place."

"I suffer through these things," says Alison the Switchzilla Goddess, who is working the forum along with Kristin the Switchzilla Goddess and Rashida the Mixmistress and a dozen other LAMP kids. "I can't stand the music these people pick."

Granning and the others take a moment now to peek out from behind the video screen, watching the Latin students as they dance and perform a string of skits. At this moment, for some inexplicable reason, a girl with a microphone appears to be attempting an imitation of Barbara Walters.

The LAMP kids watch on, shaking their heads.

"This is *so* bizarre."

"What dweebs."

"I told you so."

Just outside the dance hall, oblivious to the backstage sniping, YY and the other Largo girls are walking around in a collective panic. They had planned to attend the dance, but now they're too frazzled, pacing back and forth, railing away at themselves, at one another, at anyone who will listen.

"We are in *deep* shit."

"I *tried* to get them out."

"We're going to get in *trouble.*"

"They were *on* the balcony."

They've been like this for an hour or so, ever since the unfortunate incident in their room. It happened late this afternoon, not long after they returned from the games at Olympic Field. It was still light outside, and everybody's clothes were on, and the door to their second-floor room was open. YY and Janice Rooney and the other two girls from school were just hanging out, reading and talking and watching TV, when suddenly Elvis and a couple of the other Largo boys walked in unannounced, headed for the balcony, and started tossing a tennis ball to another kid on the ground. They weren't out there for long before a teacher and someone else from another school spotted them, and instead of doing the human thing, which would have been to simply tell the boys to clear out, she reported them to the proper authorities. Soon afterward, one of the teachers in charge of the forum phoned the room and told the girls that they were in serious trouble and that investigators would be sent to their room later, after the dance, to question them about the infraction.

YY can't believe it. Certainly she and the others have broken their share of rules at these forums. They've climbed around outside on the balconies; they've dangled each other upside down from the balconies. They've even sneaked liquor into their rooms. In fact, YY believes that one of her unofficial duties as the president of the Latin Club—Mrs. Troiano would die if she knew—is to help her younger colleagues obtain alcohol and join them in getting smashed. But this makes no sense. They're getting reamed out over a tennis ball? Don't these teachers have anything better to do on a Friday night? Are their lives that empty?

"It's so childish," says YY, leaving the other girls as she heads off to find Mrs. Troiano. "I mean, come on. I'm going to be eighteen in a couple of months. I'm going to be going off to college and living on my own. I don't need somebody all over my case because I've got somebody of the opposite sex in my room."

YY rants on and on, whipping herself into a fury. She knows what will happen when her mother finds out, she says. Helen the Hun will give her the usual speech about how that's life and how we have to learn to take responsibility for ourselves and accept the consequences of our actions, blah, blah, blah. "But me," she says, "I'm not going to say a word. I'm just going to let them yell at me. It'll be just like Ms. Westfall razzing me. Just like any adult getting on my case about stupid things . . ."

Finally she tracks down Mrs. Troiano in a conference room, huddled with other Latin teachers. The two of them talk outside in the hall. Mrs. Troiano is not surprised to see her; she has already heard the news. Scandal travels fast.

"Don't give me that look," says YY.

"What am I supposed to do, kid?" says Mrs. Troiano, putting a friendly arm around her. "It's happened. Let's see what the results are."

"Why can't they just mind their own business?"

"I agree. I figure if we just blame it all on the boys, it'll be okay."

Mrs. Troiano smiles, trying to cheer her up. She tells her not to worry, tells her there's nothing they can do until the investigators show up.

"I know," says YY, biting her lip. "But we weren't *doing* anything."

"Okay. Well, go have fun for a while."

YY wanders away, not sure where to go. She finds a table in a deserted courtyard outside the convention center and sits down for a moment. It's a cool night, and she wraps her arms around her shoulders and shivers.

"I don't feel like going to the dance, you know?"

She stares off into the distance, stares down at her hands fidgeting before her. And then she begins to talk. She is so raw, exposed so completely, that she drops her guard and lets loose with everything inside her. Words flow out with a rush, rolling from one subject to the next. She talks about how Karin has just gone onto a mega-diet, trying to lose weight and please her mother. She talks about this boy named Matt she's started going out with and how they're supposed to go to the prom together. About her father, who has just moved into a big new apartment. About her mother, who was filling out her federal income taxes a couple weeks ago, waiting until April 14 to get started and then staying up through the night to get it done. The last-minute rush didn't faze old Helen, though. She was perfectly calm, says YY. Helen the Hun is always calm these days, she says. She's so unflappable, she doesn't even seem to have noticed that YY's on the brink. She likes to minimize YY's pressures; she tells everyone how beautifully her daughter handles stress.

"She thinks I'm so happy all the time," says YY.

When YY comes to her with something that's bothering her, Helen always tells her it's nothing. She has this line about YY's problems, one of those incredible mom lines. If that's the worst thing that ever happens to you, Helen tells her, then you're going to have a pretty good life. It makes YY want to scream. She wishes her mother could understand that adults aren't the only ones who feel overwhelmed. It would be nice, she says, if Helen would take her seriously and recognize that her problems are real, too. Just once, she asks, couldn't the woman show a little sympathy? Couldn't she get upset on YY's behalf? YY's ready to sympathize with her, if only Helen would let her. YY knows the past couple years must have been rough for her, with the divorce and all, but her mother's never spoken to her about it. Helen won't open up to YY. She'll divulge her feelings to YY's older sister, Adriana, but she won't say a word to YY and the other kids. She's too discreet. She never tells YY anything, just leaves her in the dark, dangling . . .

YY trails off, closing her eyes. She's still sitting there, drained, when Elvis and Greg Hardy, another Largo boy, drift by to see how she's doing. They talk about the incident. They wonder aloud what the investigators will ask them.

"I'm not worried about it," says YY. "Are you?"

Knowing she's lying, Elvis and Greg persuade her to stand up and join them back at the dance. There's no point in going psycho yet. Why not try to forget it for a little while?

So off they go, back to Florida Hall, where the strobes are still flashing and the music is pumping harder than ever. Granning has ordered the troops to play "Funky Cold Medina," and now the crowd is getting into it. They're dancing on the floor, dancing on the chairs, dancing on the stage beside the video screen, spinning in and out of the spotlight, casting giant shadows that merge together and skip apart, playing across the walls and across the somber face of the censor, still sitting off to the side, maintaining her vigil.

Ignoring her, the kids keep moving, watching themselves and their partners on the video screen. In the middle of the crowd, where they're working up a serious sweat, girls dance with one arm crooked behind their heads, using one hand to lift their hair off their necks; one boy, surrounded by writhing bodies, stops for a moment to slick back his hair, then dives back into his routine. Through it all, trailing his umbilicals, walks the mobile cameraman. He weaves his way back and forth, searches for dancers with exotic moves, crouches and even drops onto his back on the floor so he can catch some primo low-angle shots—he admits this is what he's after—under the skirts of the girls. It's been easy getting the leg shots tonight; this is an amazingly docile crowd. When he moves through the audience at most dances, people usually flick him off and tell him to get away. But the Latin students are so polite and proper, they just smile and make room for him. The cameraman can't understand it. What the hell is wrong with these people?

Still, in its own restrained way, this crowd is doing its best to kick out the jams. And when Madonna's "Express Yourself" starts up, the energy level on the floor rises a couple notches. The kids wave their arms in the air, singing along word for word, scoping out Madonna as she slinks across the screen; when she makes the big move and grabs her crotch, they go wild, howling and whistling, instantly forming a conga line. The adult chaperones, sitting in the back, watch on with what appears to be a mixture of indignation and outright confusion. Is it possible? Did that insufferable woman in the video really fondle her privates?

When the next number comes on, something happens. It's New Order's "Blue Monday," a rolling, gliding dream of a song that sends the crowd into a trance. As the music floats through the hall, the kids close their eyes and rock together as one. It's a hypnotic moment. Even YY has been transported. She stands on a chair near the back, completely relaxed, swaying. Time has been suspended; judgment has been suspended. She nods. She smiles. She leaves all thought behind, surrendering to her spine.

''THE THREE MAJOR RULES ARE: NO BOYS OR GIRLS IN THE room at the same time, with or without the door closed; no drinking, drugs, smoking, pills; no breaking our curfew."

The lead investigator pauses, staring into the faces of the accused.

"Someone in this room broke the first one. I'm assuming all four of you did."

Another dramatic pause.

"Let me tell you what you're in danger of. Your whole delegation could be suspended for a year. Your . . ."

YY and the other three girls sit on their beds, dazed beyond belief as they listen to the charges and penalties now hanging over their heads. Mrs. Troiano listens silently beside them, not quite sure why these people are making such an unbelievable fuss. It doesn't matter what she thinks, though; rules are rules.

It's almost midnight. The two investigators arrived a few minutes ago, and now one of them, an older woman who betrays no trace of any sense of humor, is conducting the interrogation while the other takes notes.

"Who was involved in that incident?" she says. She turns to her assistant. "Get their names down."

She presses for the details of what happened. YY and the girls, taking their cue from Mrs. Troiano, place the onus entirely on the guys, insisting that they did their best to get them out of their room.

"We were all trying to get them out," one of them says.

"How did they get in?" asks the assistant.

"We had the door open."

Off to one side, Janice Rooney, whose broken thumb is hurting, has begun to quietly cry. The lead investigator looks at her and visibly softens.

"I'm so sorry this is happening to you," she says. "But I won't minimize the situation. We have two adults who saw you, and you have admitted the situation."

Still, she says, there's one thing going in their favor. At least they've been honest. "You stood up and told me the truth," she says, "and I think that speaks well for you."

Under any other circumstances, YY would have undoubtedly laughed at such a transparent line of patronizing horsecrap. Honesty? This woman has the nerve to sit here and preach to them about honesty? But this is not the time or place for such retorts. Ignoring her pride, YY sits quietly, like a good girl, and lets the insult pass.

"What we have to do," says the investigator, who won't shut up, "is we have to take you before the disciplinary board. You need to report with your sponsor tomorrow morning at seven forty-five in the Boca Raton Room."

She and her assistant stand up. "Now, do you have any questions? Okay. We're real serious about these rules."

The two investigators say their goodbyes and head downstairs with Mrs. Troiano to question the boys and get their side of the story. The moment they leave, YY calls the guys' room to warn them that the hammer is falling their way.

"Oh shit," says Elvis. "We gotta do something."

The boys, it seems, have been busy with some real infractions. Elvis and one of the others—not Greg Hardy—have been enjoying themselves tonight, smoking Marlboro Light 100s and working their way toward the bottom of a bottle of Captain Morgan rum they smuggled into the hotel. Now, knowing they only have a few seconds, maybe a minute at most, they tear around the room, hiding the cigarettes and the booze, giving the air a liberal spraying with Lysol, cramming Certs into their mouths to cover up the smell of alcohol on their breath.

They're still at it when they hear the knock at the door. Mrs. Troiano and the investigators walk in and take their seats, totally unaware of the bottle of rum that sits at their feet under one of the beds. The drill is the same this time, only more grim than ever. Now that she's facing the real culprits in the incident, the lead investigator bears down with renewed intensity. Elvis listens to her through a rum-soaked fog.

"Let me tell you the size of the embarrassment and the hurt that you caused your adviser," she says, nodding toward Mrs. Troiano. "She brought you in good faith, and she trusted you."

The boys, who've been told that they are to be the scapegoats, volunteer their guilt. It does them no good. The investigator commends them for their honesty, just as she did with the girls, but reminds them that the rules for the forum were clearly stated. She explains how the disciplinary board will decide on the punishment; in case they have any doubts about the seriousness of the charges, she informs them that in the past, when some students were caught in a similar infraction, their principal added to the board's punishment by suspending the kids for ten days.

"From school?" says Elvis, suddenly sitting up.

The investigator nods. "For ten days."

The boys stare in horror at the investigator. They can hardly believe what they're hearing. They might get suspended? For throwing a tennis ball? What dimension is this woman from?

A few moments later, the investigators get up to leave. The boys watch them go, fixing icy stares on the back of the lead interrogator as she walks out the door.

"*Bitch,*" one of them says softly.

With that, the boys flip out—and with good reason. If they're suspended for ten days, they'll go over the nine-day semester limit for absences and automatically flunk all their courses.

Elvis is beside himself.

"If they suspend me for ten days," he says, "I swear to God I'd kill them all. I swear. *I would kill them all.* I'd blow up this hotel."

Soon he begins to ramble. He talks about how maybe when he grows up he'll run for the U.S. Senate. He'll run, he says, and he'll win, and then he'll get back at this investigator—who will be well over sixty-five by then —by cutting off her Social Security benefits. And when he's asked to explain why he did it, he says, he'll talk about this day of infamy.

"Yeah," he says, practicing the speech already, "I was a kid once. And I was caught on the balcony in the girls' room. Fully clothed."

The others are ranting, too.

"Look where honesty is getting us. I move for chicanery."

"We could have stolen a video game and not gotten in as much trouble."

Sitting on his bed, Greg Hardy flips into an imitation of Ronald Reagan on the witness stand, raising his hand to take the oath as he testifies about Iran-Contra.

"I'm sorry, I don't remember that," he says, tilting his head just right, giving his voice the old Ronnie quaver. *"I wasn't informed of that . . . I can't recall . . ."*

Maybe, says one of the boys, they should plead insanity when they go in front of the board. Or maybe, says someone else, they could cry real pitifully. Perhaps they could rent a copy of *Old Yeller* tonight, one of them suggests, and watch it together, so their eyes will already be red and puffy when they walk in there and beg for mercy.

Of course, the disciplinary board isn't the only thing they've got to worry about. After the investigators have left, Mrs. Troiano calls the kids together and tells them that no matter what action the board takes, she'll still have to make a report to Ms. Westfall.

"Great."

"Will she ask for names?"

Mrs. Troiano nods. She'll have to share everything with Ms. Westfall. But not to worry, she says. "I'll beg her for the mildest possible punishment . . . She knows you're good kids."

YY laughs.

She's had enough. It's almost 1:30 A.M., well past curfew. But she doesn't care. She walks out onto the parking lot, sits down on the trunk of the Y-mobile, and starts to cry. If she weren't so tired, she wouldn't bother wasting her tears; she'd see how laughable this whole thing is. But she can't see it. Deep down, beneath all the hostility directed toward Ms.

Westfall, YY remains an old-fashioned honor student who is always eager to please, who hates getting in trouble, who longs for approval and validation. She is exactly the type of kid who takes it to heart when someone in authority feeds her guilt-trip lines. She has bought every word the investigators told her. So now, knowing that as president of the Latin Club she has just brought dishonor to her school, YY finally cracks. She knows she's overreacting, but she can't help it. It's not just this stupid Latin scandal. It's everything.

YY can't stop crying. She sits on her car, sobbing away, letting it all pour out of her.

JUST AFTER DAWN THE NEXT MORNING, THEY HEAD FOR THE hearing to meet their fate. They have it all planned. The girls are sticking to their strategy of dumping everything into the laps of the mean old boys, and the mean old boys are expected to play along. Reluctantly the guys agree when YY lays it out for them ahead of time. They know a losing battle when they see one.

"Listen," she tells them. "I'm sorry."

Elvis, already coping with a hangover, gives her the wounded look of the betrayed. *Et tu, YY?*

The hearing goes as planned. The disciplinary board buys the story and throws the book at the guys, disbarring three of the four from the league and placing the entire school chapter on probation.

The boys slink away, disgusted. The award ceremony is scheduled for that morning, but they don't want to go, since their disbarment automatically disqualifies them from winning any honors. Instead they return to their hotel room and drop onto the beds, consoling themselves with cold slices of leftover pizza. It being Saturday morning, they turn on the TV and watch Baby Scooby Doo. Once again, he's in a heap of trouble, defending himself with the usual barking apology.

"I'm sorry."

THIRTY-FOUR

TREMORS

BACK AT LARGO HIGH, MRS. Troiano makes her report to the principal, recounting every detail of the weekend of shame. Ms. Westfall listens carefully, waiting for the kicker, wondering when she'll finally hear whatever it is her students have done that's so terrible. But the kicker never comes. Whether YY knows it or not, Ms. Westfall can recognize the difference between a real disaster and a manufactured one. Just like Mrs. Troiano, she doesn't think the incident was that big a deal. True, the boys shouldn't have gone onto that balcony. But suspend them? For ten days? Please.

No. All Ms. Westfall wants is for the boys to write letters of apology to Mrs. Troiano and to the teacher who headed the disciplinary board. And for them to use their heads the next time they want to play catch with a tennis ball.

THE DEAD ZONE IS OVER. SPRING break has come and gone, already long forgotten. Inside the faculty lounge, the teachers drop onto the couches and stare out the window, praying for the arrival of summer.

"Do you know the difference between ignorance and apathy?" says one of them, telling one of the worn-out jokes making the rounds down in D Wing. "I don't know, and I don't care."

Over in the auditorium, Heather Pilcher, who has entered her second trimester and is just starting to show, stands under the stage lights in a black habit, rehearsing to be a nun. The school's spring musical is *The Sound of Music,* and Heather is one of the devoted sisters at the Nonnberg Abbey, the same convent from which Maria Von Trapp will burst forth, singing across the hills of Austria; Chris Wainscott, Heather's boyfriend, has the male lead in the production, playing Captain Von Trapp. It's a little unusual having a pregnant Baptist playing a Benedictine nun, but nobody seems to care. The habit is loose enough so that Heather's stomach isn't noticeable, and she has such a beautiful voice, it would have been a shame to waste it. Besides, she admits there's something funny about a pregnant nun.

After the trauma of the early days, when she stood in that bathroom blowing on her pink pregnancy test, desperately trying to get it to turn back, Heather has reached the point where she can laugh once in a while about her situation. She and Chris still have some rough times ahead of them, but at least they've started coming to terms with the pregnancy. The hardest part was telling their parents.

Heather didn't have to actually say anything to her mother. Unbelievable as it may sound, the women in their family tend to be a bit psychic. Heather's aunt, who lives in Georgia, is one of these people who have a sixth sense for knowing when something bad happens to a loved one; once, when Heather's sister was sick, this aunt knew it almost instantly because she had a picture of her niece on the wall and saw it crying. Heather's mother, meanwhile, has an uncanny ability to know what Heather's thinking and to anticipate what she's about to say, sort of like the Radar character on *M*A*S*H.* Ever since Heather was a little girl, her mom has been giving her the answers to questions that Heather hasn't even asked.

"Yes," her mother will reply.

"Mom, I didn't say anything."

"Yes, you did."

It was the same way with the pregnancy. A few days after using the home testing kit, Heather was at the house, still trying to work up the courage to share the news—she'd already confirmed it with a trip to a clinic—when her mother turned to her and stared into her eyes.

"You are, aren't you?" she said.

"I'm what?"

"If you are, you are going to ruin your whole life."

Stunned, Heather kept her mouth shut. She didn't say anything until a couple days later, when she told her dad. Mr. Pilcher took it hard. For days he couldn't bring himself to look at Heather or speak to her. When she tried talking to him, he'd cry. He was so crushed, he cried every time she walked in the room. Heather couldn't believe it. She understood that this was hard for him. But couldn't he see how much harder it was going to be for her? Finally one afternoon, she decided she'd had enough. She had just come home from school—she'd had to stay late that day—and there was her father sitting in his chair, sobbing again.

"I can't stand it anymore," she told him, slamming down her books. "If you're going to be like this every time I come in the door, maybe I'll just go somewhere else."

She was outside and walking away down the street, steaming, going who knows where, when both her mother and father caught up with her and coaxed her back inside. It's been better ever since that day. Her parents aren't exactly thrilled about the situation—her father still gets worked up when Chris comes to the house—but now that they're past the shock, they're both supportive and have made it clear that they'll help any way they can. They were glad to hear that Heather was planning to keep the baby, and after learning that she and Chris were thinking about eventually getting married, they've been urging them to do it as soon as possible.

In the meantime, Heather and Chris are doing their best to enjoy the rest of the year at Largo. It has not been easy. Heather has been throwing up at school twice a day, especially around lunch. She gets into line in the cafeteria, takes one look at what they're serving, then bolts for the door. Plus, with her classes and her homework and her singing and the evening rehearsals for the play—all added to the monumental changes taking place inside her uterus—she's ready to collapse by the end of the day. She's so tired, she's starting to fall behind in some of her classes, especially in biology, of all subjects.

The hardest thing, perhaps, has been the deterioration of her relationship with God. Heather is still burdened with the belief that she sinned when she had sex with Chris that day after school in her bedroom. Though they have not slept together since, she is plagued with the feeling that she has lost something that may possibly never be regained. She no longer brings her Bible to school, and she has quietly dropped out of Logos, the Bible studies group.

It wasn't like anyone in Logos chased her away, saying nasty things. Once word of her pregnancy spread, a couple people in the group seemed to look at her differently. But none of them said anything, kind or unkind. They didn't say a word, which left Heather hurt and confused. After all those mornings together, talking about Christian charity, it would have been nice if they had let her know they still cared about her, even though she'd made a mistake.

Now there is a distance between her and the rest of the group. She leaves them alone, and they leave her alone. It's as though she'd never been a part of them.

ANOTHER BELL, ANOTHER FLOW OF BODIES INTO THE HALLS. Andrea Taylor, moving through the crush in B Wing, spies a certain wispy sophomore walking in her direction. Andrea slows down and gives this person her best glare.

"Here's a girl I really don't like."

It would be hard for the sophomore not to hear these words. Still, she walks right by, obviously doing her best not to make eye contact. Andrea turns her head, watching her go.

"She gets on my nerves."

This sophomore was once another complication that stood between Andrea and John. But there's no time to worry about her now. Andrea needs to move. A full afternoon of classes awaits her.

She stands in her chemistry lab, goggles over her eyes, squeezing a few drops of chloride into a clear liquid mixture inside a test tube. She waits, watching to see if the liquid changes color, then scribbles her observations on a worksheet.

"Clear," she says. "Okay, it's just clear."

She sits in her note-taking class, listening to the teacher reviewing from *Principles of Speedwriting Shorthand*.

"Again," the woman is telling them, "remember that our cursive capital letter N represents . . ."

One of the girls in the back row turns toward Andrea and the others and whispers an astonishing announcement.

"Twenty in fifteen minutes!"

What she means is that the teacher has just said the word "again" twenty times in the past fifteen minutes. It's a little quirk the kids can't help noticing. Whether she's aware of it or not, this teacher has a habit of dropping "again" into nearly every sentence; she says it so often, the students in this class have decided to document the phenomenon. Every day, one of them keeps a precise log, noting the number and exact time of each repetition. The record is twenty-five in one class period. Today, though, that standard might be shattered. The woman is on a roll.

"Again, if it comes at the beginning of the word . . ."

Andrea smiles. She's almost always smiling these days. It's official now: She and John are a couple at last. They had to wait for a month or so after John ended it with Sabrina, but finally the time came to stop worrying about other people.

"I don't care what anyone says anymore," Andrea told John. "I want you to be mine."

John wanted the same thing, except he had one small problem. By this point, he was slightly entangled with another girl, the wispy sophomore who makes Andrea's blood boil. Her name is Tracy. She sits next to John in his third-period algebra class, and the two of them used to write notes back and forth. Around the beginning of the second semester, they even went out a few times. It wasn't anything serious, more of a friendly flirtation, a pleasant diversion during a time when John wasn't sure whether he and Andrea were ever going to work it out. John thought Tracy was nice. Even after he broke up with Sabrina and was ready to start dating Andrea, he kept going on about this girl. He'd tell Andrea that he didn't want to be too rough on Tracy and break her heart, since she was so nice and sweet.

That's when Andrea finally snapped. Suddenly all of her reservoirs of patience and understanding, the depths of which she had plumbed so often during the heartbreak of the past months, were depleted. In their place was a sense of blistering determination. After all this time, holding back so she wouldn't hurt Sabrina, Andrea was finally ready to be ruthless. She made her move on John one week when his nice little sophomore was out sick and wasn't around to defend herself. She saw an opening, and she took it. She told John to dump Miss Sweetness. To cross her out of his life, period. No more walking with her to class. No more talking to her in the halls.

John told Andrea he'd do his best. But whatever he told Tracy, it didn't make much of an impression. The girl was still writing notes to John and calling him at home. Clearly she was not ready to bow out gracefully. So Andrea went looking for her. It wasn't hard to find her, because her locker happens to be right next to Andrea's.

"Excuse me," Andrea told her, slamming her locker to get the girl's attention. "You better stay away from him."

"What do you mean?" said Tracy, blinking innocently. "I don't like him anymore."

"Don't hand me that stuff."

The face-to-face warning wasn't enough. Tracy kept writing breathless little notes to John; Andrea kept finding them and flying into a rage. She took one of the notes and ripped it up in the girl's face. Another time, she told her that she'd better watch out, that she was about to find herself in a fistfight. No one was more startled than Andrea at how violently she was reacting. She had never done anything like this before; it wasn't like her to threaten other people. But she couldn't help it. She simply was not ready to allow anyone else to get in the way of this romance.

One day Andrea and John were walking down the hall together when they passed Tracy. As she went by, Andrea jabbed at her rival's ankles with the toe of her shoe.

"Did you try to kick her?" said John.

Now it was Andrea's turn to play innocent.

"What do you mean?"

John was amazed. He could not believe that Andrea would go so far.

"You are so crazy," he said after one of these encounters. "You are *so* crazy."

But that's all long past. It's another story for the archives. Because now, with no one standing between them, Andrea and John are finally happy. Their first real date was on March 12, the day before John's eighteenth birthday. It was a Monday, and that night, after one of John's track meets, they went to see *Hard to Kill,* which was perfect, since the title could have been written to describe their romance. Andrea was surprised she was allowed to go out that night—she almost never got permission to go anywhere on school nights—but then, her mother really likes John. Like everybody else, she senses how solid John is. She thinks he and Andrea are good together.

She's right, too. Talk about a pair that was meant to be. If John's and Andrea's lives were a movie, this would be the part where the breezy love song comes up on the sound track and plays over the montage of the two of them walking hand in hand, tickling each other at their lockers, feeding nuts to the squirrels in the park, staring up at the stars at night. Because they're doing all those things. Lately they've been making plans for the prom. They can't wait. It'll be so nice for them to dance across the floor without having to worry about anyone seeing them, so wonderful to let people see how much they belong together.

Sure, it's corny. But happy couples are always corny. It's their right. Now Andrea wears John's sweetheart necklace, lets him drive her car on their dates, and faithfully sits in the stands at his track meets. John wears her necklace and cheerfully endures the ragging of the other guys, who keep talking about how tightly he's wrapped around that girl's finger, how she's turning into his wife.

The best part is, Andrea is still on speaking terms with Sabrina. Not that there wasn't a bumpy moment or two when Sabrina first confronted her. It happened on the phone one day, before Andrea had found the nerve to bring up the subject herself.

"How's John?" Sabrina asked her.

"Fine," said Andrea, trying not to sound cornered. "Why?"

"You like him, don't you? You can tell me. I'm your best friend. You can tell me anything."

Andrea took a deep breath, then stepped off the cliff she'd been skirting for so long.

"Yes," she said. "I do like him."

Turns out Sabrina already knew. In fact, she'd suspected for some time. Ever since that day she saw John's photo on Andrea's bedroom wall and almost gave Andrea a heart attack. What started the wheels turning in Sabrina's head was not the photo. It was the look that flashed on Andrea's face when Sabrina first noticed the photo.

Of course, it wasn't until the phone call later that the two girls brought the whole thing out into the open. The funny thing was, Sabrina —an independent girl whose life does not revolve around any boy—didn't care that much. She liked John, but she didn't feel as strongly about him as Andrea did. In other words, Andrea had been torturing herself all this time for nothing, worrying about her friend's feelings. True, Sabrina was a little hurt. But once she and Andrea talked it out, everything was okay between the two of them.

"You do what you think is best," Sabrina told her. "I hope we can still remain best friends."

OFF IN ANOTHER HOUSE, ANOTHER WORLD AWAY, LAURA Sheehy has just come home after another shift at the hospital. She walks into the kitchen, checks the answering machine, and finds a message waiting for her. It's from Largo High. From a Mr. Wagar, one of the assistant principals. When she hears what he has to say, she feels the bottom drop out of her stomach.

"Jaimee has been missing classes," says the voice on the tape. "She's missed nine days of school. Can you call me back?"

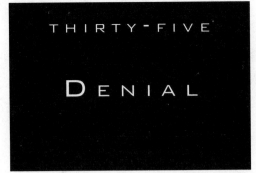

THIRTY-FIVE

DENIAL

THE SCHOOL HAS MADE A MIS-
take. Jaimee doesn't know exactly how it
happened, she says, looking at her
mother, but this Mr. Wagar is wrong.
She's not skipping again. She swears it.

"They're getting me mixed up with a
different Jaimee," she says.

Laura Sheehy listens carefully to her
daughter, not knowing whether to believe a word she says. Ms. Sheehy doesn't
know anything anymore. She had actually allowed herself to believe that Jaimee
was finally turning things around. She'd
heard Jaimee talking in detail about what
was happening in her classes; she'd seen
the homework assignments. Now Ms.
Sheehy can hardly stop herself from losing control. After all those months at
Charter, hasn't Jaimee learned anything?
What about all those promises? What
about all those times she begged for another chance?

Now Jaimee sits here in front of
her, fervently denying everything, insisting over and over that there's been
some kind of mix-up at the school. It
could have happened when they changed
her class schedule, she says. Or else

there's been some kind of glitch with the computer in the front office.

As her daughter speaks, Laura Sheehy allows herself the slightest bit of hope. She wants so much to believe. Besides, Jaimee has been so sweet lately; she's been cooperative and responsible, just like in the old days. The school did recently change her class schedule, and she has been bringing home all that math work. If she's skipping, where did those assignments come from? Computers aren't always right, are they? They can malfunction, can't they? It's possible, Ms. Sheehy tells herself, that Jaimee might be right. Maybe she has been wrongfully accused.

There's only one way to find out. Ms. Sheehy calls Mr. Wagar and makes an appointment for early one weekday morning. She wants to sit in that man's office and watch Jaimee's face when the allegations start to fly. If she can look into Jaimee's eyes, maybe she'll know what's really happened.

When the day of the appointment comes, Ms. Sheehy plays it close to the vest. She doesn't give Jaimee any warning, doesn't even hint at what she plans to do. She just tells her she'll be driving her to school that day. When they arrive on campus, Jaimee says goodbye and starts to get out of the car.

"No," her mother says. "You're coming with me."

They walk into Rick Wagar's office, another cluttered little room. Jaimee sits quietly in the corner while Mr. Wagar outlines the facts, telling Ms. Sheehy that her daughter has been skipping consistently almost since her return to school in mid-March. Just to double-check, he calls up her attendance records on the computer screen at his desk. He looks at the screen for a second, then nods. It's confirmed, he says.

"Are you sure?" Ms. Sheehy asks him.

Mr. Wagar turns the screen so she and Jaimee can see all the fives forming a line after Jaimee's name. Five is the school's code for absences. Each five, in other words, represents an absence in one of Jaimee's classes; in many of the classes, she has more than twenty of them.

Jaimee is caught. She is being forced to stare at the truth. But still she refuses. She says the computer is wrong. She says they've confused her with someone else. She wants to argue about each absence, one at a time.

"But I *did* go," she says, pointing to one of the fives. "I was at that class. I know I was there. In fourth period, three days ago, I was there."

"No, you weren't," says Mr. Wagar.

It is painful for Laura Sheehy to watch her daughter go on like this, clinging to her story. After Charter and all her other ordeals, the only thing Jaimee has apparently learned is how to tell a more elaborate and convincing lie. Ms. Sheehy feels like a fool for having believed her. The mistake, she realizes now, was putting Jaimee into regular classes instead of back in GOALS. Down in the pod, the attendance clerk, Mrs. Welch, checks to make sure that every GOALS student is in every class every period of every day. It's one of the best things about GOALS. If a kid disappears for even one period, Mrs. Welch is immediately on the phone, calling that child's mother or father at work to let them know. But in the regular classes, there are too many kids and too little time to always pay such close attention. Teachers take attendance in every class, but unless a student misses a large number of days, parents are not routinely notified. Now Jaimee is back where she started, haunting the halls.

She still won't own up to it. Even now, as she sits here, cornered by her mother and Mr. Wagar and the evidence on the computer screen, she insists they've got the wrong person. She keeps talking about how she was excused for the days she missed.

"I have a pass," she says. *"I have a pass."*

Jaimee has already piled up enough absences to fail two or three semesters, and all she can talk about is her hall pass. Her mother stares at her daughter as though she is studying an alien creature. She watches Jaimee, lying over and over. It's frightening to see how convincingly she does it. Maybe, her mother wonders, she really believes it. Maybe Jaimee doesn't even know she's lying.

PROM IS JUST AROUND THE CORNER, AND THE MEMBERS OF the Fearsome Foursome are blazing ahead with preparations. For weeks they have been shopping for the right dress, hunting for the right shoes, plotting their pre-dance dinners, finalizing every detail of what they hope will be one of the best evenings of their lives. All four of them have found dates; Amy Boyle will be going with Greg Hardy, YY's friend from the Latin convention.

Karin, meanwhile, is still on her mega-diet, fighting to bring down her weight before the big night. The others have seen her on diets before; sometimes it seems as though she's never been off one. But this time there's an extra degree of urgency to the battle. This is Karin's senior prom, and for once she wants to look as perfect as everyone else. Of course, it didn't help when her mother decided a couple weeks ago that the dress she'd picked out made her look heavy. Karin was devastated. She'd searched forever for the dress—she and YY must have hit every shop in central Florida—and finally she found a beautiful pink gown, with puffed sleeves and a puffed waist and a straight skirt. She thought it made her look thin, but when she tried it on at home, her mother said something about the skirt accentuating Karin's hips.

Karin tried to joke about it afterward, but it was obvious she was crushed. She already had planned to lose some weight, but her mother's observation made her all the more determined. For weeks she has been on this crazed liquid diet, chugging protein shakes and staying away from solid foods. When lunchtime comes and the other girls sneak off campus and head for Royal Hoagie, their favorite sandwich place, she gets depressed because she can't go with them. Her willpower is paying off— she's lost nine pounds—but YY and the others are worried about her. Isn't Karin taking this a little too far?

The truth is, they don't know the half of it. At night, when she sits down at the dinner table with her family and allows herself something to eat, Karin sometimes gets a feeling as though she has been stuffing her face for hours. When this feeling strikes, she quietly excuses herself from the table, goes to the bathroom, turns on the water in the faucet so no one will hear, then sticks her finger down her throat until she vomits.

There have only been a few of these episodes, and Karin has told no one of them. In fact, she hardly acknowledges them to herself. She is vaguely aware that she's doing it, but while it's happening she turns herself off, allowing her consciousness to go nearly blank. When she is done, she flushes the toilet, rinses her mouth, then returns to the dinner table, talking and joking with her parents.

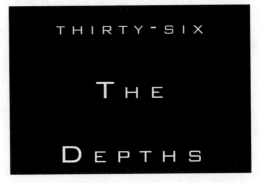

THIRTY-SIX

THE

DEPTHS

BODIES BUMPING AS THEY RACE across the stained blue carpet. Fists pounding on the scuffed-up walls, if only for the sake of pounding.

The bell has just rung inside the pod, and now Mrs. O'Donnell stands before her class, telling them that today they are going to try something different. She hands out a sheet filled with philosophical sayings, such as "We cannot direct the wind, but we can adjust the sails," and "The most important thing to goals is having one," and "The greatest mistake a person can make is to be afraid of making one." She wants them to pick one saying and write a paragraph or two on what it means to them. If they're not interested in doing that, she says, they can put down whatever's on their minds.

One boy writes his paper in a flowing stream, using almost no punctuation:

> *The most important thing about goals is having one I like that because its the shortest one and I dont wanna write a lot. This class is boring I hate doing this assignment I am Rad I AM RAD RAD RAD RAD. . . .*

A girl writes:

> *What I'm thinking of is how I don't wanna do this, plus those sayings are stupid. . . . I don't want Kevin finding out I have a boyfriend cuz I don't wanna hurt him . . .*

Another girl writes:

> *I have scared my self this pass week with strange thoughts that I don't want to be thinking. I also want to tell my boyfriend this but all he does is yell and complain . . .*

Then there is the boy who keeps making passes at Mrs. O'Donnell. The one who keeps telling her they're perfect for each other. Seeing another opening, he writes:

> *I need to have sex do you think that you can help me with my problem*

Mrs. O'Donnell reads this and laughs. At this point in the year, after losing so many students, she's happy to detect any signs of life in her classroom. She still makes time for show-and-tell, still climbs on skateboards, listens patiently to stories about Jimmy Page and other guitar heroes. Day after day she and the other GOALS teachers do whatever they can to keep the lines of communication open with the kids who are still around, hanging on. Mr. Klapka breaks down their resistance with his relentless string of awful jokes; Ms. DiLello hypnotizes them with her subatomic stare. Across the hall, inside the GOALS office, Lois Welch lets them cry on her shoulder.

Meanwhile, a new English teacher has just been hired to take over ms. trimm's classes. She arrives her first day and immediately gets down to business, calmly taking the roll among the cannibals who consumed her predecessor.

"Chris?"

"Here."

"Okay, turn your chair around, please."

She looks to the next name on the list.

"Mike?"

No answer.

"Mike Broome?"

Still no answer.

"He's up on the steps," someone says.

On to someone else.

"Philip?"

"He died."

"Larry?"

"Right here."

She looks up from the roll book.

"A couple of things I want to go over," she says. "First of all, my name's up on the board. It's Mrs. Terwilliger."

She has compiled a list of class objectives. She passes it around, explaining that they will be completing these objectives, learning each of them before the end of the semester.

"I doubt it," says a smirking boy.

Mrs. Terwilliger, a young woman with auburn hair and an air of unmistakable purpose, either does not hear this or chooses to ignore it.

"Today you can cross off number three," she tells them. "Today and tomorrow we're going to be working on business letters and completing forms."

Another boy screws up his face. "We have to write a business letter today?"

"Yeah."

Two of the other kids sit off to the side, paying no attention, talking loudly. Mrs. Terwilliger asks them to stop. When they keep it up, she walks over and stands quietly before them, waiting for them to stop.

"You know what? I don't know what you did before. But when I talk, it's just me. It's not anyone else. And that's the way I run the room."

"Well," says one of the girls, "when ms. trimm was here everybody talked."

Mrs. Terwilliger does not look impressed. That's too bad, she says. Because that's not how it's going to be anymore. She passes out their books, directs them to page 263, then starts the lesson. For a few minutes, there's still some whistling and talking. But even the rowdiest kids in the room can tell that the anarchy of the past is over. Soon they are all working quietly on their assignment.

"You like being a teacher?" one of them asks.

"Yeah."

"Don't you get tired of us?"

Mrs. Terwilliger smiles.

"I just met you."

"HOW DO YOU LIKE MRS. TERWILLIGER?" Mrs. Palmateer asks Mike Broome one day.

Mike looks confused. "Who?"

"Mrs. Terwilliger. She's in for ms. trimm now."

"Oh. I didn't know that."

Mike and Mrs. Palmateer have these conversations all the time. As his assistant principal, she makes a point of walking over to him on the steps every day at lunchtime and telling him to go to class.

"Do I have to?"

"Yes, Mike. You have to go to class."

He tries to ignore her. But Mrs. Palmateer keeps after him until he heads toward the pod. She knows it's only an act, though. Once she walks away and continues on her rounds, he sneaks back onto the steps. He still makes an occasional appearance at some of his other classes. He sticks his head in Mrs. O'Donnell's doorway almost every day to say hello; one morning he startles Mrs. Frye's critical-thinking class—several students nearly fall out of their chairs—when he shows up and actually takes a seat. No one can figure what he's doing.

"I know you're here," says Mrs. Frye. "But why?"

On another morning, he turns up in his second-period math class and does his best to sleep through a review of negative-number equations. Ms. DiLello stands near the overhead, taking the class through a series of exercises. When she gets to number five, she calls on Mike, forcing him to wake up and stare at the problem on the screen: $(-3 + -8) - -9$

"What's the sum?" she asks him.

"I don't know."

"What's negative three plus negative eight, Mike?"

"Negative eleven."

Together they work it through, subtracting the negative nine from the negative eleven and ending up with a negative two. Mike finally sits up and pays attention. Still, he does not bother to write down any of the problems. Ms. DiLello tries to get him to join in.

"Mike," she says, standing beside him, "you like this stuff."

He looks away. "I already failed this year."

"It's not too late. If you pass the six weeks, you have a chance to appeal."

She's right. If Mike could somehow get himself together and start going to his classes, he could file an attendance appeal at the end of the semester and possibly get a wavier for all the days he's skipped. If he's willing to give his teachers that much—willing to show them that at least he's trying—they might still be able to persuade the attendance committee to give him a break. But Mike doesn't see it that way. As far as he's concerned, the situation is long past salvaging. He doesn't care, he says. What's the point?

"I'm not even going to bother with an appeal," he tells his friends. "They'll still reject me. I know they will."

Mike is plunging even further into the depths these days, destroying everything he'd managed to build early in the semester. His grades. His credits. His chances of passing any of his classes. He's tearing it all apart, kicking and clawing and stomping on even the smallest blade of hope.

His mother has given up, too, having tried everything she could think of. The dirt bike was the last straw. For months, Mike had begged her to get him a dirt bike, as though he thought she had all these piles of extra money lying around. Finally Jewelene Wilson gave in, telling him that if he stopped skipping, she'd buy him the bike. So Mike got his wheels—she bought him a nice little Honda—and headed back to class. But a few days later, the school was calling to tell her that Mike was skipping again. For a while, it seemed as though the phone rang almost nonstop. But the school doesn't bother anymore.

The other day, inside his room at home, Mike had another one of his famous explosions. He was arguing with his mother, and he picked up his radio—one of his most prized possessions—and hurled it. Then he saw his mother, saw the look on her face, and he backed up.

"You do that again," she told him, "and I'll knock you through a wall."

Sometimes it's hard to believe there could be so much deadness in someone so young. He stares without interest at the TV, plays another round of Nintendo, lies on his bed for the thousandth time, and listens to the traffic outside. He had a job for a while, working at a car wash, but then he got tired of it and quit. He has a girlfriend these days—he's seeing Tabatha Turner, the girl with the Oh Shit necklace, who fought so hard not to cry that day in Mrs. Palmateer's office—but he doubts that's going to last too long, either. With Mike, not much does.

His dreams of joining the Air Force are long forgotten by this point. He doesn't even talk about it anymore. He openly admits that he plans to quit school next year when he turns sixteen. Until then, he has no choice but to keep showing up at Largo High, wandering through what's left of a wasted year.

For a time, after he started skipping his other classes, he would pass the hours with Mr. Gerber. He already had Gerber for two classes, gym during first period and shop during sixth period, but soon he began showing up three or four times a day. Mr. Gerber knew Mike was supposed to be somewhere else, but he let it go, figuring it was better than letting him roam the campus all day, getting in trouble. In the last few weeks, though, Mike has started skipping even his classes, blowing a solid A in both gym and shop. He asks him what's wrong, but Mike won't tell him anything.

"I don't know," Mr. Gerber says one morning, standing inside the gym, watching Mike and some other GOALS students shoot baskets. "I'm stumped with him."

He stares at the boys as they chase after the ball, scrambling for a shot. He's been trying to get them to go outside into the sunshine to play flag football, but they won't do it. They can't stand losing, he says. They get behind by one touchdown, and they give up, refusing to play anymore. He can't understand it. Where's their spirit? When did they become so defeated?

Mr. Gerber sighs.

"It's scary to see what's happening. It really is," he says. "I really love these kids, but geez . . ."

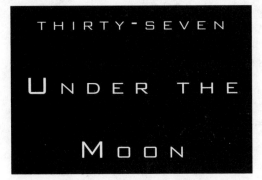

A LUMINOUS SATURDAY NIGHT IN early May. Ghostly vapor trails stretch across the sky, lit from behind by the moon. A soft breeze, touched with the scent of salt water and freshly cut grass, moves through the live oaks, stirring their tangled beards of Spanish moss.

Out on the roads, an armada of limousines makes its way northward, headed for the hall in Tarpon Springs where the prom is already under way. There are white limos and black limos, with freshly polished hoods and tires that hum across the pavement; they slip through the darkness like sharks on their way to a feeding. In the backseats, behind the tinted windows, sit the couples, who have just come from candlelight dinners and who are now bathed in the soft blue light of flickering TV screens, drinking champagne, laughing, wondering whether they will end this evening alone with each other inside a hotel room.

Behind the wheel of his older brother's white Chevrolet Cavalier, Elvis sips his rum and Coke and takes another bite out of his pre-prom burger. Elvis does not need a limo or a candlelight dinner. He does not harbor any expectations

involving hotel beds. On the biggest date night of the year, he is dateless. He was going to ask someone to the prom, a friend of YY's, but at the last second, after he spent days working up the courage to approach her, YY informed him that this particular person was already going with someone else. Elvis took it fairly well; he's used to this kind of thing. When it comes to love, it's possible that his luck is even worse than YY's. Once, last year, he sent three dozen roses to a girl at school—had them delivered to her in the front office—and asked her to a dance. The girl turned him down, telling him she didn't plan on attending.

"She wanted to be my friend instead," he says, thinking back to the moment of shame. "That f-word."

As it turned out, the girl showed up at the dance with another date. Even worse, Elvis later found out that she had tossed his roses into the back of her car and let them bake in the Florida sun for days until they rotted. Still, word of his bold gesture quickly spread and earned him the affection of other girls, some of whom he'd never even met before.

"If you send me three dozen roses," they'd say, sidling up to him in the hall, "*I'd* go with you."

Now, on the night of another romantic shutout, Elvis finds himself in

his brother's car, alone except for a friend who's also dateless. The boys
are trying to take a philosophical approach; the way they figure it, they're
saving a ton of money going stag. They each had to buy a prom ticket and
rent a tux—Elvis went with the classic black model—but otherwise, this is
turning out to be a cheap evening, since they don't have to spring for a
corsage or dinner or a limo or even a hotel room. Let the other guys drop
seventy bucks on chateaubriand for two; Elvis and his buddy just stopped
at the drive-through window of a Hardee's. Elvis got himself a burger and
fries, plus a large Coke to mix with the rum that his brother graciously
bought for him.

They're barreling along on Alternate 19, one of the county's main
north-south arteries, a winding road that skirts along the Gulf of Mexico,
which is glittering this evening under the moonlight. Onward they drive,
working on their drinks and trying not to think too much about girls. It's
a long ride, more than ten miles north of Largo, taking them through
Dunedin, through Palm Harbor, past the tiny roadside attraction known
as the Chimp Farm, past the trucking company with the huge sign that
says *Truckin' for Jesus,* past the sponge docks in Tarpon Springs, until
finally they arrive at the hall, a big building that sits alone on a slight ridge
on the outskirts of town. When they pull into the lot, there's a line of
limousines at the front, shining in the entryway lights. Couples are emerg-
ing from the back, then walking up the front steps, arm in arm.

Elvis and his friend take one last gulp of their drinks, pop some breath
mints into their mouths to cover the telltale smell, then head inside to face
the music.

IN THE CENTER OF THE PARQUET DANCE FLOOR, ANDREA TAY-
lor and John Boyd hold each other close, swaying in a sea of couples. She
is wearing a white gown with a ruffled hem; he is wearing a white tuxedo
and carrying a white cane, which he holds behind her as he dips her
backward. They are easily the most dazzling pair on the floor. As they
glide through the crowd, their bodies are dappled with the swirling reflec-
tions from the mirror ball that spins above them.

They danced like this last October, on that night after Homecoming,
when Andrea leaned against John and smelled his cologne and realized
with a start that she did not ever want to let him go. But tonight is
different. Tonight Andrea does not have to worry about anything. It's
wonderful.

The two of them are so engulfed in each other, they scarcely have a chance to notice the prom decorations, which are even hokier than usual. This year the prom committee might have outdone itself. The theme for the dance is "One Moment in Time," which is taken from the song of the same name, and to honor that theme, the committee has done its best to have the entire hall transformed into a huge time machine. When people enter the hall, they must first walk through a corridor, strewn with hundreds of flashing lights, which is supposed to be a time tunnel. Once inside, they travel through the centuries by walking to different parts of the room, where they can gaze upon various monuments that are designed to evoke the spirit of different epochs.

In one corner, representing prehistoric times, someone has erected a model of a volcano—it looks like a giant mound of melted tofu—that actually belches smoke, as though it were threatening to erupt. In another corner, the pharaohs of Egypt are commemorated with a gold-colored pyramid that rises four or five feet off the floor. At the back of the room, guests are greeted by a motley collection of tiki masks and torches and other items that could easily have been taken from the walls of a Polynesian restaurant; this display, the least impressive of the three, appears to be a gratuitous nod toward the South Pacific, though it doesn't seem to include any specific time reference. The tables where couples sit and rest their feet, meanwhile, are adorned with centerpieces made from tiny hourglasses, which people are already breaking off and stuffing into their purses as keepsakes.

"I don't get it," says Kristin the Switchzilla Goddess, staring in disbelief at the pyramid. "The prom committee must be imbeciles."

Kristin is here with Mr. Granning and the rest of the LAMP crew. Prom is no longer just a dance; like everything else these days, it has been transformed into a video event, which means that LAMP's technical services are once again in demand. This is their second prom of the weekend. Last night they did one for Northeast High, and here they are again, back with their attitudes and their monster amps and their walls of speakers and their special-effects generator. They've set up camp on the other side of the floor, just behind the giant screen, which is jumping with a series of videos, from Young M.C.'s "Bust a Move" to R.E.M.'s "Stand." The mobile cameraman is winding his way through the crowd once more, still trailing his umbilicals, getting live shots to flash up on the screen next to the videos; just like at the Latin Forum, the kids on the floor are doing the electronic hall of mirrors routine, dancing and watching themselves dance at the same time.

"Let's play something slow after this," says Mr. Granning, making sure the song list includes plenty of dreamy numbers for the lovers in the audience. Sinéad O'Connor's "Nothing Compares 2 U" comes on, and the couples hug tight, wrapped in each other's arms.

Judi Westfall, on duty as always, stands off to the side of the crowd, watching them slowly circle across the floor.

"I still get goose bumps," she says, sighing happily.

Tonight is turning out to be a relatively easy prom for Ms. Westfall. No one appears to be chanting "Get laid, get fucked," as the crowd did last year during Billy Idol's cover of "Mony Mony"—in fact, LAMP has been discouraged from playing that song this year—and only a couple of kids have been caught with alcohol out in the parking lot. The campus police officer and various administrators have been patrolling the lot all evening, keeping their eyes and nostrils open, and a couple of them are now standing guard at the front entrance, checking to make sure that no one tries to smuggle any booze inside.

Some students, who have little patience for such close supervision, only stay at the dance for a short while before they quit the hall and retreat to less restrictive venues. For many kids, prom night is not really about the prom but about what happens afterward. Showing up at the dance is almost a formality, a mere warm-up to the highlight of the evening, when they head for their hotel rooms. Not everyone rents rooms —not everyone wants to or can afford it—but for lots of students, it's the only way to wind up the night.

Getting a reservation isn't always easy, since most hotels technically don't rent rooms to minors. But most kids find a way, either getting their parents or an older friend to make the reservation or finding a hotel clerk who's willing to bend the rules. This tradition, which has become increasingly entrenched in the last decade or so, puts many parents in an awkward position. Do they act like prison wardens and refuse to let their kids spend the night in a hotel, even though half of the senior class already has reservations? Or do they give in to peer pressure, knowing that this is just another rite of passage on the way to adulthood? Because that's what prom has become: an elaborate ceremony in which kids are officially allowed—sometimes for the first time in their lives—to shake off all the restrictions of childhood and finally act like adults. They dress up, they go out to a fancy dinner and a dance, then spend the night in a hotel room, where they drink what they want and stay up as late as they want and do whatever they please with whomever they please.

For the record, whatever they please does not necessarily mean rolling around underneath the sheets. Lots of kids, especially those who aren't involved with anyone at the moment, rent a suite of rooms with a gang of their friends and throw a party. But for others, sexual expectations are never higher than on prom night. Some girls, caught up in the fairy-tale trappings of the event, actually wait for prom to lose their virginity. They might spend part of the night at a party down the hall, drinking with their friends, but the key moment in the evening is when they retire with their boyfriends to their own private room.

Of course, Ms. Westfall and the other adult chaperones here at the dance are fully aware of what kids will be doing tonight after they leave the hall. The tradition is so well known, it would be almost impossible for the administrators not to know. Still, there's not much they can do about it, other than try their best to see that no one gets drunk at the dance and then climbs behind the wheel of a car. Besides, the night is young, and the prom is still in full swing; no one's likely to be heading for a hotel room this early. Out in the lobby, kids are casting their votes for the Prom King and Queen—YY and Karin and Andrea have all been nominated for Queen—and getting in line with their dates to get their photos taken.

Inside, the crowd is slow-dancing away, working itself into another one of those mass trances. Amy Boyle and Greg Hardy are staring into each other's eyes in the center of the floor; YY and her boyfriend, Matt, are swaying not far away. Karin Upmeyer, looking considerably thinner after her weeks of dieting, leans close to her boyfriend, putting her head on his shoulder and shutting her eyes. John Boyd is quietly whispering something into Andrea's ear, making her laugh. It would not be an exaggeration to say that there's a hint of something magical floating about the room. A suggestion of possibilities. It's there in the makeup of the crowd. YY and company are all on hand, as are Heather Pilcher and Chris Wainscott and all sorts of patio people and many of those from the rail and most of the Raw Dogs—John's been clowning with them all night—and even a few GOALS students, all looking beautiful in their gowns and tuxes, all of them dancing together under the lights. For a moment, it seems as though all the walls are down, as though everyone truly were part of the same school.

Before everyone knows it, the music and the videos are being stopped for the announcement of the King and Queen. YY doesn't care if she wins; she's not even sure why she was nominated, except perhaps as a joke. Karin and Andrea don't particularly care, either. They'd just as soon see it go to Shana Denton, who is obviously dying for this crown after her disappointment at Homecoming. Shana's boyfriend, Jamie Bryant, is up for King, and if they both win, they'll get their big romantic moment together under the spotlight.

"We need everybody to move back off the floor," says the junior class president, who's holding a microphone. "Is everybody having a good time?"

The audience screams.

"Okay. Let me explain this. After we announce the King and Queen, they'll come out and do a dance to 'One Moment in Time' . . . So you guys ready? The 1990 Prom King is Jamie Bryant . . . and the 1990 Prom Queen is Shana Denton."

Shana and Jamie come up front for their coronation, and the music begins, and finally they get their dance. As the song fades away, the first jangling notes of U2's "With or Without You" wash over them, and the other couples move onto the floor, locked together, whispering to each other, tenderly kissing. Before things get too sappy, though, out come the pounding rhythms of Salt-n-Pepa's "Push It," which gives the boys a good excuse to finally toss away their jackets and gets the girls to kick off their shoes. Now it's really time to dance.

THE MUSIC IS STILL BLASTING AWAY WHEN PEOPLE BEGIN TO discreetly disappear. By midnight, the floor is almost empty.

YY and Matt, on a double date with another couple, go to Matt's house, where all four of them will be spending the night; they'd probably be having a nice time if the other couple weren't in the middle of a big fight. Meridith and her date, Justin, head for a party at another house. The two of them aren't really dating—they only went to prom as friends —and when they arrive at the party, they flirt with other people. Eventually Meridith ditches Justin and leaves with another guy she's just met from Countryside High. Amy and Greg, who've been double-dating with Karin and her boyfriend, go to Amy's house; Amy has been drinking, and on the way home, she gets her dress stuck in the car door. Later, at the house, everything goes fine until Greg makes the mistake of telling Amy that he loves her.

"Okay," she says, wondering what else she can possibly say. A guy has never told her this before, and Amy doesn't really like it. Greg is getting far too serious; the moment he says the fateful words, she begins to plot her escape from their relationship. A few minutes later, she politely leads him to the door, wishing him good night.

Elvis, still dateless, still behind the wheel of his brother's Cavalier, speeds southward down Alternate 19. He and his buddy have been joined by another passenger—another lovelorn friend, who somehow got separated from his date—and now the three of them are ridding themselves of a little excess energy by racing with a guy they know in another car. They're going seventy-five, eighty-five miles an hour, passing each other over and over again, hooting and yelling. When they're done, they pull into a 7-Eleven, where Elvis buys a gigantic Slurpee to mix with his rum. He's well on his way to getting trashed when they wind up at a party at the La Quinta Inn near the interstate, where some people they know have rented a few rooms. Elvis, drinking even more heavily now that he's no longer driving, scams on a girl whose date has wandered off. Although the massive amounts of alcohol would later cast a haze over his recollection of this encounter, Elvis somehow manages to secure this girl's phone number. It's not exactly a huge victory; it's not like he actually winds up with any meaningful physical contact. But on a night like this, he'll take it.

A mile or so to the north, in a private room at the Holiday Inn, away from all the parties and the crowds, John Boyd has just opened a bottle of berry-flavored Mad Dog and is now offering some to Andrea. But when she tastes it, she makes a face and says she doesn't want any.

"Well, fine," says John, acting hurt. He nods toward the bed on the other side of the room. "You just sleep over there, 'cause I'm sleeping over here."

Andrea's mother rented the room for them. She wasn't thrilled about it, but Andrea was straight with her, telling her that if she didn't help them, they'd find some other way to be alone that night. So her mom, who came to terms long ago with the fact that her daughter is becoming an adult, made the reservation. Still, when she called the hotel, she requested a room with twin beds.

Now here's John, playing with the situation, pretending like he's mad, telling Andrea to stay away. She keeps getting out of her bed and trying to climb into his, but he keeps pushing her away.

"Get out," he says, trying not to laugh. "Why do you think your mom got these separate beds for us?"

Finally, when he stops joking, they turn off the lights.

THIRTY-EIGHT

COLD WAR

THE MEAN STRETCH HAS BEGUN.
Now that prom is over, the brief moment
of grace that revealed itself on the dance
floor has quickly vanished. The school
has officially entered the last few feverish
weeks of the year, when the papers and
exams become a constant barrage and the
tension level skyrockets. With graduation
night fast approaching, the entire campus
has been seized with a sense of grim in-
evitability. Tempers are flaring. Nerves
are fraying. Suddenly everything seems
on the verge of falling apart.

The next step in the collapse of the
Fearsome Foursome—the widening of
the pressure cracks that first appeared
when YY broke down at the Latin Forum—comes just two days after prom.
On Monday, May 7, when Amy and
Meridith declare war against each other.

There probably wasn't any way to
avoid it. The two of them have been
headed for a blowup for weeks now.
They're like two sisters who have been
cooped up forever inside the same room.
Amy, always so perfect, always in the
right, has been getting on Meridith's
nerves, and Mer, who remains as elusive
as ever, still reluctant to open up and

share her feelings, even with her closest friends, has been bugging Amy. Naturally, when the blowup finally comes, it comes over something silly. The ostensible reason for the fight involves the dinner before the prom. Amy and Greg had planned to go out with Mer and Justin, but at the last second, Mer backed out, changing the reservations at the restaurant. When Amy found out, she was crushed. She asked Mer what had happened, and Mer said that Justin preferred that the two of them went alone, that he wouldn't have been as comfortable doubling with the others.

"Justin doesn't know Greg," she said, "and he'd feel stupid."

Technically this wasn't true. Meridith was the one who wanted a little privacy. She also didn't want a repeat of last year's prom, when she and Amy double-dated with the two guys now known as the Prom Dates from Hell. So she fudged a little, trying to get out of the dinner tactfully, without hurting Amy's feelings. Unfortunately Amy later talked to Justin, who was apparently none too thrilled about being ditched by Meridith at the post-prom party and who had no compunction about blowing the whistle on Mer's story. Now, on this Monday, as the two girls sit out on the patio together at lunchtime, selling tickets for the senior picnic, Amy lets it be known that she's angry.

"What's wrong?" Mer asks her.

"I know that you lied to me."

"I'm sorry. I thought it would hurt you. I thought it would ruin your night."

In better times, when they're not under so much stress, this apology might have been enough to take care of things. But as the minutes drag by, both girls grow angrier and more distant. They don't say another word to each other through all of lunch. In fact, they barely exchange a word the rest of that day. Or the next day. Or the day after that. Suddenly, walls of ice have descended between them. They won't even look at each other when they pass in the halls or in AB-12.

"I'm fine," says Amy, not very convincingly. "I'm just acting like she was never one of my friends."

She looks away. After all these years they've spent together, she doesn't understand Mer.

"I don't know her," she says. "I *never* have known her."

Mer, always the quietest of the four, avoids the subject entirely. She doesn't want to talk about it; she doesn't even want to acknowledge that anything is wrong. She just smiles and goes about her business. But clearly she has removed herself to the safety of some inner room.

As the days go by with no sign of a reconciliation, YY and Karin start to get desperate. They have to do something. They don't know what, but this has to stop. Because if it doesn't, sooner or later the two of them will be pushed into choosing between the two combatants. Which could mean the end of all their friendships.

It never occurs to the girls that once again they are reenacting a scene from *Heathers*. They've been doing it all year, sometimes on purpose, sometimes accidentally. First they were dressing up in the costumes and conducting the lunchtime poll. Then they were dealing with a backlash just like the girls in the picture. Now this. Just as two of the Heathers slug it out in the movie, Amy and Meridith are locked in their own battle of wills, threatening to tear apart the very thing that made them all so indestructible.

E V E N   A N D R E A   A N D   J O H N   A R E   L O O K I N G   S H A K Y .   A F T E R   A L L they've been through, John still can't seem to rid himself of other entanglements. Andrea has just heard through the grapevine that he's been hanging out with another girl and has actually kissed her. Even worse, he denies it when she confronts him.

That night, after she asks around and finds out that he's lying, that the story is true after all, Andrea tracks John down at the house of one of the other Dogs and pulls him out into the yard to talk it out. It's raining— first just a sprinkle, then hard—but Andrea doesn't want to budge. She stands there in the middle of the downpour, demanding an explanation.

"I just want to know," she says. "Are you just playing games with me?"

John pauses, watching the rain wash across her face.

PART FIVE

SOLITAIRE

LINGERING BEFORE THE BELL STRIKES FOR THIRD PERIOD.

THIRTY-NINE

WANDERLUST

ON THE TUESDAY AFTER PROM, one day after Amy and Meridith begin their split, an army of angry teachers stages an assault upon the state capital in Tallahassee. Armed with signs and banners, they have come to march, to rally, to beg, to threaten, to do whatever it takes to prod the governor and the legislature into giving more money to education.

"You know what we need right now?" says Mike Klapka, roaming with a friend through the maze of long white corridors inside the capitol building. "We need those cellular phones."

Mr. Klapka, who has taken the day off from his GOALS classes at Largo, is only half-joking. He and his partner—Marshall Koppel, a guidance counselor from Pinellas Park High—are here not just for the mass demonstration, but also to hunt down legislators so they can talk to them face-to-face, pleading the case for the public schools. It's a thankless job, especially for ordinary people like teachers, who have almost no money and almost no power and who therefore have less than zero leverage. But if they were equipped with cellular phones or beepers or one of the other status symbols commonly carried by Tallahassee's movers and shakers—if they could at least look like people with clout—then maybe someone would take them seriously.

Officially Mr. Klapka and Mr. Koppel are working as lobbyists for their local classroom teachers' association; other Pinellas County teachers are prowling these halls, too, lobbying other legislators. But it's painfully obvious that they're only amateurs at this game. Even dressed up in jackets and ties, wearing their most sober faces, they're clearly in a different league from the professional lobbyists who keep charging out of the elevators, hurrying past them with their designer suits and their designer ties and their high-voltage attitudes.

"It's tough to compete against that," says Mr. Klapka, shaking his head.

They've got to try, though. Increased funding may not be the answer to all of education's problems, but as a veteran social studies teacher who has taught everything from honor kids to dropouts, Mr. Klapka knows firsthand that the public schools are stretched to the breaking point. Classrooms are overflowing, jam-packed with so many bodies that teaching becomes an exercise in crowd control. Basic supplies are running low; at some schools, textbooks are so scarce that sometimes there's only one set per classroom, which means that kids don't always have books of their own, which means they can't take them home for homework. Last year, funds were so tight at Largo that some members of the faculty were asked to sell doughnuts to defray the costs of running the copy machine. Not surprisingly, people were offended.

"The Great Doughnut Debate," Mr. Klapka calls it. "My personal feeling was 'I'll do it this one time but don't ask me again.'"

As if that's not bad enough, Florida's teachers are shockingly underpaid, forced to make ends meet on salaries that tell them all too clearly how little they're valued. It's an amazing contradiction. In a country that supposedly cares about education, a country where every president claims to be the "education president," movie stars get millions of dollars for uttering a few lines of dialogue and quarterbacks get millions more for hurling a piece of pigskin down a field. Yet Mr. Klapka, who's thirty-three and has been teaching for nine years, shaping hundreds of lives, makes a grand total of about $24,000 a year. (That's $7,000 less than the average salary for American teachers; at this point, during the 1989–90 school year, the National Education Association reports that Florida's average teacher salary ranks twenty-eighth among the fifty states.) With a wife and a young son, it's just not enough. Despite the long hours at school, Mr. Klapka is often forced to work a second job as a sales clerk at a department store.

One time, at a party, someone asked him what he did for a living.

"I teach."

"Gee," said the other person. "I'm sorry."

Mr. Klapka doesn't regret the profession he chose. He has his moments of frustration, like anybody else, but when you see him in the classroom, it's obvious that he gets a tremendous kick out of working with students. Still, something has to be done, he says. There has to be more money, so the school systems can build more classrooms and buy more textbooks and start paying teachers a decent salary. A few years ago, Florida voters approved a new state lottery that was supposed to be a huge boon for public education. It hasn't exactly worked out that way, though. The lottery pumps tens of millions of dollars into the schools every year, but Governor Bob Martinez and the legislature keep draining away much of the increase, using the lottery funds to supplant tax dollars that would otherwise be budgeted for students and teachers. In the end, as education officials have been telling anyone who'll listen, the schools are still getting shortchanged.

Which is why Mr. Klapka and the other teachers are here today in this Panhandle town. Tallahassee is a deceptively pleasant little city, with rolling hills and streets lined with red azalea bushes and white dogwood trees —the dogwoods bloom every spring, when the legislature is in session— and barbecue joints where the waitresses serve the iced tea already sweetened, Southern style. The tallest building around is the capitol itself, a twenty-two-story concrete tower flanked by two half-domes. Taken together, the tower and the two half-domes bear a striking resemblance— people have been commenting on it for years—to a giant erect penis, nestled between two giant testicles and rising straight into the clear blue sky.

Whether it was designed to look that way or not, the effect is completely appropriate, since the capitol constantly seems to be overdosing on testosterone. It's a notoriously macho environment, known for its power plays and backstabbing and petty feuds. Some years ago, a couple of state senators almost came to blows on the floor of the chamber, cussing away at each other, with one of them threatening to whip the other's butt right there in open session.

In a place like this, teachers naturally fall to the bottom of the food chain. Though they'd never admit it publicly, many legislators loathe this point in the session, when the teachers arrive to make their annual plea for more funds. One of the legislative staffers, a former teacher who's comfortable talking off the record with Mr. Klapka and Mr. Koppel, makes no bones about how poorly they're received.

"Oh, the legislators say it all the time," she tells them. "They say, 'Yeah, it's Teacher Day. Oh God, does that mean they're going to be hounding us about money?'"

Nevertheless, Mr. Klapka and his colleagues are giving it their best shot, going for strength in numbers, hoping that if enough of them pound their message home, they'll be able to scare someone into paying attention. That's why so many of them are carrying signs that say *I touch the future, I teach. I touch your future, I vote.* That's also why the high point of today's efforts is the rally, which will begin with a march to the steps of the Capitol.

The whole thing kicks off shortly before noon. Hundreds of teachers, who've traveled from around the state in caravans of cars and buses, gather in a public park only a few blocks from the Capitol, where they cheer at some derogatory comments about Governor Martinez and wave signs with other slogans, such as *If you can read this, thank a teacher* and *Ask me about the "lottery lie"* and *Florida's education funding is child abuse.* A few minutes later, the whole crowd is off, chanting "BETTER SCHOOLS RIGHT NOW! BETTER SCHOOLS RIGHT NOW!" and brandishing their signs, which are flapping in the breeze, and moving down the street in a long but perfectly formed column—what else would you expect from teachers?—with six people in every row.

"No bunching please," says someone with a megaphone, keeping them all neatly spaced.

Marching in the middle of a weekday through the middle of a busy downtown, they are moderately successful in attracting attention. They are watched by a mother and her small child; by drivers in their cars, stopped at stoplights; by construction workers, leaning over their jackhammers; by police officers who sit on their motorcycles, gazing impassively from behind their sunglasses as they divert traffic away from the column's route.

"You're bunching," Mr. Klapka tells his partner, laughing under his breath. "Stop bunching."

By the time they reach the capitol, which looms above them, gleaming in the sun, the chanting and the enthusiasm of the most fervent marchers has infected the rest of the crowd. Everyone is pumped up, their fists raised high as they roar approval at the featured speakers who step forward to the microphone, one by one, to urge them on. The loudest cheers are reserved for Betty Castor, Florida's commissioner of education, who like them has been fighting to get the governor to pay more attention to the schools. When she is introduced, the teachers begin a new chant.

"BET-TY! BET-TY! BET-TY!"

Castor stands at the lectern, beaming.

"Today I want to talk to you about our role as educators and your specific role as teachers," she says, staring out at the sea of waving signs, "and the rewards that you deserve for putting your hearts and souls into teaching."

She tells them they deserve more money, more respect, more recognition for all they do. Because they're not just asked to be teachers anymore, she points out; now they're also supposed to be solving all of society's problems, serving as advisers, social workers, disciplinarians, and surrogate parents. Yet under this year's proposed state budget, she tells them, teacher salaries and the amount of spending per student would actually decrease when adjusted for inflation.

"You deserve better," Castor says, stirring the crowd into a frenzy, "and the children of Florida deserve better."

It's a rousing moment, and when the rally breaks up, Mr. Klapka and Mr. Koppel and the other teacher-lobbyists, fired up now with the energy of all the speeches, are sent off to continue their one-on-one efforts with legislators.

"Let's rock," says Mr. Klapka.

Once they're back inside the capitol, winding their way once again through the maze of corridors, reality sets in. As they go from one office to the next, hearing the same line from everyone they meet, the enthusiasm slowly disappears from their faces.

"I wish it could be better," one state representative says, "but . . ."

"I'm as supportive of education as any legislator," says another, "but . . ."

"We're down to the bare bones . . . Our hands are tied."

Mike Klapka doesn't argue with them. All rhetoric aside, he knows that what they are telling him is correct. Unless the voters back home are willing to pay more taxes—unless they recognize what it takes to build better schools—there's not much their representatives here in Tallahassee can do. Mr. Klapka doesn't know what to say. How can he and the other teachers make people understand? What can they do to show them how much of the future is slipping away every day?

"GOOD MORNING. OUR THOUGHT FOR THE DAY IS: EVEN IF you're on the right track, you'll get run over if you just sit there."

They would deny it down in the physics lab, but time has definitely shifted into a higher gear. There was a feeling of acceleration at the end of the first semester, but nothing to match this. The school is hurtling toward June with a rushing, roaring momentum; days are whizzing past at an incredible clip, one blurring into the next. Now that summer is so close at hand, the Florida sun is rapidly becoming unbearable, and once again the kids are fanning themselves in the halls and the teachers are turning on their classroom air-conditioning units.

Over in A Wing, Mr. Feazell's seventh-period history class is waiting for the bell to ring. Heather Pilcher, seated toward the back, takes the hand of the girl at the desk beside her and places it on her stomach.

"You feel the baby move?"

The other girl nods. "When are you due?"

"October thirty-first."

"Halloween!"

Heather nods. "A gremlin baby," she says, smiling happily.

Heather's doing her best to hang on these days. She's still tired all the time, and she's still falling behind in her biology class. And with the baby getting bigger and pushing against her bladder, she can hardly make it through a single class period without having to ask permission to go to the bathroom; it happens so often, some of her teachers don't even bother giving her a hall pass anymore. Now that she's past the first trimester of her pregnancy, however, she's not throwing up anymore. In fact, she's hungry all the time, craving lemons and Häagen-Dazs ice cream and a million other things. She even craves the cafeteria food. Doesn't matter how gross it is. The other day she actually ordered the dripping monstrosity that the cafeteria calls barbecue ribs.

The lady behind the counter thought she was joking.

"Really?" she said. "You really want this?"

Heather and Chris have set a date for their wedding. They'd talked about waiting until they both finished high school, but finally they bowed to the wishes of Heather's parents, who wanted them to do it sooner. The ceremony is scheduled for June, just a few weeks from now, right after Chris graduates. Heather's grandfather, the preacher, will preside.

Having a baby and getting married will mean some sacrifices. For one thing, Heather and Chris had both planned to go away to college—Chris had his heart set on a Nazarene school in Tennessee, where he could continue with his singing—but that's out of the question. Still, now that everything is decided, the two of them are excited. It certainly wasn't what they'd planned for their lives. But they're determined to make the best of it.

O NE GRAY AND DRIZZLY MORNING, WHEN THE SCHOOL IS wrapped in fog, Jaimee Sheehy meets with a girl named Tiffani just before the start of class.

Jaimee has been burning through friends again, discarding them or being discarded by them at an astonishing pace, and the odds are good that her relationship with Tiffani—Tiff, Jaimee calls her—won't survive much longer, either. For the moment, though, they are best friends, and when they hear the warning bell for first period, cutting through the fog, the two of them are standing together on the walkway outside D Wing, rubbing their arms against the early-morning chill. Tiff shivers and looks at the crowds of students shuffling into the building, headed for their lockers.

"I don't want to be here," she says.

Without any further discussion, she and Jaimee begin to roam, paying no attention to the final bell as they float through D Wing.

"My parents are getting divorced again," says Tiff. "I've had, like, forty-five parents."

The two of them glide past Jaimee's first-period class, past Tiff's first-period class, past friends in other classes who wave through the open doors. If they see others they know, floating just like them, they scold them in their best teacher voices.

"Stephanie! Get to class!"

Dipping is what they call this. They keep saying they're on their way to class. They really should go today, they say. Especially Tiff. She has a test to take in her French class. But no. They decide instead to head down to the office. Down to guidance, where they can ask for schedule sheets and ponder what classes to take next year. Or maybe what classes to dip next year.

Jaimee and Tiff are sitting at a table in the guidance area, flipping aimlessly through their curriculum guides, pretending to fill out the schedule sheets, when Tiff sights her English teacher.

"Hey," she says. "Is that paper due today?"

The teacher smiles politely. "No. Friday."

"Does it have to make sense?"

"Yes."

"I mean, does it have to be like a paragraph that goes together?"

"You have a good mind . . . I know you can do it."

Another friend—her name is Dawn—takes a seat beside Jaimee and Tiff and begins working on her own schedule. Dawn's thinking of taking floral design. She's heard there's good money in arranging flowers.

"That stuff pays off, man."

Tiff stands up and announces she's leaving. She has to go to class, she says. Really.

"I love you," says Jaimee.

"I love you, too. Ciao."

Dawn and Jaimee stay at the table. Jaimee opens her purse, pulls out a compact, gazes in the tiny mirror. She does not like the situation currently developing with her hair.

"I'm going to cry," she says.

Not to worry, says Dawn. "I just use oodles of hair spray. If it doesn't work, it wasn't meant to be . . ."

Once again, Jaimee has thrown everything away. This will be her second year of high school without earning a single credit. She is back to her haunting full-time, dipping all day nearly every day. Now that Mr. Wagar has shown her mother the truth about her attendance, Jaimee's wandering is tinged with a barely concealed desperation. She's constantly smiling and laughing, telling jokes and making funny remarks about her teachers, talking about what a bunch of weenies they are. But there's something hollow to it all. Anyone who looked closely could sense the panic; it's there in the way she can hardly hold still, the way her voice wavers, the way her eyes are always darting in another direction. She seems more scared than anything else.

Still she keeps it up, maintaining the illusion. She exists on massive denial, refusing to go to class but also refusing to acknowledge that she's not going. Mr. Wagar tries to keep an eye on her, listening to all her excuses and stories, doing his best not to be taken in. But it's too much work for any one person. One day, when she's caught skipping class and leaving campus, she swears to Mr. Wagar that she'll never skip again. The next day, though, she breaks the promise and is already missing. Another time, when Mr. Wagar manages to find her in the halls, he asks her what class she's supposed to be in, then escorts her to the door of the classroom, only to later discover that it wasn't Jaimee's class at all; once he leaves, she simply slips back outside.

"She knows all the games," he says.

Jaimee's mother, caught in the middle once again, doesn't have the faintest idea what to do. Mr. Wagar and everyone else she talks to at school keep reminding Laura Sheehy that the year is almost over, that there's nothing much they can do this semester, that Jaimee's about to turn sixteen, that they've tried everything they can think of. But Ms. Sheehy isn't ready to let it go. She's still trying to understand what's happening with her daughter. She's pushing for Jaimee to be tested and evaluated, for some expert to take a look at her and figure out what's happening. Maybe Jaimee's stuck. Maybe she's gotten so far behind that she's paralyzed. Because it's not like she's destructive or anything; she's a good kid who just got lost somewhere along the way. Only now, the cycle's getting worse. Jaimee's starting to sneak out her bedroom window again. Her mother wakes up, finds her gone, wonders what's happening. Is Jaimee at some friend's house? Is she driving around in a car? What if there's an accident? That's when the dream comes back. The one where Ms. Sheehy gets the phone call in the middle of the night . . .

Jaimee has been sitting in the office, fiddling with her schedule for almost an hour—and making almost no progress—when Alan Willey, her guidance counselor, steps out and asks her to come into his office. He has just received a note, he says, from Mrs. Badders, Jaimee's math teacher. The one whose doorway she floated past this very morning.

"I was in her class," Jaimee says.

Mr. Willey does not bother arguing with Jaimee. He tells her that Mrs. Badders reports that she has not seen her for days.

"Well," says Jaimee, "I was sick for like two weeks, 'cause I had strep throat."

"For two weeks?"

"Well, for like a week and a half."

Jaimee tries to change the subject, talking about how she wishes Largo High offered hockey. If they had hockey, she says, that would be great.

"In Florida?" says Mr. Willey.

"Yeah."

Mr. Willey quickly tries to get the discussion back on track. "How are you doing in school?"

"Better. I like my third- and fourth-period classes."

Jaimee leans forward in her chair, resting her arms on top of the counselor's desk and resting her chin on top of her arms. She watches him call up her name on his computer terminal. She sighs.

"Okay," he tells her, looking at the screen. "What I see is, you haven't been going to school . . . You need to be in school, or you're not going to pass."

"I'm in school."

Suddenly Mr. Willey looks very tired. He is assigned to watch over approximately 450 students. He does not have time for this. Yet, he wants Jaimee to pull it together. He tells her it may not be too late. She might still be able to get through the semester with some credits. She'll have to fill out an attendance appeal, but there's a chance.

"You're going to have to work hard for the rest of the year," he says.

Jaimee gives him a reassuring smile.

"Okay."

There's nothing more Mr. Willey can do. He gives her a pass and sends her off to class. On her way out of the office, she runs into a boy she knows.

"Hi," he says. He glances at her pass. "What are you doing?"

"Going to school," Jaimee tells him.

The boy looks confused.

"What do you mean?" he says.

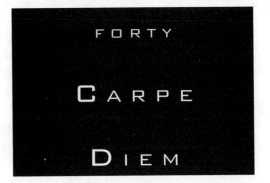

FORTY

CARPE

DIEM

THE WAR BETWEEN THE HEATH-
ers rages on.

Almost two weeks have passed since
it began, and still Amy and Meridith are
not speaking to each other. They have
been closest friends for years, and yet neither of them is ready to declare a truce.
YY and Karin can't believe it. After all,
Amy and Meridith are in class together,
eat lunch at the same time in AB-12, constantly hang around with the same
friends. They must spend at least several
hours a day within a few feet of each
other. How can they avoid talking? Yet
somehow they do. Amy and Mer are two
strong and independent spirits, both of
them equally stubborn. If they don't put
a stop to this thing fairly soon, they're
going to end their senior year this way.
One of them's got to give. But who?

Wisely the other AB-12 rats are doing
everything possible to stay neutral. With
the sketch index already soaring, even
before the war began, the newspaper
kids are flipping into altered states of
consciousness without the aid of any
drugs other than No Doz. They're hurling paper wads at each other, dragging

forks across the blackboards, openly forging teacher signatures onto hall passes.

"Have you ever thought of becoming a professional criminal?" one of them says, watching a girl fake the scrawl of Mrs. Amburgy, the newspaper adviser. "Because you're awesome. Really."

In wilder moments, some of the students are actually yanking each other's pants down.

"No more de-pantsing in the room, guys," says Mrs. Amburgy, doing her best to look sternly at Jason Davenport, who has just helped a girl perform the procedure on another girl.

"I didn't do it," says Jason, feigning innocence. "I just held her hands."

Now that the prom is over, various romances are predictably biting the dust. Amy, for instance, has already broken up with Greg Hardy. YY is calling it quits with Matt. They've been dating since February, but the truth is, she never fell head over heels for him. How could she? She tried to make it work, but Matt was always so awkward; when he wrote her love notes, he'd sign his first and last names. Plus, for the past few weeks, he's treating her like a nonentity, preferring to do the macho bonding routine with his friends. Whenever he's around the guys, he acts like she's not there. So one night, in between her marathon study sessions, YY tells him it's over.

Matt doesn't take it too well. In fact, he flips out. The next day at school, he goes into the Y-mobile and leaves a nasty note on the dashboard, telling YY how angry he is.

"Was it totally necessary for him to break into your car?" Amy says when she hears the news.

YY can hardly believe it, either. "He ignores me for a month, and he's getting mad," she says. "He doesn't have to go all psycho on me, you know."

It gets worse. Later that day, after giving her the note, Matt is riding his bicycle when he's hit by a car. He's not seriously hurt—he escapes with some minor damage to an ankle—but his bike is totaled, and when YY asks him what happened, he tells her the whole thing's her fault. The only reason he was in the accident, he says, is that he was so overwrought, so utterly consumed with thoughts of their shattered relationship, that he forgot to pay attention to traffic.

"Guys," she says afterward, shaking her head. "When you break up with them, they go through this upset stage and then they go through this hate-your-guts stage."

As if that's not enough, YY is still wrestling with her perpetual career crisis. After all this time, she is no closer to making up her mind about what she wants to do with her life. One morning—the morning of Friday, May 18, to be precise—she brings it up in Mrs. Hay's English class. The subject arises naturally, because Mrs. Hay is talking to them about college and careers and all the other decisions that await them.

"This is such a tough time that you're going through," she says. "It really is. You know that, don't you? It's hit you that this is a little stressful?"

YY and the others nod, laughing nervously. Mrs. Hay waits a moment, then asks each of them what they plan to do after graduation. One by one, they answer, talking about the University of Florida and the University of Miami and several other schools.

"Now you have to decide what you want to be," says Mrs. Hay. "The way we make decisions in life, a lot of times it's just whim."

With that, she turns to them once more and asks what they're thinking of doing for a living. One girl wants to be a teacher, just like Mrs. Hay. Another says she'd like to become a nun, but she doesn't think she could handle a vow of silence. YY, however, says she's not sure. Her parents, she says, are still pushing for some kind of math-related career. They're still talking about how she needs to be practical.

"What do *you* want to do?" Mrs. Hay gently asks.

YY laughs again—the same nervous laugh she always uses when she's forced to talk about something painful—and says she doesn't know.

"It's getting confusing," she says.

"How are you going to handle that?"

"I don't know."

At that moment, when she hears YY's dilemma, Mrs. Hay decides it's time to give the speech. Every spring, on the day before finals, she makes the same speech to her seniors. But this time, there's no reason to wait.

"Maybe I need to share something with you," she tells them. "Maybe now's the time."

She pauses and gazes into their faces.

"When I was thirty-four years old," she says, "something happened to me."

It was spring fifteen years ago. She was already at Largo High; at that point in the semester, she was teaching her students *Richard III*. Anyway, she says, she went to the doctor one day, and for some reason, she asked him if he'd do a Pap smear. She doesn't know why she requested it; she'd had the test only a short while before. But something made her ask, and so the doctor performed the procedure, and that's when he discovered what he called a "possible cancer."

"I was thirty-four years old," she says again, "and my daughter was what?" She thinks a second. "Seven?"

Before Mrs. Hay knew it, she was on an operating table in the hospital, with a surgeon ready to cut inside her. As she was fading out under the anesthetic, she remembers looking at the clock on the wall—it was a little after 10:00 A.M.—and thinking about how she was supposed to be in class, working with the kids on *Richard III*. In fact, the doctor would later tell her that as she lost consciousness she'd been quoting from that play and from *The Tempest*.

When she came out of it, she asked the doctor if she was going to live.

"I don't know," he said.

They had to wait two days before they could be sure one way or the other, she says. So she lay in her hospital bed, thinking about what it would be like if she died and her seven-year-old daughter were left without her. What would her little girl do? It was then, says Mrs. Hay, that she realized how lucky all of us are to be alive. How every hour we are given is a gift. And when the two days passed and she learned she was going to survive, she told herself she would never forget that realization.

"I swore I was going to hang on to that feeling."

Which is why she is so delighted, she says, to still be alive—she's forty-nine now, she tells them proudly—and to still be doing what she loves, which is to teach. Especially with kids like the ones in this class. She wants them to know that, she says. She wants them to understand how wonderful it is to sit here and be surrounded by kids who give her such joy. And she wants the same for them. She wants them to understand, she says, that they need to do whatever it is that brings them joy.

"I love you, you know. I know I told you that before, but I mean it," she says. "You've got to live your life, because you only have one, and you don't know from day to day. *You don't know*. And you can't take it for granted."

This is her lesson for the day. It is her lesson, she says, for the year. More important than iambic pentameter. More important, she says, than anything else she could ever teach them.

"What could be more important that I could say to you than to take care of yourself and be true to yourself and love one another? . . . After all, what is life anyway but today? We don't have a guarantee on tomorrow. We have today."

She pauses again. She's crying a little. She's also smiling.

"I get paid for this," she says, shaking her head with wonder. "I get paid today to sit with you. It's incredible. An *incredible* thing."

The bell rings as she finishes. Some of the kids walk up and hug Mrs. Hay. Fighting back tears, they slip away into the hall, then start to sob.

YY, WHO UNDERSTANDS HOW DIRECTLY THIS MESSAGE WAS aimed at her, leaves quietly without allowing herself any outpouring of emotion. She's not sure what to say. She's not sure of much of anything anymore. She loves Mrs. Hay, and she knows that what she told them is right. Still, it would be so hard to go against her parents. She doesn't know if she's strong enough. Besides, there are so many other things to worry about right now. YY is still rationing her emotional energy during this final onslaught of exams and papers; she cannot afford, she says, to think about anything else right now. She can't worry about graduation, or about what she should study in college, or what she should do with the rest of her life. Later, she tells herself, there'll be plenty of time to think all these things through.

Amy Boyle is not so sure. Amy was in that class, too, and when she listened to Mrs. Hay, what occurred to her was that time is running out. At least, it's running out for her and Meridith. Once the year's over, what's left for them? How are they supposed to work it out then? Maybe, Amy tells herself, she should forget her pride and break the silence. Maybe she should go to Mer, tell her she's sorry, try to work it out. But that would be so hard. It would take so much . . .

FORTY-ONE

NATURE

THE PYTHON IS A BIG DRAW IN Mrs. Adler's second-period speech class. Her students are giving demonstration speeches, and on this quiet Thursday morning, word has spread that one of them will be speaking about the care and handling of his ten-foot pet reticulated python. Now kids from other classes are showing up at Mrs. Adler's classroom door near the end of C Wing, asking permission to stay and watch.

Helene Adler doesn't mind the visitors. But she's not sure why they're so anxious to see this young man and his pet.

"He's not going to feed it, is he?" she asks.

"Oh no," the kids tell her.

Soon the owner of the snake, a tall dark-haired boy, is ready to begin. He shows the class his python, a female named Elie, which is curled up in a cage, and spends the next several minutes talking calmly about the history of snakes and their habits and their anatomy. Then he says he would like to show how the snake eats.

"You're not going to feed it, are you?" Mrs. Adler asks again.

The boy smiles. He reaches into a box and pulls out a live rabbit. A big black rabbit. Before Mrs. Adler has a chance to object—before most of the people in the room can emotionally register what's about to happen, even though many of them obviously knew it was coming—the boy drops the rabbit into Elie's cage.

The rabbit wiggles its nose, gets its bearings, hops over toward the snake to say hello. Lunchtime arrives without warning. In a flash, Elie strikes, wraps her coils around the animal, takes its head into her mouth, and swallows it whole. The rabbit goes slowly, kicking its hind legs as the rest of its body disappears down Elie's digestive tract.

Mrs. Adler shakes her head and sobs. "Oh my God, no!" she says. "No!"

It's too late. Some of the girls jump from their seats and run crying from the room. The boys move up front for a better view and beat their desks with their fists, chanting, *"Yes! Yes! Yes!"*

The boys can't get over it. As Elie finishes, they're laughing and cheering and giving one another high fives. One guy keeps saying, "What's up, Doc?"

Later, after it's over and everyone has had a chance to calm down, Mrs. Adler grades the boy's speech, giving him a B+. He loses points for his dramatic ending—"Not the best!" she writes on his paper—but earns high marks for "clarity of purpose," "poise and self-control," and "use of visual aids."

JOHN BOYD, WHO HAPPENED TO BE IN THAT SPEECH CLASS, tells the whole story afterward to Mr. Feazell.

"I knew it was in there," John says, meaning Elie's main course. "But when he pulled it out of the box, I couldn't believe how big it was. I thought it was going to be a baby rabbit. I was stunned." He smiles, shaking his head. "The rabbit, he didn't know what time it was."

Mr. Feazell laughs. "He found out real quick, didn't he?"

John can't get over it. He goes on and on, talking about how big this rabbit was and how hard it fought.

"Oh, *man* . . . That was a healthy rabbit. You should have seen it kicking . . ."

Mr. Feazell likes talking to John when he's this pumped up. It's good to see him happy, to see him doing so well these days. Still on track, still bearing down on his homework, John spends most class periods poring over his notes. He's working hard, plowing through reports and work-sheets, getting ready for finals. At the top of one of his papers, he writes a single word: *STUDY!!* Still, even though he has his nose to the grindstone, John can't seem to avoid the attention of the opposite sex. When he walks down the hall, girls come up to him all the time, flirting, joking, asking him why he's always ignoring them. One day a girl walks up to him with a pass in her hand and a teasing smile on her face.

"You need to come to the library," she says. "The rest of your life may depend on it."

It's nothing serious—she just wants to get him alone to talk for a few minutes—so John goes with her and talks. That's all he does, though. Despite the flirting, he's trying his best to stay faithful to Andrea. Some-how the two of them are still a couple, even after their big fight in the rain. John felt terrible that night, seeing how much he'd upset Andrea. He's crazy about her. He still can't resist flirting with other girls; he keeps telling himself how young he is, how there's no need to get too serious. But Andrea's special.

"You can break up with me if you want to," he told her after the fight. "I just want you to know that I didn't do any of that to hurt you."

Andrea made it clear she didn't particularly trust him anymore, but she wanted to try to work it out. So now they're doing just that, spending all their spare time together, enjoying their last couple weeks of high school. Actually it's only Andrea's last weeks of high school. John, who repeated a grade in elementary school, is still just a junior, which means that next year he stays at Largo while she heads for Florida State. Never-theless, Andrea seems determined to stay together, even though it will mean a long-distance romance. Now that she and John are finally to-gether, she's not ready even to consider letting him go. She's already talking about how she's going to drive down from Tallahassee on the weekends, just so she can sit in the Largo stands at the football games and cheer him on.

John tells her there's no way. He says she'll be too busy hanging out with her college boyfriend.

Andrea hugs him.

"You're still going to be my boyfriend," she says.

John, who wants to make the most of what little time they have left, doesn't push the issue. But he knows the odds.

Even if Andrea can't bring herself to face it, John recognizes that the two of them are caught up in one of those nearly inescapable patterns that have been playing themselves out, year after year, since the dawn of high school. They could try to fight it—they could tell themselves that they're different, that they're immune, that they're stronger than everyone else— but in the end they'd probably break up anyway. It's like what's happening with the Fearsome Foursome. Now that they're all about to graduate, it's part of the natural order that YY and the others are struggling to hold their friendships together. How could it be otherwise? This school is the place that brought them together, and now they are leaving it and everything that came with it. Sooner or later, all of them will have to learn to say goodbye.

MRS. FRYE WAITS FOR HER THIRD-PERIOD CRITICAL-THINKING class to get settled down, then passes out the worksheet with the unfinished sentences.

You are like an untraveled path when . . .
You are like starlight when . . .
You are like a mountain when . . .
You are like a flower when . . .

"Wayne," she says, looking at one of the boys, "you are like a flower when what?"

He says nothing.

"What is a flower? How would you describe a flower?"

"Ugly."

"Wayne, finish the sentence. You are like a flower when . . ."

"It smells."

Mrs. Frye goes to someone else.

"Chris, you finish it. You feel like a flower when . . ."

"I don't know."

Still not ready to give up, she turns to a boy wearing a Metallica shirt. A boy who has not bothered coming to this class in many days.

"Mike?"

Mike Broome scowls. "I ain't a flower."

"I didn't say you were a flower."

"I don't feel like no flower, either."

Kim Frye, a young teacher with a soft voice and an air of perpetual calm, has this fantasy. When her students are like this, she imagines storming into class wearing a hockey mask and carrying a chain saw. She sees herself ripping the cord, starting the saw with an ominous growl. She sees the looks of surprise and terror on the kids' faces. She hears her voice, muffled behind the mask, telling them, *"Now you're going to pay attention."*

But at this moment, confronted by the vast indifference of Mike Broome, Mrs. Frye does not have the option of waving a chain saw. Not unless she wants to end up on the six o'clock news. So she moves on, handing out another worksheet.

Mike puts his head down on his desk.

"What's wrong?" she asks.

"I'm tired."

"Why are you tired?"

"I don't know."

"Why are you here?"

"I don't know. So I can get my license."

He tries to put his head back down, but Mrs. Frye won't let him.

"You're not going to sleep."

"Fine. I'll just go home."

He gets up, moves toward the door.

"I'm fixin' to leave," he says.

Mrs. Frye is up front now, working with another student. She's trying to ignore Mike; she has no time for this. Maybe a month or so ago, when there was still a chance for him to turn it around again. But not now.

"Can I leave?" he asks.

No answer.

"Can I leave, then?"

He storms out, slamming the door like he always does. Outside, he tries to walk off his rage. He's so filled with it, he's almost running. He bounces from one end of the school to the other, heading first for the AA building, then down the long cement walkway over to D Wing, then back to the AA building, then over to his old spot on the auditorium steps.

"I just didn't feel like sitting in that class," he says. "I didn't see no use in it. I've already failed this year."

He's right. It's too late now. There's no way the attendance appeal committee would give him a waiver and allow him to pass any classes. So now he wanders the campus, day after day. Mrs. Terwilliger has only seen him once. When he finally showed up at her class for the first time, she had no idea who he was.

"Do you belong in here?" she asked him.

Mrs. O'Donnell and Mr. Gerber and his other teachers can hardly bear to watch Mike end the year this way. They've tried so hard to reach him. They have kept trying long after almost anyone else would have written him off. But they also know that sooner or later there comes a point where it's up to him and only him. They can't force him to straighten up; if he's determined to drop out, there's no way to stop him.

Mike has decided to stay deep inside his hole. Either that, or he does not know how to get out. Like Jaimee, he is stuck in a different kind of pattern, a pattern far more destructive and even more difficult to escape than the ones confronting Andrea and John and the Fearsome Foursome. He is trapped in something larger than himself, swept up in a cycle that began before he was born and that he only partially understands. Someday he may find a way to break free, but for the moment he has given up any notion of shaping his own future. In fact, the future seems to hold no meaning for him; he doesn't know what he's going to do tomorrow, or the next day, or the day after that. He walks the halls, running the tips of his fingers along the walls. He sits in front of the auditorium, smoking his Marlboros and feeling the wind in his face and making fun of any other students he sees ducking out of class.

"Skipping school again?" he says one morning, laughing at a couple other guys who join him on the steps in the middle of third period. "You skippers."

Suddenly this serious look comes over his face.

"I've never skipped a day of school in my life," he says to no one in particular, looking down at the ground. "I've never skipped a *full* day. I always go to at least one class a day."

Mike's personal life is just as impermanent. He's not going out with Tabatha Turner anymore. After seeing her for a couple of weeks, he says, he asked one of his friends to tell her that he wanted to break up with her. Now he has a new girlfriend; his mother doesn't know it yet, but he and this girl are already sleeping together. Their first time, Mike's first ever, was just the other night. Mike was spending the night in a tent in a friend's yard, and his girlfriend surprised him and joined him in the tent. One thing led to another; now the two of them are having sex whenever they can. They're not using any birth control, though. They're just hoping she doesn't get pregnant.

Still, at least Mike has something to look forward to. At least he's got something to care about. Because here at school, it's getting hard for him.

Without a chance of earning even a single credit, coming to campus is an exercise in futility. With nothing to do, of course, he repeatedly gets into trouble. Sometimes he does it on purpose—he admits it—deliberately creating confrontations, triggering his famous temper so that the school will kick him out and send him home. Sometimes he's not sure why he does it. But it keeps happening, over and over.

The final display of fireworks, the moment when Mike gets his wish at last, comes early one Wednesday afternoon.

It's sixth period, and for once he is actually where he's supposed to be, in Mr. Gerber's shop class. The problem is, Mr. Gerber is out that day, and the substitute teacher doesn't have a key to let the students into the wood shop. So the sub takes the class down to the basketball courts in the back of the school, letting them run around in the sun and shoot baskets. Everything's going fine until Mike gets into an argument with another kid over possession of one of the basketballs. It's the kind of thing preschoolers fight about, but Mike and this other kid take it dead seriously. They're cursing at each other and getting ready to start swinging, making such a commotion that they attract the attention of another teacher, a veteran coach who's working with a class on the nearby tennis courts. Sensing trouble, the coach comes over and tells the two of them to knock it off or they're both going to the office with a referral.

That's when Mike goes over the top.

"I ain't fucking going anywhere," he says. "Shut up, you fat old asshole. I ain't going to take any fucking referral."

He tells him there's no way he can order them around, since he's not their teacher. He says he can't give them a referral and he can't send them to the office.

"Kiss my ass, you faggot. I'm leaving."

With that, Mike turns around and starts to walk away. The coach tells him to come back, tells him he's just causing himself more problems, but Mike says he doesn't care. He heads over toward the stadium, where—to prove how little he does care—he lights up a cigarette and begins puffing away in full view of everyone.

Once he calms down, Mike faces the inevitable and makes his way to the front office, where he takes a seat across the desk from Mrs. Palmateer. She already knows what's happened; the coach has sent down a referral that cites him for the profanity, the disrespect, and the smoking. The coach, who had never met Mike before, gets his name wrong, identifying him as "Mike Broom," but other than that, the whole incident is laid out very clearly. After she gives Mike his copy, Mrs. Palmateer tells him she has no choice but to suspend him for ten days, which amounts to two full weeks of school, which is the bulk of what's left of the semester. Even after he finishes the suspension, she says, there's not much point in his coming back to school unless he intends to go to class.

Mrs. Palmateer looks at Mike. Has he thought about next year? Perhaps, she says, he should consider going into the IBIS program, a special school for students who always find themselves chafing against the rules.

"There's so much good in you," she says. "If I could just figure out a way to channel it into school . . ."

Mike refuses to even consider the IBIS program. Mrs. Palmateer tells him not to be hasty, that he doesn't have to make up his mind today, but he says there's no way. He is not going to any special school.

He sits there in the chair, fuming. He keeps talking—partly to her, partly to himself—about the fact that, once again, someone has misspelled his name. This man has just sent him up on almost every infraction in the book, and yet he doesn't know his name. He's going to get even with the coach, he says. Somehow, he's going to get him.

Mike gets up and walks out. He wanders for a while, then goes to his locker and cleans it out. There are no books inside the locker, no paper, no pencil, no pen, but he does have his gym clothes and a few other belongings, and he gathers them together and takes them to the car of a friend who's driving him home. Before he leaves, he stops by Ms. DiLello's room to say goodbye. After all, she was his favorite teacher. She was the one who stood there with Mrs. O'Donnell at the beginning of the year and put her arm around Mike and told him she cared about what happened to him. Now she listens carefully as he gives the details of the suspension. That's it, he says. He won't be returning for the rest of the semester.

Ms. DiLello asks him why he did it. "Were you looking for a permanent vacation?"

"Yeah."

She asks him if he'll be back next fall.

"I don't know."

THAT SAME DAY, AS MIKE IS SAYING GOODBYE, MRS. Palmateer calls his mother and tells her the whole story. Jewelene Wilson is not surprised; she could see this moment coming, like everyone else. But the news hits her hard anyway. She tells Mrs. Palmateer that she still wonders if she's somehow responsible for Mike's problems.

"You really shouldn't blame yourself," Mrs. Palmateer tells her. "I know you tried."

Afterward, Mrs. Wilson sits in her chair in the living room, smoking and staring blankly at the TV. She's so sick of it, she says. So tired of struggling with Mike and never getting anywhere. She's had enough, she says. Enough of worrying about Mike and worrying about Wade and wondering when they'll all ever have enough money to afford a decent house and trying, week after week, to find some way to scrape by on her disability pay and Jerry's salary. It's just too much. There is too much bearing down on her. She wishes she could scream, she says. If she could get out into the country, go somewhere far away from everyone else and then scream at the top of her lungs, then maybe she'd be all right.

"You know what I feel like doing sometimes?" she says. "Packing my bags, getting in my car, and hightailin' it."

Whenever she talks about these feelings—and she talks about them all the time these days—Mrs. Wilson works herself up, growing more and more agitated. She leans forward in her chair, one hand gripping her cane. Her voice rises; her light blue eyes ignite with the same fire as her son's. Suddenly she is on the edge of her own explosion.

Sometimes, she says, she wishes she could lash out at everyone around her. Earlier in the year, when there was still a chance for Mike to turn it around, she'd go to conferences in the pod and meet with his teachers, and as she listened to them, going on and on about all the things Mike had done, she'd find herself wanting to stand up and tell them to shut their mouths. She wanted to pummel every single one of them. The teachers. Mrs. Welch. Mrs. Palmateer. Even Mike.

"Do you ever get that feeling you'd like to use somebody as a punching bag?" she says. "I just get so nervous, so frustrated, I want to take it out on somebody."

At last she leans back in her chair. She takes another puff on her cigarette, then lets out a long sigh.

"Maybe next year will be a whole different ball game, I hope. It doesn't hurt to hope."

FORTY-TWO

SURVIVORS

Now that final exams are nearly upon them, most of the students are mentally locking and loading, burrowing into their books for the last push before finals. Others, realizing that it's too late, are walking around campus with the fatalistic smiles of those who no longer bother worrying about their GPAs.

Of course, even in the middle of the crunch, kids are finding a few spare moments to enjoy all the usual rituals that mark the close of a school year. The votes for this year's senior superlatives—the annual contest to decide who should be named Most Likely to Succeed, Most Spirited, and so forth—have been collected and counted, and now people are waiting to hear the final tally.

The winners are announced at the senior picnic, which takes place on a glorious Thursday afternoon down at the stadium. The picnic is a time-honored perk, a chance for the seniors to lounge in the sun for a couple hours while the luckless geeks in all the other grades are still slaving away in class. As picnics go, this one is pretty good. Over on the track, a reggae band is pulsing away on a portable stage—in honor of the band, Karin Upmeyer and some other girls are sporting some wicked dreadlocks—and off to the side are tables filled with chicken wings and hamburgers and potato chips and punch. The seniors are taking full advantage, piling the food high on their plates and then plopping themselves down onto the grass of the football field, a rare treat since it's so much softer and less scratchy than the thick St. Augustine grass found in so much of Florida. Frisbees and footballs are flying through the air; a throng of kids stands by a net erected near the center of the field, smacking a volleyball back and forth.

When it's time to announce the superlatives, the reggae band takes a rest and everyone else gathers by the sidelines, where the senior class president reads out the names of the various winners. It's a long list, with one boy and one girl winning in each category, but the president runs through it quickly. To no one's surprise, Jen Belzel—the sweet girl who was so shocked when the Seminole kids flicked her off at the quiz team match—wins Most Likely to Succeed. Smiling politely as always, she walks up to the front and accepts her ribbon, which like all the other ribbons to be awarded happens to be green; they were supposed to be blue, to match the school colors, but the class officers ordered them too late and had to settle for what they could get.

Karin is named Class Clown among the girls; Shana Denton wins Best Personality; Troy Vaughn, the mastermind behind this year's toga scavenger hunt, is awarded the title of Party Animal. Andrea Taylor wins Most Involved, an honor she's not sure how to interpret.

"Most involved?" says Andrea. "Involved in what?"

The winners in the more humiliating categories—including Most Obnoxious, and Class Airhead—are announced to the predictable hoots and cheers. Still, the recipients seem to take the abuse fairly well, laughing and telling their friends to pipe down. Perhaps the most embarrassed is the girl who wins Best Buns, since once her name is called out, she's forced to walk up front and get her ribbon, giving the crowd a brief but well-appreciated view of the behind in question.

"Oh my God," she says, blushing at the chorus of whistles.

The best part of the picnic is not the superlatives, however. The best part—the moment that lingers—is when Ms. Westfall coaxes everybody on the field into joining her for a dance.

It's a gutsy move, the kind of gesture you never expect from a principal, but somehow Judi pulls it off. Until she steps forward, almost nobody is willing to dance. The seniors are standing off to the side, looking awkward and slightly guilty as they ignore the lead singer of the reggae band, who has been pleading for them to get into the beat.

"This is your party," he says. "I want to see you getting down."

Apparently this man does not realize that the worst way in the world to induce teenagers to dance is by urging them to "get down."

"Come on," he says, sounding increasingly desperate. "I want to see everybody shaking their waistline."

That's when Ms. Westfall puts down her walkie-talkie and takes the plunge. She's no fool. She knows how stupid she'll probably look to most of these kids. But she does it anyway. For a moment she's out there by herself, strangely vulnerable as she rocks and turns to the band's version of "Stir It Up." Then it works. First a few kids join her, and then a few more, and then suddenly, before she knows it, she is surrounded by swaying bodies. Teachers are joining in; so's the campus police officer, who moves along with them in her dark blue uniform.

Smiling, Ms. Westfall raises her arms and dances on.

AFTER MAKING IT THIS FAR, THE CLASS OF '90 HAS EVERY right to celebrate. Still, when they're together like this, it's hard not to think about all of their classmates who are no longer on hand to join the party.

The raw numbers tell the story well enough. Back in 1986, when these kids were just gangly freshmen, there were 571 students in their class. Today, as they prepare to pick up their diplomas, there are only 334. What happened to the other 237? Some transferred to other schools or moved away. But most dropped out. Even now, this late in the year, kids from every grade level are still disappearing from the rolls at Largo High. Some formally quit, filling out their withdrawal papers and emptying their lockers. Others just leave without a trace, not saying a word to anyone about where they've gone.

In the GOALS program, so many students have quit that the pod feels like a war zone where the casualties keep mounting. Lisa, the seventeen-year-old girl who dropped out once and then returned—the one who used to babysit for the children of exotic dancers—just dropped out again, giving her teachers some excuse about how she thought she'd be better off away from high school. Tabatha Turner, the girl who briefly dated Mike Broome, quit only the other day, announcing that she was transferring to a technical school. Added to the ranks of the departed are at least five GOALS seniors, kids who have walked away on the verge of graduation. The teachers can't believe it. These kids have made it all this way, and now they're quitting?

"I look at my roll book, and I'm thinking, 'What happened to all these kids?'" says Mrs. LaVassaur, who's working with the seniors. "It gets depressing."

Of course, it's not just GOALS kids who quit. By year's end, 12.5 percent of the student body—a total of 228 kids, some from inside the pod, the rest from other classes—will have dropped out. However, that figure is a little misleading, since it only tells what's happened during this school year. Largo's annual dropout rate has been hovering around 10 percent for several years now, which is about one and a half times the state average, and that's in a state which already has one of the worst dropout problems in the country. Add four of those years together, accounting for every year between ninth and twelfth grade, and you'll find that roughly 40 percent of the kids who enter Largo are gone by the time their classmates reach graduation.

None of this would be so bad if it were just a question of statistics. But when the teachers look at the list of dropouts, they remember the names and faces and personalities that went with them. It hurts to realize that no matter how hard they've worked, they've still lost all those kids. It hurts especially in GOALS, where the teachers have lost such large numbers. Sometimes it makes them wonder if they're reaching anyone at all. Are they really doing any good?

"Should we scrap GOALS?" Ruth Riel says one day to her colleagues in the pod.

Miss Riel asks this question only a few days after Mike Broome's final eruption. It's just after seventh period, the end of another grinding day, and she and some of the other GOALS teachers are sitting around the scarred wooden tables in Mr. Klapka's room, talking about all of the students they've tried and failed to reach. Miss Riel tells them about a kid she's just spoken with, an eighth grader on his way to Largo next year who needs the kind of help GOALS is supposed to offer. But this kid, says Miss Riel, wasn't so sure he wanted to be in the pod. After all, he told her, GOALS hadn't done much of anything for Mike Broome.

With that, the teachers launch into an impromptu critique of their efforts. They agree that they've gone the extra mile for Mike Broome; as far as they're concerned, Mike's failure is his own. But what about the program in general? Is it working? Are they too easy on the kids? Are they so desperate to keep them in school that they allow them to get away with too much?

"Are we doing justice?" says one teacher. "I don't know."

Kim Frye says she asks herself the same question. When she sees so many intelligent kids coming into the program and then dropping out anyway, she wonders what went wrong. Some of the others, listening on, point out that there are teachers outside the pod who simply don't think they're pushing the kids hard enough.

"Assigning homework," says Miss Riel, nodding. "We need to be more consistent on that next year with kids."

"None of them will do homework," says Mrs. Glidden. *"None of them."*

This is the dilemma the GOALS teachers face every day. If they assign homework, many of the kids will refuse to do it, which means they'll earn Fs on those assignments, which means they're more likely to get frustrated and drop out. But if they don't give them homework, if they don't push them to study and reach higher, are their students learning anywhere near what they should? What does it say about their education if these kids can earn a diploma without ever cracking open a book at home?

Now, as they debate these questions, the teachers begin trading some of the excuses their students give them for why they can't do homework.

"My favorite was 'My mom won't let me,' " says Mr. Klapka.

The homework issue is only one of many problems, though. Many GOALS kids clearly believe that being in the program means they don't have to work as hard or follow as many rules as other students. Mrs. Terwilliger, who's still the newest teacher in the pod, says she can't believe how many kids take advantage, knowing that the teachers are willing to bend over backward for them.

"What can you do about that?" she says.

"GOALS needs an attitude change," says Mrs. Glidden.

Others in the room agree. A few years ago, when they were starting the program and trying to strike the right balance with the kids, they needed to be more lenient. But now that GOALS is established, it's time to get tougher and demand more of their students. Just as crucial, they say, will be finding some way to get more mothers and fathers actively involved in their children's education. The memory of last semester's parent workshops, the ones attended by almost no parents, still cuts deep in these teachers' minds; Miss Riel brings it up now. If they could get past this hurdle, she says—if they could get parents to support what they're doing—then maybe the kids would stand a chance.

"That's never going to happen," says Mrs. Frye, pointing out how deeply ingrained the apathy is. "That's generation to generation."

The teachers talk on and on, debating back and forth. In the end, they agree that for all its shortcomings, GOALS is still worth fighting for. They'll need to keep fine-tuning, rethinking the rules, trying to figure out what works and what doesn't. But they still believe the program can make a difference in the lives of hundreds of kids.

"I just think there needs to be a major revamp," says Miss Riel.

Even with all the kids they've lost this year, Miss Riel and the other teachers try not to get too discouraged. With the kinds of problems their students are dealing with, it's a victory to keep any of them in school. And for all the ones who've quit, there are still dozens of other students who are already responding to the one-on-one attention. The most tangible proof of this—the proof that keeps the teachers going—is the seniors. In a few days, Largo's first class of GOALS graduates, the ones who didn't quit, will walk across the stage in their blue caps and gowns and pick up their diplomas. Altogether, there will be nineteen of them, each living proof of what GOALS can accomplish.

There's Craig McCray, a sweet kid who's talking about heading for junior college and possibly studying to become a TV cameraman. There's Cathy Turner, who started skipping school in fifth grade—her older sisters used to sneak her out—and who was planning to drop out before she entered GOALS.

"If I wasn't in there," she says, "I don't think I would have made it."

Then there's Donny Campbell. Donny's a great kid, with long curly hair and a perfect tan. He's one of the surfers who watches the weather reports on TV, waiting for a low-pressure front to move in and pump up the waves. Back in his sophomore year, when he first came into GOALS, he was a handful, getting into fights, skipping constantly, failing classes. Today his attendance and grades are so solid he's earned an honor card; he wears shorts to school almost every chance he gets. Mrs. LaVassaur and the other GOALS teachers, he says, have made all the difference in the world.

"The teachers in here have a better attitude," he says. "They have a sense of humor."

Donny's aware of how many other kids have gotten lost along the way. One of his best friends is a GOALS student who dropped out last year. One Sunday night a couple of months ago, after the two of them had been out riding the waves at Sunset Beach, Donny got a call from his friend. He'd had a fight with his girlfriend; now he sounded odd.

"You can have my surfboard," he said. "I don't need it anymore. I don't need anything."

Donny's heart sank. "Don't do anything stupid."

"I already have."

Donny raced over to the friend's house and found him sitting in front of the garage, slicing his wrist over and over with a kitchen knife. Donny grabbed the knife, threw it into the yard, then drove his friend to a hospital. Both of them were covered with blood; both were crying. But the friend lived.

"He still talks about doing it sometimes," Donny says. "I tell him to shut his face. I don't want to hear it."

Donny has no time for negative thinking these days. He's moving forward with his life, talking about going to junior college and maybe studying to become a veterinary technician.

"I just can't wait to get out of here," he says, echoing the words of nearly every senior in the school.

As a graduation present, he says, his parents are sending him on a trip to the Caribbean. Donny's still deciding where to go. Maybe Barbados. Maybe Costa Rica. Someplace where the surf is just right . . .

On the evening of Thursday, May 24, the GOALS graduating seniors and their parents gather in the library for an awards ceremony. Ms. Westfall gives an emotional speech about the strength of the kids and the tireless efforts of all their teachers.

"If caring and love came in bushel baskets," says Ms. Westfall, gazing out at Mrs. LaVassaur and Mr. Klapka and the others, "we'd be able to fill semi-tractor-trailers by the miles."

The room is electric with enthusiasm. Awards are handed out. Hugs and presents are exchanged. Kristina Hadley, another senior, stands up to talk about how she probably wouldn't have stayed in school without the program.

"On June seventh," she says, her voice wavering a little, "I will proudly receive my high school diploma and be ready to face the challenges of tomorrow. Thank you."

That same evening, over in the auditorium, another glittering ceremony is under way. Out in the audience, the rows are filled with beaming parents. Up in front, sitting under the lights, are some fifty of Largo

High's most accomplished students. YY is here to pick up her PRIDE writing award; Amy Boyle is here, too, ready to receive a citizenship award from the Daughters of the American Revolution. So's Carolyn Hanson, the valedictorian, who has honored the school by being selected as a Presidential Scholar, one of the highest academic honors available to a high school student in America; next month, in recognition of her achievement, Carolyn will visit the White House.

Meridith Tucker is sitting next to YY, who is next to Amy, who is next to Andrea Taylor. Andrea does not know what award she is to receive; the school has simply sent her family a letter, informing them that Andrea will be honored in some way. Her mother is out there now, along with John, both of them waiting proudly to see what she gets.

They find out once the man from St. Petersburg Junior College stands up and begins reading off the names of students who qualify for scholarships to the college. He begins with the ones awarded to students with GPAs of 3.8 or higher. Then he reads off the list of those who have qualified for the next type of scholarship, which is given to students with GPAs above 3.5. Then he comes to the final list, which is for those who have won the college's Black Incentive Award.

"For students that have received a 3.0 or better," the man explains.

Andrea hears these words and blushes. She feels the heat rising in her cheeks—feels the other kids staring at her—not just because of the graceless way in which the man has emphasized the differing standards, but also because she is the only black student seated in this group at the front of the auditorium. When Andrea began high school, her class included many other talented African-American students, but now most of them are gone. Either they've dropped out or become pregnant or been sidetracked some other way. For whatever reason, Andrea is the only black senior in the school with a GPA above 3.0.

And now this man has slapped her with that fact in public. This is what she and John and her mother came for tonight?

She hears the man call out her name, and no other name. She laughs, because the only alternative would be to cry. Burning, she walks up onstage, shakes the man's hand, and politely accepts his patronizing little certificate.

"I don't believe this," she says.

A few minutes later, when the ceremony is over and they're driving away, Andrea rips up the paper and tosses it out the window. She doesn't need sympathy. She's already going to college.

''LET'S GO AHEAD AND GET started," says the team leader, making notes at the head of the long Formica table, shining under the gleam of the ceiling lights. "First on the agenda, let's discuss the situation with Jaimee Sheehy."

The other members of the team turn to Mr. Willey, Jaimee's guidance counselor.

"Okay, I've spoken with some of you individually about this," he says. "Since she's been here, she has not been going to class. I've checked with all her teachers . . . She's here every day, but we can't get her to go to class."

"What's she doing at home right now?" asks the school psychologist, seated across from Mr. Willey. "How's she getting along with Mom?"

"I'm not sure on that. Mom doesn't think she can control her."

The team leader leans forward. What does Jaimee want to do? he asks. Does she want to earn her credits and eventually graduate?

Mr. Willey shrugs. "She *says* she does. But what she says and what she does are different things . . ."

Every Thursday morning, the

school's PASS team—a team that includes Mr. Willey and the other guidance counselors, a social worker, a school psychologist, and an occupational specialist—gathers in this crowded little conference room in the front office to review the cases of troubled students, students who for one reason or another have stumbled and are now slipping from sight. The team's job is to figure out what has gone wrong and to find ways to help these kids.

Laura Sheehy, still fighting for her daughter, has urged that Jaimee be included on today's agenda. But as they analyze Jaimee's situation, studying her history of almost incessant skipping, her stay at Charter Hospital, the many attempts to get her back on track, the team members agree that it's too late in the year to do much good. Jaimee's mother wants the school psychologist to evaluate her, to test her for a learning disability; maybe, she says, that would explain why Jaimee's acting like this. But with only a short time left in the semester, the psychologist's schedule is already overflowing. Besides, as she now points out, flipping through Jaimee's file, another school psychologist already evaluated Jaimee when she was in middle school. There was no evidence of a learning disability, she says; in fact, there's no evidence of emotional problems or other special circumstances that would offer some deeper explanation for Jaimee's behavior. At this point, it appears that Jaimee is simply unwilling to come to grips with the fact that sooner or later she will have to face the future.

"Have we considered other alternative programs for her?" asks the social worker.

Mr. Willey explains that Jaimee has already been in GOALS and that she was in supervised probation after she stole her mother's car, neither of which seemed to work.

"She needs to be in a classroom where she can't get out," says someone.

"We don't have that, do we?" says the social worker. "A locked classroom?"

Mr. Willey reminds them that Jaimee's mother is insistent that they come up with some kind of plan. Ms. Sheehy, he says, does not understand why the school can't do something.

"She's looking to us to solve the problem," says the social worker.

"Some of the responsibility has to go with her," says someone else.

Laura Sheehy sits outside the conference room, waiting anxiously for the meeting to end. Just a few minutes ago, she saw her daughter floating through the office, making one of her usual tours of the campus. As hard as it was for her to accept other people's descriptions of Jaimee's behavior here at school, it's even more difficult for her to witness it firsthand, to hear the bell ring and then see Jaimee come floating in with her carefree smile and endless supply of excuses.

"Why aren't you in class?" Laura asks her.

"I'm talking to them." Jaimee nods toward a couple other girls standing nearby.

"How come you're not in class?"

Jaimee goes on for a few minutes about how these girls are peer counselors, about how she has to meet with them to discuss her math teacher. Her mother listens, dumbfounded. Once Jaimee leaves, she sits down and waits for the PASS meeting to end, wondering aloud how it could have come to this. She just doesn't get it, she says. Why does Jaimee bother coming to school if she won't go to class? What does she do all day?

A few minutes later, Mr. Willey steps out and invites her into his office to talk with him and the social worker. They explain to her that Jaimee's already been tested, that she does not have a learning disability, that they're willing to test her again but that there's nothing they can do until after the semester is over. But whatever program they put her into, says Mr. Willey, it won't work unless Jaimee wants it to work.

"Some of this has to come from within her, too," he says.

The social worker asks the mother if she's considered going to court and asking a judge to formally declare Jaimee as an ungovernable child. If that happened, the judge would take control of the situation, ordering Jaimee to class and sending her to a juvenile detention center if she refuses.

Laura Sheehy sits across from the two of them, drowning. She is trying to make them understand how special Jaimee is.

"I don't think she's ungovernable. I don't know . . ." She trails off and pauses for a moment, looking down at her lap. "I think she needs help."

Outside, Jaimee wanders on. That same morning, while her mother sits in the office, Mr. Wagar catches her in the middle of second period, chatting away on one of the pay phones in front of the administration building. Mr. Wagar is not sure what she's doing. Maybe she saw him coming and picked up the phone to avoid a conversation with him. But when he grabs the receiver from Jaimee's hand and puts it up to his ear to find out whom she's talking to, the only thing he hears is a dial tone.

• • •

"Good morning. Our thought for the day is: The person who is cockeyed finds it hard to succeed."

The voice of wisdom refuses to go quietly. With only a week or so left and half the student body teetering on the brink of nervous exhaustion, it remains as relentlessly, absurdly perky as ever. Even now, though, no one seems to notice. As so often happens at this time of year, the entire school is caught up in a state of intense, nearly religious preoccupation. The campus is rapt with a sense of magnified reality, as though there were no place other than the school and no time other than the next few harried days.

Predictably, waves of regret have begun to sweep through the seniors. All year they've been talking about how wonderful it will be to finally escape from Largo, laughing at the teachers who warned them that someday they would look back on this time of their lives with tears in their eyes and a knot in their throats. Now the reality of the situation has hit home. Suddenly they are deeply and passionately in love with the place they are about to flee. They step slowly down the halls with a slightly stunned expression, their eyes wide open as they try to commit every brick, every locker, every smudge on the floor, into the memory banks of their brains. They sit in class, talking in hushed voices about how they'll never occupy these desks again, how they'll never take exams in these rooms again, how nothing will ever be the same.

"This could be the last pencil you ever use," someone tells YY one afternoon in calc class, watching her scribble a note in someone's yearbook.

"Who cares!" says YY, still doing her best not to get emotional about all this. She reaches for the Bic on her desk. "This could be the last pen I'll ever use! This could be the last paper I ever use!"

The yearbooks were handed out only yesterday. Now kids all around the school are driving the teachers crazy, passing the books up and down the rows in the middle of class, signing their names for the ages. The inscriptions in YY's book are filled with private jokes; pledges of eternal loyalty; promises, soon to be broken, of always keeping in touch, always remembering, never changing; plus a long list of references, veiled and not so veiled, to many fabled misadventures, including the kidnapping of Wooter and the challenging of Timothy "I Challenge" Burrows and one terrible/wonderful night when YY was dubbed "Yak-Yak" after she spilled the contents of her stomach in front of a crowd of people outside a party. Not surprisingly, one of the girls from the Latin Club reminisces about their scandal at the forum:

Who would have thought we'd get busted for guys and not alcohol!

One of the boys from YY's English class, remembering what Mrs. Hay told them, urges her to stick with writing:

You have such talent in writing and I hope one day that you use that. No matter what you decide to do, just remember that you are the one who has to work for it, so don't let anyone change your mind.

There is also a long and rambling note from Matt, who has apparently recovered from being hit on the bicycle and who now wants to apologize for his cloddish behavior in the last days of their relationship:

Christine, you were so nice to me and I treated you like crap at least one time that I can think of . . . I want to be friends with you and make the best of the summer vac.

Not everyone is thrilled with this year's edition of the book. To some, the whole enterprise has been turned into a giant tribute to the patio people, filled with pictures of the cheerleaders and the jocks and all the AB-12 rats. Though none of the Fearsome Foursome had anything to do with it—they're all on the newspaper staff, not yearbook—YY and Amy and Meridith and Karin are all shown repeatedly. YY's in there at least eight times, Amy at least nine times. Students from other parts of the school, however, are hardly pictured at all. Jaimee Sheehy is in there only once, with her name spelled wrong. Mike Broome doesn't show up anywhere, not even in the class photos. Many black kids, meanwhile, are upset because there are relatively few pictures of African-American students. After the book is released, several of them approach Ms. Westfall to complain.

The pages of the yearbook, they point out, are crammed with white faces. White kids at their island parties. White kids with their surfboards. White kids out in the parking lot, showing off the monster stereos in their boom cars. There's some nice shots of Andrea, including a couple from Homecoming night, and John Boyd is shown tearing down the football field in his uniform, eluding a tackler. But where's everybody else? Are there any shots of African-American kids hanging out at their parties? Standing with their cars? In the entire book, is there one shot of kids sitting on the rail? No. In fact, one of the more prominent displays of black faces comes in a section on students who are sent to the office. "Breakin' the Rules," the section is called.

Ms. Westfall agrees that these kids have a point. She finds the editors for next year's book and shows them the problem.

"What this would say to me," she says, flipping through the pages, "is that no black kids have parties, no black kids have jobs, no black kids have cars. What are they doing? They're in the discipline office."

Ms. Westfall knows the editors mean well. But when they put together next year's book, she says, she wants them to make sure they step outside their own lives and show what Largo is like for other kids, too.

"We've got to do a better job," she says, "about fairly representing everybody in the school."

As the yearbook debate continues, other end-of-the-year dramas are playing themselves out. As usual, the seniors are engaged in a massive guessing game, wondering which of their classmates will be unfortunate enough to crash and burn in their finals, thereby coming up short of the credits they need to graduate. Down in the pod, the teachers are wrestling with the opposite problem. Donny Campbell and several other GOALS seniors, it seems, have decided to skip the graduation ceremony, even though they've earned the credits to be there. Mrs. LaVassaur and Ms. DiLello have put on the full-court press, trying to persuade them to change their minds; after all, isn't this the moment these kids have been struggling toward all these years? But Donny and the others keep saying no. They have no intention, they say, of putting on a cap and gown and walking across a stage in front of all those people.

"That's gay," Donny says. "It doesn't matter. I get my diploma anyway."

The teachers aren't sure what's really behind the refusal. After watching so many of their friends drop out, are Donny and the others self-conscious about their success? Knowing how GOALS is mocked in other parts of the school, do they feel like everyone else on the field will be looking down on them? Who knows. But they show no sign of budging. They're not going to the graduation rehearsal. They haven't even ordered caps and gowns.

In the meantime, something strange has happened. After serving his ten-day suspension, Mike Broome has returned.

"Why'd you come back?" someone asks him.

"I don't know. I just did."

Sitting at home, it turns out, was even more boring than coming to school. At least here Mike can see his friends, say hello to the teachers, talk to Mrs. Palmateer. When he first showed up after the suspension, he came to her office, smiling, friendly, obviously glad to be back. She told him that he couldn't stay unless he actually went to class, but he soon disregarded the warning, settling back into his old routine, roaming the halls, smoking on the steps, sneaking over to the Wendy's next door, playing basketball with the other kids in Mr. Gerber's gym classes.

On the day when final exams are starting, Mrs. Palmateer calls Mike to her office and tells him she's kicking him off campus. If he comes back this semester, she says, she'll be forced to have him removed.

When he leaves the office, Mike is upset. Afterward, Mr. Gerber sees him with tears in his eyes and speaks to him for a few minutes, asking about his plans.

"Do you want to live with your father?"

"No."

"Do you want to live with your mother?"

"No."

M s . W estfall's surfing the airwaves again. A s the fi-nal days fly by, she keeps coming onto the P.A. system, asking the Largo Packers to petition the school board on behalf of the shorts experiment. Technically the experiment and all its incentives were approved only for this year, but Ms. Westfall is hoping that the board will agree to extend it. Now she wants students to flood the board members with "positive letters," telling them how wonderfully the honor card system has worked.

"We're looking for student opinions on the value of the incentive program," she says.

In the newspaper office, the AB-12 rats greet these requests with the usual snorts and laughs. Actually YY and the other seniors have been thinking about Judi a great deal these past few days. They're trying to decide what to give her at graduation. At high schools in this area, it's considered tradition for the graduates to hand their principal some kind of a gag farewell gift as they walk across the stage and pick up their diplomas. Last year, each Largo senior handed Judi a 1989 penny—they were the Class of '89, after all—but this year no one seems to know what to give her. Among the possibilities that have been discussed are apples, rotten bananas, toothpicks, marbles, or possibly honor cards.

Karin Upmeyer has a better idea.

"I say we go with the condom motif," she announces one day to her colleagues. "I say instead of apples or pennies, everybody should give her a condom."

For all the joking, the pressures are taking a physical toll on the Fearsome Foursome now that finals are under way. Amy has come down with one of her famous fevers, and Meridith is feeling nauseous, throwing up at home. YY, cramming for a calculus exam and a Cicero test, is digging into her private stash of No Doz and tugging on her eyelashes once again. Karin, meanwhile, is back on another diet, struggling to lose a few more pounds before graduation night.

Worst of all, there's been no thaw in Amy and Mer's battle of wills. They're still maintaining that bizarre state of mutual nonrecognition, spending hours every day in close proximity but somehow refusing to acknowledge or utter a single word to each other. Now the war is escalating, edging into a new and potentially more destructive phase. The two of them are starting to push YY and Karin into choosing sides, just as YY and Karin had feared.

The situation finally reaches a breaking point on Friday, June 1. The catalyst is a concert that's being given that night in Clearwater by Jason Davenport and his band, Science+Spirits. As Jason's biggest fans, YY and company definitely plan to attend the show. But the travel arrangements are getting stickier by the hour. Amy's asking the others for a ride, but only if Mer isn't going; Mer wants to come along, but feels compelled to ask if Amy is going.

That's it. YY and Karin can't take it anymore.

"I think we should talk to them," YY says, pulling Karin into the hall outside AB-12 to plot a course of action.

"You want to do it right now?"

With that, the two of them head back into the newspaper room, approach Amy and Meridith—who sense that something's up—then drag them both into the privacy of the darkroom to tell them how stupid they're acting.

"This is totally uncool," Karin tells them.

"We're tired of it," says YY, wrapping an arm around Karin for moral support.

Amy and Mer are seated at opposite sides of the room. Amy is playing with her hair; Mer is hugging a pillow. Neither will look at the other.

Watching them, seeing how stubborn they are, Karin finds herself getting angry. She's not usually the type to try to order anybody around, but this is too important. She can't hold back now. This whole thing has gone far enough, she says. Amy and Mer have been friends for so long, and now they're going to throw that all away? After everything they've been through together? Karin says it makes her sick. She can't believe that they're being this ridiculous. But there's no way, she says, that they're going to suck her and YY into their petty little game. She and YY, she says, are not going to choose sides, play favorites, give anybody a ride anywhere without letting everyone in the car.

For a few minutes, Amy and Meridith are silent. Then Amy speaks up, saying she'd like to work things out.

"But I just don't know where Mer stands," she says.

Mer looks over at Amy and apologizes for not being straight with her about the prom. She didn't mean for everything to turn out this way, she says.

"I'm really sorry."

Karin and YY, who know when their job is done, excuse themselves quietly, shutting the door to the darkroom behind them so the two combatants can work it out between themselves. Sensing victory, Karin and YY give each other high fives out in the newsroom. They're smiling and laughing. Karin can't believe how worked up she got.

"Did I go off?" she says. "Or did I go off?"

A few minutes later, the door to the darkroom opens, and out walk Amy and Mer, smiling bashfully, with the traces of a few tears still glistening on their cheeks.

"Guess what," says Mer, grinning. "Amy and I made up!"

It's not that simple, of course. Even though a truce has been declared, it's not like they're suddenly back to being soulmates. Rebuilding their friendship will be long, hard work. But at least they're on their way.

OVER IN C WING, HEATHER PILCHER SITS INSIDE HER BIOL-ogy class, trying not to panic as she stares at the final exam.

Heather, who's been on the honor roll for years now, is not used to the idea of failing an exam. But with the pregnancy wearing her down this semester, she's just never managed to get caught up in this class. Now, looking at the multiple-choice questions on the final, she realizes she only knows a few of the answers.

She knows what to do, though. Instead of Christmas-treeing the test, she has decided to get a little help from the baby. She knows he's a boy— she just had a sonogram—and she knows he likes to move when she holds still. So sitting as motionless as she can, she looks at the first question that stumps her and reads through the possible answers.

"Is it A?" she says silently. "Is it B? Is it C? Is it D?"

She waits for his kick, then marks the answer. She turns to the next mystery question and goes through it again.

"Is it A? Is it B? Is it . . ."

If people were to realize what Heather's doing, it's impossible to predict how they would react. Would they laugh? Would they feel for her? Would there be room inside them to reconcile the beauty and grace of the moment along with its undeniable sorrow? What exactly are we supposed to feel about a sixteen-year-old girl who asks her unborn child to help her pass a biology exam?

Heather has no time to worry about such things right now. She and her son have too many other questions awaiting them.

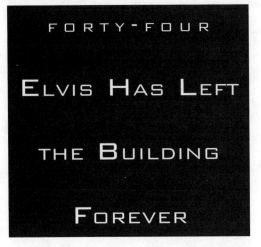

FORTY-FOUR

ELVIS HAS LEFT

THE BUILDING

FOREVER

THEY CAN'T TAKE THEIR EYES OFF
the clock.

"What time do we get out of here?"
says Karin, turning to Elvis, sitting directly behind her.

"Twelve-sixteen."

Actually the bell will ring at twelve-
fifteen. But according to Elvis's calculations, it will require another minute before he makes it to his car and opens his
first beer of freedom.

"I've already got it waiting," he says.

It is Wednesday, June 6, and now the
seconds are ticking away from the final
class of the final day of school. From one
end of campus to the other, kids are taking their last exams, turning in their
books, listening to the usual dire warnings from their teachers that no one—
absolutely no one—is to move an inch
from their seats until the tolling of the
year's last bell.

The natives, not surprisingly, are
growing more restless with the passage of
every minute. Down in the pod, they're

cranking up the volume on their Walkmans, playing desktop football with tiny triangles of paper, taking advantage of this final opportunity to torment their teachers. Over in B Wing, YY and Amy and the other students who put out the literary magazine are throwing a little farewell party, listening to the radio and munching on Cool Ranch Doritos.

"The best chip known to man," says YY, grabbing another handful.

John Boyd is camped in Mr. Feazell's history class, swapping stories with another football player. Andrea Taylor is roaming around her chemistry lab with a camera, taking pictures of her friends.

"I'm not a senior anymore," she tells them. "I'm a college freshman!"

Karin and Elvis, meanwhile, are bidding farewell to high school with one last fateful appearance in Ms. Fish's Algebra II class. Since they're both failing this subject anyway, and since neither needs this credit to graduate, the two of them held a race a few minutes ago, seeing who could whip through the final the fastest. Elvis won hands down—Karin was at a handicap, since she actually tried to come up with the right answers—and now they're doing their best to wait calmly for the bell. Elvis is sitting quietly, anticipating the first sips of his beer. Karin is eating wheat crackers and trading final jabs with almost everyone around her.

"Karin?" says the girl in the next row.

"What?"

"It's been enlightening having you in this class."

At twelve-thirteen, a slight hum comes over the P.A. system. It's Ms. Westfall again, making her final address of the year.

"Good afternoon, teachers and students."

"Judiiii!" says someone in Karin's class.

"Well, we've come to that time of year . . . We hope that everybody had a lot of success in their exams."

Karin blows a raspberry.

"I think we've really had a very successful year, and students, much of that is due to you . . ."

The kids keep standing up, and Ms. Fish keeps telling them to sit down. But it's no good. They can hear the buzz of excitement building in other classrooms; they can look out the door and see the throngs of people already congregating in the halls. Even Ms. Westfall senses that time has run out.

"Have a good summer," she says, wrapping it up. "The day is over."

The bell rings. As Karin and the others rush for the door, a wall of noise fills the hall. Kids are screaming and crying and pounding on the lockers; they're shouting to their friends, to their teachers, to no one in particular. Suddenly, rising over the din, there comes the sound of someone letting loose with a long and mighty Tarzan yell. It hangs in the air for a moment, savage and mysterious, every trembling note commanding attention.

The lord of the jungle, calling to his people.

THE CLASS OF '90.

FORTY-FIVE

POMP AND CIRCUMSTANCE

EARLY THE NEXT EVENING, WHILE other parents are checking the film in their Instamatics, straightening their ties, and heading for the festivities at the school, Laura Sheehy sits alone in her house, wondering where her daughter could be.

Jaimee has disappeared again. Only this time, it's worse. She has been gone for most of the past two weeks—it's been days since she's slept in her own bed—and now her mother is racking her brain, frantically trying to figure out a way to find her. Jaimee hasn't exactly run away. She's around somewhere. But never in a place where her mother can put her hands on her. She visits the house during the day, when she knows her mother is at work. She calls the answering machine at odd hours and leaves vague messages as to where she'll be.

"I'm at the beach," the messages say. "I'm going to Melissa's house."

Laura Sheehy checks. She goes to the beach. She calls the house where her daughter is supposedly staying. But Jaimee is never where she claims. Since the day of the PASS team meeting, she's been spinning even further out of control, ignoring her mother's every attempt to keep track of her, putting her off with one bald-faced lie after another. If by chance she happens to come home, she only stays for a little while and then sneaks out.

It happened again just last night. Her mother came home and found Jaimee in the house. It was the first time she'd seen her in several days, and yet when she tried to talk to her, Jaimee was impatient and distracted, clearly in a hurry as she searched through her room for a new pair of shorts her mother had just bought her. She said she was picking out something to wear for the next morning, but it was obvious that she was merely packing a few clothes before she took off again. Her mother didn't confront her. She tried to be calm, tried not to yell, did her best not to scare her away. Maybe if she backed off, she thought, Jaimee would at least spend the night at home. But a little while later, Laura Sheehy heard a voice outside the house along with the sound of Jaimee trying to pop out the screen in her bedroom window. Laura ran into the bedroom and found Jaimee at the window, with a boy waiting outside on the lawn.

"Forget about it," her mother told her, sending the boy away.

An hour or so afterward, Jaimee tried it again, and again her mother heard the telltale noises at the window and stopped her. Eventually, though, Laura Sheehy had to give up her vigil, since she was due at work early the next morning. She tried to stay up, listening, but finally she drifted off to sleep. When she woke at 4:00 A.M., she went immediately to Jaimee's room to check on her. The window was wide open. Jaimee was gone.

Now, on this Thursday evening—which looks to be a nasty one, with a large storm building in the east—Laura Sheehy waits at the house, worrying and trying to decide what to do. Should she call the police and report Jaimee missing? Should she call some other agency? She has no idea anymore. But somehow she has to find Jaimee. She goes to Jaimee's room, gets her new yearbook, then pores through it, flipping through the pages, studying the inscriptions, looking for some familiar name she can call and ask for help. She sits by the answering machine, listening to incoming messages from Jaimee's friends. She knows that if she answers, they'll probably just hang up. But this way, maybe one of them will slip. Maybe they'll leave some clue as to where Jaimee might be . . .

BACK AT THE SCHOOL, THE WEATHER IS THREATENING TO drown out graduation. It's been sunshine and clear skies most of the day, but now the heavens are looking positively ominous, with a massive line of black clouds—a line illuminated by stabs of lightning—sweeping rapidly in this direction from across the bay.

At six thirty-seven, exactly fifty-three minutes before the Class of '90 is due to walk out onto the football field, the first few drops of rain fall across the campus. The seniors, who are already gathered on the walkway beside the patio in their blue caps and gowns, look at one another and shake their heads. A few minutes later, when the winds kick in and the sprinkling surges into a driving downpour, the graduates-to-be are quickly ushered into the shelter of the auditorium. Immediately they begin to pray for the rain to stop. Because if it doesn't, they'll all have to come back tomorrow morning.

No way. They've waited four years for this. They are not prepared to wait a moment more.

"This sucks!" someone cries out.

Down the rows, the students are becoming increasingly restless, grumbling and protesting to every adult in sight. Mr. Wagar and a couple other adults are up front, trying to calm them, but it's no good. Now that these kids are about to graduate, there's nothing left to threaten them with. They're screaming, exchanging jungle bird calls, chanting at the tops of their lungs.

"WE WANT BEER, YES WE DO! WE WANT BEER, HOW 'BOUT YOU?"

Someone lets out another Tarzan yell. Someone else starts a wave, which ripples across the hall from side to side. Mr. Wagar, who knows when he's up against an insurmountable force, stands back with his walkie-talkie and listens to the cries rising toward the rafters.

"WE WILL, WE WILL, ROCK YOU . . . WE WILL, WE WILL, ROCK YOU . . ."

With every passing minute, the situation grows more grim. The clock is ticking, families and friends are arriving outside—among hundreds of others, John Boyd has come to cheer for Andrea—and yet the rain still falls. Inside the auditorium, the chanting grows more fervent; the kids are standing up and stomping their feet on the floor.

"NA-NA-NA-NA, NA-NA-NA-NA, HEY-HEY-HEY, GOOD-BYE!"

Then a miracle occurs. The clouds part and the rain dies down at almost exactly seven-thirty, the ceremony's starting time. Sensing that everything will be all right, the seniors quiet down.

"Class of 1990," says Mr. Wagar, "on behalf of the administration, we want to wish you all the luck and success in the world. Once a Packer, always a Packer."

The seniors rise and quickly form into two great lines that move out of the auditorium and across the campus, heading for the stadium. Suddenly someone looks up at the sky and lets out a squeal of delight.

"You guys! We have a rainbow!"

Not just any rainbow. A monster rainbow. A mega-rainbow. The storm has left it behind, and now it hangs shimmering over the stadium. The seniors, who have been asked to hold up for a moment on the sidewalk, stare upward, oohing and aahing.

Mr. Wagar's walkie-talkie crackles with the go-ahead signal, and the two long blue lines resume their march. As they approach the stadium, they see the lights towering over the field, shining in the dusk, and hear the school band playing the familiar strains of *Pomp and Circumstance.* The music grows louder as they enter the back of the stadium, snaking through the locker rooms—one line going through the home locker room, one line through the visitors locker room, the boys yelling and pounding on the lockers as they pass—and then make their way out onto the field. The moment they stride into view, their gowns glowing in the glare from above, the crowd in the stands lets out a roar. Moms are crying and waving. Dads are firing off their cameras. Joyous pandemonium.

From that moment, everything happens so fast. The national anthem is played, and some of the students actually sing along. Introductions are made. Speeches are delivered by a series of people, and then the Madrigal Singers—including Heather Pilcher, who passed her biology final and who is here not just to sing but to celebrate the graduation of Chris Wainscott, her fiancé—join the band in a rousing rendition of "America the Beautiful." Then Ms. Westfall briefly addresses the rows of seniors, congratulating them and saying she hopes they will all have the privilege of "carrying life's honor card."

Ms. Westfall turns to the school registrar, seated nearby.

"Ms. Bachman," she says in her most official voice, "as registrar do you certify that the members of this graduating class have met all the requirements?"

The registrar stands up and solemnly nods, confirming that she does so certify.

"The graduates will please stand," says Ms. Westfall, who informs them that they may now move their tassels from the right side of their caps to the left.

That's it. Before anyone knows it, names are being called out, and one by one, the students are walking carefully across the stage, their hearts pounding as they step into the future.

YY walks. Karin walks. Andrea Taylor and Carolyn Hanson and Jennifer Belzel and Amy and Meridith and Elvis and Donny Campbell—who was persuaded at the last minute, along with most of the other holdouts, to take part in the ceremony—and Cathy Turner and Craig McCray and the other GOALS graduates . . . All of them walk. They shake Ms. Westfall's hand, take their diplomas—actually just their diploma cases, since the real documents are waiting inside, where they won't get wet—and hand their principal an honor card, which is what they decided to give her. It's incredible. All these months later, after the guerrilla warfare and the hurling of the sacred darts at Judi's smiling mug, YY and Amy and all the AB-12 rats who have ever aligned themselves against Ms. Westfall now end up shaking her hand, staring into that same face, being forced to acknowledge, if only for a second, that she has always wished them well. After all, this is the moment that Ms. Westfall and the rest of the faculty and administration have worked so hard for, too.

"Oh my God," one girl says as she picks up her diploma cover. "I don't even believe this is happening."

Across the field they go, through a reception line formed by the teachers, who are clad in their black gowns and who are now distributing hugs, handshakes, whispered words of miscellaneous advice.

"You guys all made it. This is a minor miracle."

"Be good!"

"I love you," Mr. Feazell tells Andrea, squeezing her tight.

A few minutes later, when the last student has walked across the stage and through the line and back to his seat, there's a huge round of applause and all the graduates hurl their caps into the air. They've been instructed not to, but they don't care. Once they've retrieved their caps and returned to their seats, they listen to one more playing of the alma mater. The song the kids have ridiculed for years now sets them gently rocking, tears forming in their eyes.

Then suddenly it's over. They hoot. They scream. They pose for a quick shot with their families before dashing off with their friends.

"You ready to fly now?" says one grinning boy. "I'm flying like the wind."

• • •

THAT SAME NIGHT, AS THE GRADUATES ACCEPT KISSES FROM their parents outside the stadium, Mike Broome sits in his mother's easy chair, coughing and smoking another Marlboro and staring at the TV.

Everyone else in his family has gone to bed. Mike is up alone, watching *Trinity Is Still My Name,* a dubbed Italian western. He has already seen one movie tonight; when *Trinity* is over, he plans to watch another. Quietly he looks at the screen. He hears the gentle creaking of the overhead fan, hears the traffic cruising by on Belleair Road, hears his mother getting up so she can drink some milk to soothe her ulcer. He waits for a slow stretch in the movie, then finds a deck of cards. Without turning off the TV, he begins to play a game of solitaire. He lays out his seven piles, then starts flipping cards and searching for places to build.

He turns up the king of spades.

Nothing.

Jack of spades.

Nothing.

Queen of hearts.

Nothing.

EPILOGUE

EVERY YEAR, MORE THAN TWO million students graduate from public high schools in the United States, hearing the same joyous roar that greeted YY and Andrea and the others. Unfortunately many other teens never make it to graduation. At the moment, according to the U.S. Department of Education, there are close to four million dropouts in this country between the ages of sixteen and twenty-four. In Florida alone, more than twenty thousand students drop out every year.

GOALS and other dropout prevention programs continue to spread through the country, working with every grade from kindergarten to high school, searching for ways to turn back the tide. In Pinellas County, the GOALS program is now in place in eight high schools as well as at two technical educational centers. Exact numbers are hard to come by, but school officials report that since the program began, at least several hundred GOALS students have graduated in this county—several hundred who may well have dropped out had it not been for GOALS. Fine-tuning continues: At Largo, the GOALS teachers report that they now place stricter demands on their students and have curbed some of the disruptive behavior that plagued Mrs. O'Donnell and the other teachers in the pod.

Largo's shorts experiment is no more. There's no need for it, since the superintendent and the school board of Pinellas County decided during the 1990–91 school year—the year after YY wrote her editorial criticizing the experiment—to revamp the dress code and allow all students to wear shorts to school. Thus far, there is no report of mass chaos in the wake of the code's relaxation.

Many of the teachers described in this story are still plugging away in Largo's classrooms. Judith Westfall, however, no longer serves as Largo's principal. In recognition of her achievements, she received a promotion at the start of the '90–'91 school year and was named the county's associate superintendent for curriculum and instruction, making her one of the area's top school officials.

UNFORTUNATELY THERE'S NOT ENOUGH ROOM IN THESE pages to tell what's happened to all of the students described in this story. Many have done well, others have not. In one of the saddest cases to come out of Largo in years, a case that shows just how desperate the lives of some teenagers can be, Tabatha Turner—the GOALS student who briefly dated Mike Broome—was arrested in February of 1992 and charged with manslaughter in the death of her newborn son. Tabatha, now nineteen, was living with her parents at the time and already had a fourteen-month-old daughter. According to the police, when she became pregnant again, she did her best to hide the situation from her parents, eventually delivering the baby herself in secret late one night at home. In statements to officers, Tabatha reportedly admitted that after the birth she wrapped the seven-pound baby in a sheet, put him on the floor of her closet, then placed a pile of clothes on top of him and left him. The infant's body was found the next day by another member of the family.

While she awaits her trial, currently scheduled for June 1993, Tabatha has been released on her own recognizance. After the arrest, her daughter was temporarily placed in the custody of other family members.

LIFE HAS BEEN KINDER TO HEATHER PILCHER, WHO MARRIED Chris Wainscott in the summer of 1990, just nine days after Chris's graduation. Her grandfather, the Baptist minister, presided at the ceremony at their church, and then Heather gave birth the following October to a boy named Steven. Heather, who still had a year of high school to go, left Largo High and finished her senior year with the help of a special program run by the YWCA for pregnant teens, graduating in June 1991. Today the Wainscotts live in an apartment just south of the school. Heather is in the honor program at St. Petersburg Junior College, studying to be a nurse and working part-time to help pay the bills; Chris, who has put off his college plans until Heather finishes her studies, works as a laboratory courier at a local hospital. Both of them still take advantage of their singing talents, performing together at churches around the area.

AGAINST ALL ODDS, JAIMEE SHEEHY APPEARS TO BE RE-covering from her self-destructive cycle of behavior. The turnaround hasn't come easily, though. In 1990–91, she continued to habitually skip her classes, piling up so many absences that she failed every subject for the third year in a row. But when the following September arrived, Jaimee— who told her mother it would be too easy to continue skipping if she stayed at Largo—asked to be enrolled in a small alternative school where the teachers can provide even more one-on-one attention than in GOALS. In the summer of 1992, after completing the program, she took her GED exam and passed, earning her diploma.

Jaimee now bears hardly any resemblance to the ghost who haunted Largo High. She has lost weight; she has regained the color in her face; when she talks, she makes eye contact. No longer does it appear as though she might dematerialize at any second and vanish into the ether. Jaimee has had the same boyfriend for more than a year. She's continuing with her studies, heading for technical school in hopes of becoming a respiratory therapist, like her mother. She's been working hard at various jobs and uses her earnings to pay for her own car insurance and car repairs. She's even talking about saving up to buy another horse.

What accounts for the reversal? Neither Jaimee nor her mother can completely explain it, any more than they can account for why she went so far astray in the first place. Among other things, Jaimee believes that the time had simply come where she had no choice but to move forward. After all, she says, she couldn't wander the halls forever.

• • •

JOHN BOYD AND ANDREA TAYLOR BROKE UP IN THE SUMMER of 1990 shortly after Andrea's graduation. The end came less than two weeks after the ceremony, when John told her he wasn't ready to settle down with any one person. Today, Andrea is a junior at Florida State University in Tallahassee, majoring in accounting, with her sights still set on becoming a business executive. She is still close with her old friend Sabrina, who also attends FSU. John, meanwhile, graduated from Largo in June 1991 and moved to the Midwest to play football for the University of South Dakota, which awarded him a full scholarship. Today, John has settled into his sophomore year at the university and is majoring in education and scoring touchdowns as the school's starting running back. Though he would love the chance to play professional ball someday, John knows the odds of that are slim. When he finishes school, he says, what he'd like to do is work with kids. He's thinking about becoming a guidance counselor or a teacher.

"Like Mr. Feazell," he says.

Something else has happened. John has become a father. In the spring of 1992, a Largo girl he'd dated briefly over the previous summer gave birth to his daughter, Jada. John and the girl's mother are no longer together, but John visits Jada whenever possible during his trips home from South Dakota. He is determined, he says, to be there for her.

"A child is a part of you," he says. "I don't want my kid not knowing who her father is."

LIKE ANDREA AND JOHN, THE FEARSOME FOURSOME HAVE gone their separate ways.

Karin Upmeyer is now a junior at Florida Southern College. Amy Boyle, Meridith Tucker, and Christine Younskevicius are all juniors at the University of Florida. Several years after the summit in the darkroom of AB-12, Amy and Meridith have managed to rebuild their friendship. But during their freshman year in college, Amy and Karin had a major falling-out and no longer speak to each other.

"It's hard," says YY, who still talks to all of them. "I try to stay out of it."

Sad as the split may be, the four girls understand that such things are a part of growing up, and all of them have gotten on with their lives. Amy is studying to be a pharmacist; Meridith has entered journalism school. Karin is not sure what she wants to become, but she is majoring in psychology and is relieved to report that she has conquered her fear of math; in fact, she's doing so well at school that she recently made the dean's list. She also learned to deal with her bulimia and quit purging in the second semester of her freshman year, after she heard a speech on the dangerous and sometimes fatal effects of the eating disorder. As for her feelings of insecurity about her mother, Karin says that the two of them have long since moved past those days. She knows that her mother never meant the comments about her weight to sting, that she was only trying to look out for her. Karin says that she and her parents are closer today than ever.

YY, meanwhile, has come to terms with the aching sense of loss that so disturbed her in the aftermath of her parents' divorce. She no longer curls up in a ball when she's alone; she also has tried to quit pulling her eyelashes. After years of disastrous high school romances, YY is happily involved in a long-term relationship with a boyfriend. The two of them are considering marriage, but not until after she's finished with her studies. As for her career crisis, YY reports that although she still loves writing, she has decided to take the math route and is now majoring in computer science. She seems happy about her choice. Echoing her mother's words, she says she realized that she truly does have a gift for numbers and that it would be a shame not to take advantage of that gift.

AND MIKE BROOME?

After that graduation night when he played solitaire in front of the TV, Mike plunged even further into the depths, getting into trouble repeatedly until he dropped out of school in April 1991, ten days after his sixteenth birthday. The following November, Mike left Largo when his mother and her husband decided to move the family to Chipley, the small town in the Florida Panhandle where Jewelene Wilson was raised.

Months later, when I spoke to Mrs. Wilson over the phone, she told me that the change of scenery seemed to have helped. Mike had calmed down, she said, and was going to night school and working on his GED. Furthermore, he was engaged to be married and soon to become a father. The notion of Mike settling down with a wife and child was too startling to ignore. So this past September, shortly after the wedding, I drove to the Panhandle to see for myself how he was doing.

Just as with Jaimee, the change in Mike was immediately apparent. It's as though the sweet kid his teachers were always trying to reach had finally stepped out into the open. He smiled, told jokes, was actually willing to hold a conversation. Furthermore, it was obvious that he is deeply in love with his wife, Amanda, a straight-talking girl who's a half-year older than him and who speaks with a gentle north Florida accent. The two of them were already engaged when Amanda became pregnant, and when I saw them, Mike doted on her, holding her hand as he talked happily about how he couldn't wait to become a father.

Many good things have happened to Mike since he came to Chipley. He's gone back to church and been baptized. He's cut down on his smoking and is learning to control his temper. He has also become a walking testimonial to the importance of staying in school. Dropping out, he said, was the biggest mistake of his life. Although he hopes eventually to become an auto mechanic, about the only job Mike had been able to find was a part-time stint washing dishes in a nursing home. Amanda, meanwhile, was working part-time as a cashier at the local Piggly Wiggly's. Since the wedding the two of them have been living with Mike's mom, but they've been saving money, trying to get enough so they can afford a place of their own. Still, on their combined yearly income—roughly $5,500—it may take some time. When the baby comes, they said, they'll have to apply for food stamps.

"How much money have you saved so far?" I asked.

Amanda thought for a second, then said they had about ten dollars, counting their change.

Mike was still struggling to come to terms with his father. He talked at length that day about how much it would mean to him to get to know his dad and for his dad to know him. Without his father's example, he said, he feels lost.

"As I get older and become a man, how am I supposed to act?" he said, sitting across from me at the family dining room table. "What are some of my responsibilities?"

Mike vowed that he would be a better father to his own child, which he insisted would be a son. He said he wants to spend time with him, to take him hunting and fishing, to let him know that someone cares about him. He'll do everything he can, he said, to make sure his boy doesn't make the same mistakes he did, that he stays in school and gets an education.

As I sat there listening to Mike, I could not help but think about the obstacles ahead. There was no doubt of Mike's sincerity. But with almost no education or money, with all the pressures that will come to bear on him and Amanda in the next few years, what are the chances of it turning out the way he hopes? Isn't it possible that the cycle is about to begin again and that his child will end up as embittered as he was?

When I asked Mike this question, he looked down at the table, his face clouding over. For a moment, as a light breeze floated through a nearby window, he said nothing. Finally he looked up and answered. He knows there are no guarantees, he said. However hard he tries, he understands there's still a chance that it will all go wrong in the end. But he doesn't think that will happen, he said. If he's a good father, if he makes sure that his child feels the strength of his love, then he believes everything will work out.

In the months that followed our conversation, things continued to look up for Mike. He finished night school and obtained his GED. He got a better job, working at a dairy. And on March 6 of this year, he and Amanda became the parents of a baby boy. Michael Keyth Broome weighed in at eight pounds and fifteen ounces, measured twenty-one and a half inches long, and entered the world hollering.

His father, who was in the delivery room coaching Amanda, fought back the tears as he cradled his son in his arms for the first time. Smiling, Mike carried the boy into the nursery and held him for a moment before handing him over to the nurses. Later, Mike took him to the hospital room where Amanda was recovering and held him some more. He sat on the bed with the baby in his lap and stared at him, memorizing every detail of his face. He stood up and rocked him and spoke to him quietly, calling to him by name. Mike didn't seem to want to let go. He was determined, no matter what, to let his son know he was there.

"It's Daddy," he whispered.

—Thomas French
April 1993

A F T E R W O R D

More than two years have passed since I finished *South of Heaven,* and I am still asked for updates on YY, Mike, and the other young men and women I followed so closely for so long. I am glad readers feel such a strong connection to my subjects' lives—I certainly felt it, from the moment I met them—and am happy to report that, by and large, most of the central figures in the book are doing well.

Mike Broome, still living in the Florida Panhandle, has found a steady job that he enjoys on a surveying crew and is studying computer drafting at night school. Unfortunately, Mike and his wife, Amanda, separated recently, and he tells me they're unlikely to get back together. Mike, however, continues to stay close to his son, and when we talk over the phone, he proudly reports Keyth's latest achievements. Andrea Taylor, who retains the glow of her high school years, has just graduated from Florida State with a business degree and has been hired as a concierge at one of the hotels at Walt Disney World. John Boyd, still attending the University of South Dakota on his football scholarship, is within a year of earning an education degree. Although he hopes to be drafted by a professional team, John says it's more likely that he'll put football behind him after graduation and begin a career as an elementary school teacher. Like Mike, John is a proud father; when I spoke to him not long ago, he was bragging about his daughter's latest birthday.

Unfortunately, I do not know what has happened to Jaimee Sheehy. I lost touch with her and her mother some time ago, just before the book was published, and have not heard from them since.

As for the Fearsome Foursome, they have continued along their separate paths. Amy Boyle has graduated from the University of Florida and is now married and attending pharmacy school at Mercer University in Atlanta. Meridith Tucker recently graduated from the University of Florida with a journalism degree and is also living in Atlanta, working as a copy editor. Karin Upmeyer, who once worried that she would never make it into college, has graduated from Florida Southern and plans to seek her master's degree; at the moment, she is working full-time for the college as—strange but true—an admissions officer. YY, meanwhile, has graduated from the University of Florida, is working as a software designer, and has just married her college boyfriend. The wedding was this past May, and when YY stepped forward to the altar to take her vows, Karin and Meridith were standing only a few feet away, serving as bridesmaids. It was a beautiful ceremony, and as I sat in that church, watching YY hold hands with her new husband, I was struck not only by how radiant she looked but by how much she resembled her mother.

Of course, when I think of YY in her wedding gown and Mike Broome holding his son, it seems as though that year at Largo High, the single year I tried to chronicle in this book, existed an eternity ago. In reality it was only yesterday. These days, when I walk the halls of other high schools, I am struck by the number of students I meet who remind me of YY and Mike and Andrea and John and Jaimee. The names and faces of the freshmen change, and different songs blast out of the seniors' car stereos. But high school goes on forever.

Over the years, I will confess, it has become impossible for me to write with complete detachment about the public schools, especially since I became a parent. My oldest son, who was born not long before I started reporting on *South of Heaven,* has just finished kindergarten inside the same school system I have written so much about. My son attends one of the so-called magnet schools, special public schools that attract families by emphasizing certain areas of study. Some magnets focus on math or computers or writing; my son's school has a special curriculum built around the arts and international studies, which means that even as kindergartners the children are taking dance and drama and music, as well as learning Spanish daily. So far it has been a tremendously affirming experience. My son is happy and excited, and every time I step onto the campus and see the work he and the other students are doing, I feel a surge of renewed hope.

Still, having spent so many years reporting inside the schools, I am aware that the prognosis for many children is uncertain, even at a good school such as my son's. Sometimes I sit in his classroom, studying him and his young friends as they draw and play and listen to stories, and I wonder what will happen to each of them. Who will grow up with the self-confidence and drive of YY and Andrea? Who will burn with Mike Broome's anger and isolation? Who will wander the halls, smiling and disconnected, like another Jaimee Sheehy? Which of them, God forbid, will feel so trapped, as did John Boyd, that they will find it necessary to carry a loaded gun to school?

As a journalist and a parent, I am continually surprised by the cynical assumptions people make about the public schools. I was particularly taken aback when some of these critics—who often condemn from a distance, without any concrete appreciation of what's involved—cited *South of Heaven* in support of their biases and declared the book an indictment of public education. If anything, this book was an attempt to get past simplistic discussions that insist on labeling the public schools as either "good" or "bad," when in fact the quality and nature of students' experience varies greatly, depending on where they live, what school they're zoned for, what teachers they wind up with, and most important, what their personal backgrounds and home lives are like. Parents are the key. Without our support and involvement, it is impossible for even the best of schools to educate our children.

Since I completed *South of Heaven,* people frequently ask me what's gone wrong with our public schools. My first instinct, always, is to hand them a mirror. What has gone wrong with our schools is what has gone wrong with us. What can we do to begin turning the situation around? I don't pretend to have the answers, but when asked, I say that nothing will change until we reawaken ourselves to our responsibility to our children. I am not speaking solely about what we owe our own flesh and blood, but what we owe to every child. Not long ago, I was talking to a friend, a wonderful mother so troubled by the shortcomings of the local school system that she has decided, reluctantly, to send her son to a private school.

"I just want him to be safe and get a good start," she said. "I want him to have a cocoon."

I wasn't sure how to respond. As I can attest, the problems inside our schools are very real and frightening. But I wondered about the children whose parents cannot afford to send them anywhere else. What happens to them? What happens

to them, and to public education, if the most active, involved parents we have—
parents such as my friend—continue to remove their kids and their own energy
and creativity from our classrooms? Where does that leave the children who are left
behind? Ultimately, when you look down the road ten or twenty years, where does
it leave our country?

This is not intended as a diatribe against parents who choose private schools.
My wife and I were very fortunate to have gotten our son into the magnet school
I've described. I understand that, in the end, parents have to do what they think is
best for their child. But I also believe, at a fundamental level, that each of us can
make a tangible, material difference in the lives of many children. I have seen it
repeatedly during my reporting, witnessing firsthand the heroic influence of teachers like the ones described in this book. I have also seen it while volunteering at
my son's school.

There are many simple, basic steps we can all take to improve the education
of our young. To start with, our political leaders might find the backbone—and cit-
izens might summon the will to support them—to ensure that teachers are paid at
least a semblance of what they're worth. The politicians might also drop the ridiculous pretense that teacher-pupil ratios are irrelevant, and build enough schools to
reduce overcrowding and thus give students more individual attention. As long as
they're waving the flag and making speeches about the hallowed importance of
education, the politicians should immediately dismiss and discard forever any proposal to allow parents to use vouchers for private school tuition; such proposals
are inherently elitist and would gut the public schools. It would also be great—
mind you, I'm not holding my breath—if politicians pledged to send their own children to public schools and honored those pledges. Come to think of it, it would
be helpful if all community leaders—corporate heads, ministers, and newspaper
editors who insist on issuing proclamations about the quality of education—sent
their children to public schools. You'd be astonished at how quickly things would
improve if that ever happened.

What else? As long as I'm making a wish list, I would love it if more business
leaders stopped whining about the sorry quality of our high school graduates and
joined the corporations that are already forging partnerships with the schools, offering financial support and giving their employees time to volunteer in the classroom.
Retirees, who have a lifetime of experience to share, could tutor more school-
children as well, teaching everything from the alphabet to thermodynamics.

And parents? We need to turn off the TV, learn how to say no, pay attention,
be physically and emotionally present at some point in our children's day, read to
them at night or listen to them read to us, teach by example and pick up a book
once in a while ourselves, set boundaries and stick to them, listen better, reacquaint
ourselves and our kids with the notion that learning is its own reward, know the
names of our children's teachers, make sure those teachers know our names, and
stop dumping our sons and daughters at the classroom door expecting the school
to fix everything.

Ultimately, we must recognize that all of us are parents and that all children
are our children. And no matter how exhausted we are, no matter how busy or
overworked, we must find a way—find the will and make the time—to become a
part of their schooling, their raising, their everyday existence. Without us, they are
orphans.

ACKNOWLEDGMENTS

Hundreds of people have generously given their time and effort to this project, but none deserve higher thanks than the students, parents, teachers, staff members, and administrators of Largo High School, who opened their doors to a stranger and allowed me to wander into their lives. I am especially grateful to John Boyd, Amy Boyle, Mike Broome, Jaimee Sheehy, Andrea Taylor, Meridith Tucker, Karin Upmeyer, Chris and Heather Wainscott, and Christine Younskevicius, as well as many of their parents; to Jan Amburgy, Helen Atkinson, Susan Bachman, Joann Burrows, Annette DiLello, James Feazell, Kim Frye, Andy Gerber, Jim Gill, Vicki Glidden, Lucia Anne Hay, Tracy Howard, Mike Klapka, Len Koutney, Janet LaVassaur, Barbara McDivitt, Barbara McGraw, Pat Mahoney, Mary O'Donnell, Pat Palmateer, Richard Penberthy, Rayshall Poinsette, Ruth Riel, Renny Taylor, laura trimm, Zelda Troiano, Rick Wagar, Lois Welch, and Leah Whitehead, all of whom were indispensable in helping me make sense of what unfolded before me; to Barbara Thornton, who has made me feel welcome at the school in the years since; and to Judith Westfall, who constantly pushed me to remember the best interests of her students and faculty, regardless of how she was to be portrayed. Without Judi's candor and encouragement, this book would not have been possible. I am also indebted to many people in the Pinellas County school system, including Howard Hinesley, the superintendent of schools, as well as Marilyn Brown, Mary Ellen Leonard, Jan Schwartz, and Dee Walker.

This project would not have gone forward without the unflagging support of numerous people at the *St. Petersburg Times.* Among others, I would like to thank Andrew Barnes, Don McBride, Steve Small, Sandra Thompson, and Nancy Waclawek, as well as Barbara Hijek and everyone in the *Times* library. I am also grateful to Terri McKaig, for technical advice; to George Rahdert and Pat Anderson, for their continuing counsel;

to Susan Earley, David and Melinda Galaher, Mark Granning, Janie Guilbault, Jana Ham, Rik McNeill, Shirley Moravec, Nora Moulton, Mary Osborne, and Lou Zulli, for their years of teaching and listening; and to Suzanne Klinkenberg, for once again identifying the flora and fauna. Turning this story into a book, meanwhile, would not have been possible without the tireless efforts of my agent, Jane Dystel, and my editors at Doubleday, Joel Fishman and Deb Futter, as well as assistant editor Wendy Goldman, all of whom showered me with guidance and care.

Many writers and writing coaches have given me their suggestions and friendship through several years of reporting and writing. Among them are Roy Peter Clark and Donald Fry of the Poynter Institute for Media Studies; David Finkel of the *Washington Post;* Sheryl James of the *Detroit Free Press;* Tim Nickens of the *Miami Herald;* Christopher Scanlan of the Knight-Ridder Washington bureau; and Anne Hull, Jeff Klinkenberg, Chris Lavin, Mary Jane Park, Karl Vick, and Tom Zucco of the *St. Petersburg Times.* I am especially indebted to Michael Foley, whose idea this was in the first place, even if he doesn't remember it; to Rick Holter, whose talent and enthusiasm shaped this project in a thousand ways; to Wilma Norton, for selflessly sharing her knowledge and support; and to Maurice Rivenbark, for his remarkable photos. Deepest thanks to Neville Green, managing editor at the *Times,* who has been the greatest teacher, protector, and friend any writer could wish for.

Finally, love always to my sons, Nat and Sam, and to my wife, Linda, who kept me going when nothing else could.